Furthe

"Judith Rich Harris calls *No Two Alike* a 'scientific detective story.' The mystery is why people—even identical twins who grow up in the same home with the same genes—end up with different personalities. The detective is Harris herself, . . . who takes on the academic establishment armed only with a sharp mind and an Internet connection. Harris the author scrupulously follows clues; Harris the protagonist drives the story forward through force of character."

—William Saletan, *New York Times Book Review*

"With neither a doctorate nor a university behind her, Harris more than compensates with intelligence, dogged research, lively writing, a love of mystery, and droll humor. . . . Harris makes behavioral genetics and evolutionary psychology enjoyable and accessible to general readers as well as scholars. Essential for general and academic libraries."

—E. James Lieberman, *Library Journal*, starred review

"Harris's writing is highly entertaining, which will help readers stick with her through the elaboration of a fairly complex theory."—*Publishers Weekly*

"Harris delivers an answer (and, yes, it's sure to be controversial), but it's the quest itself that will prove most fascinating for general readers, who will marvel at the step-by-step accumulation of facts, as the author marshals her argument by adeptly juggling a wide array of tools, from new theories of evolutionary psychology to behavioral genetics and linguistics."

—David Pitt, *Booklist*

"There are many books about 'human nature,' but very few on the important question of why humans differ from one another. Judy Harris's book is terrifically well written and interesting." —Robert Plomin, author of *Nature and Nurture: An Introduction to Human Behavioral Genetics*

"As a parent, as a social psychologist, and as a human being, I was enlightened and enthralled. Harris is an extraordinary thinker and writer: wise, witty, learned, scientifically rigorous, and absolutely fearless. Contemporary psychology has no sharper critic—and no better friend."

—Joshua Aronson, editor of *Improving Academic Achievement: Impact of Psychological Factors on Education*

"Readers interested in evolutionary psychology and human development will find a lot to ponder here."
—*Science News*

"Harris's books are well worth reading for many reasons. With its roots in old-fashioned curiosity and wide learning, her exposition is a tour de force of arresting anecdotes, lively reportage, and lucid analysis."
—Amy L. Wax, *Policy Review*

"When this book arrived, I pretty much sat down and read it from cover to cover—hardly my typical reaction to a nonfiction book. *No Two Alike* is a deeply impressive accomplishment."
—Paul Bloom, author of *Descartes' Baby: How the Science of Child Development Explains What Makes Us Human*

"There are lots and lots of goodies, including fascinating studies of memory and learning and observations of chimpanzees, chickens, paper wasps and ants. Harris shows why relationship and socialisation skills don't necessarily go together; why bullies *don't* have low self-esteem, as normally proposed; why height and earnings are related; and so on. . . . Her work is enjoyably well worth reading and, in this reviewer at least, stimulated much thought."
—Denise Winn, *Human Givens Journal*

"Harris is not a professional scientist and isn't afraid of ranging widely across disciplines in search of an answer. She writes with breezy good humour too, as she attempts to explain variations in personality that can't be attributed to variations in genes."
—*Scotland on Sunday*

"Why are we the way we are? Why do identical twins, raised in the same house by the same parents, turn out to have such different personalities? For years, psychologists and other professionals thought they had the answers, but this grandmotherly, iconoclastic outsider may force us to revise our thinking about these basic questions. . . . Mrs. Harris is an amazing woman. . . . As an independent scholar, she took a broader view of the issue than was possible for many of the certified experts. Perhaps that is why she has been able to see the forest, as well as the trees."
—Peter Pettus, *New York Sun*

"Harris makes waves again with a new theory of personality to explain why no two people are alike. . . . Expect some lively rebuttals."
—*Kirkus Reviews*

"I enjoyed reading this book; Harris has a conversational and engaging style that nonetheless manages to convey quite a bit of information clearly. . . . The evidence Harris produces to support [her theory of personality] is not only persuasive but fascinating to read."

—Mary Hrovat, *Thinking Meat* (thinkingmeat.com)

"Judith Harris has produced a top-notch social science text. The book takes a fresh look at research from behavioral genetics, developmental psychology, sociology, personality, and social psychology to explain, in new ways, the non-genetic causes of individual human differences. . . . A well-researched and thought-provoking analysis of fundamental issues in psychology."

—Eric Lang, *Science Books & Films*

"The chapters on gene-environment interaction and birth order differences within families contain some fascinating detective work. . . . I very much enjoyed reading this book."

—Dorret Boomsma, *Nature Genetics*

"Marshaling an impressive range of evidence—social psychology, anthropology, genetics, neuroscience, and, crucially, evolutionary biology—Harris demolishes entrenched orthodoxies and opens new avenues. This book will intrigue, amuse, and greatly enlighten you, whatever your personality."

—Helena Cronin, author of *The Ant and the Peacock: Altruism and Sexual Selection from Darwin to Today*

"Why are identical twins reared together so different when they share all of their genes and all of the environment? Why were the Iranian conjoined twins Laleh and Ladan so different when their genes and environments seemed all but identical? *No Two Alike*, this wonderful new book by Judith Rich Harris, takes on this most difficult of questions. . . . And Harris, a devotee of mystery writing, is a great storyteller. . . . This is a very important book."

—John Mullen, *Metapsychology*

"A truly engaging, moderately challenging take on what makes people tick. [Harris is] a plucky, ridiculously informed writer who brings potentially droll scientific studies to life, and synthesizes and picks holes in the most influential psychology studies relating to personality in the past several decades. The result is a new theory that covers all bases and explains why we are the way we are."

—Karla Starr, *Willamette Week*

Also by Judith Rich Harris

The Nurture Assumption: Why Children Turn Out the Way They Do

No Two Alike

Human Nature and Human Individuality

JUDITH RICH HARRIS

W. W. NORTON & COMPANY
New York • London

To Steven Pinker

Printed in the United States of America
First published as a Norton paperback 2007

For information about permission to reproduce selections from this book, write to Permissions, W. W. Norton & Company, Inc., 500 Fifth Avenue, New York, NY 10110

Manufacturing by Courier Westford
Book design by Dana Sloan
Production manager: Amanda Morrison

Library of Congress Cataloging-in-Publication Data

Harris, Judith Rich.
No two alike : human nature and human individuality / by Judith Rich Harris.—1st ed.
p. cm.
Includes bibliographical references and index.
ISBN 0-393-05948-0 (hardcover)
1. Individual differences. 2. Individuality. 3. Personality. I. Title.
BF697.H3765 2006
155.2—dc22

2005025837

ISBN 978-0-393-32971-1 pbk.

W. W. Norton & Company, Inc., 500 Fifth Avenue, New York, N.Y. 10110
www.wwnorton.com

W. W. Norton & Company, Ltd., Castle House, 75/76 Wells Street, London W1T 3QT

1 2 3 4 5 6 7 8 9 0

Contents

Preface

HUMAN INDIVIDUALITY is a mystery. The theories of personality (or of personality development) that are currently in vogue cannot explain why no two people are alike or why they differ in the particular ways they do. Even identical twins reared in the same home differ in personality and behavior. Identical twins have identical genes, so the differences between them cannot be genetic.

The interesting differences among people are not due to genes. Nor are they due to any of the other things that the word "personality" probably made you think of. That's why human individuality is a mystery.

My goal in this book is to solve that mystery. This is a scientific detective story.

The time is ripe for such a quest. I have tools at my disposal that the earlier theorists lacked: in particular, a new view of the human mind, based on the work of evolutionary psychologists such as Steven Pinker, Leda Cosmides, and John Tooby. The human mind, we now understand, is not simply a complex organ: it is a *collection* of complex organs, each serving a separate purpose, each operating according to its own rules.

But evolutionary psychology is not the only tool I bring to this quest. As an independent investigator, I have the freedom to ignore the territorial markers of the academic world and follow the trail wherever it leads me. The fields I've strayed into include social psychology, developmental psychology, psycholinguistics, neuroscience, and behavioral genetics. I've found useful clues in lots of unlikely places. Even in entomology, the study of insects.

In order to solve a mystery, one of the things a detective has to do is to examine alternative solutions and eliminate the ones that don't work, the so-called "red herrings." I am well equipped for that job, too: I'm a doubting Thomas, an asker of impertinent questions. If some stuffed shirt with a string of letters after his name tells me that such-and-such is true, my response is "Show me the data." I was impertinent and skeptical even as a child, but my experiences over the past seven years—since the publication of *The Nurture Assumption*—have made me more so. You'll hear that story, too, because it's relevant to this quest.

But I don't mean to suggest that my experiences during the past seven years have been mostly negative. On the contrary. Though health problems have kept me more or less housebound, I've met (mainly through e-mail) many interesting and open-minded people. One of the things I've learned is that a string of letters after someone's name doesn't necessarily make him or her a stuffed shirt.

It has been, in fact, an extraordinary seven years. You wouldn't think that someone in my situation—no longer able to travel or to go to parties—could have such a good time. But while I've been stuck here in the backwaters of New Jersey, *The Nurture Assumption* has traveled all over the world, translated into fifteen different languages. That e-mail I mentioned comes not only from my own country but from parts of the world I've never seen and never will. This is my opportunity to thank all the people who have shared their thoughts with me. I've been edified, gratified, challenged, entertained, and sometimes moved by what you've told me.

I owe a debt of gratitude to many other people as well. My agent, Katinka Matson of Brockman, Inc., has always been there when I needed her, lending an ear and giving good counsel. My editor at W. W. Norton, Angela von der Lippe, made many suggestions that improved this book by making it clearer in meaning and gentler in tone. Other people at Norton whose help has been instrumental are Vanessa Levine-Smith and Renee Schwartz.

I am especially grateful to the colleagues, friends, and relatives who helped me immeasurably by reading earlier drafts of this book and giving me wise and useful feedback. A thousand thanks to the following people: Stephen L. Black, Marie Bristol-Power, Helena Cronin, Joan Friebely, Charles S. Harris, David G. Myers, Steven Pinker, Robert Plomin, Richard G. Rich, and Frederic Townsend. The advice and information they gave me were worth more than rubies.

Much more than feedback was provided by my husband of forty-four years, Charles Harris. Quite literally, he has made it possible for me to go on writing books. For the help and encouragement I've received from him, he has my gratitude and my love. My love, too, to the other members of my understanding and supportive family: my daughters, Nomi and Elaine, my sons-in-law, Chris and Tim, and my brother, Richard. May I mention my grandchildren, please? There are four, all bright and beautiful: Jennifer, Abigail, Jeremy, and Eleanor.

I've dedicated this book to Steven Pinker, who has been my e-mail friend and colleague since 1995. He has listened to my ideas, cheered me up when I've gotten discouraged, and argued with me when he thought I was heading in the wrong direction. Though we still don't agree on everything, Steve has influenced my thinking more than anyone else has. Equally important, he has allowed me to influence *his* thinking.

Writing that, I realized that there is one more group of people who deserve my thanks: the inventors and developers of the Internet. They made it possible for someone in my situation to toss around ideas with some of the leading scientific thinkers of our time. The miracles of modern medical science have kept me alive, but the miracles of modern technology enabled me to write this book.

No Two Alike

1

An Appreciation of Differences

On the day I began writing this book, Laleh and Ladan Bijani were buried in Iran, in separate graves: apart in death as they had never been in life. Laleh and Ladan were conjoined identical twins, twenty-nine years old, born attached at the head. They died during the surgery that separated them.

In their twenty-nine years of enforced togetherness, Laleh and Ladan had accomplished more than most Iranian women of their generation: both had graduated from law school. They were able to sit and to walk because they were joined side by side, facing in the same direction. But the only way each twin could see the other's face was by looking into a mirror.

Laleh and Ladan went into the surgery knowing the risks; physicians had told them that they had only a 50–50 chance of surviving it. They were willing to take that risk for the chance of living separate lives. "We are two completely separate individuals who are stuck to each other," Ladan explained to reporters before the surgery. "We have different world views, we have different lifestyles, we think very differently about issues." Laleh wanted to move to Tehran and become a journalist, while Ladan planned to remain in their hometown of Shiraz and practice law. Ladan was the more outspoken of the two, described by a close acquaintance as "very friendly, she always liked to joke."[1]

The conflict in career goals was one reason they gave for undergoing the surgery. Another was their desire to see each other face-to-face without a mirror. There may have been other reasons that they didn't admit to reporters—their desire to marry, perhaps, and to have children. Having to go everywhere with one's sister can be a bit awkward at times. Researchers have found (and Laleh and Ladan might have discovered on their own) that someone who falls in love with one identical twin may not even *like* the other one.[2]

Though identical twinning is nature's way of making a clone, twins are separate and unique individuals, to themselves and to the people who know them. Laleh and Ladan had identical genes and identical environments—they went everywhere together, they had no choice—but their personalities, opinions, and goals in life were different. That individuality was what they died for.

Most identical twins are not born fastened together, of course, and most conjoined twins do not seek surgical separation in adulthood. But identical twins invariably differ in personality. Why they differ is a mystery that science has so far been unable to solve and that twins themselves are puzzled by.

"Why am I me?" That question was put to Freeman Dyson, professor of physics at the Institute for Advanced Study at Princeton, by his eight-year-old grandson George. I don't know what he said to George, but Dyson later told an adult audience that the question "summarizes the conundrum of personal existence in an impersonal universe." Um, I suppose so. But the question had a more specific meaning for George, because he is an identical twin. According to his grandfather, George knows the difference between identical (monozygotic) and fraternal (dizygotic) twins, and he knows that he and his twin brother Donald are genetically identical. He is also aware, according to his grandfather, that he and his twin "have the same environment and upbringing"—they are growing up in the same home with the same parents. When George asked "Why am I me?" he was asking, his grandfather gathered, "how it happens that two people with identical genes and identical nurture are nevertheless different."[3] If their nature is the same and their nurture is the same, how come they have different personalities?

Human individuality and human differences are the subject matter of this book. Though twins present the problem in a nutshell, the differences between ordinary siblings are just as mysterious and just as unexplained. And if scientists cannot explain why twins are different and why ordinary siblings are different, it means they also can't explain why you and I, or any two people picked at random, are different.

In fiction and in real-life law enforcement, the solving of a mystery involves something called "proof." Science works a little differently. In

Ladan (left) and Laleh Bijani. *(Reprinted courtesy of AP/Wide World Photos.)*

most cases there's no way to provide absolute proof that a solution to a scientific mystery is correct; often the best you can do is to demonstrate that alternative solutions fail to account for crucial aspects of the evidence. Sherlock Holmes, who prided himself on his scientific methods, was fond of saying, "When you have excluded the impossible, whatever remains, however improbable, must be the truth."[4] A real scientist would say something much less quotable—something like, "When you have excluded the highly improbable, whatever remains is, for the time being, in the realm of viable possibilities."

Mysteries are my favorite leisure reading, but I usually choose something more up-to-date than Sherlock Holmes—for example, Sue Grafton's alphabetical series, starting with *"A" Is for Alibi*. These mystery novels feature a detective named Kinsey Millhone, details of whose life have been revealed gradually over the course of the series. Learning about Kinsey is part of the fun of reading these books.

Like me, Kinsey doesn't kowtow to authority, cuts her own hair, and is curious to a fault. She speaks in the first person and her books usually contain a passage like this in the first page or two:

> My name is Kinsey Millhone. I'm a private investigator, licensed by the state of California. . . . I'm thirty-two years old, twice married, no kids, currently unattached and likely to remain so given my disposition.[5]

You might call me a private investigator too, since I investigate things on my own. In other respects, though, Kinsey and I are a continent apart. I live in New Jersey. I'm sixty-seven years old, still married to my first and only husband. Two nice kids, four lovely grandchildren. Currently attached to a number of people and likely to remain so in spite of my disposition.

But the most important difference between me and Kinsey is that she is strong and healthy and I am not. I have been ill for almost thirty years with a disorder that has been diagnosed as a mixture of systemic sclerosis and lupus, two autoimmune diseases that can each affect a variety of organs. Over the years, my immune system has launched attacks on many parts of my body. Now it has taken aim at my heart and lungs. About half of patients with systemic sclerosis eventually develop a debilitating malfunction of the heart and lungs called pulmonary hypertension. I was diagnosed with this malfunction in 2002.

To keep fit, Kinsey goes for three-mile runs; I get out of breath just walking at a normal speed. Kinsey is able to jump into her car and travel to distant places in search of clues; I can't do that. I'm not entirely confined to my home—I do get out occasionally—but my physical stamina is so limited that I seldom venture farther than the local library or office supply store. When I go to the hospital for tests, my husband pushes me around in a wheelchair.

But there are fictional detectives more handicapped than I. In a mystery called *The Daughter of Time*—the title comes from an old proverb, "Truth is the daughter of time"—the detective does all his detecting while he's flat on his back in the hospital. The novel, written by Josephine Tey and published in England in 1951, begins like this:

> Grant lay on his high white cot and stared at the ceiling. Stared at it with loathing. He knew by heart every last minute crack on its nice clean surface.[6]

Alan Grant of Scotland Yard, hospitalized due to injuries he suffered while pursuing a malefactor, didn't let his immobility stop him. With the aid of friends who brought him books and reproductions of old paintings, he found a mystery to solve: Who killed the Little Princes in the Tower?—a crime usually attributed to Richard III. Since the events in question occurred in the fifteenth century, Grant couldn't have interviewed witnesses and suspects even if he had been sound in body. His detective work consisted, as one of his friends put it, of "academic investigating."[7]

Academic investigating is a good description of what I do. There are many ways to collect evidence from far and wide while staying put. Unlike unlucky Alan Grant, I have access to the Internet and a wide circle of friends and colleagues with whom I correspond in e-mail. Some of my correspondents are privy to information that I wouldn't have been able to obtain even if I were as healthy and mobile as Kinsey Millhone. But most of my evidence comes from published sources: scholarly books and articles in professional journals (see the endnotes and reference list at the back of this book). Other people do the legwork—the actual collecting of data—but once the outcome of their labors is published, it becomes grist for my mill. Even if I don't agree with the researchers' conclusions or approve of their methods—which, as you will see, is often the case—the published reports might contain something useful.

My first job is the same as Alan Grant's: to convince you that there is a mystery in need of solving. Most of Grant's contemporaries thought that the mystery had already been solved: "everyone knew" that it was Richard III who dunnit. Before Grant could set about identifying the real perpetrator, he had to show that the widely accepted solution was wrong. Almost three-quarters of the novel is devoted to convincing the reader that Richard did not kill the princes, the two young sons of his dead brother, Edward IV. With the aid of a young American researcher who has access to old documents stored in the British Museum, Grant establishes that Richard had no motive to have the boys put to death, that it would have been out of character for him to do so, and that in all probability they were still alive when Richard was killed at Bosworth—yelling, according to the account Shakespeare wrote a century later, "My kingdom for a horse!"

Most of my contemporaries think that the mystery of personality—of individuality, as I have called it in the subtitle of this book—has already been solved. It is commonly accepted that people turn out the way they do—different from one another, different from their brothers and sisters—because of "nature," "nurture," and/or some kind of interaction between the two.

"It is a capital mistake," asserted Sherlock Holmes, "to theorize before one has data. Insensibly one begins to twist facts to suit theories."[8] In the real world, theories seldom spring to life in the total absence of data: one has to have something to begin with. But a theory may be formulated on the basis of inadequate, ambiguous, or misleading data. Then, insensibly one begins to collect more data in such a way that the new data tend to confirm the theory.

That sort of thing can go on for a remarkably long time: in psychology, for more than a hundred years. Then a new broom comes along and sweeps out the cobwebs by approaching the problem from a new angle. In psychology, there are two new brooms, both of which will be put to good use in this book: evolutionary psychology and behavioral genetics. Two new brooms that sweep in different directions—not opposite, but perpendicular to each other.

Evolutionary psychology is a science that regards the human mind as the product of Darwinian selection. At first glance it doesn't look like a promising way to study human individuality. On the whole, evolutionary psychologists aren't much interested in human differences: they are interested chiefly in what all humans have in common. Take, for example, the book *How the Mind Works*, by the evolutionary psychologist Steven Pinker.[9] The "the" in the title is a giveaway. Pinker's book is not about how my mind works or how yours does, but how everyone's mind works. It's about the standard equipment, not the optional stuff. Not the little blips and dings that make my mind work a little differently from yours.

Steven Pinker is actually an exception among evolutionary psychologists: in his latest book, *The Blank Slate*, he does talk about individual differences. But not until chapter 19. Here's how *The Blank Slate* begins:

> Everyone has a theory of human nature. Everyone has to anticipate the behavior of others, and that means we all need theories about what makes people tick.[10]

True enough, but the trouble is that having a theory of human nature doesn't get us very far, because people don't all behave alike. Knowing what makes one person tick—or a hundred people, for that matter—doesn't help much in anticipating the behavior of the hundred and first.

Case in point: Matthew, the son of one of my e-mail friends, recently proposed to his girlfriend in front of a large group of people assembled at a formal dinner party. Fortunately, Alison said yes. But what if she had refused him, or said she'd have to think it over, or pointed to another man and said "I'd rather marry *him*"? How brave Matthew was, I thought, to take that risk in front of all those people.

Then it occurred to me that Matthew knew exactly what h doing: he wouldn't have proposed when and where he did (in fact, h probably wouldn't have proposed at all) if he hadn't been pretty sure of Alison's response. His prediction of her behavior wasn't based on his understanding of human nature—on his theory, let's say, that women have a natural urge to get married. It was based on his understanding of Alison.

Admittedly, that interpretation of Matthew's behavior is itself based on a theory of human nature. My belief that he wouldn't have proposed in front of an audience if he hadn't been pretty sure that Alison would say yes is based on my knowledge that humans do not, as a rule, enjoy being humiliated in public. So it is possible to predict human behavior to some extent. But that isn't good enough. We need to be able to predict the behavior of *specific* others, and to do that we need to know what makes *them* tick. Not many people fly airplanes into office buildings, but some do.

People differ in behavior, and some of these individual differences persist over time. Some people are chronically more law-abiding, or less trusting, or friendlier, or more apt to get upset than others. Psychologists attribute these differences among individuals, and the consistencies within individuals, to differences in personality.

In a classic study, the social psychologists David Napolitan and George Goethals asked their subjects—undergraduates at Williams College—to have a brief face-to-face discussion with a woman posing as a graduate student in clinical psychology. The "graduate student" was actually a trained confederate of the researchers—trained to act in either a friendly or unfriendly manner with the subjects. With half the subjects she was warm and supportive; with the others she was aloof and critical.

After the discussion, the subjects were asked to fill out a questionnaire that included items about the personality of the graduate student. They were specifically instructed to evaluate her true personality, not just her behavior. But since the subjects had met the woman only once, they had nothing to go on other than her behavior during the discussion. Naturally, the ones who had seen her unfriendly persona rated her as cold and rejecting, and the ones who had seen her friendly persona rated her as warm and accepting.

The surprise came when the procedure was changed a little and new subjects were informed in advance that the graduate student was required, for the purposes of the study, to behave in a friendly or unfriendly manner.

The additional information made no difference at all! Even when a student knew, while he was talking to the woman, that she had been *instructed* to behave in an aloof and critical way, he nonetheless rated her "true" personality as cold and unfriendly. He disregarded the fact that the situation demanded a certain kind of behavior from the grad student and attributed her behavior to an enduring characteristic—to her chronic predisposition to behave, and presumably to feel, in an unkind and unfriendly way.[11]

Many variations on Napolitan and Goethals' experiment have been carried out, with similar results. The subjects always lean too far in attributing people's behavior to their enduring characteristics; they invariably underestimate the power of the situation to compel a person to behave in a particular way. Only in regard to their own behavior are they likely to give adequate weight to the exigencies of the situation.

Social psychologists call it the "fundamental attribution error"—a grandiose name for something most people have never heard of, but "fundamental" is only a slight exaggeration. Though the magnitude of the error may vary somewhat across cultures, it is a human universal.[12]

"Everyone has to anticipate the behavior of others," as Pinker pointed out. How do we do that when people vary so much in behavior? The answer, as shown by the fundamental attribution error, is that we take into account not just human nature in general but also the nature of particular humans. We are predisposed to see other people as having enduring characteristics that cause them to behave in predictable ways, and to interpret samples of behavior—even hopelessly inadequate samples—as clues to their characteristics. Our theory of human nature leads us to expect that people will be consistent—that if we meet the graduate student in the supermarket, she will be as nice or as nasty as she was in the laboratory.

The predisposition to attribute someone's behavior to something within them that's relatively stable and enduring—something that nowadays is called *personality* and that used to be called *character*—actually causes us to make errors in prediction: we expect people to be more consistent than they really are. It's a reasonable error to make, however, because (in the absence of other information) the best predictor of how an individual will behave in the future is how he or she behaved in the past.[13]

At least to some extent, people *are* consistent. Some are habitually friendly; others are persistently hostile. In a classroom full of children (a classroom is a situation designed to produce uniformity of behavior), some children keep bothering their neighbors or talking out of turn, while others turn red and stammer if the teacher calls on them. They behave this way year after year, despite the turnover in teachers and classmates.

Evolutionary psychologists generally don't say much about such differences, but they can't do business without them. Individuality is incorporated into their theories, often without being explicitly acknowledged. Take mate selection, a major topic in this field. If you ask people what's important to them in choosing a mate, both men and women list qualities like kindness, dependability, sincerity, and intelligence.[14] If these are qualities that cause people to prefer some potential mates to others, then potential mates presumably differ in these ways. Some are judged to be kinder, more dependable, and more intelligent than others.

Of course, there are also differences in physical appearance; we find some individuals more attractive than others. But physical appearance has another, equally important function in mate selection: it's the way we recognize individuals, the way we tell them apart. Though hearing and the sense of smell may also play a role, humans rely primarily on vision to identify individuals. If the selection of a long-term mate means learning about the qualities of specific individuals, then we have to be able to tell potential candidates apart and remember which one has which qualities. Choosing a mate is not just a matter of choosing someone of the right sex, the right shape, and the right age: it's a matter of choosing a particular *individual.*

The ability to recognize and remember specific individuals also plays a crucial role in another aspect of human nature much discussed by evolutionary psychologists: altruism, which means helping someone else at a cost to oneself. At first glance, altruism seems at odds with a Darwinian viewpoint. Rescuing someone from a burning building entails a risk to the rescuer; yet, people do it. Since dying to save someone else's life is hard to justify from a "survival of the fittest" point of view—death being the ultimate in unfitness—evolutionary theorists needed a way to explain it. In 1964, William Hamilton pointed out that altruism makes sense in terms of fitness (he called it "inclusive fitness") if the one you are helping shares your genes. He even gave a formula for deciding, on the basis of how many genes you share with the other person—50 percent with a parent or child or sibling, 25 percent with a half-sibling or grandchild—whether you should bother.[15]

Hamilton's theory, called kin selection or kin altruism, predicts that human and nonhuman animals should provide for their own offspring in preference to providing for the offspring of others. But in order to do this, the animal must have some way of identifying its own offspring. Evolution has come up with a variety of solutions to this problem. A female sheep, for instance, has alternative ways of recognizing her offspring. Close up, the ewe relies on vision and her sense of smell to distinguish her own lamb from the others in the flock. When the lamb is too far away for scent or sight to be useful, she relies upon hearing. A ewe can recognize the sound of her own lamb's voice.[16]

Consistent with the predictions of kin selection theory, animals of most species are nicer to their relatives than to nonrelatives. But humans also help others who are *not* related to them. That is the puzzle that led evolutionary psychologist Robert Trivers, in 1971, to propose the theory of reciprocal altruism.[17] The idea is that helping others can increase your fitness because the others may be disposed to return the favor if you are ever in need. An example in nonhuman animals—in vampire bats, believe it or not—soon turned up. Drinking blood, as every moviegoer knows, is a precarious way to make a living; bats sometimes return home from a hard night's work with an empty stomach. But vampire bats are a social species: they live in groups. And they help each other out. An unsuccessful hunter is usually able to get a handout, so to speak, of regurgitated blood from one of its more successful den mates. The successful hunter has gotten more than enough to meet its requirements, so it shares with the needy. Another night it might be the one in need, and then the recipient of its gift is expected to return the favor.[18] Evolutionary psychologists, and economists in the field of game theory, call it "tit for tat."

The thing about tit for tat is that it works only if the participants in the game are able to recognize and remember each other.[19] Evidently vampire bats can do this, because they know which of their comrades owes them a favor and that's the one they go to for a handout. Social animals that rely on reciprocal altruism to get them through hard times need to be able to tell one another apart. They need to know which members of their group are beholden to them and which can be relied upon to reciprocate. So they must be able to connect particular past experiences with particular individuals. They need a memory with a separate cache for each individual, because knowing that you're talking to George and not to Donald is useless if you can't remember whether it's George or Donald who owes you a favor.

Though theories of mate selection and reciprocal altruism are interesting, they are not the most important contribution of evolutionary psychology. The most important contribution is a new view of the human mind.

The harbinger of the breakthrough was a series of elegant experiments done in the 1960s by the psychologist John Garcia and his colleagues. The subjects were not humans but rats; the procedure was a variation on Pavlov's. Pavlov found that it was possible to train dogs to salivate at a signal—say, the sound of a bell—by presenting the signal and then giving them food. The linkage in time between the sound of the bell and the taste of food resulted in what American psychologists called a "conditioned reflex." The assumption that Pavlov made—and that most American psychologists never questioned—was that any arbitrary stimulus can be associated with any innate reflex to produce conditioning.

Garcia showed that Pavlov's assumption was wrong. He demonstrated that rats quickly learn to associate a particular taste (water sweetened with saccharine) with nausea induced by exposure to X-rays, even though the X-ray-induced illness occurs hours after they drink the water. The result of this association is that the rats develop an aversion to sweetened water, despite the fact that the water was not what caused their nausea. They can also learn that when a certain light goes on, it is a warning that they're about to receive a painful electric shock to the feet. But they do not learn to avoid the sweetened water if drinking it is followed by a shock, and they do not learn to avoid water associated with the light if drinking it is followed by an upset stomach.[20]

Garcia and his coauthors had a good deal of trouble getting their research published; they were turned down by journal after journal. A traditional behaviorist expressed the opinion that Garcia's findings were "no more likely than birdshit in a cuckoo clock."[21] But the findings held up to repeated tests. Nonhuman animals, and humans too, learn certain associations more readily than others, and the associations they learn make sense. It makes sense to expect dinner when you hear the dinner bell. It also makes sense that if dinner includes some kind of food you've never had before, and you eat it and a little while later get sick to your stomach, you will (rightly or wrongly) associate your nausea with that food and thereafter avoid it. A single bad experience can put you off a food forever.

Garcia's rats were just the beginning. A growing assortment of research, mostly with humans, led to the same conclusion: that the vertebrate brain is not equally disposed to perform all kinds of learning tasks. Some associations are made readily, some only with difficulty, some not at all. The human mind is poised—prepared in advance—to learn certain things with dazzling ease and speed.

The best example is language. It was Noam Chomsky who argued that language is in fact an extremely difficult thing to learn from the skimpy and imperfect examples of it that babies hear, and that in order to learn it as quickly and competently as they do, human babies must have a special aptitude for learning language. But it was Steven Pinker who turned Chomsky's "Language Acquisition Device" (a hypothetical mechanism in the brain) into something the rest of us could understand, and who linked the theory to the brand new field—this was the early 1990s—of evolutionary psychology. Here's what Pinker said in *The Language Instinct*:

> Language is not a cultural artifact that we learn the way we learn to tell time or how the federal government works. Instead, it is a distinct piece of the biological makeup of our brains. Language is a complex, specialized skill, which develops in the child spontaneously, without conscious effort or formal instruction, is deployed without awareness of its underlying logic, is qualitatively the same in every individual, and is distinct from more general abilities to process information or behave intelligently. For these reasons some cognitive scientists have described language as a psychological faculty, a mental organ, a neural system, and a computational module. But I prefer the admittedly quaint term "instinct." It conveys the idea that people know how to talk in more or less the sense that spiders know how to spin.[22]

Language is only one of many special abilities, some of which we share with other species, that humans are provided with. Evolutionary psychologists believe that the human mind is full of devices—mental organs or mechanisms or instincts—that were designed by evolution to perform special tasks. The mind is not like the mythical kitchen gadget that can do anything. It is a collection of specialized gadgets: one for cutting up the onions, another for frying them in, a third to keep you from burning your hand on the thing you fry them in.

Mental organs or mechanisms provide the wherewithal to accomplish jobs that, during the evolution of a species, were important to the members of that species. In many cases the devices also provide the motivation to do these jobs. Babies do not have to be rewarded, or even encouraged, to learn language: they are born wanting to learn it. They are predisposed from Day 1 to listen to human speech and to try to make sense out of it.

Another thing humans are good at is identifying individuals and telling them apart. It's not just a matter of distinguishing males from females, or nubile females from those who are too young or too old: we recognize and remember specific people. "Humans are obsessed with individuals," Pinker noted.[23] I propose that members of our species are equipped with a mental device dedicated to this purpose and that this mental device supplies its own motivation. Just as babies are born wanting to learn the language, they are born with a tremendous interest in learning to tell people apart. From birth they stare avidly at faces; from birth—or even before—they listen avidly to voices. A very young baby can recognize his mother by looking at her face or hearing her voice.[24] He can see or hear his sister, or his aunt, or the babysitter, and know that she is someone else—not his mother.

The human brain is about nine times larger, relative to body size, than that of a typical mammal. Why do we have such big brains? A number of explanations have been offered; many of them probably contain at least a grain of truth. Though possessing a big brain has some serious disadvantages, being smart has some even more serious advantages. *Homo sapiens* didn't colonize the earth and become the master of most of its other species through brute force. In the brute force department, humans, taken singly, are pathetic. Richard III died, according to Shakespeare, because he didn't have a horse.

Robin Dunbar, a British evolutionary psychologist, believes that brains got larger during hominid evolution because of the need to collect and store social information. Most species of monkeys and apes (orangutans are the notable exception) are highly social animals; they live in groups. Living in groups enabled them to survive in a hostile environment, even though, taken singly, most primates are pathetic in the brute force department. Our ancestors made a point of not being taken singly. Those who didn't do well in groups didn't become our ancestors.

But for a primate, doing well in groups involves more than sticking together for protection against predators. Within a primate group, there is a complex network of coalitions and enmities, of paid and unpaid obligations and affronts. Living successfully in a group means being aware of who is friends with whom, who is enemies with whom, who can beat up whom. If Clyde gets mad at you, not only do you have to watch out for Clyde—you also have to watch out for Clyde's friend Jake. You are less likely to get beaten up by Clyde and Jake if you can enlist the aid of an ally who ranks higher in the pecking order than they do.

The bigger the group, the more individuals and relationships between individuals you have to keep track of. Dunbar discovered that there is a strong correlation between the size of a primate's group—the typical group size for a given species—and the size of the neocortex for that species. The neocortex, the layer of brain cells just beneath the skull, is, as Dunbar put it, "what you might call the 'thinking' part of the brain."[25] With a few exceptions (the orangutan again), primates that have larger neocortices tend to associate in larger groups.

Armed with this correlation, Dunbar went on to calculate the natural group size for humans, based on the average size of the human neocortex. The answer he got was 150.

Today humans are found almost everywhere on our planet, in great numbers in some places. But until quite recently, *Homo sapiens* was a relatively uncommon species. Until our ancestors invented agriculture—a mere ten thousand years ago, only yesterday in evolutionary time—they lived a catch-as-catch-can existence as hunters and gatherers. It takes a lot of land to support a hunting and gathering lifestyle, so their groups tended to be smallish and thinly spread. For hundreds of thousands of years, our human and prehuman hominid ancestors lived and traveled together in small groups. Based on what we know from studies of surviving hunter-gatherer and tribal peoples, these groups were probably somewhat unstable. Small groups would coalesce, perhaps temporarily; larger ones would split in two. Individuals or families would occasionally switch from one group to another.

As Dunbar explained, hunter-gatherer and tribal societies are organized in tiers. At the bottom are temporary "overnight" groups of 30 or 35 people who travel together for a while. At the top is the tribe, a linguistic group that speaks the same language or dialect and typically numbers about 1,500 to 2,000 people. In between is the clan, which averages about 150. This, Dunbar believes, is the natural group size for humans, and he found other examples to support his claim. The villages of the earliest farmers. The optimal size for business organizations or church congregations or military fighting units. The maximum size of Hutterite communities. The Hutterites (a religious group that practices communal farming) divide their communities in two when their size exceeds 150 people. According to Dunbar, they've found that above this number it becomes more difficult to maintain compliance to the sect's rules.[26]

The inhabitants of a community of 150 or less all know one another. They know everyone's name and face; they can recite everyone's ancestry and life history. And they have opinions about everyone's personality. The members of an Eskimo group in northwest Alaska told an anthropologist that in the old days incorrigible troublemakers were quietly pushed off the ice.[27] The opinion that a man is an incorrigible troublemaker is an opinion about his personality. It is also a prediction about his future behavior: this man will continue to make trouble if somebody doesn't stop him.

Among the special-purpose devices with which evolution has provided our species is a face-recognition module. Neuroscientists found it fairly easy to demonstrate that this device is modular because most of its wiring happens to be located in one place in the brain. There is no necessity for a brain mechanism that performs a particular task to be localized in one small area of the brain—some mental mechanisms have widespread components—but localized mechanisms are easier to study. Did you ever hear of the man who mistook his wife for a hat? His face-recognition module was so badly damaged that he couldn't even tell the difference between a human face and an object.[28] More commonly, damage to the face-recognition area of the brain results in recognizing that something is a human face but not knowing whose face it is. A person with this disability, called prosopagnosia, doesn't ordinarily mistake his wife for a hat: he mistakes her for a stranger. Even his own face in the mirror is unfamiliar to him. He hasn't only forgotten faces he already knew: he is unable to learn new ones.[29]

One of the remarkable things about the neurologically intact human brain is how many new faces it is able to learn. "The human features and countenance, although composed of but some ten parts or little more, are so fashioned that among so many thousands of men there are no two in existence who cannot be distinguished from one another," said Pliny the Elder, back in the days when thousands seemed like a large number.[30] Pliny wasn't claiming that he himself could distinguish each of these thousands of men from all the others, but he clearly felt that he could do so, given the opportunity.

The inhabitants of modern industrialized nations are given that opportunity. They live, work, and go to school in places where there are hundreds of people. Every time they change schools or jobs or residences, they meet a whole new set. Television, movies, newspapers, magazines, books, and the Internet bring them still more faces. They can remember and identify an amazing number of them. If the students who took part in the experiment with the nice or nasty grad student met her in the supermarket a month later, most of them would recognize her.

If our brains were constructed to enable us to live in groups of 150, how come so much storage space was provided? There appears to be no limit to how many new faces we can learn. No limit to our ability to collect and store other information to go with those faces—their names, or where you encountered them, or whether they are nice or nasty.

Unlike the language acquisition device, which did its best work before your twelfth birthday and then rested on its laurels, your people-information acquisition device will keep chugging away all through your life. I am sixty-seven years old and in poor health; often a week will go by in which the only people I see in person are my husband and the woman who cleans our house. But about five years ago I developed an interest in watching professional golf tournaments on TV. Today I printed out a list of the top two hundred of the world's male golfers and found that I can mentally call up a face for at least seventy of them, including twenty-three of the top twenty-five. I can also tell you other things about many of them. This one spends long hours on the practice range; that one is lazy. This one just got married; that one has two kids. This one wears his emotions on his sleeve; that one keeps them well buttoned up.

What's the point of learning all this stuff? Why am I wasting my brain cells on this useless information? I'm never going to run into Tiger Woods or Ernie Els in the supermarket!

But I've found it enjoyable to acquire this useless information and in this respect I'm by no means unusual. It is to serve this acquisitive drive that magazines fill their pages with articles about people and photographs of their faces, and bookstores load their shelves with biographies and autobiographies of real people and novels about fictional ones. In the *"A" Is for Alibi* series, detective Kinsey Millhone reveals a little more about herself in each new mystery; she keeps her readers coming back for more. In *The Daughter of Time*, Alan Grant spends hours in his hospital bed gazing at a portrait of Richard III. "I want to know," he explains, "what made him tick."[31]

I've seen that portrait; it's reproduced in a little book I own, *The Kings and Queens of Britain*, by Sir George Bellew. To me, Richard looks worried and a little sad, as though he already had an inkling that his cry for a horse would go unanswered. But according to Sir George, "This portrait gives more than a hint of the unscrupulous nature of Richard III."[32]

Not to me it doesn't, and not to Alan Grant. Grant thought Richard looked like a saint. But remembering faces is a lot easier than deciphering them. "There's no art," said Shakespeare, "to find the mind's construction in the face."[33] Shakespeare didn't mean that it's easy to read people's minds by looking at their faces; he meant just the opposite. Those words are spoken in *Macbeth* by a character expressing his dismay that someone he trusted had turned out to be a traitor.

We want to know what makes people tick. Not just people in general: we want to know what makes *particular* people tick, because people don't all tick alike. We are fascinated by the differences among people because our brains are built that way. And they're built that way for a reason: during the evolutionary history of our species it paid off to know what makes particular individuals tick, because it made it easier to predict their behavior. To decide whether to share with them, to mate with them, to trust them, to fear them. The proposal—not the only one I will make in this book—that the human brain contains a specialized mechanism for collecting people-information is consistent with the principles of evolutionary psychology.

The people-information acquisition device not only does the work of collecting the information: it also provides the motivation to do so. It makes collecting people-information something we do without effort or training and without the expectation of reward: doing it is its own reward. The face-recognition module is one component of this mechanism, but not an essential component. We store information about people even if we don't have a face to attach it to. I have no mental image of Kinsey Millhone's face. Nor do you, I daresay, but you may nonetheless remember that she runs to keep fit, lives in California, and is currently unattached.

Though the people-information acquisition device is part of our innate equipment, its innateness doesn't imply that we're all exactly alike in this respect. Just as the desire to engage in sex, or take care of a baby, or learn the meaning of a new word varies from one individual to another, so does the interest in acquiring people-information. There are individuals—the journalist Malcolm Gladwell calls them "Connectors"—who are champion collectors of people-information. But even ordinary people possess huge stores of such information. Gladwell has devised a test that he has given to hundreds of people. The test consists of a list of about 250 surnames, some common, some rare. Here are the first 50 names on the list:

> Algazi, Alvarez, Alpern, Ametrano, Andrews, Aran, Arnstein, Ashford, Bailey, Ballout, Bamberger, Baptista, Barr, Barrows, Baskerville, Bassiri, Bell, Bokgese, Brandao, Bravo, Brooke, Brightman, Billy, Blau, Bohen, Bohn, Borsuk, Brendle, Butler, Calle, Cantwell, Carrell, Chinlund, Cirker, Cohen, Collas, Couch,

> Callegher, Calcaterra, Cook, Carey, Cassell, Chen, Chung, Clarke, Cohn, Carton, Crowley, Curbelo, Dellamanna.[34]

To take the test, you give yourself a point every time you see the surname of someone you know personally—someone whose name you know and who knows yours. If you know two people with the same surname, you give yourself two points.

Among a group of college students who took the test, the average score was 21. Among a sample of Gladwell's friends—many of them journalists, most ten years or more out of college—it was 41, ranging from a low of 9 to a high of 95.

If you scored 9 on Gladwell's test, it doesn't mean you have only nine friends and acquaintances in your social circle; you have vastly more than that, since the 250 names on Gladwell's list are only a small fraction of all the names there are. And Gladwell asked only about friends and acquaintances. What if he asked about all the people, living and dead, you can identify by name—movie actors and politicians, sports figures and scientists, authors and musicians, even fictional characters in TV shows and books? It has been at least fifty years since I last read *Little Women* but I still remember Meg, Jo, Beth, and Amy. My brain didn't have to toss out Meg, Jo, Beth, and Amy to make room for Tiger Woods and Ernie Els.

The ease with which we collect information about people, and the pleasure we take in collecting it, are matched by the ease and pleasure with which we share it. The sharing is called "gossip"—a pejorative term that takes note of the fact that it's fun while denying that it might have a serious purpose. As soon as children can talk to each other they begin to talk about each other. "Do you like Jamie?" "No, Jamie broke my crayon." Older children spend much of their lunchroom and playground time gossiping. Too bad they don't enjoy learning math and science as much as they enjoy exchanging information (which might not even be true) about people (whom they may never have met).

Grownups gossip too, of course. Robin Dunbar and his students listened in on people's conversations and found that two-thirds of conversation time is spent on "matters of social import. Who is doing what with whom." Dunbar believes that the ability to share information about people had important survival and reproductive benefits for our ancestors. "In a nutshell," he says, "I am suggesting that language evolved to allow us to gossip."[35] To propose that gossip is the primary purpose of language is, I think, carrying it a bit too far; language serves many important functions and is unlikely to have evolved just so A can tell B what C is doing with D. However, a weaker version of Dunbar's proposal is plausible: *one* of the reasons that language evolved is to allow us to gossip.[36]

Whatever A wants to tell B about C, their language is sure to provide a way of saying it. In 1936, a couple of obsessive-compulsive American psychologists went through *Webster's New International Dictionary* from A to Z and marked every word they judged to be "descriptive of personality or personal behavior." They counted 17,953 of them.[37] English is exceptionally rich in vocabulary, but all languages provide a variety of words to describe personality and personal behavior. Gossip is a popular activity all over the world—a human universal.[38]

Universals often go unnoticed. We tend to take for granted things that everyone can do. That's one of the reasons why atypical individuals—people who can't do these things because there is something wrong with their brains—are of particular interest to researchers. The British cognitive scientist Simon Baron-Cohen has learned a great deal about the normal human mind by studying children with autism.

Autistic children, as we now know, are born that way; it's not something their parents did to them. Something went wrong—neuroscientists don't yet know exactly what—in the development of their brains. Genes clearly play a role; identical twins are generally concordant for autism. When one twin has the disorder, the other is likely to have it too.[39]

Autism doesn't knock out a single ability; it knocks out a whole family of them. To an evolutionary psychologist (Baron-Cohen is an evolutionary psychologist as well as a cognitive scientist—an increasingly common combination), this means that the mental mechanisms that normally serve these abilities are missing or malfunctioning. Indeed, it is hard to explain autism without invoking mental mechanisms, because some abilities are spared while others are absent.

One of the abilities that is missing or badly impaired in autistic children is the ability to recognize faces. There is neurophysiological evidence that autistic people visually process faces the way nonautistic people process objects.[40] It is a tedious business, learning to tell people apart the way we learn to tell objects apart, and autistic children take no pleasure in it. Normal babies, as I mentioned, gaze avidly at people's faces; autistic babies do not. Their lack of interest in learning to tell people apart is evidence, not only that their people-information acquisition device isn't working properly, but that this device, when functioning normally, supplies the motivation as well as the ability.

Individuals with autism not only lack an interest in finding out what makes people tick: in some sense they are unaware of the ticking. They lack what cognitive scientists call a "theory of mind." Simon Baron-Cohen wrote an interesting book on this topic, titled *Mindblindness*, in which he worked out the specifications of the theory-of-mind mechanism. Autistic children are mindblind because they don't automatically realize that other people have minds. They don't realize that other people have thoughts and knowledge that may differ from their own. They don't realize that, simply by telling a person something, they can put a thought—possibly a false one—into that person's mind. Normal children develop the abilities that underlie these realizations by the age of four.[41]

What I haven't seen mentioned in the literature on autism is that these children not only fail to appreciate that other people have minds: they also fail to appreciate the variation among minds. They don't seem to be aware of, or interested in, the fact that people differ in personality. They don't seem to realize that people *have* personalities, and that knowing something about their personalities can help to predict their behavior in the future. They also lack the motivation to share information about individuals. Autistic children don't gossip.

Earlier in this chapter I described a mental bias called the fundamental attribution error. I gave the example of the subjects who thought that a grad student was cold and unfriendly because she behaved that way during a brief conversation. A few pages later I provided another example, without drawing your attention to it. Did you notice that I called the researchers who went through the dictionary counting personality words "obsessive-compulsive"? The only thing I knew about them was that they went through the entire dictionary and counted 17,953 personality words, but from that meager information I concluded something about their personalities.

Neurologically normal humans have a strong tendency to draw conclusions about an individual's personality on the basis of a sample of behavior, even if there are other possible explanations for why she behaved that way. The conclusion that an individual has a certain personality is a prediction about how she will behave in the future. We jump to the conclusion that a sample of behavior is a clue to someone's personality because our minds—more precisely, our people-information acquisition devices—are built that way.

Mental organs are expensive to build and to run, and the fancy ones require a lot of evolutionary time to get them working properly. They don't evolve by chance; they don't evolve unless they provide their owners with some benefit in terms of survival or reproduction. The way the people-information acquisition device works implies that the following things were as true during the evolution of our species as they are today: that people had personalities, that personalities differed from one individual to another, that behavior was an indication of personality, and that it was useful to learn something about a given individual's personality because people were, at least to some extent, consistent. The information was worth acquiring because it told us what to expect in the future from that individual.

Today we store information about individuals we will never meet because the people-information acquisition device, which was designed a long time ago, doesn't know we will never meet them. In ancestral times, when there weren't so many humans around, anyone you encountered once had a good chance of showing up again. They might turn out to be important, one way or the other, to your survival.[42]

There are websites where you can search for articles that have been published in psychology journals. If you type the word "personality" in the search box you will be deluged: 165,620 relevant articles published since 1985, when I just tried it. But if what you want is a definition of the word "personality," those 165,620 articles are not the place to seek it. Look instead in a textbook of introductory psychology. A good example is the definition offered in the textbook written by the psychologist Peter Gray:

> Personality refers to a person's general style of interacting with the world, especially with other people—whether one is withdrawn or outgoing, excitable or placid, conscientious or careless, kind or stern. A basic assumption of the personality concept is that people do differ from one another in their styles of behavior, in ways that are at least relatively consistent across time and place.[43]

This definition captures two essential components of the concept: variety and consistency. Personality is about the ways in which people differ from one other but remain true to themselves. A third component is the emphasis on social interactions. To a large extent, we're talking about differences in styles of *social* behavior.

People differ from one another in a great many ways; consequently, articles about personality cover a wide range of topics. Here, for example, are some of the topics—presumably aspects or manifestations of personality—touched on in a single eighteen-page review article:

> The ability to delay gratification, the ability to process social information, aggressiveness, agreeableness, behavioral inhibition, carelessness, coercive behavior, conformity, conscientiousness, criminal behavior, curiosity, distractibility, driving while intoxicated, emotional expressiveness, extraversion, fearfulness, impulsiveness, industriousness, irritability, job satisfaction, leadership ability, moodiness, narcissism, neuroticism, openness, political attitudes, religious attitudes, restlessness, self-confidence, self-control, self-directedness, shyness, sociability, social potency, social responsibility, spouse abuse, submissiveness, substance use, the tendency to feel mistreated or deceived by others, the tendency to have temper tantrums, and the tendency to seek or avoid danger.[44]

This article was titled "Personality Development Across the Life Course." It had to do with children as well as adults, which means that the research reviewed by the authors didn't come only from standard personality tests. You can't sit six-year-olds at a table, hand them a pencil and a sheet of paper, and ask them to check off their degree of agreement or disagreement with statements like "When people don't treat me right, I get angry." Self-report personality questionnaires are used mainly with adults. In fact, the term *personality* is applied primarily to adults; researchers who study children generally just talk about the particular characteristic they are interested in: aggressiveness, self-confidence, emotional expressiveness, whatever.

Because there are so many different things to measure, and because paper-and-pencil tests are not always appropriate or possible, the behaviors and characteristics that fall under the rubric of personality are measured in a variety of ways. Aggressiveness in children may be judged by their parents, teachers, or peers; or by researchers who observe them in their homes, on the playground, or in a laboratory. Assessments of criminal behavior may be based on court records; of spouse abuse, on the say-so of the spouse.

But because self-report personality tests are easy to give and produce lots of data that can be processed by computers, a good deal of what we now know about personality is based on this method. I'm not talking about tests (such as the Minnesota Multiphasic Personality Inventory) used in the diagnosis of mental illness, or tests (such as the Rorschach or the Myers-

Brigg) that have not held up to scientific scrutiny. The kind of tests I'm talking about have been honed over the years, through trial and error, to be reliable and accurate; their accuracy is judged by how well they agree with other methods of assessment. They are designed to assess personality within the normal range by giving quantitative estimates of where an individual falls in terms of a few basic personality dimensions. The number of dimensions varies from one brand of test to another, but the most popular format uses five: conscientiousness, agreeableness, neuroticism, openness, and extraversion. Each of these dimensions is bidirectional: agreeableness–disagreeableness, extraversion–introversion, and so on. (Neuroticism means the tendency to get upset easily or to feel anxious or depressed; its opposite is emotional stability. Openness means the willingness to entertain new ideas or try new experiences.) The idea is that the infinite variety we see in human personality can be cooked up from only five ingredients, just by varying the recipe a little.[45]

You might be skeptical about self-report personality tests—many people are—but the truth is that every method of assessing personality has its drawbacks and we have to start somewhere. Unsupported by other evidence, data produced by a single method aren't worth much. Be assured that no conclusion I come to in this book is based solely on the results of personality tests.

Oh, about personality development across the life course: the authors of that article concluded that there is "modest continuity" of personality from childhood to adulthood, and that personality gradually becomes more stable as people get older. But even in mid-adulthood there remains some flexibility. If your life changes, so might you.

Though evolution has provided the members of our species with built-in curiosity about how people tick, it has provided no built-in explanation of why they tick that way—why one individual is excitable and another placid, one withdrawn and the other outgoing. Stories about the origin of personality, like stories about the origin of the universe, are products of their culture—cultural myths that may be passed on for generations or overturned and supplanted by new ones almost overnight.

The developmental psychologist Jerome Kagan provided a good example: the contrast between the autobiographical writings of Alice James (sister of Henry and William) and those of the writer John Cheever. Both were subject to spells of depression that plagued their adult lives. But Alice

James, writing in the latter half of the nineteenth century, "believed with the vast majority of her contemporaries that she had inherited her nervous, dour mood," Kagan reported, whereas Cheever, writing in the latter half of the twentieth, "assumed that his bouts of depression were due to childhood experiences . . . the conflicts that he imagined his family had created."[46] In the nineteenth century and the first half of the twentieth, explanations of why people differ in personality were based mainly on "nature"—heredity. Cultural myths changed rather abruptly in the middle of the twentieth century. Since then, explanations of why people differ have been based mainly on "nurture"—how their parents treated them while they were growing up. Notice that I do not define *nurture* as a synonym for *environment*. The word *environment* has a broader meaning; it means everything that isn't heredity. But *nurture*, from a verb meaning "to take care of" or "to rear," singles out one particular part of the environment: the part provided by the parents. It is nurture in particular, rather than environment in general, that plays a starring role in our cultural myths about the origin of personality.

Earlier I mentioned two new brooms for sweeping out the cobwebs in psychology: evolutionary psychology and behavioral genetics. Practitioners of both these disciplines are often accused of believing that "everything is genetic." The accusation is true in neither case, but what is often overlooked is its double meaning: *nature* or *genetic* means one thing to an evolutionary psychologist, something else to a behavioral geneticist. An evolutionary psychologist uses "nature" to account for the ways that all human beings (or all those of the same sex) are alike; a behavioral geneticist uses it to account for the ways that human beings differ from one another.

Evolutionary psychologists were not breaking new ground when they proposed that human beings come with some built-in abilities and predispositions. All theories of personality include as one of their axioms—whether explicitly stated or not—that something is built in. For behaviorists it is the ability to learn from one's experiences; for social learning theorists (who believe in observational learning) it is the ability to learn from someone else's. For Freudians it is the libido, powered by the unconscious drives of sex and aggression; for the followers of Abraham Maslow it is the drive to self-actualize. Like evolutionary psychologists, believers in these theories use "nature" mainly to explain the ways in which all people are the same. To explain why they differ, they rely mainly on differences in environment or experiences.

Behavioral geneticists are psychologists who specialize in studying human differences. They have shown that one of the reasons people differ—not the only reason, but *one* of the reasons—is that they have different genes.

But neither different genes nor different environments can solve the mystery of individuality. Neither can explain why Laleh and Ladan Bijani—conjoined identical twins who, in Ladan's words, were "stuck to each other" for twenty-nine years—had different world views, different lifestyles, different goals in life, different personalities. Neither can explain why George and Donald—identical twins who are not stuck together but who are being reared in the same home at the same time by the same parents—are different individuals, each with a unique personality.

Yes, identical twins (even those who are reared in separate homes) share lots of little quirks. But people who know both of them say things like "Ladan is the friendly one." Whether reared together or apart, identical twins are by no means identical in the answers they check off on personality tests: the correlation between their scores is only about .50. This is a moderate correlation, not a strong one. Alice James believed that her depression was inherited, but the identical twin of someone who has experienced a major depression has only a 40 percent chance of becoming seriously depressed. The identical twin of someone with schizophrenia has only a 48 percent chance of developing the disorder.[47]

Identical twins have identical genes; they were formed from the same fertilized egg. Alice James's theory—heredity—cannot explain the differences between identical twins. Neither can John Cheever's. Ladan and Laleh went everywhere together; how different could their childhood experiences have been? If one was exposed to family quarrels or misfortunes, so was the other. If one was kept sequestered at home or taken daily to the playground or the marketplace, so was the other. If one was subjected to harsh and early toilet training, would their caregiver have been relaxed and laissez-faire with the other? An overbearing mother, a wimpy or absentee father, parents who get along well, parents who get along poorly, exposure to privation and violence, exposure to books and museums—all these things are shared by identical twins who grow up together. And yet identical twins who grow up together have different personalities.

In a classic British mystery novel such as Dorothy Sayers' *Five Red Herrings*,[48] the detective spends most of the book examining the suspects one by one and showing why each of them couldn't have, or wouldn't have, committed the crime. The one who's left after everyone else has been eliminated is declared the perpetrator.

In this case, one suspect can be eliminated right off the bat. Nobody believes that "everything is genetic" or that behavior or personality is "determined" by the genes. Clearly, it's not just genes—it can't be—that make twins who have identical genes differ in personality.

But I'm not interested only in twins. People also differ from their brothers and sisters, even though siblings have many genes in common and share a home environment. The differences between siblings are a familiar theme in literature. In Shakespeare's *King Lear*, two of Lear's daughters say flattering things about him but the third refuses to do so, to his bafflement and anger. In Beatrix Potter's *The Tale of Peter Rabbit*, Flopsy, Mopsy, and Cotton-tail are good little bunnies who do as they're told, but Peter is always getting into trouble. Such stories are not confined to fiction. You may have read newspaper accounts of a pair of brothers in Boston: one a college president, the other a gangster on the run from the law.[49]

But I'm not interested only in siblings, either. Twins and siblings are useful, as I will show in the next chapter, because they make it possible to test some theories of personality development. A detective has to have some tools; new tools lead to new methods of detection and often to new conclusions. A suspect found guilty in Shakespeare's time might today be exonerated on the basis of fingerprint or DNA evidence. Modern methods of testing theories of personality make use of the fact that twins and ordinary siblings are similar in some ways and different in others.

We are all similar in some ways and different in others. I stand with the evolutionary psychologists in believing that humans come with quite a lot of standard equipment. But a good way to find out how the standard equipment works is by seeing how it responds when it receives different inputs from the environment. All normal human babies have a language acquisition device, but which language they learn depends on what their environment provides. It would have been very difficult for psycholinguists to figure out how the language acquisition device works if everyone spoke the same language.

My goal in this book is to show how things we all have in common can make us different. Human nature—the ways in which we are all alike—can lead to human differences. This is not a novel idea; as I said earlier, all theories of personality include an axiom (whether stated explicitly or not) that something is built in. The trouble is that none of these theories can explain why Laleh and Ladan Bijani had different personalities.

2

That Damn Rectangle

THOUGH I WAS often sick as a child and missed a lot of school, the health problems in the first half of my life were intermittent rather than chronic. My healthiest years were in late adolescence and early adulthood. I went to college, spent two years in graduate school, and married one of my fellow graduate students. I managed to produce one child, a daughter. Our second daughter was adopted.

Both daughters were grown, out of the house, and doing well by the time I had the idea that led me to write *The Nurture Assumption*. But by then my health had worsened and I was unable to travel around interviewing people to gather human interest material for my book. I had to make do with what was on hand. So, with their permission, I used my two daughters as examples of how two siblings reared in the same home can be very different. "Merely corroborative detail," Pooh-Bah explained in *The Mikado*, "intended to give artistic verisimilitude to an otherwise bald and unconvincing narrative."

As a Gilbert and Sullivan fan, I should have known better: the corroborative detail got Pooh-Bah into a lot of trouble. But I didn't make a big deal about one of my children being adopted; it's mentioned only once, in a casual way, in the book:

> I do not believe that parents have a consistent child-rearing style, unless they happen to have consistent children. I had two very different children—one of them is adopted but the same thing can happen with biological siblings—and used two very different child-rearing styles.[1]

The press nevertheless pounced on it. They were intrigued by the unusual composition of my family: one biological daughter, one adopted daughter.

It didn't escape their notice that one of the things I talked about in my book was differences between siblings and I just happened to have a perfect example right in my own family. Many journalists jumped to the erroneous conclusion that my rejection of traditional theories of child development, and my proposal of a new theory, were based on my personal experiences as a mother.[2]

No doubt some theories *are* based on the theorists' personal experiences, but mine wasn't. In fact, it is seldom necessary to think up a new theory in order to account for one's personal experiences: one can almost always find a way to explain them in terms of existing theories. Neither Alice James, in the nineteeth century, nor John Cheever, in the twentieth, had any trouble explaining their spells of depression in terms of the culturally accepted theories of their times. James blamed heredity; Cheever blamed his childhood family environment. His mother neglected him, he claimed.[3]

During the years when I was personally experiencing motherhood—the years when my children were young and living at home—my theories were entirely conventional: the culturally accepted theories of the latter part of the twentieth century. My job at that time was writing college textbooks in child development, and there was nothing out of the ordinary about the textbooks I wrote.[4] All I was doing was parroting the recognized authorities in the field. It wasn't hypocrisy: I believed them!

I stopped believing them long after my daughters were launched on their successful adult lives. What led to the sudden and dramatic revision in my thinking was not motherhood but a year spent reading widely in diverse areas of psychology, in preparation for writing another textbook.[5] What I noticed in my reading was that something was wrong with the current theories: results that didn't fit kept turning up. These embarrassing findings weren't anecdotes or case studies—they came from data based on large numbers of children. Only in data collected from many subjects can one see the forest; otherwise it's just trees.

The Nurture Assumption was my attempt to explain the puzzling findings turned up by researchers. I put together a lot of evidence showing that parents have no direct influence on how their children turn out and proposed that children are socialized by their peer groups. But socialization is a process that makes children more alike, more similar in behavior to others of their age and gender. If they're getting socialized, why do they continue to differ from one another in personality? Though group socialization could account for the similarities, my attempt to account for the differences ("differentiation within the group") was vague and unconvincing.

At least mine wasn't the only failure. Neither evolutionary psychologists (who focus mainly on the ways that people are alike), nor behavioral geneticists (who focus mainly on the effects of genes), nor developmental psychologists (who focus mainly on the effects of the environment) have provided an adequate explanation of personality differences. We know that genes cannot account for all the differences, but no one has answered the question of how the environment can make people more alike in some ways and less alike in others. No one has explained why identical twins who grow up together have different personalities.

Here's an important clue. The unexplained—that is, nongenetic—differences in personality between identical twins reared in the same home are about as wide as the unexplained differences between ordinary siblings. And the unexplained differences between ordinary siblings are about as wide as the unexplained differences between two people of the same sex and about the same age, plucked at random from a city street or college classroom.

It's an important clue but a baffling one. If this were a mystery novel and the important clue had to do with fingerprints, I wouldn't have to explain what fingerprints are or how that kind of evidence is obtained. But understanding my clue depends on having some knowledge of the methods and findings of behavioral genetics. In Dorothy Sayers' mystery *Five Red Herrings*, the important clue has to do with trains, and the reader is expected to pick up a fair amount of knowledge about the timetables and operating procedures of the trains that chugged their way through rural Scotland in the 1930s.[6] I promise you it will be quicker and more useful to learn a little about behavioral genetics.

But I too have five red herrings to let off the hook before I can solve the mystery of individuality. In this chapter I will look closely at the first two suspects: that personality differences are mainly due to differences in environment, or that they're due to a combination of "nature" (genes) and "nurture" (the part of the environment provided by parents).

The study of individual differences has been part of psychology from the beginning. IQ tests, for example, were first devised about a century ago as a tool for studying differences in intelligence. If every child gave the same response to a question on an IQ test, that question would be useless. The point of an IQ test, or of a personality test, is that different individuals answer the questions differently. Researchers who give IQ tests or personality tests are studying human variation. So are researchers who study children's aggressiveness by observing them on the playground, or who study their emotional expressiveness by putting them in contrived situations in the laboratory, or who study adolescents' use of illegal drugs by asking them to fill out questionnaires.

Expressed as numbers, the results may vary widely or fall within a narrow range. The amount of variation will depend on what you're measuring and how you're measuring it, and on the sort of subjects you've got. There's likely to be more variation in IQ in a group of basketball players than in a group of physicists, but the physicists will vary more in height. No need to be vague about it: variation can be quantified. The two statistics that are generally used for this purpose—you may already be familiar with them—are the standard deviation and the variance; the first is simply the square root of the second.[7] The standard deviation for IQ scores in the general population is 15 IQ points; the variance is 225. It would be a smaller number in the group of physicists. The word "variance" is going to crop up often in this chapter, but all you really need to know is that it's a way of specifying precisely how widely a given bunch of people vary in some way.

I'll trouble you with only one other statistical term and it's one that is in common use: correlation. A correlation is simply a relationship—a statistical linkage—between two sets of measurements. A positive correlation between children's aggressiveness, say, and how often these children were spanked by their parents would mean that children who received frequent spankings tended to be more aggressive than average and those who received few or none tended to be less aggressive than average. (If children who received frequent spankings tended to be *less* aggressive than average, the correlation would be negative.) Theoretically, positive correlations can range from zero (meaning that the two sets of measurements are unrelated) to 1.0, but in psychological research they seldom go above .50 and are usually much less than that. Developmental psychologists break open the champagne if they find a correlation as high as .30 between an outcome variable such as aggressiveness and an environmental variable such as frequency of spankings.

The developmentalists' goal is to explain the differences among their subjects. They want to discover why some individuals are more aggressive, or smarter, or more apt to reveal their emotions, or less apt to use illegal drugs than their fellows. To put it in technical terms, they want to "account for the variance" in the outcome variable they are measuring. They use correlations for this purpose. The trouble is that correlation does not imply causation. If frequency of spankings by parents and aggressiveness in children are found to be correlated, that doesn't mean that the former caused the latter. It could be the other way round: aggressive children more often try their parents' patience to the spanking point. Or the correlation could be due to a third factor, genetic influences on personality. If aggressiveness is to some extent inherited, then aggressive parents (who are quick to resort to physical punishment) will tend to have aggressive children. Perhaps all three things are going on at once. There's no way of telling, just from a correlation.

The goal of the behavioral geneticists is exactly the same as that of the developmentalists: they want to explain the differences among their subjects. They want to account for the variance in the outcome variable they are measuring. They use correlations for this purpose, just like the developmentalists. But there are crucial differences in methodology. The methods used by the behavioral geneticists, unlike those used by the developmentalists, permit them to estimate how much of the variance in outcome can be attributed to genetic influences on personality.

The first discovery to emerge from the behavioral geneticists' research lets my first red herring off the hook: differences in personality are not due entirely, or almost entirely, to differences in environment. Individuals differ from one another in part because they have different genes. Though this was not really news, its timing was unpropitious: the results started appearing in psychology journals in the early 1970s. At that time there were many people who didn't want to admit that genes had any effect at all on personality; as a result the first red herring flopped around for years. Environmentalists are still plentiful but—well, I can't say that the scales have fallen from their eyes, but over time they have become more modest in their claims and less strident in their denunciations.

The behavioral geneticists' second discovery *was* news: the environment doesn't work the way everyone thought. "Nature" was performing as expected, but "nurture" turned out to be a dud. There is variation in personality that cannot be blamed on genes, but neither can it be blamed on the environment that everyone (including me) believed was the most important to a child's development: the home in which he or she grew up.

Put into numbers, the behavioral geneticists' research showed that somewhere between 30 and 50 percent of the variance in personality among their subjects could be attributed to "heritability"—the effects of genes.[8] Across studies, heritability for personality characteristics averages about 45 percent. The expectation was that the effects of the home environment would account for most of the remaining variance, but it didn't. In fact, it accounted for only a tiny fraction of the variance and often for none at all.[9]

The behavioral genetic findings can be summed up like this. Differences in genes cause people to differ in personality, but people also differ for reasons other than genes. Differences in environment of the sort experienced by two children who are reared in different homes appear to have no effect on personality. Being separated in infancy and reared in two different homes does not make identical twins any less alike in personality. Being reared in the same home by the same parents does not make adoptive or step-siblings any more alike.

Though these results puzzled the researchers who discovered them, I noticed that they dovetailed with other unexpected findings that had been cropping up in research on children. The years of effort devoted to finding something peculiar about the "only child" were a failure; though this child's home life differs markedly from that of a child with siblings, no consistent differences in social behavior or psychological adjustment have turned up.[10] Nor have researchers found any reliable differences between children who spent the daylight hours of their first five years in a day-care center and those who spent that time at home in the company of a parent.[11] Children conceived by *in vitro* fertilization, despite the intense form of parenting they are likely to receive, are indistinguishable from those conceived in the far more common way: accidentally, often *in vino*.[12]

In short, whenever a research method is used that controls for, or is not much affected by, the genetic differences between families, the home environment and the parents' style of child-rearing are found to be ineffective in shaping children's personalities.

Two red herrings eliminated, right off the bat. The evidence produced by the behavioral geneticists shows that personality differences are not mostly due to differences in environment: genes matter too. The evidence also shows that personality differences are not due to a combination of genes plus the home environment—not due, in other words, to "nature" and "nurture." And the behavioral genetic evidence doesn't stand alone. There are many other findings to back it up, reported by developmentalists, social psychologists, anthropologists, and psycholinguists. I put all the evidence together in *The Nurture Assumption*. My conclusions about personality differences were mainly negative: I showed what the answer *couldn't* be. It's not the way the parents raise the kids.

It was that—the negative part of *The Nurture Assumption*, not my theory of group socialization—that got all the publicity. DO PARENTS MATTER? was the typical headline. Professors in psychology departments all over the country were asked for their opinion and most of them disagreed with me. The developmentalists were especially vehement in their opposition. According to *Newsweek*, "Many of the nation's leading scholars of child development accuse Harris of screwy logic, of misunderstanding behavioral genetics, and of ignoring studies that do not fit her thesis."[13] Actually, I had spent many pages taking apart those studies and showing exactly what was wrong with them. As for misunderstanding behavioral genetics, the behavioral geneticists didn't think so.

The charge that I misunderstood behavioral genetics was replaced, as time went on, by the charge that I relied on it too heavily, too trustingly. My conclusions, however, were not based solely on behavioral genetic evidence; most of the research I discussed in that book (and most of the research I will tell you about in this one) came from other areas of psychology. Nevertheless, understanding the behavioral genetic evidence is essential because it provides some important clues. Clues about the *environment.*

In order to understand how the environment produces differences in personality, we first have to allow for the differences due to genes. We have to know what the genes contribute before we can figure out what the environment does. Those who don't take genes into account are likely to jump to the wrong conclusions about how the environment affects personality. Psychologists from Freud on down have made that mistake. Freud noticed that finicky, uptight patients tended to have finicky, uptight mothers and attributed their plight to the way they were toilet trained.

Behavioral geneticists have been likened to Nazis and denounced as racists. They have been accused—are still being accused[14]—of being genetic "determinists," though no one seems to worry much about environmental determinists. I'm not going to go into the politics of the nature-nurture debate; see Steven Pinker's *The Blank Slate*. But one persistent—and misguided—criticism of behavioral genetics really gets my goat: that damn rectangle. Here, for example, is Paul Ehrlich, a professor of biology and population studies at Stanford, writing in *The Chronicle of Higher Education* in the year 2000:

> We can't partition the responsibility for aggression, altruism, or charisma between DNA and upbringing. In many such cases, trying to

> separate the contributions of nature and nurture to an attribute is rather like trying to separate the contributions of length and width to the area of a rectangle, which at first glance also seems easy. When you think about it carefully, though, it proves impossible.[15]

Ehrlich is saying that it's impossible to figure out how much heredity and environment contribute to personality. They're both important!

He is right in a way: it is nonsense to say, about a particular individual, that a certain percentage of his or her personality is due to heredity and a certain percentage to environmental influences. But no behavioral geneticist has ever made such a statement. That's not what behavioral genetics is about. It's about human variation, human differences. Not variation within a single individual, but differences from one individual to another within a population or group of people.

For a single rectangle, it indeed makes no sense to say that it owes its area more to one dimension than the other. But it makes perfect sense to make that statement about the variation in a group of rectangles—the ones in the top diagram, for example. These rectangles vary considerably in vertical length but are about the same in width, so most of the variation in area is due to the differences in length. In contrast, the rectangles in the bottom diagram vary considerably in width and are about the same in vertical length, so most of the variation in area is due to the differences in width.

Let's say you have a bunch of rectangles that vary in area. You want to figure out how much of the variation—the differences in area within this set of rectangles—can be attributed to differences in width and how much to differences in length, but you can't measure either dimension directly. How would you go about it? Right, you'd try to hold one dimension constant and see what happens to area when you vary the other. That is the principle behind behavioral genetic methods.

The innovative feature of these methods is that subjects (children or adults) are measured in pairs, usually pairs of twins or siblings. By choosing pairs that vary in genetic similarity, the researchers can study the effects of being more or less alike genetically. By choosing pairs that vary in environmental similarity, they can study the effects of having more or less similar environments. So, to vary the genetic dimension, the researchers might compare identical twins with fraternal twins, or ordinary siblings with adoptive or step-siblings. (Genetic similarity, defined as the proportion of genes shared by common descent, is 1.00 for identical twins, .50 for frater-

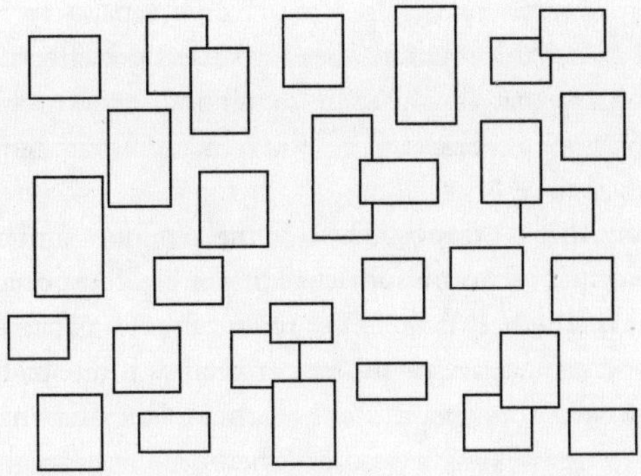

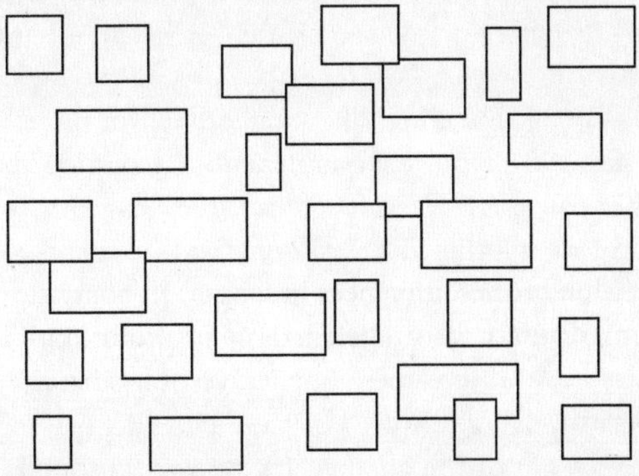

nal twins and ordinary siblings, and zero for adoptive siblings.) To vary the environmental dimension, they compare pairs reared in the same family with pairs of the same genetic similarity reared in different families.

As expected, genetic similarity makes identical twins more alike in personality than fraternal twins, and ordinary siblings more alike than adoptive siblings. Environmental similarity was expected to have a corresponding effect, but it did not. Twins who grew up together are no more alike in personality than those reared in different families, and adoptive siblings reared in the same family aren't alike at all.

Admittedly, the environmental measure is not as well calibrated as the genetic one. Only two levels of environmental similarity are considered: either a pair grew up in the same home or they didn't. However, it is not necessary to assume that the two who grew up in the same home had identical environments, or that the two reared separately had altogether different ones. What this method does is to assess the effects of any aspects of the environment that are the same for siblings reared together but that might differ for siblings reared apart. These include most of the things that developmentalists have been talking about for years: whether the home is headed by one parent or two, whether the parents (if there are two of them) get along well or poorly, whether they are college graduates or high school dropouts, whether their philosophies of child-rearing are autocratic or laissez-faire. The mother might stay at home or go out to work every day, as John Cheever's mother did; she might be in robust mental health or subject to depressions like Alice James. The home itself might be urban or rural, crowded or spacious, well organized or chaotic, stocked with art supplies or strewn with used auto parts. All these things are alike for two siblings reared together—particularly if they are twins—but may differ for two reared apart.

And that's not all. The things that might differ for the reared-apart pair also include features of the environment found outside the home. The reared-together pair not only share a home: they also grow up in the same neighborhood, attend the same schools, and—particularly if they are twins—may belong to the same peer group.

In effect, the same-home/different-home contrast skips to the bottom line. It captures most of the environmental variables that the developmentalists have been studying for fifty years and puts them all together. This is good in one way and bad in another. It's a powerful tool, because even if each little difference between two homes has only a small effect, something should show up when they're added together. On the other hand, it's a blunt instrument: it can't discriminate these effects from one another. In particular, it can't separate the effects of family life from the effects of what happens to children outside the home. Everything is lumped together.

And yet this lumped-together environment has little or no measurable effect on the siblings who share it. The most common outcome in behavioral genetic studies, especially in the newer, larger ones, is that the estimated effects of the "shared" environment—the environment shared by two siblings who grew up together—do not differ significantly from zero. Growing up in the same home does not make twins, ordinary siblings, or adoptive siblings more alike in personality.[16]

In the clarity that hindsight brings, some developmentalists denied that they ever expected the home environment to make siblings more alike.[17] This expectation, however, didn't come out of the blue; it was based on the same reasoning as research based on traditional methods. Consider an article, written by three developmentalists, that is typical of their field: a survey of research on emotional expressiveness in children. The studies reviewed in this article showed that parents who express emotions freely tend to have emotionally expressive children, and those who keep their emotions buttoned up tend to have emotionally unexpressive children—a correlation the authors attributed to "parental socialization of emotion."[18]

Let me rephrase those results. There was a statistical trend for the children of expressive parents to be above average in expressiveness and for the children of inexpressive parents to be below average in expressiveness. This means that two children, growing up in two different homes, whose parents happen to be equally expressive are, on average, more alike in expressiveness than two whose parents happen to differ in that respect. Which implies, in turn, that two children raised by the *same* parents should be more alike in expressiveness than two raised by different parents.

So the prediction that two children raised in the same home should be more alike in behavior than two raised in different homes follows logically—indeed, mathematically—from the results of studies using traditional methods. Prevailing theories of development, such as the theory that children are socialized by their parents to express emotions or to bottle them up, had led researchers to expect (if they thought about it at all) that being reared by the same parents *would* make siblings more alike.

The developmentalists found that the children's behavior was correlated with the parents' behavior and attributed the correlation to the effects of the home environment. Though they realized that heredity might account for some of the correlation, they never considered the possibility that heredity might account for *all* of it. But that is exactly how it turned out. Once the effects of genetic similarities were estimated and skimmed off, the correlation declined to zero. The putative effects of the home environment disappeared.

In other fields too, new methods of research sometimes produce results that conflict with prevailing theories. In medical science, for instance, according to epidemiologist Alvan Feinstein, "almost every plausible concept that has been held throughout the centuries about the causes, mechanisms, and treatment of diseases has been either wholly wrong or so deficient that it was later overthrown and supplanted by other concepts."[19] But plausible concepts don't give up the ghost without a struggle. For some reason humans don't like to admit—even to themselves—that they were wrong. Nevertheless, physicians eventually gave up their faith in purging and bloodletting, which gives me hope for psychology.

In science, the struggle between old concepts and new ones often focuses on research methods. Quoting Feinstein again,

> When the conclusion suggested by the research is compared with the belief held by the reader or by the scientific community, all further aspects of rational analysis may vanish. If the results confirm what we believe, the customary human tendency is to assume that they must be right. The research methods need not be examined closely because there is no need to do so. Having produced the right answer, the methods must also be correct. Conversely, if the results are contrary to what we believe, the research methods must be wrong, no matter how good they seem.[20]

If the behavioral geneticists' research had produced the expected results—that sharing genes makes people more similar in personality, and that growing up in the same family also makes people more similar—no one would have complained about their methods. Since the research didn't produce the expected results, many members of the scientific community concluded that there must be something wrong with the methods. The jurors in the O. J. Simpson trial rejected the DNA evidence rather than give up their belief in his innocence.

But the strength of behavioral genetics is that it isn't a single method: it's a set of methods, designed to home in on an answer from two or more directions at once. Depending on which kinds of subject pairs take part in the study, different formulas are used to calculate the contributions of genes and environment. There is no mathematical necessity for these formulas to produce the same results—no a priori reason why estimates of environmental effects based on identical twins reared apart should agree with those based on adoptive siblings reared together—but they do. Estimates of genetic effects vary somewhat from one study to another, which is what we'd expect. But estimates of the effects of the shared home environment seldom stray far from zero, regardless of the method that is used.[21]

In the past three decades, the behavioral geneticists have examined a wide variety of human behaviors and psychological characteristics, measured in a variety of ways: standard personality tests; judgments by parents, teachers, spouses, or peers; observations by researchers. Objective measures—

whether or not subjects got divorced or had run-ins with the law—have also been used. The remarkable thing about these results is their consistency. Occasionally an aberrant result does turn up—somebody finds a significant effect of the home environment on something or other—but aberrant results, like the glove that didn't fit O. J., turn up occasionally in every field. One has to look at the overall pattern of the evidence, not at just a single finding. The behavioral genetic results obtained in different studies, using different subjects and measuring different things in different ways, back each other up to a degree that is rarely found in psychology.

The rectangle criticism is generally made by people who know nothing about behavioral genetics. Those with a little knowledge are more likely to base their criticism on the pie. The claim is that there's something dodgy about the notion that variation in behavior or personality can be cut up, like a pie, into genetic and environmental sectors.[22] That's not exactly what behavioral geneticists do, however. In fact, what they do is quite conventional: like researchers in other areas of psychology, they look for correlations in their data and use them to account for some of the variation in the measured outcome.

Traditional developmentalists count their research a success if they find a correlation between the outcome variable they are interested in and one of the environmental variables they've measured. If they find a correlation of .30 between children's aggressiveness and how often they were spanked, it would mean that the researchers have, in a technical sense, "accounted for" some of the variation in aggressiveness (though, as I said, the correlation doesn't prove that spanking *caused* the aggressiveness). A correlation of .30 accounts for 9 percent of the variance—you square the correlation to get the proportion of variance accounted for.

Correlations are used in a somewhat different way by behavioral geneticists but the principle is the same. They look at pairs of subjects who vary in genetic or environmental similarity and use that variation to account for the variation in the outcome. To the degree that subjects who are more similar genetically are more similar in aggressiveness, they've accounted for some of the variation in aggressiveness. To the degree that subjects who have more similar environments are more similar in aggressiveness, they've accounted for some additional variance. Instead of using an environmental variable—spanking—to account for variance, they're using similarity in genes and similarity in environment.

But what the behavioral geneticists are doing with the pie is no different from what the developmentalists have been doing for so long: they're slicing off whatever portions of the variance they can explain by the correlations in their data. The main difference is that the behavioral geneticists can take a much bigger slice, which naturally has aroused some resentment. The developmentalists have to content themselves with morsels; to them, 9 percent is a feast. But the behavioral geneticists help themselves to a whopping wedge—the 45 percent of the variance that can be attributed to the effects of being more or less similar genetically.[23] If the effects of sharing or not sharing a home are detectable in their data (in most cases they are not), they can take another little sliver.

But they can't have the whole pie. A little more than half still remains after the behavioral geneticists have taken all the slices their data entitle them to. What they've done in their published reports is to attribute this portion to a mysterious perpetrator they've dubbed "the nonshared environment." I suspect they would have had fewer public relations problems if they had simply admitted their ignorance and left the uneaten portion on the plate.

The 55 percent of the variance in behavior or personality that the behavioral geneticists attribute to the nonshared environment is variance they can't account for, variance they don't know how to explain. It is not

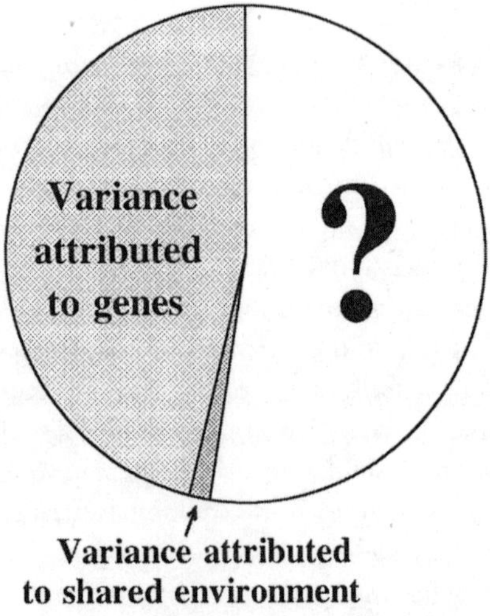

genetic, so by default they call it environmental. A more accurate name for it is "unexplained variance," and that is what I will call it. The unexplained variance is the variance that remains after all the correlations—all the measured similarities between siblings—are taken out. It includes something called "measurement error": imprecisions in measuring the outcome variable. But mainly it represents differences in personality—real differences—among the subjects who took part in the study. Not just differences between siblings but differences among all the subjects. All the variation that can't be explained by the differences in the subjects' genes or in the homes in which they grew up.

I don't want you to get the idea that the unexplained variance is a mathematical abstraction. On the contrary, it's plainly visible to the naked eye. The poster children of the unexplained variance are reared-together identical twins: two people with identical genes who grew up in the same home at the same time, and yet they are different. Even conjoined twins who live their entire lives together, like Laleh and Ladan Bijani and the famous "Siamese twins," Chang and Eng, have different personalities.[24]

There is one more objection to behavioral genetic methods that I'll have to deal with: the charge that twin studies are invalid because they're based on a fatal error the critics call the "equal-environments assumption." Since behavioral geneticists don't assume that a pair of twins reared in the same home have equal environments, it should really be called the "equally-similar-environments assumption." It's the assumption that the home environments of reared-together fraternal twins are as similar as those of reared-together identical twins. This assumption is wrong, the critics claim, because parents treat identical twins more similarly than fraternal twins.[25] If identicals actually have more similar environments than fraternals, then the greater environmental similarity might explain why identicals are more alike in personality than fraternals. This means that the estimates of the heritability of personality might be too high: environmental effects on personality may have been mistaken for genetic effects.

It is true that behavioral geneticists make the equally-similar-environments assumption. The reason is historical: their methods were first used to answer the question of why children tend to resemble their parents in intelligence. How much of this resemblance, the researchers asked, is due to the intellectually enriched or impoverished environment the parents provided and how much to inherited genes? This is where the "nature-nurture controversy" had its roots and why it was so bitter: it involved the politically charged question of the heritability of intelligence. There were people in the 1970s who very much wanted the heritability of intelligence to be zero.[26] They have since been reduced to bickering about whether it's closer to .60 or to .30.

When the variable being studied is intelligence, it is reasonable to assume that identical twins and fraternal twins have equally similar environments. Parents do not, as a rule, provide an intellectually enriched environment for one of their children and not for the other, especially if the children are the same age. The features of the home that are assumed to play a role in the development of mental abilities—the parents' education and their attitudes toward academic achievement, the vocabulary they use in conversation, the dictionaries and computers that the home does or does not contain, the family excursions to the museum or the ballpark—all are likely to be the same for two siblings reared in the same home, whether or not they are identical twins.

But the equally-similar-environments assumption becomes less tenable when it comes to personality. In fact, there's no question about it: parents behave in a more similar fashion to identical twins than to fraternal twins, and in a more similar fashion to ordinary siblings than to step- or adoptive siblings. How a parent behaves toward a child is in part a reaction to the child's behavior; the parent-child relationship is a dialogue to which both parties contribute. That was the point I was making in the quote from *The Nurture Assumption* that appears at the beginning of this chapter, the passage in which I mentioned that one of my children was adopted. It is impossible to treat two children the same if they behave differently.

Two children who have similar genes are more likely to be similar in behavior, as the behavioral genetic studies showed. Therefore, they are more likely to be treated similarly by their parents.[27] So if you believed that the way children are treated by their parents has long-term effects on their personalities, and if you believed that being treated in the same way by their parents makes children more alike, then you would conclude that studies that compare reared-together identical twins with reared-together fraternal twins produce inflated estimates of heritability.

Fortunately, behavioral geneticists don't have to rely on a single method for calculating heritability; as I mentioned, they generally use two or more methods to home in on a result. Since each method has its own strengths and weaknesses, the critics have had to resort to thinking up a different, ad hoc criticism for each one. But let's say, for the sake of argument, that they are right in this case: that there might be some overestimation of heritability in twin studies. What would that mean? Why should I care?

The answer is, I don't. I'm not trying to explain why identical twins are so alike—I'm trying to explain why they are so different. It's immaterial to me whether heritability accounts for 30 or 60 percent of the variance: I'm interested in the variation in personality that is *not* due to genes—the unexplained variance. If identical twins are treated so similarly by their parents, how come they're not more alike? How come a sizable portion of the variance remains unexplained by their shared genes plus the presumed effects of the presumably similar treatment by their parents?

Whether or not the behavioral geneticists have overestimated heritability, they have provided us with valuable information. Their evidence has eliminated from contention all aspects of the environment that siblings who grow up in the same home do in fact share, whether or not they are twins. All the things that siblings do have in common have been shown to be ineffective; these environmental factors can explain no more than a negligible fraction of the variation in personality. But any aspects of the environment that can differ for two siblings raised in the same home, including how they are treated by their parents, are still in the running.

Also still in the running is the possibility that some aspect of the home environment might be the same for two siblings and yet they might react differently to it. If, for instance, their parents are always quarreling, and one child withdraws from the tumult and becomes an introvert while the other reacts by becoming a hail-fellow-well-met type, these dissimilar reactions will contribute to the unexplained variance—the variation in personality I'm trying to explain.

The behavioral geneticists have not ignored these possible sources of differences between siblings. Nor am I planning to sweep them under the rug. I'll return to them in the next chapter and the chapter after that.

The violation of the equally-similar-environments assumption means that identical twins actually have more similar home environments than fraternal twins do. Since they are genetically identical, they might also be expected to react more similarly to environmental events such as parental quarreling. And yet the unexplained differences between them are as wide as the unexplained differences between other kinds of sibling pairs. They are as wide as the unexplained differences between a pair of unrelated strangers. This is the important clue that I mentioned earlier. What makes it hard to understand is the fact that identical twins are so much more alike. Shouldn't there be less variation to account for?

It isn't an illusion; identical twins really are more alike in personality than other kinds of sibling pairs, though the resemblance is a long way from perfect. The correlation between their scores on personality tests is around .45 or .50, whether they were reared together or apart.[28] The correlation is considerably lower for fraternal twins and ordinary siblings, and is approximately zero for adult adoptive siblings who were reared in the same home; adoptive siblings aren't alike at all.[29] Heritability—the effects of genes—accounts for virtually all of the resemblances between the biologically related pairs. (The effects, if any, of the greater environmental similarity of identical twins would be included in the heritability estimate.)

What confuses people is that they expect the amount of variance attributed to heritability to equal the correlation, but in most cases it does not. The reason is that correlations represent only similarities between siblings, whereas genes are responsible for differences as well as similarities. Some of the differences between siblings who aren't identical twins are due to the fact that they have different genes. For example, fraternal twins sometimes differ in eye color. This difference is entirely due to the fact that they inherited different eye-color genes. In a given population, the correlation for eye color in fraternal twins might be only .75, but the amount of variance accounted for by genes is nonetheless 1.00. Whether you're a identical twin or a fraternal twin, your eye color is completely a function of your genes (that's what a heritability of 1.00 means), but genes for eye color can vary.

Personality isn't completely a function of genes; only about half of the variance in personality is genetic. But the genes that affect personality vary, and they may differ in fraternal twins and in ordinary siblings. Only for identical twins is the heritability estimate approximately equal to the correlation. Genes cannot produce differences between identical twins because they have the same genes.

Here's how the estimate of about .45 for the heritability of personality can hold true for identical twins, fraternal twins, and adoptive siblings alike. For identical twins, heritability accounts for all of their similarities and none of their differences. For fraternal twins, heritability accounts for some of their similarities and for some of their differences. And for adoptive siblings, heritability accounts for none of their similarities (there are no similarities to account for) and for about half of their differences.[30] The upshot is that the amount of variance *not* explained by genes is roughly the same, around 55 percent, in each case. In one major recent study, five different types of sibling pairs—reared-together identical twins, fraternal twins, ordinary siblings, half-siblings, and step-siblings—were all assessed with the same exhaustive battery of tests, and the conclusions held true across the board. There were no important differences among the sibling pairs in the proportion of variance that was unexplained.[31]

This counterintuitive finding has an important implication. It implies that whatever causes reared-together identical twins to differ in personality also causes ordinary siblings and step-siblings to differ, and to differ just as much.

So the perpetrator I'm looking for is not heredity; nor is it the environment your parents provided for you and your siblings. It doesn't care where you got your genes and is indifferent to your childhood address. The perpetrator I'm looking for widens the personality differences between identical twins in the same way, and to the same degree, as it widens the differences between ordinary siblings. It produces nongenetic differences between two people raised in the same family that are as big as those between a pair plucked at random from the population.[32]

One suspect whose modus operandi could fit that description is chance. I'm not even going to count this as one of my red herrings, because if chance—randomness—is responsible, then my mystery would have no solution. It would be like one of those irksome books where it turns out that the victim died of natural causes or faked his death and is living with his mistress on an island in the Bahamas.

Could differences in personality all be due to random things that happen during development? A neuron zigged instead of zagged and you are impulsive rather than cautious? A bully knocked you down in fourth grade and you are shy rather than outgoing?[33]

If it were true—if the unexplained variance were all due to random perturbations of one sort or another—then my quest for a solution would be in vain. In psychology there's no good way to study random things because you can't combine data from different subjects in order to look for overall trends. If each subject turned out the way he or she did for idiosyncratic reasons, there wouldn't be any overall trends. Whatever made one person impulsive would be different from whatever made the next one impulsive. All trees, no forest.

It isn't difficult to find evidence that favors the no-solution conclusion. There is a certain amount of randomness—or what appears to be randomness, given our current understanding of biological processes—in all human characteristics. The human genome is not capacious enough to specify every whorl of the fingerprints, every synapse in the brain. To some extent the details of construction have to be worked out on the construction site, which adds variability to the outcome—"developmental noise," biologists call it. The result is that identical twins aren't exactly alike physically. They may differ slightly (occasionally more than slightly) in height and weight and in appearance; the family and friends of identical twins generally have no trouble telling them apart. MRI scans show subtle differences between their brains.[34]

I mentioned in the previous chapter that the identical twin of a person with schizophrenia has only a 48 percent chance of also being diagnosed with the disorder. Similar findings have been reported for physical malfunctions. If one twin falls ill with type 1 (childhood onset) diabetes, the other has only a 40 percent chance of developing the disorder. The heritability of the tendency to get ear infections in childhood is .73; the remainder of the variance is unexplained. As far as physicians can tell, it's random. Sharing a home does not make children more alike in whether they do or don't get ear infections, any more than it makes them more alike in aggressiveness or conscientiousness.[35]

There are biological differences between identical twins, due to unpredictable things that happen before and after they are born. A neuron zigs instead of zags. One fetus occupies a better position in the uterus. One twin falls down the stairs or contracts a virus. Exposure to pathogens has been proposed as a possible etiological trigger both for schizophrenia and for type 1 diabetes.[36] The schizophrenic twin may have developed the disorder not because her life was more stressful but because she happened to encounter a virus at the wrong time.

A few pages ago I admitted that heritability of personality characteristics might be somewhat overestimated due to the violation of the equally-similar-environments assumption. It is possible that some of the variance attributed to genes should really have been attributed to shared environment. But now it appears that some of the variance *not* attributed to genes isn't environmental at all: it's biological. Some of it may even be genetic. Medical researchers recently described a case in which one identical twin was born with a cleft lip and palate, the other with a normally formed face. It turned out that the birth defect was due to a genetic mutation, present in one twin and not the other.[37] The mutation must have occurred after the fertilized egg that gave rise to both twins split in half and formed two separate embryos.

The biological perturbations that affect the outcomes of identical twins also affect nontwins. A virus or a mutation, a neuron that zigs instead of zags, can happen just as easily to babies born singly. So these random biological events—developmental noise—could explain some of the unexplained variance in personality.

But orderly genetic effects plus developmental noise can't explain all of it, because that would mean that virtually all the variation in personality was built in, one way or the other. It would mean, in other words, that the environment has no lasting effects on personality—that young humans are incapable of making long-term modifications of their behavior on the basis of their experiences. This is implausible both on theoretical and empirical grounds. Much of the evidence I will discuss in this book has to do with the ways that children modify their behavior in response to their experiences.

What about randomness that isn't biological? What about environmental randomness? One twin gets knocked down by a bully in fourth grade and the other doesn't. One gets the upper bunk bed, the other gets the lower. One stays home sick from school on a particular day and that makes all the difference.[38]

Again, I have to admit that this kind of randomness can't be ruled out; no doubt it accounts for some portion of the unexplained variance. There are many opportunities for random events to occur in people's lives, and random events sometimes do have dramatic long-term consequences. It is a familiar theme in real life and in fiction. Here's Pip, in Charles Dickens' *Great Expectations*, describing the consequences of his first visit to Miss Havisham's house:

> That was a memorable day to me, for it made great changes in me. But, it is the same with any life. Imagine one selected day struck out of it, and think how different its course would have been. Pause you who read this, and think for a moment of the long chain of iron or gold, of thorns or flowers, that would never have bound you, but for the formation of the first link on one memorable day.[39]

It was a random event of a much less memorable sort that changed the course of my life and led me to become a writer of books and articles about psychology. I had a friend who had a dog she needed to find a home for, and I helped her write an ad for the classified section of her local newspaper. A few months later she needed help rewriting an article that had been turned down by a psychology journal—my friend was an assistant professor of psychology at Rutgers University—and she thought of me. "You have a way with words," she told me. Her opinion was based on the ad I had helped her write, a classified ad about a dog. The shortest writing job I've ever had. It started me on the path that ended up here.

On second thought, perhaps I would have become a writer anyway. At any rate, writing the classified ad was only one link—one zig where I might have zagged—in a long chain of thorns and flowers that may or may not have been random. I probably wouldn't have become a writer if I hadn't been rejected by my peers for a crucial four years of my childhood.[40] Those years as a social outcast turned me into an introvert; previously I had been a boisterous, outgoing child. If my parents had decided to buy a house in some other community, perhaps my schoolmates wouldn't have rejected me. When, after four years, my family moved to a different part of the country, I stopped being an outcast. But by then the link had been forged; my personality had changed.

Personality can change; evidence from large numbers of subjects shows that it can change, to some extent, even in adulthood, if one's circumstances change.[41] But it is considerably more plastic, more flexible, in childhood. Children are adaptable. They adapt to their society, their culture—they become socialized. And they also adapt to their individual circumstances, as I adapted to being a social outcast.

Evolution has provided the members of our species with a large, intricately wired brain and a lengthy period of immaturity: the prerequisites for an education. Natural selection favors attributes that contribute to their owner's reproductive success. Costly attributes—the ability to be modified by experience is a costly attribute—are unlikely to be selected if the modifications are made on a random basis, because random modifications would have random effects on an individual's chances of surviving and reproducing. Making personality plastic but leaving it at the mercy of chance, to be buffeted this way and that by unpredictable events, doesn't make sense from an evolutionary standpoint. Natural selection would favor any alternative to randomness that produced results that were better than chance.

That statement isn't something I've proved: it's a hypothesis, derived from Darwinian reasoning. I am hypothesizing that evolution made personality plastic so that children can profit from their experiences—so that they can learn ways of behaving that will serve them well in adulthood. I am hypothesizing an adaptability that gives children some advantage, or ameliorates a disadvantage, in the competition to survive and reproduce. That hypothesis has to be backed up with evidence, which I will do my best to provide.

I have given randomness an arm and a leg: I've admitted that some of the unexplained variance in personality is due to biological noise and some to environmental noise. Now it is following me around like the crocodile that followed Captain Hook: it wants *all* the unexplained variance. But I'm not going to give in to it that easily. Randomness is the explanation, or the excuse, that a scientist resorts to when all else fails. It is a shrug of the shoulders, an admission of defeat.

Let us proceed on the premise that there is a real solution, a satisfying solution, to this mystery.

3

Monkey Business

I BECAME A WRITER of college textbooks because it was something I could do at home. I gave up writing textbooks when it suddenly occurred to me that what I had been telling my undergraduate readers was wrong. But the first thing I did after that realization struck was not to write a book of a different sort: first I wrote an article, laying out some of the evidence against the prevailing theories of child development, and submitted it to the *Psychological Review*. Despite my lack of the usual credentials—I have neither a Ph.D. nor a university affiliation—the journal accepted my article and published it.[1]

It caused very little stir, at least among the people who taught the courses for which I used to write textbooks, the professors of developmental psychology. But not everybody in the academic world ignored my article. In fact, the American Psychological Association gave me an award for it: the George A. Miller Award, named in honor of an eminent cognitive psychologist and presented each year to the writer of an outstanding article in psychology. The award came with a check for five hundred dollars, a bronze plaque (hanging right here on the wall of my office), and an invitation to give a fifty-minute address to a large audience of APA members at their annual convention, held in San Francisco that year.

The year was 1998. Although I hadn't reached the point of being unable to travel, California is a long way from New Jersey and the trip would be exhausting and somewhat risky for me. And I had had very little experience speaking in public. Nevertheless, I accepted the invitation. I arrived in San Francisco a day and a half before my talk and spent that time resting in my hotel room.

I began my address[2] by reading aloud the letter I had received, thirty-eight years earlier, from the Harvard Department of Psychology. The letter explained that the department had decided not to let me stay on for the Ph.D. degree. They had decided that I wasn't worthy of a Ph.D., the letter said, because they didn't think I had the "originality and independence" to live up to Harvard's standards. The punch line came when I told my audience who signed that letter: the acting chairman of the Harvard Department of Psychology, George A. Miller.

The audience's reaction to my revelation—the fact that I was receiving an award named after the very man who had kicked me out of graduate school—was just as I'd hoped: they burst into laughter. Perhaps that moment of shared merriment helped to diffuse some of the hostility I might otherwise have received; they were pretty gentle with me during the question period. The flak came afterwards, when the APA was publicly criticized for giving me the award and angry letters were published in the organization's monthly magazine.[3]

But the real cause of the angry letters was not the article: it was my book, *The Nurture Assumption*, which—as luck would have it—appeared in print just a few days after my talk in San Francisco. The developmentalists had paid no attention to my article but it wasn't so easy to ignore the book. I had gone over their heads, as it were, and taken my case directly to the general public.

That got the developmentalists' attention, all right. It was like giving them a wedgie. What I was saying—that parents have no power to mold their children's personalities—was heresy to their ears. Many of these people had spent their entire professional lives doing research designed to show how parents mold their children's personalities. Not *whether* parents mold their children's personalities but *how* they do it. That parents have this power was something the developmentalists simply took for granted. That's what I meant by "the nurture assumption."

With the publication of the book, my life changed in an eyeblink. For years I had worked quietly at home, seldom seeing anyone outside my family. Suddenly journalists were clamoring for interviews and TV producers were asking if they could come to my home to film me. Though I was unable to go on book tours or appear on talk shows, essays about the book were printed in newspapers and news magazines around the country.

The media attention hadn't yet died down when I got a phone call from Marie Bristol-Power, of the National Institute of Child Health and Human Development (abbreviated NICHD), part of the National Institutes of Health. She wanted to organize a conference on parenting, she told me, at the NICHD campus in Bethesda, Maryland. The purpose of the conference would be to discuss some of the issues I raised in my book. Would I give the keynote address? I said yes.

It wasn't until much later that I heard about the dispute that erupted after Marie proposed the conference. "Why would you want to invite *her*?" she was asked by her colleagues. "Hasn't she gotten enough publicity already?" One prominent developmentalist who was invited to the conference said she wouldn't come if I was going to be one of the speakers. Marie didn't waver. "What, are you afraid of a little woman from New Jersey?" she asked. "But there's so much evidence against what she's saying," protested the developmentalist. "Fine," said Marie. "Tell the audience about it."[4]

"I had to fight to get that conference," Marie told me. "I had to fight to get you on the program." Marie won those fights: the conference was held and I was invited to it. But she had had to make some concessions. The program was packed with developmentalists who were opposed to me, and there were two keynote speakers rather than one. The other, who got top billing, was Eleanor Maccoby, the grande dame of developmental psychology. Though officially retired from a long teaching career at Stanford, she was still quite active and mentally sharp.

Being an amateur at public speaking, I am always very nervous beforehand. At the NICHD conference I would be facing an audience that had already taken up arms against me. Only one of my allies—David Rowe, a behavioral geneticist at the University of Arizona—had been invited. My talk was scheduled right after Maccoby's, and Maccoby was a pro who had been speaking in public for years.

To my surprise, she stepped up to the podium, pulled out a thick sheaf of paper, and began to read from it. That's how Maccoby gave her talk: she read it from a typescript, rapidly and dryly, hardly ever looking up at her audience. She said I was wrong, but the evidence she cited didn't worry me and her humdrum performance gave me courage. Nevertheless, the audience was friendly to Maccoby and not to me. They sat there stony-faced while I talked. My little jokes evoked no more than scattered titters.

Afterwards Maccoby and I took questions. All the questions were addressed to me and most of them were hostile. But the one I remember—the most overtly hostile of them all—came from a heavyset fellow at the back of the room. He stood up and told me, in a scornful voice, that I was ignoring interactions. *Naturally* the behavioral geneticists hadn't found any effects of the shared home environment: they had forgotten about interactions. Nature and nurture don't act directly to produce developmental outcomes: they *interact.*

The heavyset fellow turned out to be Stephen Suomi, head of the Laboratory of Comparative Ethology at NICHD. He does research on rhesus monkeys, not on human children. His comment—it wasn't really a question because he clearly wasn't expecting an answer—had to do with interactions between genes and environment. Gene-environment interactions are my third red herring.

Stephen Suomi wasn't afraid of a little woman from New Jersey. Maybe he should have been.

If you took a biology course in college you may have seen a drawing, similar to the one in the diagram here, of a bunch of plants.[5] Each of the seven plants in the top row is the "identical twin" of the one directly below it in the bottom row: they were both grown from cuttings from the same parent plant, which means the two in each pair have identical genotypes (the

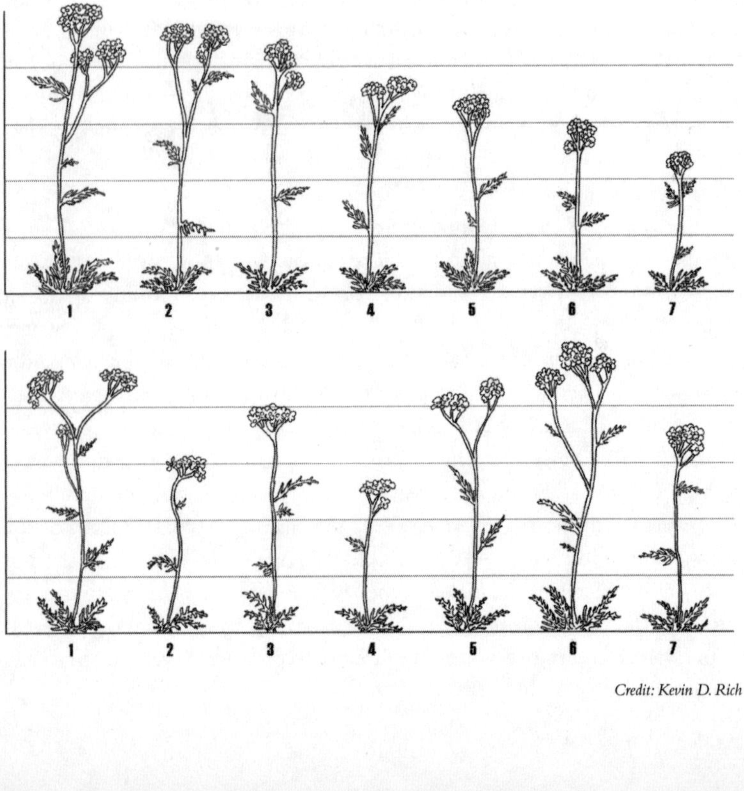

Credit: Kevin D. Rich

biologists' way of saying they have exactly the same genes). So what we have here are seven different plant genotypes, all from the same species, grown under two different environmental conditions: the top ones, let's say, at sea level, the bottom ones at a higher elevation. The point of the picture is that some genotypes grew taller in one condition, others grew taller in the other condition. If this result is obtained reliably—if certain genotypes consistently grow taller in one environmental condition and other genotypes consistently grow taller in the other—then we have evidence of a gene-environment interaction.

But there is a curious thing about this diagram: it shows no "main effects," to use the statisticians' term, either of genotype or of environment. A main effect of genotype would mean that some genotypes tended to grow taller than others in every environment. A main effect of environment would mean that some environments are more favorable to plant growth than others. The second diagram illustrates both of these effects; this is in fact a far more likely

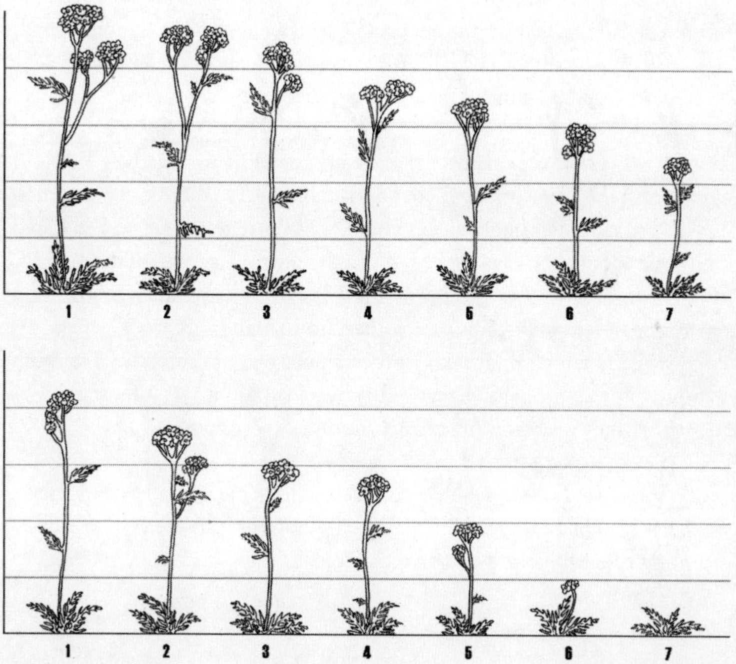

Credit: Kevin D. Rich

outcome than the one shown in the first diagram. In nature, main effects of genes and of environment are common. When interactions occur, they usually are superimposed on main effects. Often they are not apparent to the naked eye and special statistics must be used to tease them out.

At the NICHD conference it soon became clear that cutting-edge developmentalists, shaken by the revelations of the behavioral geneticists, had regrouped. The most knowledgeable among them, including Eleanor Maccoby and Stephen Suomi, had pretty much given up hope of finding main effects of the home environment on children and were pinning their hopes on gene-environment interactions.

In casual use, the word *interaction* just means that two things have something to do with one another, as in "Ginger Rogers interacted with Fred Astaire." But the people at the NICHD conference were using the term in its technical, statistical sense. Here's how Maccoby put it:

> Nowadays, interactions between parenting styles and possible genetic attributes are a matter of active interest in developmental psychology. . . . [One group of researchers] found that a given parenting style has a different effect on a child who is temperamentally bold and adventurous than it does on a timid, shy child. . . . If we were to aggregate the two kinds of children together, some of the parenting effects would wash out.[6]

There was a good reason for the developmentalists to pin their hopes on interactions: the behavioral geneticists' data didn't rule them out. Any effects of gene-environment interactions would contribute to the unexplained portion of the variance in personality, not to the portion attributed to the shared home environment or to the portion attributed to heritability. So this was a way for the developmentalists to nod their heads at the behavioral genetic evidence while retaining their faith in the importance of the home. The home environment might be important—they were certain it was important!—but it doesn't make children more alike. Quoting Maccoby again,

> If a given kind of household or a given style of parenting has different effects for children with different predispositions, this means that parenting often functions to make children in the same family different rather than alike.[7]

It was Maccoby's answer to the question posed a dozen years earlier by behavioral geneticists Robert Plomin and Denise Daniels: "Why are children in the same family so different from one another?"[8] Maccoby had interpreted "children in the same family" to mean siblings, ordinary siblings. Ordinary siblings have different genotypes, and people with different genotypes might indeed react differently to the same environmental conditions. But Plomin and Daniels' question wasn't just about ordinary siblings: much of the data they summarized in their groundbreaking article came from twins. Identical twins have the same genotype. A gene-environment interaction cannot explain why genetically identical individuals reared in the same household turn out differently. Genetically identical individuals are presumed to be born with the same predispositions, and therefore should react in the same way to a given kind of household or a given style of parenting.

Perhaps the reason why it never occurred to the developmentalists that they might be called upon to explain the personality differences between identical twins is that so little has been said about their differences. On the contrary, we're always hearing about how amazingly alike they are. You've heard, I'm sure, the stories about the pairs who were separated at birth, reared in different homes, and reunited in adulthood. There were the twins who both enjoyed startling people by sneezing in elevators. The twins who, at the beach, were afraid to confront the waves straight on and always went into the water backwards. The twins who both married women named Dorothy Jane Sheckelburger. Okay, I made the last one up, but it's only a little more bizarre than some of the actual reports.

That there are some striking similarities in personality between identical twins is beyond dispute. These similarities, however, are entirely due to their matching genotypes. As I explained in the previous chapter, once you take into account their identical genes, the differences between identical twins—the *nongenetic* differences—are as wide as the nongenetic differences between ordinary siblings. So an environmental mechanism that produces differences between ordinary siblings, but doesn't work for identical twins, is not going to be the answer to the developmentalists' prayer. Nor is it the perpetrator I'm looking for.

But let me put the question of identical twins aside for the moment—I have other bones to pick in this chapter—and just consider whether gene-environment interactions can account for the differences between ordinary siblings.

What the behavioral genetic data showed is that the home environment has no main effects. The plants grown in one environmental condition were, on average, as tall as the plants grown in another. The net effect of the home environment was essentially zero. Can a gene-environment interaction explain how the net effect of environmental conditions can average out to zero, or near zero? Yes, if it's the crossover kind of interaction, illustrated in the first of the two sets of plant diagrams. Some genotypes—plants or children—do better in one environmental condition, others do better in another. Perhaps having parents who fight all the time causes some children to become more outgoing, less agreeable, and less conscientious, while others in the same household react by becoming less outgoing, more agreeable, and more conscientious.

Crossover interactions, however, are rare in nature. The authors of biology textbooks have to grope for genuine examples. One involves the eyes of fruit flies. It seems that normal (wild-type) fruit flies grow smaller eyes if they're kept at temperatures above 25 degrees Celsius, but a mutant variety, called "infra-bar," grow *larger* eyes at higher temperatures.[9] So if you had an even mix of wild-type and infra-bar fruit flies and didn't know you had two different kinds, you might think that growing them at high temperatures had no effect on eye size.

The kind of interaction that is far more common in nature doesn't involve a crossover but only what might be called "sensitivity." Some genotypes are more sensitive than others to certain environmental conditions. Some genotypes respond, positively or negatively, to conditions that have little or no effect on other genotypes. A sensitive genotype might not develop properly if exposed to an environmental condition that wouldn't bother a tougher sort. On the other hand, a sensitive genotype might profit from an environmental condition that would provide no benefit for an insensitive one.

It's easy to find real-life examples of the sensitivity kind of interaction and we don't have to call on mutant fruit flies. Put a child who was born with musical talent into a musical environment and you might get a Mozart. Put a child who was born tone deaf into the same environment and what you will get is an adult who can't carry a tune. Put a child who has a predisposition to become depressed into a stressful environment and you might get a depressed adult. Put one who lacks this predisposition into the same environment and what you will get is an adult who tells you how stressful her life is but who sounds more annoyed than despondent.[10] Your results will vary because what you get depends on what you start with.

Unlike crossover interactions, sensitivity interactions don't average out to zero. If some genotypes respond to a certain environmental condition and others do not, then what you would get on average is a weaker response—a main effect, though a smaller one.

In her talk, Eleanor Maccoby presented evidence for sensitivity interactions. Much of her evidence had to do with IQ. She also mentioned criminal behavior and schizophrenia. Adopted children whose biological parents were criminals are more likely to become criminals themselves if reared in an environment where crime is a viable career option; adopted children whose biological parents were law-abiding are unlikely to become criminals regardless of the circumstances in which they are reared. The biological children of schizophrenic parents are more likely to develop a mental illness if reared in adoptive families in which the parents aren't functioning well themselves.[11]

Statistical interactions tend to be evanescent; those found in one study often fail to turn up in the next. But Maccoby had hit upon the three areas—IQ, criminal behavior, and mental illness—where reliable interactions have been demonstrated. None of these interactions, however, are found in the absence of main effects. There are main effects of genes on all three outcomes: the biological children of intelligent, schizophrenic or criminal parents are more likely to be intelligent, develop a mental illness, or commit crimes no matter where they are raised. There are also main effects of environment on all three outcomes. Socioeconomic status affects IQ. Criminal behavior and schizophrenia both occur more commonly in crowded urban settings. For schizophrenia, this finding fits with the hypothesis that virus infections may trigger the disorder in susceptible individuals. For criminal behavior, the evidence suggests that it's the neighborhood, not the home, that determines whether or not a child will become a lawbreaker. There is nothing newsworthy about the observation that crime rates are higher in some neighborhoods than in others.[12]

In fact, nothing in Maccoby's talk came as news to me. Nothing she said at the NICHD conference on parenting provided convincing evidence that parents can influence a child's personality by the way they bring up the child. The most convincing evidence presented at the conference had to do, not with human parents and children, but with rhesus monkeys. It was Stephen Suomi who provided what appeared to be rock-solid evidence of an effect of parenting on child outcomes. That is, on monkey outcomes.

Suomi started his talk[13] by contrasting "peer-reared" monkeys with monkeys that were reared in the normal way by their mothers (all these monkeys were born and raised in laboratory cages). The peer-reared monkeys were taken from their mothers at birth and bottle-fed, but from an early age they were caged together with three or four other monkeys of the same age. Peer-reared monkeys develop strong attachments to one another; they cling to each other when frightened. Although monkeys reared in isolation turn into socially abnormal adults, monkeys reared with peers are reasonably normal. However, statistical differences between peer-reared and mother-reared monkeys do show up in certain circumstances.

Does it surprise you to hear that I would expect such differences? The headline DO PARENTS MATTER? appeared above so many of the newspaper and magazine articles about *The Nurture Assumption* that many readers got the impression that my answer was no. But I've never said that parents don't matter; certainly they matter! That's why evolution provided parents with the motivation to take care of their children. And it's not just a question of keeping the baby alive: having a mother (or mother substitute) may be necessary for optimal development of the baby's brain, the parts of the brain involved with social behavior. "In order to complete its development," I explained in *The Nurture Assumption*, "the brain requires certain inputs from the environment. . . . You might say that the developing brain 'expects' certain stimuli to be present in the world outside the womb and relies on them in producing the finished product."[14]

Since an infant mammal cannot survive in the wild without a mother, its developing brain "expects" a mother to be present. The fact that peer-reared baby monkeys turn out nearly normal is testimony to the adaptability of the primate brain. The fact that subtle statistical differences can be found, if you look for them, between peer-reared and mother-reared monkeys didn't worry me—it's what I would predict.

But Suomi went on to tell his audience about a second study with baby rhesus monkeys. He described a "cross-fostering" experiment in which infant rhesus monkeys were reared by adoptive monkey mothers. Some of these infants came from strains known to produce nervous, high-strung animals: "high-reactive," he called them. Other infants came from calmer "low-reactive" strains. Infants from both strains were reared either by good foster mothers or by bad ones. Evidently the baby monkeys from the calmer strains turned out okay regardless of which kind of mother reared them, but—here's the interaction—the high-reactive baby monkeys were sensitive to the way they were mothered. High-reactive monkeys reared by bad mothers turned into social failures who couldn't handle stress, but those reared by good mothers did very well. The effects of good mothering persisted even after they were separated from their foster mothers and caged with same-age peers. They ranked high in the dominance hierarchy of their peer group, Suomi reported.

These results were clearly at odds with the theory presented in *The*

Nurture Assumption. What I was trying to do in that book was not to argue that parents don't matter but to answer a question about *differences* in parenting: Are differences in the kind of care parents provide, or in the way they provide it, responsible for the differences in how the children turn out? My conclusion, based on a good deal of evidence, was no, as long as the kind of care the parents provide is within the normal range for our species. But the normal range for our species, I pointed out, is very wide. Baby-care and child-rearing practices vary tremendously across the globe and through history. You don't have to go back very far to see this. At the time I was born, American babies were fed on a strict schedule and mothers were warned against "spoiling" them by picking them up too often. Children were routinely spanked for minor infractions of household rules. Household rules were made for the grownups' convenience, without regard for the children's wishes. This was only sixty-seven years ago!

Of course, differences in child-care practices are going to have visible effects on the way the child behaves in the parents' presence. What I didn't expect were differences that persisted into adulthood and that could be measured even in social settings that were not associated with the parents. Researchers have found no systematic differences in adult personality between people born in the first half of the twentieth century and those born in the second half, despite the sweeping changes in child-care practices and parent-child relationships that occurred during that period. Despite the reduction in corporal punishment, adults born in the latter part of the century are not less aggressive. Despite the increase in emotional closeness between children and their parents—in particular between children and their fathers—they are not happier or less neurotic. Despite the fact that they received more praise and less criticism, they are not more self-assured.[15]

So I was taken aback by the results of Suomi's cross-fostering experiment. What surprised me was not that the monkeys with good foster mothers did well while they were with their mothers, but that the effects of the good mothering persisted even after they were separated from them. Suomi was describing long-term effects of differences in parenting on baby rhesus monkeys and I didn't expect them. I couldn't explain the results of his cross-fostering study. All I could do was to shrug my shoulders and mutter, "Well, it's monkeys, not humans."

But it wasn't so easy to sweep those monkeys under a rug. They popped up again six months after the NICHD conference, when an article by five prominent developmentalists, including Eleanor Maccoby, appeared in the most widely read journal in psychology, the *American Psychologist.* The article was titled "Contemporary Research on Parenting: The Case for Nature *and* Nurture." It was the establishment's response to the charges I had made in *The Nurture Assumption* and that David Rowe—my sole ally at the conference—had made in his book *The Limits of Family Influence.*[16]

Despite the "contemporary" in the title, most of the article was the same old same old. Almost a third of the references cited dated from the 1980s or earlier; fewer than half had been published after 1993. I had already explained what was wrong with most of that evidence.[17] But not all of it. Stephen Suomi's study of cross-fostered baby monkeys figured as prominently in the *American Psychologist* article as it had at the NICHD conference. I could no longer ignore his research.

My notes on Suomi's NICHD talk were sketchy, so I had to rely on the description of the cross-fostering experiment given in the *American Psychologist* article. Baby monkeys from a genetically high-reactive strain were reared, the article reported, either by high-reactive foster mothers or by calm foster mothers. Here's how the results of Suomi's experiment were summarized:

> Genetically reactive young animals that are reared by calm mothers for the first six months of their lives and then placed in large social groups made up of peers and nonrelated older adults develop normally and indeed rise to the top of their dominance hierarchy. . . . By contrast, genetically reactive infants who are reared by reactive mothers typically are socially incompetent when placed in the larger living group at the age of six months and are particularly vulnerable to stress.[18]

The reference cited for this experiment was Suomi, 1997—a chapter in an edited book with a mouthful of a title: *Neurodevelopment and Adult Psychopathology.*[19] It was time I learned more about Suomi's research—the details of his procedure and results. I can request books like *Neurodevelopment and Adult Psychopathology* from my local library (without even having to pronounce their titles) by filling out a form. But it usually takes two or three weeks to obtain a book on interlibrary loan. So I got in touch with Joan.

In *The Daughter of Time*, the mystery novel about Richard III and the murdered Little Princes, detective Alan Grant manages to do his investigating despite being flat on his back in the hospital. He does it with the help of a research assistant named Brent Carradine, a young American who has access to historical documents stored in the British Museum. There is a Brent Carradine in my story, too. Her name is Joan Friebely and she has access to the riches of the Harvard libraries.

Brent Carradine is described in *The Daughter of Time* as "a tall boy, hatless, with soft fair curls crowning a high forehead."[20] I can't give you a physical description of Joan because we have never met in person (I've met few of my friends in person), but she has an upbeat personality and an offbeat sense of humor. Joan and I met in what I have come to think of as the conventional way: in e-mail. She came across my *Psychological Review* article in 1997 and wrote to me. Her doctoral dissertation, she explained, had been based on the work of developmentalist Diana Baumrind, whose work I had deconstructed in that article (and would later criticize in greater detail in *The Nurture Assumption*). Joan had ended up with serious doubts about Baumrind's work and was glad to have someone to share them with. Thus began our e-mail friendship.

Joan is the one I turn to when I need access to a university library. I can make it to my local library on my own, and when I'm not in a hurry I can use their interlibrary loan service to borrow books from university libraries. But some books aren't loaned out, and I'm often in a hurry, and much of the reference material I need is published in journals, not books. Those are the times when a Brent Carradine comes in handy.

In e-mail, I asked Joan to send me a copy of Suomi's chapter in *Neurodevelopment and Adult Psychopathology*, the source cited in the *American Psychologist* article for the cross-fostering experiment. I read it the minute it arrived and was puzzled to discover that it didn't say anything at all about the cross-fostered baby monkeys—they weren't even mentioned. The chapter was about the differences between mother-reared and peer-reared monkeys.

The first author of the *American Psychologist* article was Andrew Collins, a developmentalist at the University of Minnesota. On Valentine's Day 2000, I wrote to Collins and told him that the reference he had cited for the Suomi work didn't contain the research mentioned in his article. "Can you give me the proper reference for the Suomi study you described?" I asked.

Collins replied in a few days, saying that Eleanor Maccoby had drafted that portion of their coauthored article. After he received my e-mail he asked her about the Suomi research, he said, and she told him that her sources were a phone conversation with Suomi, some unpublished papers by him, and a 1999 chapter in an edited book.[21] But the chapter, Collins warned, contained only a brief summary of the experiment—no data. "We suggest that you contact Steve directly for the data," Collins told me. "He has been slower than many of us would like in publishing the actual data, so you can goad him a bit perhaps!" He ended by thanking me for alerting him to the problem of the incorrect reference.[22]

What I had been hoping for was a journal article describing Suomi's cross-fostering experiment. A chapter in an edited book isn't good enough because there is no requirement to meet the standards of journal publication. To get a research article into a peer-reviewed journal, an author has to give a detailed account of the procedure. The number of subjects who contributed data to the study—what researchers call "the N"—has to be specified, along with pertinent information about the subjects, such as their sex. The results have to be given precisely; this almost always means that they have to be expressed in numbers, not just words. Tests of statistical significance also have to be reported.

This was the kind of information I needed for the cross-fostering experiment, so I followed Collins' advice and wrote directly to Stephen Suomi. "Can you tell me if the cross-fostering experiment has been published," I asked him, "and if so, where? If unpublished, can you give me more details about the procedure and results? For example, how many high-reactive and low-reactive baby monkeys were there, and how many mothers of each type?"

Suomi's reply was lengthy and packed with details about the cross-fostering experiment. He explained that cross-fostering is a difficult procedure because two monkey mothers have to give birth at around the same time in order to make it possible to switch their infants. It took four years to complete the experiment. "In all," he told me, "36 infants (18 high-reactive, 18 low-reactive) were cross-fostered, 2 of which died during their first year of life. Half of the high-reactive and half of the low-reactive were foster-reared by 'nurturant' females, etc."[23]

I read it twice before it dawned on me that Suomi's e-mail contained a lot about the procedure but nothing about the results. Collins had advised me to "contact Steve directly for the data," but there were no data in Suomi's e-mail. However, he did mention three papers that he said contained information about the cross-fostering experiment. He also said that he was currently preparing a monograph "that will describe the results of the entire study in comprehensive fashion" and that he expected to complete by the end of 2000. "I'd be happy to send you a copy of it when it's done," he said, "if you so desire."[24] "Yes, please," I replied.

There was plenty of other stuff to read in the meantime. Joan was finding and sending me a steady stream of papers by Suomi and his colleagues. By the time she was done she had located more than three dozen book chapters and journal articles, including the three he had recommended to me, on the effects of rearing conditions on rhesus monkeys. Writer's block does not appear to be an occupational hazard for monkey researchers.

The cross-fostered monkeys, Joan and I discovered, made their first appearance in print in a 1987 chapter in an edited book. This chapter contained preliminary results from the "first cohort of rhesus monkey infants in a major cross-fostering longitudinal study." How many monkeys were in this first cohort? No N was given in the chapter (see why I was hoping for a journal article?), but clues dropped here and there strongly suggested that there were fewer than eight. The foster mothers in the experiment varied in two ways: high- versus low-reactive, and nurturant versus punitive. In this first cohort, Suomi admitted, "there were not enough infants and foster mothers to fill all cells of the 2 × 2 × 2 (Infant Reactivity × Foster Mother Reactivity × Foster Mother Maternal Style) design matrix."[25]

It would take eight baby monkeys to fill a 2 × 2 × 2 design matrix, and only half of them—four—would be of the high-reactive type that Suomi claimed were affected by the type of mothering they got. These four baby monkeys would be reared by four different kinds of foster mothers. Suomi's description of the results of this first cohort, I realized, was based on individual monkeys, such as "the one high-reactive subject who also had a punitive and high-reactive foster mother" and who ended up "at the very bottom of the dominancy hierarchy of its group."[26]

Any number of things can affect the status of an individual monkey. The monkey's size, for instance: bigger, heavier animals dominate smaller ones. Punitive monkey mothers push their babies away and don't let them nurse as much as they want to. Were the monkeys with nurturant mothers heavier than those with punitive mothers, and is that why they were dominant? With such a small study, it would be impossible to control for body weight.

Okay, Suomi had told me in e-mail that it took four years to cross-foster thirty-six baby monkeys. So I turned to a paper he published four years later, in 1991—another chapter in an edited book—and found another summary of the cross-fostering experiment, now described as "recently completed."[27] But there were no new data and again no N was given. There were four panels of numerical graphs, showing behavioral measures of the cross-fostered monkeys in the first months of life, before they were permanently separated from their foster mothers. But these were the same graphs that had appeared in the 1987 chapter: every line was identical.[28] Suomi had had four years to update his graphs; why hadn't he done so? In 1987, he had sounded apologetic about not having enough subjects to complete a 2 × 2 × 2 experimental design. If his N was larger in 1991, why didn't he say so?

Joan and I spent weeks searching for traces of the cross-fostered baby monkeys in published papers by Suomi and his colleagues. There were some journal articles that did contain an N, but they were about other things—not about the social behavior or dominance status of high-reactive monkeys reared by calm or nurturant foster mothers. When an N was given in a paper by Suomi and his colleagues, it wasn't for the cross-fostering experiment described by Andrew Collins and Eleanor Maccoby in their *American Psychologist* article. When the cross-fostering experiment was mentioned, no N was given, just a reference to the 1987 or 1991 chapter.

Joan and I never found any evidence, in the published works of Suomi and his colleagues, that the cross-fostering experiment had ever progressed beyond the small "first cohort" of baby monkeys. If thirty-six monkeys were in fact cross-fostered, I suspect that the results from the larger N didn't support the findings described in the 1987 chapter. Anyone who has done research knows how risky it is to get excited about preliminary results. The drug that seemed so promising when given to fifty patients may fail to live up to its promise when given to five hundred. It's the law of small numbers and it means you shouldn't bet the ranch on early results.

In July 2000, I informed Eleanor Maccoby and Andrew Collins of the results of the investigation that Joan and I had carried out. I told them that the claim they made in their *American Psychologist* paper, that high-reactive baby monkeys reared by calm foster mothers "develop normally and indeed rise to the top of their dominance hierarchy," was based on evidence that appeared to involve fewer than eight cross-fostered monkeys and that had been published only in chapters in edited books. I also pointed out a discrepancy between what they reported in their article and what Suomi had said in his chapters. Collins and Maccoby had claimed that high-reactive babies reared by *calm* foster mothers did well after they were separated from their mothers, but what Suomi had been saying since 1987 was that high-reactive babies reared by *nurturant* mothers did well.

I never heard back from Collins, but Eleanor Maccoby replied. She was apologetic about having confused calm foster mothers with nurturant ones. For the other things she said about Suomi's monkeys, she told me, she had relied mainly on one of Suomi's book chapters, one of the ones I had read. "True," Maccoby admitted, "the chapter gave us only a summary, not the numbers we are all eager to see when the new monograph becomes available."[29]

Are you familiar with the term "vaporware"? It's a word used to describe a product announced and promoted by a software company, but that hasn't yet been delivered and probably never will be. Suomi's monograph proved to be vaporware. He never sent me a copy of it and, as far as Joan and I have been able to determine, it was never published. We have searched repeatedly and never found an account of the cross-fostering experiment containing the details that would be required for acceptance by a journal.[30]

Two things of interest did appear in print, however. The first, in 2002, was a book based on the NICHD conference, *Parenting and the Child's World*. It contains a chapter by everyone who participated in the conference—a written version of their talk—and naturally I was curious to see what Suomi would say in his chapter. By the time he was preparing the final draft he must have known, not only what I had discovered about his research, but also that I had been informing others of my discoveries. What would he do? Would he repeat what he said at the conference? Nope, he backed down. Those high-reactive baby monkeys who had played such a prominent role in his talk—the ones who rose to the top of their dominance hierarchy because they were reared by the right kind of foster mothers—do not appear in Suomi's chapter.[31] They had been left on the cutting room floor.

The second thing was an article by another primatologist, Dario Maestripieri of the University of Chicago, which appeared in 2003 in the journal *Developmental Psychobiology*. Maestripieri reported the results of a cross-fostering experiment with baby rhesus monkeys, the same species Suomi had studied and pretty much the same method. But Maestripieri had followed his subjects for three years (Suomi's monkeys were only fifteen months old when he summarized his findings in the 1987 chapter), and Maestripieri's results were quite different from Suomi's—in fact, opposite to them. He made quantitative observations of the young monkeys' social behavior and reported that "no clear behavioral similarities between offspring and foster mothers were observed at any age"; in fact, the offsprings' social behaviors "resembled those of their biological mothers."[32] Their biological mothers, not their foster mothers.

But what really clinched it was what Maestripieri said about his N. He had to report it, of course, since this was a journal article. Only ten baby monkeys took part in the study, and Maestripieri explained why there weren't more. "Cross-fostering experiments are difficult to perform because [monkey] mothers adopt unrelated infants only under very restricted circumstances," he said. "As a result, very few studies have used this procedure to investigate the intergenerational transmission of behavior, and these studies typically involved very small sample sizes."[33] Here he cited Suomi's 1987 chapter—the only work by Suomi he referred to.

Primatologists studying rhesus monkeys keep informed about one another's work. If Suomi had really run thirty-six baby monkeys in a cross-fostering experiment, I'm sure Maestripieri would have known about it. What Maestripieri was suggesting was that his ten baby monkeys might not be much, but they were more than Suomi's "very small sample."

Perhaps you're wondering why I'm making such a fuss about a bunch of monkeys. After all, they're not humans; they're not even apes. Why should I care whether Suomi's evidence on cross-fostering in monkeys was or wasn't genuine? Why should I care if the monkey mothers whose foster children allegedly turned out well were nurturant or calm?

I'll tell you why. The nurturant monkey mothers, as Suomi described them in his 1987 chapter, sound very much like the kind of human mothers sometimes described as "overprotective." The nurturant monkeys and the overprotective human mothers both spend a lot of time holding their babies; both are relatively tolerant of disobedience. This kind of indulgent mothering has been reported (by Suomi) to have good effects on high-reactive infant monkeys, but it has been reported (by the developmentalist Jerome Kagan) to have *bad* effects on high-reactive infant humans.[34] And these conflicting results have both been used as evidence that I'm wrong: that mothering style does have important effects on how the offspring turn out, but that the effects come in the form of an interaction—only high-reactive infants show these effects.

High-reactive infant humans (also called timid, fearful, inhibited, or shy) featured prominently in a *Newsweek* cover story about *The Nurture Assumption*. In that article, I was accused of "ignoring studies that do not fit [my] thesis," and a study by Kagan was presented as "Exhibit A" among the studies I had allegedly ignored. Here's how it was described:

> Exhibit A: the work of Harvard's Kagan. He has shown how different parenting styles can shape a timid, shy child who perceives the world as a threat. Kagan measured babies at 4 months and at school age. The

> fearful children whose parents (over)protected them were still timid. Those whose parents pushed them to try new things—"get into that sandbox and play with the other kids, dammit!"—lost their shyness. A genetic legacy of timidity was shaped by parental behavior, says Kagan, "and these kids became far less fearful."[35]

The evidence does sound impressive. These were not short-term results; according to *Newsweek*, the children in this study had been followed to school age. The fearful babies whose parents had refrained from overprotectiveness had lost their timidity by school age.

Your question now should be: Have these results been published in a peer-reviewed journal? Funny you should ask; the answer is no. Joan and I found no evidence that the study described in *Newsweek* was ever done or, if it was done, that it produced the reported results. It wasn't just that it hadn't been published in a peer-reviewed journal—as far as we could determine, it hadn't been published anywhere.

What had been published was a preliminary report. In his book *Galen's Prophecy*, which came out in 1994, Jerome Kagan described a study carried out by his student Doreen Arcus. It was the research she did for her 1991 doctoral dissertation at Harvard. Arcus studied twenty-four babies who were judged high-reactive on the basis of a test given when they were four months old, and twenty-six babies who were judged low-reactive. She found that the high-reactive babies whose mothers were relatively indulgent—who picked them up and held them when they cried and who were relatively wimpy about setting limits when they began to crawl—were more likely to be fearful at fourteen months. At twenty-one months, the high-reactive babies who were still fearful tended to be those whose mothers said that they didn't particularly value obedience. The low-reactive babies were unlikely to be fearful at fourteen or twenty-one months regardless of their mothers' child-rearing practices or philosophies.[36]

Galen's Prophecy summarizes fifteen years of research on fearful children by Kagan and his students. Doreen Arcus's unpublished dissertation research—twenty-four high-reactive babies followed to the age of twenty-one months—is the only evidence Kagan gives in the book to support his conviction that the way parents raise their children plays a role in whether or not the children are fearful.

The problem here is not the N: it's that twenty-one months is not school age, and the *Newsweek* article had said that the babies were measured "at 4 months and at school age."

In 2001, three years after the *Newsweek* report, a chapter by Arcus appeared in an edited book. The chapter is about biological and social influences on temperament, and the stability of temperament during development. In it, Arcus refers to a "longitudinal study of 98 infants" and reports data on stability of temperament for these subjects from the age of four months to four and half years. (At four and a half years, the children who had been judged high-reactive at age four months were, on average, less chatty and outgoing than those who had been judged low-reactive.) Clearly, these children had been followed at least to the age of four and a half years. And yet when Arcus describes her research on the relationship between mothers' child-rearing style and children's fearfulness, she reports results only up to the age of fourteen months.[37]

Promising preliminary results often fail to hold up when more subjects are added to a study. The same thing can happen when subjects are followed for a longer period of time.

Assume, for a moment, that *Newsweek*'s description of the research by Kagan and his students was correct, and that correlations between mothers' child-rearing style and children's fearfulness could still be detected at school age. What would that show? The findings for fourteen and twenty-one months are presented in *Galen's Prophecy* as evidence of a gene-environment interaction: an interaction between a particular kind of infant temperament, assumed to be genetic, and a particular mothering style, part of the infant's environment. Babies who are born with a genetic predisposition to be fearful can, according to Kagan, avoid this fate if they are reared in the right kind of environment.

Kagan and his students used a test given at four months to classify babies as high-reactive or low-reactive. This is a method often used by developmentalists: instead of using twin or adoption studies as a way of controlling for genetic predispositions, they use some kind of pretest. They test or observe a bunch of children at an early age, look at them again at a later age, and assume that any changes between Time 1 and Time 2 must be due to environmental factors. They assume that genetic effects show up early, like inherited money, and that environmental effects show up later, like compound interest.

But genetic effects can show up at any age. There are genes that kick in early and genes that bide their time; this is one of the reasons why you become more like your parents as you get older. Genes that determine whether a female will grow large or small breasts at puberty don't begin to reveal their intentions until the biological clock strikes twelve. Genes that determine male baldness work on an even more leisurely schedule. You can't tell by looking at a baby how much hair he's going to have in middle age. Counting the hairs on the baby's head is not a good control for genetic influences on hairiness at age forty.

The environmental side of the alleged interaction is equally problematic. First of all, the way a mother takes care of a baby is in part a reaction to the baby's behavior. A baby destined to be fearful may be sending out signals that Kagan's four-month test misses but that get through to its mother. The mother might respond by being more protective.

Second, a mother's style of caring for her baby is a function, not only of the baby's characteristics, but also of her own.[38] Mothers who hold their infants a lot, especially when they cry, and who are wimpy about enforcing discipline sound to me like anxious mothers. Anxious mothers may have fearful children (and fearful children may have anxious mothers) for genetic reasons. The heritability of personality traits is about .45. A child who is anxious or fearful may have inherited this characteristic from one or both of his parents.

It's an odd thing. Though many developmentalists are now willing to admit that babies differ from one another at birth and that these differences are largely genetic, they still haven't come to terms with the fact that babies get their genes from their parents. They still haven't figured out how to deal with the fact that babies and their parents are likely to resemble each other in personality for genetic reasons alone. One sign of this unwillingness to face facts is their avoidance of the word "heredity." They tend to use euphemisms such as "genetic" and "nature" (as in "nature and nurture"), which acknowledge that children have genes without acknowledging where they get them from.

Behavioral geneticists, who are keenly aware of where children get their genes, study adopted children for this very reason. Adoptees get their genes from one set of parents and their home environment from a different set. Suomi's cross-fostering study of monkeys is an adoption study; the idea is that you can do things with monkeys that you cannot do with humans. But even though high-reactive human babies aren't systematically placed with calm or nervous adoptive mothers, or with nurturant or punitive ones, we have enough data from human adoptions to know that the adoptive mother's personality and her philosophy of child-rearing have no long-term effects on the personality of her adopted child. The near-zero correlation between adoptees' personalities and those of their adoptive parents means that adoptees reared by nervous adoptive mothers are, on average, no more anxious or fearful than those reared by calm ones.[39]

Reports of Kagan's timid babies and Suomi's nervous monkeys have traveled beyond the academic world into publications aimed at a general audience. Suomi's cross-fostering experiment was recently described, for example, in a book titled *Liars, Lovers, and Heroes*, by neuroscientists Steven Quartz and Terrence Sejnowski. Here's the description these authors gave of Suomi's experiment:

> Suomi, a primatologist at the National Institute of Child Health and Human Development, selectively bred monkeys for both inhibited and bold temperaments. Then, he rearranged their rearing environment to explore how environmental factors and temperament interact, all while tracking their neurotransmitter levels. In Suomi's experiments, a fearful infant monkey was put in the care of an uninhibited, nurturing foster mother. . . . The young monkey became less fearful, and its levels of noradrenaline dropped. Regarding temperament, Suomi notes, "Our work shows that you can modify these tendencies quite dramatically with certain types of early experiences."[40]

No reference was given in the endnotes for the experiment or for the quote from Suomi, so I wrote to the authors and asked for their source. Terry Sejnowski replied. He said the description of the procedure and results came from a talk Suomi had given at his institute a few years earlier, and that the quote came from a 1997 article in *Discover* magazine.[41]

I looked up the article. What Suomi was referring to when he told the *Discover* journalist "You can modify these tendencies quite dramatically with certain kinds of early experiences" was not the cross-fostering experiment Quartz and Sejnowski described in the passage I quoted from their book: Suomi was talking about peer-reared versus mother-reared monkeys. But later on in the same article the *Discover* journalist did refer to the cross-fostering experiment:

> Suomi . . . has shown that even monkeys who are born anxious and inhibited can overcome their temperamental handicap—and even rise to the top of the dominance hierarchy in their troop—if they are

raised by ultra-nurturing super-moms. Kagan's work confirms that mothering can alter the course of an inhibited child's development.[42]

The *Discover* journalist did not point out that "ultra-nurturing super-moms" are alleged to alter the inhibited monkey's development one way and the inhibited child's development in the opposite way. Nor did she mention that both results were evidently based on small samples followed for an insufficient length of time and that neither has been published in a peer-reviewed journal, despite the fact that years have gone by since the preliminary reports.

A good story—especially one that appears to confirm what people already believe—acquires a life of its own. Once it becomes folklore it is highly resistant to disproof.[43] I am showing you how these myths get started. Suomi gives talks about his cross-fostered monkeys; Kagan tells journalists about his overprotected kids. The stories, perhaps improved a bit by the journalists, get into the popular press—the *Discover* article, the cover story in *Newsweek*—and then are repeated, with further improvements, by other writers. When you can no longer remember where you heard or read something, you are unlikely to question its accuracy. It's just something you know.

In 1951, when Josephine Tey's *The Daughter of Time* was published, every schoolchild in Britain could tell you that Richard III was a heartless villain. Tey spent more than two-thirds of her book trying to persuade her readers that what everyone knew wasn't true. The case against Richard III, she showed, had been trumped up. The histories of Richard's brief reign—one of which was the basis for Shakespeare's play—had been written by people who had something to gain from the posthumous trashing of Richard's reputation. They were allies of his enemies.

Josephine Tey's first job was to convince her readers that the mystery of what happened to the Little Princes hadn't already been solved—that the solution everyone had accepted for so long was just a myth. That's my first job too, though I will make shorter work of it than Tey did. But I'm fighting the same uphill battle. People see what they expect to see; ambiguous results, like ambiguous pictures, are interpreted in accordance with preconceived notions. Sir George Bellew, author of *The Kings and Queens of Britain*, looked at the portrait of Richard III and saw in Richard's face clear indications of his "unscrupulous nature."[44]

Seven months after I told Andrew Collins and Eleanor Maccoby about the errors in their *American Psychologist* article, the journal published some letters to the editor commenting on the article, along with the authors' reply. This would have been their opportunity to set things straight, at the very least by correcting the wrong reference they gave for the Suomi study and their mixup of "calm" and "nurturant." They didn't do it. They admitted no errors in their reply.[45]

What's worse, Collins is evidently still telling students who take the introductory psychology course at the University of Minnesota about Suomi's cross-fostered monkeys. The website for this course currently includes the following item among its "learning objectives":

> Describe the findings of the Suomi study that Dr Collins will tell us about. It's a good piece of evidence in the nature/nurture controversy—the biological infants of reactive rhesus monkey mothers were fostered by 'calm' & 'reactive' rhesus monkey mothers. What happens?[46]

Yes, tell us, Dr. Collins. What happens?

Collins, Maccoby, and the three other authors of the *American Psychologist* article summed up their conclusions as follows:

> This new generation of evidence on the role of parenting should add to the conviction, long held by many scholars, that broad, general main effects for either heredity or environment are unlikely in research on behavior and personality. Statistical interactions and moderator effects are the rule, not the exception.[47]

Main effects are unlikely; interactions are the rule. Maccoby had said pretty much the same thing at the NICHD conference:

> If a given kind of household or a given style of parenting has different effects for children with different predispositions, this means that parenting often functions to make children in the same family different rather than alike.[48]

What they are saying is that a given style of parenting has no predictable effects: the same parental behaviors can cause one child to become more cheerful and another more depressed, one more honest and the other more deceptive. If a given style of parenting had predictable effects even *on the average*—if certain parental behaviors led to cheerful or honest children more often than not—then we would see main effects of parenting. Since the effects of parenting depend, according to the developmentalists, on the predispositions of the child you happened to get, it would seem pretty clear that no one could give you advice on how to raise that child, unless they had some secret way of finding out about his or her predispositions. Right?

A few months after the conference I got a letter from the director of NICHD. All the participants in the conference were invited to contribute to a booklet of parenting advice aimed at the general public. "Consider it this way," the letter said. "If you could give parents one piece of advice from your research, what would it be?"[49]

My advice would be to run the other way if you see an advice-giver coming toward you, but I didn't think that was what the director wanted to hear so I didn't bother to reply. The booklet, with NICHD's imprimatur on it, came out in 2001; *Adventures in Parenting*, it's called. Here are two samples of the advice it contains:

> Much "acting out" stems from children not knowing how to handle their emotions. Feelings can be so intense that usual methods of expressing them don't work. Or, because feelings like anger and sadness are viewed as "bad," your child may not want to express them openly. Encourage your child to express emotions in a healthy and positive way.
>
> Because you can't be with your child all the time, you should know who is with your child when you're not. Friends have a big influence on your child, from pre-school well into adulthood. Much of the time, this influence is positive, but not always. With a little effort from you, your child might surround him or herself with friends whose values, interests, and behaviors will be "pluses" in your child's life.[50]

According to the acknowledgments page of the booklet, the 1999 NICHD conference on parenting "provided the impetus for this publication." But a major theme of that conference was that parenting doesn't have any main effects: only gene-environment interactions. If parenting doesn't have any main effects, it means that if you encouraged your child to express emotions in a healthy and positive way, it might have a beneficial effect, but then again it might have a deleterious one. If you spent a little effort to see that your child surrounds him- or herself with the right kind of friends, your efforts might pay off, but then again they might backfire. Your results will vary because what you get depends on the kind of kid you started out with, and the writers of the advice booklet have no idea what kind of kid you started out with.

The developmentalists are speaking out of both sides of their mouths. In the *American Psychologist* article, five of America's most prominent developmentalists said that "broad, general main effects for either heredity or environment are unlikely in research on behavior and personality." But all they really want to deny is the existence of broad, general main effects of heredity (the evidence for which is incontrovertible). They don't really want to deny the existence of broad, general main effects of the home environment. If the developmentalists gave up their belief in broad, general main effects of the home environment, they would be forced to admit that giving advice to parents is useless.

In reality, it is worse than useless. Advice-giving has moral repercussions. If there are good parents—the ones who provide just the right amount of nurturing but who avoid being overprotective, who encourage their children to express their emotions in a healthy way, who take the time and trouble to make sure that their children have the right kind of friends—then there must also be bad parents, the ones who fail to do these things. And if the right kind of parenting produces good kids, then bad kids must be the product of the wrong kind of parenting. If your child is timid, you must have overprotected him or failed to provide sufficient nurturing. If your child acts out or bottles up emotions, it's because you didn't encourage her to express emotions in a healthy way. Even if there are no main effects, only interactions, that doesn't let you off the hook: you could have prevented your high-reactive baby from turning into a timid kid, if only you hadn't overprotected him!

The detective in *The Daughter of Time* was up against four centuries of unquestioned belief in Richard III's culpability. I am up against only fifty years of unquestioned belief in parents' culpability. Sixty-seven years ago, when I was born, parents didn't get blamed when their children turned out badly; according to the cultural myths that were prevalent at that time, bad kids were "born that way." Alice James attributed her depression to heredity, not to her parents' child-rearing methods.

The unquestioned belief in the good and bad effects of parenting has resulted in a systematic bias in the reporting of research results. In addition to the exaggeration of supporting evidence and the slanted interpretation of ambiguous evidence, there has also been a suppression of negative evidence. I mentioned one case in *The Nurture Assumption*: a study of the effects of child-rearing practices, done in the 1950s, that failed to produce the expected results. The null outcome went unpublished until Eleanor Maccoby—one of the researchers on the study—mentioned it in print, thirty-five years later.[51]

Jerome Kagan's first noteworthy publication was a book titled *Birth to Maturity*, which came out in 1962.[52] It was the final report of a major research project in which almost a hundred subjects had been followed from infancy to young adulthood. Periodic assessments were made of the subjects themselves and of the "maternal practices" of their mothers. Of the large number of correlations the researchers calculated between maternal practices and child outcomes, only 6 percent—about the percentage you'd expect to occur by chance—were statistically significant.[53] This failure to find meaningful results was apparent, however, only to readers who carefully scrutinized the appendixes of the book, where the correlation coefficients were reported. In fact, it was apparent only to those who carefully scrutinized the *first* edition of the book. The reprint edition of *Birth to Maturity*, published in 1983,[54] has suffered an appendectomy.

Some years ago I had a brief e-mail interchange with a developmentalist. She told me that in the early 1970s she and a colleague—an older man with an eminent reputation—had carried out a large and elaborate research project of the sort called an "intervention study." Intervention studies, which I will discuss in a later chapter, are designed to improve child outcomes by training parents to use better child-rearing methods. This study, according to my correspondent, "yielded NO effects. . . . These data were never published unfortunately."[55]

Medical researchers testing the efficacy of a new drug are expected to disclose any financial ties they have to the manufacturer of the drug, but conflicts of interest occur all the time in developmental research and nobody raises an eyebrow. The researchers themselves and the granting agencies that fund their research—NICHD, for example—are united in their faith in the efficacy of parental influence.

A physician commenting on medical research in the *Journal of the American Medical Association* said, "If possible, the effectiveness of an effort should be determined by someone outside the effort who has nothing to gain by its perpetuation."[56] The corollary of this good advice is that the effectiveness of an effort shouldn't be determined by those who have a lot to lose if the effort turns out to be a failure.

There's an old story about two ladies in Victorian England who have just heard the news about the theory of evolution. One exclaims, "According to Mr. Darwin, our ancestors were apes!" The other replies, "That cannot be true! But if it is true, let us pray that it will not become generally known."

The developmentalists sincerely believe in the efficacy of parental influence. But if parental influence turns out to be a dud—if the best kind of parenting they can think of is really no better than the placebo—they are praying that it will not become generally known. This prayer is not motivated entirely by self-interest. In the *Newsweek* article, psychologist Frank Farley of Temple University warned of possible consequences:

> [Harris's] thesis is absurd on its face, but consider what might happen if parents believe this stuff! Will it free some to mistreat their kids, since "it doesn't matter"? Will it tell parents who are tired after a long day that they needn't bother even paying any attention to their kid since "it doesn't matter"?[57]

Farley's statement is absurd on its face. Thousands of generations of hominid parents took good care of their children (have you any idea how much trouble it was to keep a child alive in the days when there were no permanent homes, no baby carriages or strollers, no jars of baby food, and no disposable diapers?), even though it never occurred to these parents that what they were doing might have long-term effects on their children's personalities. But what bothers me about this statement is not so much the ignorance of evolutionary psychology it reveals: it's the arrogance. Farley seems to think that he and his colleagues have the right to decide what American parents should be told about the efficacy of parenting—that he and his colleagues have a right to withhold or suppress information if, in their opinion, it wouldn't be a good idea to have it become generally known.

In the past, researchers looking for gene-environment interactions often relied on imprecise methods for estimating the contribution of genes. Subjects were presumed to have an inherited tendency to be fearful or irritable on the basis of a pretest given in infancy.

In the future, researchers will look for gene-environment interactions by decoding their subjects' genes. A few studies of this sort have already been published. One, for example, showed an interaction between stressful life events and a gene associated with anxiety and depression. People who have one variant of this gene are at risk of becoming depressed, but this generally happens only if they experience multiple stressful events, such as the loss of a job or the breakup of a romantic relationship. People who have the alternate version of the gene are unlikely to become depressed no matter how stressful their lives are.[58] It's a sensitivity type of gene-environment interaction: the gene makes its owner more vulnerable to the slings and arrows of outrageous fortune.

There is a paradoxical danger in this kind of research: it sounds so frightfully scientific that the reader is discouraged from looking too closely at it and may simply accept the researchers' conclusions. But let the buyer beware: a scientific approach to the genetic component of a gene-environment interaction may be coupled with a naive, old-fashioned approach to the environmental component. The example I have in mind is the study—you may have read about it—in which researchers found that a variant of a certain gene, which codes for an enzyme abbreviated as MAOA, greatly increased the likelihood of antisocial behavior in adulthood, but only in males who had been treated badly in childhood.[59] The low-MAOA variant of the gene allegedly increases a child's sensitivity to what the researchers called "maltreatment" but that was generally referred to as "abuse" in the news coverage.

The results, it was claimed, can explain why some, but not all, maltreated children grow up to become violent criminals. The conclusion might be true but the data from this study offer scant support for it. There is a well-known correlation between abuse in childhood and unfavorable outcomes of one sort or another in adulthood, but correlations are uninformative about causes. The study that focused on the low-MAOA gene is simply a correlational study packed together with a genetic study that controlled for only one gene. Maltreatment (which was defined by the researchers as any of a variety of unfavorable experiences,[60] such as more than one change of primary caregiver in childhood or a "soiled, unkempt appearance" at age three) is statistically associated with a number of other environmental factors. And complex outcomes such as antisocial behavior are highly unlikely to be influenced by only a single gene—it usually takes many, working together. I can think of several alternative explanations for the results of this study.

For example, the low-MAOA gene might lead to antisocial behavior only if it is coupled with another (unknown) gene that produces a high activity level. Highly active children try their parents' patience and are more likely to be treated harshly;[61] thus the maltreatment could be a consequence of having the high-activity gene, and the antisocial behavior could be a consequence of having both genes. This would be a gene-gene interaction, not a gene-environment interaction. Another possibility is a gene-environment interaction that is due to environmental factors other than maltreatment by parents. The unfavorable experiences included in the researchers' definition of maltreatment occur more commonly in homes of lower socioeconomic status, and such homes are more likely to be located in neighborhoods where crime and violence—antisocial behavior—are prevalent. As I mentioned earlier, neighborhood effects on antisocial behavior are well known.

Nobody questions that child abuse is cruel and immoral. But evidence that is in accord with deeply held beliefs should be looked at just as critically as evidence that goes against these beliefs.

The term "red herring" comes from the sport of foxhunting. A red herring is a smelly smoked fish (the reddish color appears when it is smoked) that was sometimes dragged across a trail in order to distract the hounds from following the track of the fox. When this was done in training, rather than as a way of sabotaging a hunt, its purpose was to teach the hounds not to be sidetracked from their real goal, which was to find the fox.

My goal is to find out why people differ from one another in personality. This chapter was about gene-environment interactions, which turned out to be a red herring. That makes three now. Mind you, I'm not claiming that gene-environment interactions don't occur: just that they are not the perpetrator we are hunting for. They're fish, not fox.

Gene-environment interactions exist, but the ones that have been convincingly demonstrated are all of the same sort: certain genotypes are more sensitive to certain environmental conditions. Such interactions do not produce null effects; they cannot explain why the behavioral geneticists found that differences in home environments had little or no effect on adult personality.

Nor—to return to a point I made at the beginning of the chapter—can they account for the differences between identical twins reared in the same home. Imagine, for a moment, that Kagan's high-reactive infants came in sets of two: identical twins, two babies with the same genotype. If the test given at four months is a valid measure of their genetic predisposition to be nervous, both will be judged high-reactive. What happens next? Will their mother be indulgent with one and strict with the other? Will she tell one twin, "Get into that sandbox and play with the other kids, dammit!" and the other, "Better stay here by my side"? It's possible, of course—I will examine this possibility in the next chapter—but in all likelihood, as the critics of behavioral genetics keep pointing out, she will treat them much alike. So can we attribute their personality differences in adulthood to the fact that "a given style of parenting has different effects for children with different predispositions"? No, because identical twins have the same predispositions. A gene-environment interaction can produce differences between two individuals only if they have different genotypes. Since identical twins have the same genotype, a gene-environment interaction cannot produce a difference between them. It would take a difference in environments—a main effect, not an interaction.

The behavioral geneticists found no main effects (or only negligible ones) of the home environment on personality characteristics related to fearfulness, and yet there are substantial differences in such characteristics between identical twins reared in the same home. Often, one twin is more outgoing—less inhibited—than the other. Why?

Three red herrings eliminated, two more to go.

4

Birth Order and Other Environmental Differences Within the Family

IT IS NO SECRET that the academic world—the so-called "ivory tower"—is as riven with rivalries and hatreds as any other venue in which humans compete with one another for status, money, and access to desirable mates. Such animosities are the source of a recognized genre of fiction: the academic murder mystery. The murderers in these novels usually turn out to have been motivated by things like ill will associated with tenure decisions or pique that their work was ignored and their rival got the credit.

Outside of fiction, academic animosities more often involve groups—opposing schools of thought—than individuals. But as you will see later in this chapter, animosities sometimes do occur between individuals, and though I haven't heard of them leading to murder, they can be very bitter. The case in question involves a dispute over birth order—a dispute between one man who is certain that birth order has deep and lasting effects on personality, a second man who is certain that the first is wrong, and a third who risked his career to ensure that both voices would be heard.

The fact that this topic arouses strong feelings in some people is not, however, why I'm going to devote most of this chapter to it. Birth order is important to my purposes for two reasons. First, looking for birth order effects on personality—for systematic differences between firstborns and laterborns (or firstborns, lastborns, and middle children)—turns out to be an excellent way to test hypotheses about personality, including some that would be extremely difficult to test in any other way. Second, birth order is—or at least appears to be—a simple thing to study; hence we have loads of data on it.

Although the developmentalists and the behavioral geneticists could serve as a textbook example, so to speak, of the opposing-schools-of-thought type of academic animosity, they are not as far apart as you (or they) might think. Behavioral geneticists have their cherished beliefs just like anybody else. They too have been reluctant to give up their faith in the efficacy of parental influence. Some behavioral geneticists actually *are* parents. That's right, some of them have mated and produced offspring of their own, and I daresay they are as proud of their offspring as the developmentalists are of theirs.

So when the behavioral geneticists discovered that differences among home environments can't account for differences in adult personality (which is another way of saying that growing up in the same home doesn't make siblings more alike), they didn't straightway announce to the world that "parents don't matter." Only one behavioral geneticist, David Rowe, even hinted at that possibility.[1] The others searched for ways to reconcile the results of their research with the beliefs they held before the data started coming in.

The behavioral geneticists realized almost from the start that gene-environment interactions weren't going to save the day for the home environment. They pinned their hopes on something else: environmental differences within the family. Two children can grow up in the same home and yet have very different experiences there. One might get more of their parents' affection; the other, more of their parents' anger. One might be labeled "the thinker"; the other might be the athlete of the family. If they differ in age, one has to put up with a pesky younger sibling, the other with a bossy older one.

Environmental differences within the family exist. They are real and they matter. But can they account for the differences in personality between twins or siblings reared in the same family? Can they explain the variations in behavior that cannot be attributed to variations in genes? Does it all boil down to "Mom always loved you best"?

Robert Plomin is the world's most eminent behavioral geneticist. He is a tall, scholarly-looking man with a high forehead and a graying beard (I've seen him interviewed on television science programs). Born and raised in the United States, Plomin moved to England several years ago and currently heads a division of a research institute in London.

Plomin's 1987 paper with his student Denise Daniels, titled "Why Are Children in the Same Family So Different from One Another?", laid out the problem boldly and clearly. Biological siblings are not altogether different; they tend to be somewhat alike in personality and intelligence. But their similarity is due to their shared genes. Adoptive siblings aren't alike at all in adulthood. The evidence, said Plomin and Daniels, doesn't show that environmental influences are unimportant: it shows that they don't work the way everyone expected them to. Instead of making siblings more alike, "these environmental influences make two children in the same family as different from one another as are pairs of children selected randomly from the population."[2] These mysterious environmental influences are responsible for about half of the variation in personality among the subjects in behavioral genetic studies—the half I call the unexplained variance.

It was Plomin's challenge to academic psychology: If you guys are so smart, let's see you explain the unexplained variance. He offered some tips: Study at least two children per family and focus on *nonshared* aspects of their environment—ways in which their environments differ. Don't bother with the aspects of the environment they have in common; such things have no noticeable effects on personality.

Researchers geared themselves up for the challenge. Proposals were written and funded.

In 2001, Robert Plomin, in an article coauthored by two other colleagues (Daniels had left the academic world), issued an update: "Why Are Children in the Same Family So Different? Nonshared Environment a Decade Later."[3] Actually, it was fourteen years later. How time does fly!

Alas, not much progress had been made in those fourteen years—much less than Plomin had hoped for. This was partly because the developmentalists had largely ignored his advice to study more than one child per family and were still using the same outmoded research methods. But not all of that research funding had been wasted. Two major studies provided relevant, though discouraging, results.

The first, by Eric Turkheimer and Mary Waldron of the University of Virginia, was a meta-analysis—a statistical technique for combining data from a number of smaller studies in order to get an overall result. Turkheimer and Waldron found forty-three research reports that addressed the question of the unexplained variance. They put them all together and found it was hardly worth the trouble. The nonshared environmental variables measured in the forty-three studies "do not account for a substantial portion of the nonshared variability," Turkheimer and Waldron concluded.[4]

Differential treatment by parents—the tendency of parents to treat their children differently—accounted for only 2 percent of the total variance. Differential sibling interaction also accounted for 2 percent. Family constellation variables such as birth order and age differences between children accounted for only 1 percent. The most successful studies were those that looked at outside-the-home variables such as differential interaction with peers or teachers, but even those accounted for only 5 percent. And these meager results came, in many cases, from studies of dubious quality. In some, there were no controls for genetic differences between siblings. In others, multiple measures were collected but the researchers reported only the ones that reached statistical significance.

The second major study was carried out by a team of researchers who made none of these methodological errors, which is not surprising, given that one of them was Robert Plomin. The study was called NEAD, short for Nonshared Environment in Adolescent Development. I mentioned the NEAD study in chapter 2; it's the one in which five different kinds of sibling pairs—reared-together identical twins, fraternal twins, ordinary siblings, half-siblings, and step-siblings—were all assessed with the same exhaustive battery of tests.

The study was exhaustive—or do I mean exhausting?—in every respect. The researchers managed to find 720 sibling pairs living in 720 stable two-parent families (no easy task in itself). Each pair of siblings was examined twice, three years apart; the age range was ten to eighteen years. Many measures of the home environment were collected, including the mother's and father's behavior toward each sibling and their agreement or disagreement over how to handle them, the relationship between each parent and each child, and the relationship between the siblings. Multiple points of view were obtained and combined; for example, judgments of parental warmth and rejection toward each sibling were made by both parents and both siblings and also by trained observers. There were also many measures of the siblings themselves, including assessments of their antisocial behavior, depressive symptoms, industriousness, autonomy, school performance, sociability, social success, social responsibility, and self-esteem. Because almost all the measures were based on the combined judgments of two or more people, they were exceptionally accurate and reliable.

As expected, the results showed sizable differences between siblings that could not be attributed either to genes or to aspects of the home environment they shared. The results also showed that the parents did indeed behave differently toward different offspring—again, no surprise. What came as a surprise, and a big disappointment to the researchers, was the complete failure to find any explanation for the sibling differences. Differential parental behavior could be linked to genetic differences between the siblings but not to the nongenetic differences between them. In other words, the results showed that parents were *reacting* to the genetic differences between their children, rather than *causing* their children to be different.

As I mentioned in the previous chapter, a highly active child is likely to be disciplined more harshly than a quiet one. A child born with a predisposition to be disagreeable isn't treated the same way as one who was born amiable. Genetic predispositions affect the child's behavior, and the parent's behavior toward the child is in part a reaction to the child's behavior. I call such reactions "child-to-parent effects."[5]

Child-to-parent effects explain or contribute to many of the correlations reported by developmentalists: for example, the finding that when parents keep a close eye on their teenagers' activities, the teenagers are less likely to get into trouble. Monitoring, as it's called, is not simply a matter of the parents deciding to make the effort; it's more a question of how much the teenager chooses to tell the parents. Teenagers intent on getting into trouble are unlikely to keep their parents informed about what they're doing.[6] So the developmentalists are right that there's a correlation, but wrong in assuming that the parents' behavior is the cause and the teenagers' behavior the effect. The causal arrow points in the other direction.

The NEAD data showed that parents do treat identical twins more similarly than fraternal twins, and biological siblings more similarly than step-siblings, but that the differential treatment was due to child-to-parent effects. None of the environmental factors the NEAD researchers looked at could account for more than a negligible fraction of the unexplained variance in the outcomes they measured (antisocial behavior, depressive symptoms, industriousness, self-esteem, and so on). The results of the study were summarized by one of the researchers, David Reiss:

> We can say with confidence that, on the basis of the data we collected, the following family characteristics do not reflect nongenetic, non-shared influences on the adolescent: differential marital conflict about the adolescent versus the sib, differential parenting toward siblings, and asymmetrical relationships the sibs construct with each other. . . . Given that our very large twelve-year study was designed to identify nongenetic, nonshared factors, this dearth of findings is not only disappointing but galvanizing.[7]

Reiss put it more bluntly in an interview with a journalist. "I was shocked," he confessed.[8] David Reiss is a psychiatrist and a psychodynamic family therapist, poor chap.

The NEAD researchers didn't expect within-the-family differences in environment to account for *all* of the unexplained variance. Some of that variance is no doubt due to randomness. Any errors of measurement—personality measures have a fair amount of play in them—would contribute to the unexplained variance. So would developmental noise, the little random zigs and zags that make physical development somewhat unpredictable; even identical twins don't have precisely identical brains. But the researchers didn't expect to come up empty-handed. In his 2001 update, Plomin ruefully admitted that it had been shortsighted of them to look for environmental differences only within the home and to ignore outside-the-home experiences:

> Perhaps some sources of nonshared environment can still be found in NEAD. . . . In retrospect, however, as Harris (1998) has trenchantly pointed out, it seems odd to have looked for differential experiences of siblings solely in the family because siblings live in the same family.[9]

But NEAD is only a single study and not necessarily an ideal one. The subjects might have been too old, or the environmental measures too coarse, for the kinds of effects the researchers were looking for. Differential treatment by parents might have its effects in the early years. Or the differential treatment might be subtle. Parents might favor one child over another and yet not show it in ways that the NEAD researchers were able to detect.

Parents might behave differently, in subtle ways, even to identical twins. There are personality differences between identical twins even in infancy, apparently due to developmental noise. In newspaper accounts of seventeen-month-old conjoined twins Carl and Clarence Aguirre, born attached at the tops of their heads, Clarence is described as lively and cheerful, Carl as quieter and more serious.[10] If that's how their parents see them, aren't they likely to treat the two babies somewhat differently? In fact, even in the case of twins whose personalities match very closely, aren't there bound to be little random differences in the experiences they have at home? One gets the upper bunk bed, one gets the lower. One falls into the salmon mousse and ruins their mother's dinner party and she never entirely forgives him.

There is a way to answer all these questions: the well-designed birth order study. Like twinning and adoption, birth order is a "natural experiment," but unlike twinning and adoption it is a common one. The reason it is such a valuable research tool is that the experiences a child has within the home *differ systematically* depending on his or her ordinal position in the family. Most sources of differences in experiences within the home are either genetic—Mom always loved you best because you were cuter or more amiable than your sibling—or random—developmental noise, bunk beds, salmon mousse. Differences in experiences due to birth order are not genetic (as far as we know, firstborns and laterborns are genetically equivalent on average), and they're also not the result of developmental noise (whether a neuron zigs or zags doesn't depend on whether it's in a firstborn or a laterborn). So looking for personality differences between firstborns and laterborns reared in the same family gives us a way to examine the effects of purely environmental differences, while controlling for the effects of all biological differences, those due to genes and those due to developmental noise.[11]

And studying birth order has another advantage over other research methods: it provides a way to separate the effects of within-the-family environmental differences from those of outside-the-family differences. In contemporary societies—at least those not ruled by monarchies—being a firstborn or a laterborn matters only at home. When children go to school, their classmates don't care (and often don't know) that Luke is the baby of the family and has four older siblings, or that Michelle has two younger ones whom she helps to take care of. At home, Luke is the smallest among his siblings, but at school he may be one of the largest in his class. This imperfect correlation between the home environment and the outside-the-home environment will prove useful to us.

The nonsystematic, nonbiological differences in children's experiences at home—differences of the bunk bed or salmon mousse sort—are impossible to study, because each case is unique and there is no way of putting together enough data for statistical analyses. But the environmental differences due to birth order are predictable, sizable, and go on for a long time. We can study them.

The differences begin at birth. The firstborn comes into the world and finds herself in the hands of inexperienced parents who hover over her nervously but proudly. Every cry gets an immediate response; every smile is an occasion for fetching the camera. This child is the center of her parents' life.

Until her little brother is born. Every firstborn in a family with more than one child has had to experience what some psychotherapists call "dethronement."[12] John Cheever, the novelist and autobiographer who blamed his own depression and alcoholism on his mother's alleged neglect of him (she worked outside the home), blamed his older brother's depression and alcoholism on the dethronement that occurred when he, John, was born. Cheever referred to his own birth as the "turning point" in his brother's life:

> He was happy, high-spirited, and adored, and when, at the age of seven, he was told that he would have to share his universe with a brother, his forebodings would, naturally, have been bitter and deep. . . . His feeling for me was always violent and ambiguous—hatred and love—and beneath all of this must have been the feeling that I challenged him in some field where he excelled—in the affections of his parents.[13]

But perhaps Cheever was overstating the case, as was his wont. Some people believe that parents continue to favor their firstborn even after they have other children. Those who hold this belief point to the custom of primogeniture: when the crown or the farm must be handed down to a single offspring, the honor almost invariably goes to the firstborn son. Data on infanticide and homicide also support the view that parents favor firstborns—or, more accurately, favor older children over younger ones. In traditional societies in which infanticide was practiced, a common reason for deciding to abandon a new baby was that the previous child had not yet been weaned. When it came down to a choice between saving the newborn and saving the two-year-old, the two-year-old would almost invariably be chosen. In contemporary societies, homicide rates are highest for infants and decline with the child's age.[14]

Evolutionary psychologists explain that there is a good evolutionary reason for parents to favor older children over younger ones when faced with life-or-death decisions. Under ancestral conditions, when at least half of all newborns never lived long enough to have children of their own, the older ones were a better bet. They had survived the most hazardous stage of life and were closer to the time when they could pay back their parents' investment by providing them with grandchildren.[15]

But infanticide statistics may be a poor indication of how parents behave after they have committed themselves to rearing the newborn. Infants are at risk precisely because they require so much care; nevertheless, most parents are able and willing to provide that care. Robert Trivers, one of the founders of evolutionary psychology, pointed out that parents should actually be more concerned about the well-being of their youngest and neediest offspring, because that is where their investment can make the most difference. That is where a failure to pay sufficient attention can do the most harm.

> The offspring is typically more helpless and vulnerable the younger it is, so parents will have been more strongly selected [by natural selection] to respond positively to signals emitted by the offspring the younger the offspring is.[16]

Trivers' statement is consistent with child-care practices all over the world. In hunter-gatherer and tribal societies, babies and toddlers are cosseted—carried around and nursed on demand—but paradise ends when a younger sibling is born. The older child is sent out to join the local play group and thereafter receives a minimum of attention from his mother. Her attention is now focused on the new baby.[17]

Favoritism toward the younger child is less blatant in industrialized societies but still clearly visible. In a recent study of 3,762 families with two or more children from four to eleven years old, researchers found that the youngest children received the most attention and affection, the oldest ones the least. When parents have more than one child to take care of, they pay more attention and give more affection to the younger one.[18] A surprisingly large number of parents are even willing to admit that they love the younger one best. In two separate studies, British and American parents of two small children were asked whether they felt more affection for one than the other. More than half admitted that they did. The overwhelming majority of these parents—87 percent of the mothers and 85 percent of the fathers in the American study—said they favored the younger child.[19]

These are big differences in parental affection. They don't occur in every family—there must be many in which the older child happens to be more lovable than the younger one—but on the whole parents love their younger children best, at least while they're still small and living at home.

So firstborns experience not only the "turning point" of dethronement: it goes on for years. The one Mom loves best is their little brother or sister. And this is by no means the only difference between the family experiences of firstborns and laterborns. Parents give more responsibility to firstborns. Their expectations for them are higher; they tend to be stricter with them.[20] But there are compensations. Firstborns are bigger and stronger than their siblings and they know more. They can push around their little brothers and sisters. The dominance hierarchy—also known as "pecking order"—is seen in many social species, from chickens to humans, and in almost every case the dominant one is the biggest and strongest. An individual low in the hierarchy has to learn to avoid evoking the anger of the higher-ups. The home life of a laterborn isn't all milk and honey.

Plomin and Daniels' question—why are siblings so different?—reached the ears of investigators outside of behavioral genetics and developmental psychology. One ear it reached belongs to a historian of science named Frank Sulloway. Sulloway has wide-set blue eyes (or so they appear in photos) and an old-fashioned, pencil-thin mustache. Since receiving a Ph.D. from Harvard in the history of science, he has followed an unusual career path that enabled him to remain in the academic world without becoming a member of a university faculty. Instead, he has made a career for himself as a visiting scholar, giving an occasional lecture and supporting himself primarily by writing books (he has written two, both quite successful) and receiving research grants.

In his 1996 book *Born to Rebel*, Sulloway proposed that sibling differences are due to birth order and presented a well-worked-out theory of how birth order shapes personality. I'm going to examine Sulloway's theory in detail, partly because it's the best one around (most of the books you see on birth order are complete balderdash), partly because it makes use of concepts derived from evolutionary biology and evolutionary psychology.

According to Sulloway, the source of nongenetic sibling differences in personality is competition for family resources. "Disputes over these resources, especially over parental affection, create rivalries." Firstborns, being bigger and stronger, have an edge in this competition: "They arrive first within the family and employ their superior size and strength to defend their special status." Thus, he says, "Firstborns tend to be dominant, aggressive, ambitious, jealous, and conservative." Laterborns develop their own counterstrategies to the firstborn's attempt to dominate: "Although laterborns often manifest a distinct inclination to rebel, they also work hard to improve their lot through good-natured sociability and cooperation."[21] In short, firstborns compete by being nasty, laterborns by being nice. At this point a disclosure is in order: I am a firstborn. Yes, Sulloway is a laterborn.

Sulloway's explanation for why competition leads to personality differences is couched in Darwinian terms. "Siblings become different," he wrote, "for the same reason that species do over time: divergence minimizes competition for scarce resources." Although full siblings are close relatives—as similar genetically as parents are to their children—that doesn't mean they will necessarily behave benevolently toward each other. "Because siblings share, on average, only one-half of their genes, altruism among siblings—while considerable—has its limits. Siblings will tend to disagree about the allocation of shared resources." Each sibling wants the lion's share of the goodies for himself; his brother or sister can have whatever is left.[22] Every parent of two or more children will sigh and nod.

Though Sulloway's description of sibling relationships sounds convincing, there are some theoretical problems with his explanation of the personality differences between siblings. The first is that siblings don't "become different" from each other as a result of their interactions with each other or with their parents. The notion that behavioral genetic data provide evidence for sibling differentiation or sibling contrast effects is an error. Sulloway is not the only one who has been misled; the misunderstanding is a common one. Let me see if I can clear this up.

The primary source of confusion is what the behavioral geneticists have said about the unexplained variation in personality. They attributed it to the "nonshared environment," which is often defined as environmental influences that "make siblings different."[23] So it sounds as though something in the home environment was actually creating or widening personality differences between siblings, causing them to become more dissimilar than they would have been if they were reared in separate homes. But the behavioral genetic evidence doesn't show that growing up in the same home makes siblings different—only that it fails to make them more alike. Prevailing theories of development, such as the theory that children are socialized by their parents to express emotions or to bottle them up, had led researchers to expect that being reared by the same parents *would* make siblings more alike. The question "Why are siblings so different?" is the mournful cry of unfulfilled expectations. What the behavioral geneticists really wanted to know was: Why aren't siblings more alike?

It isn't growing up together that makes them different. If sibling differences were due, say, to the siblings' own efforts to differentiate themselves from one another, then siblings reared in the same home should actually be less alike than those reared in separate homes. The evidence doesn't support this prediction; in fact, pairs reared together are neither more alike nor less alike than those reared apart. Adoptive siblings are not less alike than adoptees reared in different families. Identical twins separated at birth are as similar (and as dissimilar) as those who grow up together.[24] So defining the nonshared environment as "environmental influences that make siblings different" is misleading. A more accurate definition is "environmental influences that are *uncorrelated* between siblings." The difference-making effects on a pair of siblings are the same as the difference-making effects on a pair of unrelated people who never set eyes on each other.

Another source of confusion is an often-cited article titled "Growing Up and Growing Apart."[25] According to its authors, identical and fraternal twins growing up together become less alike during childhood and adolescence. That certainly sounds like sibling differentiation—it was probably this report that led Sulloway to tell a journalist in 1996 that "the longer [siblings] live together, the more different they become"[26]—but again, the evidence has been misinterpreted. What really happens is that sharing a home produces some transient similarities in the early years, especially in IQ. These shared environment effects gradually fade as the twins get older, eventually falling to zero or near zero. But the similarities attributed to sharing a home do not fall below zero and turn into differences. Growing up together may temporarily make twins or siblings a little more alike, but it doesn't make them different.

What about contrast effects? Behavioral geneticists do use that term, but what they mean by it is the tendency for parents to see their children as more different than they really are. Contrast effects are in the eyes of the beholder, not in the children themselves. Parents who see their firstborn as "difficult" tend to see their secondborn as "easy," and vice versa. Both children may actually be more difficult than average, or both may be easier, but what the parents notice is that one is more so than the other. Sibling differences tend to be exaggerated in parents' reports.[27]

The idea of sibling differentiation is sometimes invoked to explain away the failure to find effects of the shared home environment. The reasoning goes like this: Maybe being raised by the same parents *does* make siblings more alike, but the sibling relationship itself, or some other aspect of the home environment, has the opposite effect—it makes siblings more different.[28] Maybe the two effects cancel each other out, so that the bottom line, the net result, is zero!

Good try, but there's no evidence for either of these effects. In any event, postulating effects that increase the differences between siblings doesn't help to account for the unexplained variation in personality if, in order to postulate such effects, it is also necessary to postulate countervailing effects that make siblings more similar. If the two hypothesized effects cancel each other out, then nothing has been gained, because a cancelled-out effect can't explain why siblings differ.

I should mention that this discussion of sibling differentiation applies specifically to personality and to behaviors (such as aggressiveness) that reflect personality. The evidence I've looked at doesn't rule out the possibility that differentiation or divergence might operate in other areas, such as choice of interests or careers. Twins or siblings who have similar personalities and aptitudes might choose to specialize in different things, like the identical pair described by twin researcher Nancy Segal: "Both twins are talented in performing arts, but Julie specialized in dance and Lisa specialized in drama."[29]

The second problem for Sulloway's birth order theory is the fact that the behavioral genetic findings hold true for all kinds of sibling pairs. Whether the subjects are identical twins, fraternal twins, ordinary siblings, half-siblings, or adoptive or step-siblings, the conclusions are the same: all, or nearly all, of the nongenetic variance is of the nonshared kind. The unexplained variance is approximately the same—about 50 percent of the total variance—for all these sibling pairs.

I described this counterintuitive finding in chapter 2 and said it was an important clue. Now you can see why. The consistency of the behavioral genetic results implies that the *same processes* are responsible for the differences between all sibling pairs. We need an explanation for sibling differences that will work as well for twins as for children born singly.

Can a theory that attributes the personality differences between ordinary siblings to birth order explain the differences between twins? Don't be too quick to say no. After all, twins have to emerge from the uterus in single file, and virtually all parents of twins know which one came out first. Moreover, as Sulloway pointed out, "Birth order can be seen as a proxy for differences in age, size, power, and status within the family. Common sense tells us that causation probably lies in these other variables, not in birth order per se."[30] Although identical twins do not differ in age, they may differ in power or status within the family.

But twins are a problem for Sulloway for another reason. According to his theory, the engine that drives sibling divergence is competition. Siblings compete because their interests do not coincide. Their interests do not coincide because they share only 50 percent of their genes. But identical twins share 100 percent of their genes.

Identical twinning is uncommon; no one believes that the human mind comes equipped with a set of instructions that tell you what to do if the person seated next to you at the dinner table happens to be your clone. But kin selection theory—one of the cornerstones of evolutionary psychology—leads us to expect that animals will respond to cues of biological relatedness by being nicer to relatives than to nonrelatives and nicer to close relatives than to distant ones.[31] Evidence of the ability to make such distinctions has been found in many species, including our own. Though scientists haven't yet figured out how they do it, even immature humans appear to have some way of estimating the proportion of genes they share with the people in their lives. In polygamous communities, children feel closer to their full siblings than to their half-siblings. Identical twins cooperate with each other more and compete less than do fraternal twins. When one twin dies, the other feels more grief if they were identical.[32]

If competition were the source of sibling differences, kin selection theory would generate the following prediction: nongenetic differences should be large between adoptive siblings, moderate for fraternal twins and ordinary siblings, and small for identical twins. This prediction is at odds with the evidence. Though identical twins compete with each other less than other sibling pairs, the nongenetic differences between them are as wide.

The third problem for Sulloway's theory has to do with the proposition that siblings diverge "for the same reason that species do over time: divergence minimizes competition for scarce resources."[33] Is there any evidence that divergence is indeed a successful strategy for children—that behaving differently from their siblings will gain them more parental attention or family resources? None that I know of. In the absence of evidence, is there any theoretical reason to expect that diverging from one's siblings will increase what evolutionary psychologists call "parental investment"?

If anything, theoretical considerations would seem to generate the opposite prediction: that older children would profit from behaving more like their younger siblings. As I mentioned earlier, the evolutionary psychologist Robert Trivers said that parents should devote more attention to younger offspring than to older ones, because "the offspring is typically more helpless and vulnerable the younger it is." He continued,

> This suggests that at any stage of development at which the offspring is in conflict with its parent [over the distribution of resources], it may be selected to revert to the gestures and actions of an earlier

stage of development in order to induce the investment that would have then been forthcoming. In short, it may be selected to *regress* when under stress.[34]

Regression, especially around the time of weaning or when a younger sibling is born, has been observed in nonhuman animals as well as in humans. But acting younger and needier than they really are doesn't seem to be a strategy firstborns stick to. On the contrary, the terms often used by family members to describe firstborns—responsible, conscientious, serious, bossy—are usually associated with greater maturity.[35] Sulloway interpreted this kind of behavior as a way of "currying parental favor." Firstborns, he said, "are likely to seek parental favor by acting as surrogate parents toward their younger siblings."[36]

I have a different explanation for these observations. Firstborns behave in a more mature manner in the presence of their younger siblings, not to curry favor with their parents, but because this behavior is *evoked* by the presence of younger children. Whether or not they are close relatives, older children react in predictable ways to younger ones. In an overview of children's behavior in societies around the world, the cross-cultural psychologist Carolyn Edwards noted that younger children evoke two responses from older ones: nurturance and dominance. Which response gets the upper hand depends in large part on the age of the younger child: with children under the age of two and a half, it's mainly nurturance; above that age, dominance comes into play. As Edwards defines it, *dominance* includes not only efforts to control, but also efforts "to protect, socialize, or involve the child in socially useful activity."[37] In other words, to act as a surrogate parent.

The same predisposition to behave in a nurturant and/or dominant manner toward younger members of their species has been described in chimpanzees. According to Jane Goodall, "Chimpanzees (like other group-living mammals) tend to behave in varied and predictable ways to members of the several age-sex classes." Age and sex distinctions are made on the basis of physical cues; thus, "small body size, pale skin, and white tail tuft indicate infancy." Juvenile chimpanzees of both sexes are attracted to infants and are usually gentle with them. Play gets rougher as the younger animal grows and the older one begins to assert its dominance.[38]

In our own species, studies have shown that children as young as four "talk down" to still younger children, just the way parents do, in an effort to make their speech understandable to the younger child. The four-year-olds use shorter, simpler sentences when conversing with two-year-olds than with children of their own age. They do this whether or not the younger child is their sibling and whether or not their parents are present. They do it even if they don't *have* a younger sibling.[39]

Firstborns spend much of their time at home in the company of their younger siblings and they talk to them in short, simple sentences.[40] No one, however, expects firstborns to simplify their speech when conversing with adults or with children of their own age: it is taken for granted that children adjust their style of speech to their interlocutor, and this is in fact what they do. Yet many people also take it for granted that other patterns of behavior that children acquire through interactions with their siblings will be generalized to other social partners and other social contexts. It is assumed that these behaviors, used habitually at home, become so ingrained or "internalized" that they become a permanent part of the personality.

This assumption, which is seldom stated explicitly, is the fourth problem for Sulloway's birth order theory, and it applies to other birth order theories as well. Sulloway doesn't think that firstborns are more bossy and aggressive only at home: he thinks they're like that everywhere they go, all through their lives. As a result of their interactions with their younger siblings, they've grown accustomed to getting their way by being bossy and aggressive, so they apply this strategy in other situations and continue to do so in adulthood. Of course, they don't make a conscious decision to behave like this: it happens automatically.

Once stated plainly, this assumption becomes testable. If birth order has effects on personality, these effects must occur in childhood, because that's when people have the experiences that birth order theorists believe are important. So if behaviors acquired at home are generalized to other social contexts, we should be able to see that happening in childhood. If anything, the effects should show up more clearly in childhood than in adulthood, because it's possible that firstborns learn to keep their aggressiveness under wraps as they get older.

This is where a well-designed birth order study comes in handy. Most evidence on children's behavior comes from studies that looked at only one child per family (due to a failure to heed Robert Plomin's advice) and hence are useless; the method provides no way of controlling for genetic influences on behavior. Genetic influences on behavior can look exactly like generalization and may be responsible for many of the modest correlations that developmentalists find between a child's behavior in two different contexts.

For example, a group of developmentalists found a weak (but statistically significant) correlation of .19 between children's behavior with their parents and with their peers: the children who behaved in a bossy or uncooperative manner with parents were slightly more likely to behave in a bossy or uncooperative manner with peers.[41] The researchers assumed that the obnoxious behavior in both contexts resulted from the parents' inept child-rearing practices: the child had learned that he could get his way at home by being obnoxious, so he was obnoxious on the playground too. But the researchers didn't consider the possibility that some children may inherit a predisposition to behave in an aggressive or disagreeable fashion wherever they go. The heritability of these traits—around .45—is more than enough to account for the weak correlation between obnoxious behavior with parents and obnoxious behavior with peers.

One cannot conclude that behavior has generalized from the home to outside the home unless one has a way of controlling for genetic influences on behavior. Birth order studies can do that because, as I said, there are no systematic genetic differences between firstborns and laterborns. The genes that might predispose a child to be aggressive or disagreeable are dealt out evenhandedly to firstborns and laterborns. So if firstborns behave more aggressively than laterborns both at home and outside the home, that would suggest that generalization does occur—that learning to behave in a certain way in one context causes children to behave that way in other contexts as well. It wouldn't be *proof* of generalization, however—the similarity in behavior could be the result of similar learning processes occurring separately in the two contexts. On the other hand, if firstborns behave one way at home and a different way outside the home, that would be good evidence *against* generalization.

Two well-designed studies provide useful data; in both, the researchers looked at two children from the same family and assessed their behavior both at home and outside the home. The first was carried out by the developmentalist Rona Abramovitch and her colleagues. The researchers observed children playing with their siblings and noted that firstborns do tend to dominate their younger siblings, often by behaving aggressively. Then the researchers observed the same children playing with their peers. They saw "no evidence of individual differences in sibling interactions carrying over into peer interactions." Firstborns who dominated their siblings were not more likely to try to dominate their peers; laterborns were not more likely to allow their peers to dominate them. As the researchers put it, "Even the second-born child, who has experienced years in a subordinate role with an older sibling, can step into a dominant role when the situation permits."[42]

The second study, by Kirby Deater-Deckard and Robert Plomin, used behavioral genetic methods to look at aggressive behavior in pairs of adoptive and biological siblings. The aggressiveness of both children was judged five times by their parents and by five different teachers, over a six-year period. What the parents were judging, as the researchers explained, was mainly their children's behavior at home; what the teachers were judging was behavior at school. The results showed again that older siblings are more aggressive at home but not at school: parents judged the older one to be more aggressive, teachers judged the two siblings to be about the same.[43]

Based on the teachers' reports, the heritability of aggressiveness in Deater-Deckard and Plomin's study was .49; the estimate for shared environment was not significantly different from zero. As usual, about half the variance could be attributed to the effects of genes and none to the home environment, which means that half the variance remained unaccounted for.

Even in studies that provide no control for genetic influences, when researchers look at children's behavior in more than one social context, the reported correlations are very low—often statistically insignificant, occasionally negative. In particular, children who fight like cats and dogs with their siblings are not at greater risk of getting along poorly with their peers. Nor are children who have no siblings in jeopardy of social failure: only children are not handicapped (nor helped) in their peer relationships by their lack of experience in interacting with siblings.[44]

The studies I've reviewed show that birth order definitely does affect behavior at home; older siblings dominate younger ones and behave more aggressively. Dominance hierarchies have predictable effects on their members: dominant individuals are more aggressive because they can afford to be. Those lower on the totem pole behave in a more conciliatory manner because they don't want to risk evoking the anger of someone who could beat them up. The personality characteristics Sulloway attributes to firstborns and laterborns—nasty and nice—are the predictable behavioral consequences of being the dominator or the dominated. However, the evidence shows that these behaviors are not generalized to social contexts outside the home.

And why should they be? The child who is the oldest and biggest at home might turn out to be the smallest on the playground. It wouldn't make sense for this child to try to dominate his peers the way he dominates his younger siblings. A strategy that works at home might be useless or even hazardous elsewhere. Children are capable of generalizing—of learning

"Don't force me to invoke my rights of primogeniture."

something in one context and applying it in another—but they do not do it blindly. The question of when and how generalization occurs is an important one and relevant to my quest; I will come back to it in the next chapter.

Earlier I said that two major attempts have been made in the last few years to find the source of the unexplained variance: Turkheimer and Waldron's meta-analysis and the NEAD study. Turkheimer and Waldron reported that, of the environmental factors that had been studied, family constellation variables, including birth order, accounted for the smallest amount of variance: only 1 percent. The NEAD researchers didn't look specifically at birth order (many of their sibling pairs were twins), but they did look at "asymmetrical relationships" between siblings. These would include any in which one dominated the other and any in which sibling A was nasty to sibling B but B was nice to A. In summarizing the results of the NEAD study, David Reiss reported that their data had ruled out asymmetrical relationships between siblings as a source of the personality differences between them.[45]

These are the results for children and adolescents. Next I will look at data from adults. Actually, the subjects in most of these studies were college students. Researchers classify them as adults even if their parents don't.

Designing a birth order study is not as simple as it appears at first glance. Small families produce as many firstborns as large families, but fewer laterborns; and small families tend to be higher in socioeconomic status. This means that a firstborn is more likely than a laterborn to come from an upper-class family. Most of the birth order studies you read about in the newspapers are worthless because the researchers failed to control for family size and/or socioeconomic class. Without these controls, statistical differences between firstborns and laterborns that are really due to social class are likely to be mistaken for birth order effects. It takes a very large N to do a properly controlled birth order study.

Studies that do control for family size and/or socioeconomic class, and that use standard methods of assessing personality in adults, seldom find significant differences between firstborns and laterborns. Frank Sulloway agrees with me on this; here's what he said in an article published three years after *Born to Rebel*:

> When assessed by self-report questionnaires, birth-order effects are typically modest and nonsignificant. Yet systematic differences by birth order are generally found when parents rate their own offspring or when siblings compare themselves with one another.[46]

Most of the personality data we have on adults come from standard self-report personality questionnaires. When researchers give these tests to large numbers of subjects, they generally find that firstborns are not significantly more (or less) open, conscientious, extraverted, agreeable, or neurotic than laterborns. Since a lot of researchers have done this, and each one typically looks for birth order effects in several different dimensions of personality, significant differences do turn up from time to time—they're bound to. But there's no consistency in these occasional successes (as such they are generally regarded): in one study there's a significant result for conscientiousness; in another, it's something else. Moreover, in many cases the significant result involved only some of the subjects, not all of them, or showed up only in one test out of two or three the researchers administered. For example, a significant result might be found for female subjects but not for males, or for subjects from large families but not from small families. And again there's no consistency: in one study a birth order effect might be found only for females; in the next it might be only for males.

Sulloway has attempted to explain away the null or inconsistent outcomes found with self-report personality questionnaires by calling into question the validity of the tests themselves. He has claimed that they're unreliable and potentially misleading.[47] But casting doubt on self-report personality tests is a counterproductive strategy for Sulloway, because he can't get along without them. These tests are responsible for producing the very finding he is trying to explain: the mystery of the unexplained variance in personality. "The crux of my argument," he said in the introduction of *Born to Rebel*, "stems from a remarkable discovery. Siblings raised together are almost as different in their personalities as people from different families. This finding [was] firmly established by studies in personality psychology."[48] Perfectly true, and almost all of these studies used self-report personality questionnaires.

Most of the personality data that led Plomin and Daniels to ask why siblings are so different came from standard self-report personality tests. If there are no differences between firstborns and laterborns on standard self-report personality tests, then birth order cannot account for any of the variance in studies that used those tests. Which means that birth order cannot be the answer to Plomin and Daniels' question about why siblings are so different.

Sulloway was quite correct when he pointed out that the likelihood of finding significant birth order effects depends on the method used to assess personality: consistent and statistically significant birth order effects are usually found when subjects' personalities are judged by their parents or siblings, or when they're asked to compare themselves with their siblings. The difference in outcome doesn't depend on whether or not self-report tests are used (the subjects who compared themselves with their siblings did so on self-report tests) but on whether the behavior is assessed within the family context or outside of it. Judgments by family members are necessarily based on behavior within the family context and do show birth order effects. But no birth order effects were found when children's behavior with their peers was observed by researchers or judged by their teachers. Nor are birth order effects found when researchers look at school grades or high school graduation rates (we have voluminous data on such things). If firstborns are more conscientious, as Sulloway claims, it doesn't help them do better in their schoolwork. If laterborns are more rebellious, it doesn't make them more likely to drop out of high school or less likely to go to college.[49]

Then why, when people are asked to name the academic achiever in their family, do they more often than not name the firstborn? And why, when they're asked to name the rebel in their family, do they more often than not name a laterborn?[50]

The first question is easy to answer. Firstborns evidently give their siblings the impression that they are more conscientious about their schoolwork. The probable reason is that firstborns are older than their siblings. Older children tend to be more responsible than younger ones and generally spend more time doing schoolwork. In judgments made by family members, age differences are inevitably confounded with birth order.

The answer to the question about rebelliousness is a little more complicated. In fact, research does confirm that laterborns are more rebellious in one respect: they are more likely than firstborns to engage in "problem" teenage behaviors such as early onset of sexual activity, drinking, or drug use. In general, birth order effects are not found when personality or behavior is assessed outside the family context, so this is an exception to the rule. It's one of those exceptions that turns out to be informative, because there's also an exception to the behavioral geneticists' rule that shared environment accounts for little or no variance in behavior: there are shared environment effects for adolescent delinquency. Notice that both these exceptions involve teenage problem behaviors, and that none of the behaviors first occurs at home. Shoplifting, vandalism, drug use, underage sex and drinking—these are things that teenagers do outside the home, in the company of their friends.

The explanation for both exceptions is the same: teenagers like to hang around with their older siblings and their older siblings' friends. The same heightened risk for problem teenage behaviors has been observed in teenage girls who are physically mature for their age and whose friends consequently tend to be older than themselves.[51]

The fact that laterborns are often exposed to the temptations of teenage life at an earlier age than firstborns, and sometimes succumb to these temptations, is probably the reason why the members of their family tend to characterize them as rebellious. But evidently their rebelliousness doesn't extend to other types of behavior, such as doing their schoolwork, and it doesn't show up on personality tests given to adults.

Many people, including some evolutionary psychologists, were impressed by the tables and graphs in Sulloway's *Born to Rebel* and by the magnitude of the birth order effects he reported. No one before (or since) found such striking effects, such gaping differences between firstborns and laterborns in personality and behavior. Firstborns, reported Sulloway, were far less likely to accept new scientific theories. Laterborns were far more likely to be politically liberal and rebellious.

But doubting voices soon began to be heard. Many of the reviewers had the same criticism: that despite all the graphic presentation of data, the book failed to provide the information a reader needs in order to evaluate the evidence. "No tables of descriptive statistics," complained the psychologist Toni Falbo in the book review journal of the American Psychological Association. "No simple presentation of the frequency of people falling into key categories." And, she said, there were other omissions:

> One of the most troubling concerns a meta-analysis [Sulloway] conducted of a subset of the birth order literature presented in a book by Ernst and Angst (1983). Sulloway does not list which studies he selected for his analysis, an essential element in any presentation of meta-analytic results.[52]

Ernst and Angst might sound like a good name for a rock group, but in fact they are a team of hardworking Swiss researchers who published a comprehensive review of birth order research in 1983 and concluded that birth order has no important effects on personality. Sulloway disagreed. He reanalyzed the data in Ernst and Angst's review and claimed to have found results that strongly supported his theory: of 196 findings from properly controlled studies, 72 were in line with his predictions, versus only 14 that came out in the wrong direction. (The remaining 110 did not differ significantly from zero.)[53]

I was not the only one who questioned this claim. I was not the only one who decided to check it by going through Ernst and Angst's book to see if I could find 72 positive findings from controlled studies (I couldn't).[54] A sociologist who reviewed the book for the journal *Science* also tried and failed to figure out where Sulloway got so many positive findings. Another who admitted bafflement was Jules Angst himself. An American science writer who asked him about Sulloway's meta-analysis reported, "Angst informed me by e-mail that he could 'neither reconstruct nor understand' how the data gathered by him and Ernst for their 1983 book had been reanalyzed by Sulloway."[55]

But of all those who tried to get to the bottom of the data presented in *Born to Rebel*, no one worked longer or harder at it than Frederic Townsend. Like me, Townsend is an independent scholar, lacking in academic credentials—he has a law degree but that doesn't count. Though he gave up being an attorney some years ago (he is currently a bond options trader at the Chicago Board of Trade), he hasn't lost the motivation that led him to go to law school in the first place: an urge to see truth and justice prevail. I presume that is his motivation in this case. It can't be a desire for fame or fortune—he will never receive either for the hundreds of hours he has put into his investigation of Sulloway's methods. Townsend is a married man with young children, but for seven years he dedicated much of his free time to this investigation.

The problem Fred Townsend and Toni Falbo and the *Science* reviewer and I had with Sulloway's tables and graphs was that *Born to Rebel*—though tail-heavy with 245 pages of appendixes, endnotes, and bibliography—does not contain the kind of information Sulloway would have had to provide in order to get his work through the peer-review process of a journal. It's like the missing N in Suomi's story of the cross-fostered monkeys. If Sulloway's reanalysis of Ernst and Angst's data had been held to the standards of a peer-reviewed journal, he would have had to provide a list of the studies that produced the 196 findings.[56]

"The principal reason for keeping science secret," observed the physicist Robert Park in his book *Voodoo Science*, "is that the science is questionable." Townsend sent Sulloway a letter requesting a list of the 196 findings. Sulloway turned him down. He was not obligated, he told Townsend, to make the results of his research available to "unqualified individuals." Sulloway also refused to send Townsend his list of 24 Protestant martyrs who died during the Reformation—of whom, he claimed in *Born to Rebel*, 23 were laterborns. Townsend was persistent and Sulloway was evidently annoyed. "You have identified yourself," he told Townsend in a letter, "as a kind of small-minded and ill-informed crank."[57]

If Sulloway thought he could discourage Townsend by calling him names, he had misjudged his opponent. Townsend kept plugging away. Since Sulloway wouldn't send him the list of 196 findings included in his meta-analysis, Townsend attempted to reconstruct the list himself. He used two different methods, based on what Sulloway had said at various times. Neither produced results close to those reported in *Born to Rebel*. And Townsend doesn't ask us to take his word for it: he has published lists of the studies he included in his analyses, and their positive, negative, or null findings.[58]

Townsend discovered many other anomalies and inconsistencies in Sulloway's work. For example, *Born to Rebel* contains a table (table 2) showing support for various scientific revolutions as a function of birth order. Later in the book, the data in this table are replotted as a graph (figure 14.1). The graph shows a linear relationship between firstborn/laterborn support and "trend for social attitudes." Townsend found that the points in the graph don't always agree with the numbers in the table. Out of seven data points that are different, six had moved in the "correct" direction—closer to the diagonal line drawn through the graph.[59]

Each of Townsend's examples sounds trivial in itself—"nitpicking," as Sulloway later complained to a journalist. But taken together they are devastating. A few errors or discrepancies could be put down to carelessness, but Townsend found too many of them and a very high percentage were in the direction favorable to Sulloway's theory.[60]

In 1998, Townsend turned the results of his investigations into a sharply worded critique of *Born to Rebel* and submitted it to the journal *Politics and the Life Sciences*. The editor, Gary Johnson, chair of the political science department at Lake Superior State University, sent it out for peer review. Three of the four reviewers recommended publication and Townsend's article was provisionally accepted, contingent on his making appropriate revisions in response to the reviewers' comments.[61]

Johnson didn't plan on publishing Townsend's critique by itself. He intended to make it part of a "roundtable" issue of the journal. Sulloway was invited to contribute a reply, and both he and Townsend were asked to nominate other people who would provide commentaries on Townsend's paper. I was one of Townsend's nominees and I accepted the invitation from Johnson to contribute a short commentary.[62]

Townsend revised his manuscript, it was accepted, and copies were sent to Sulloway and to the commentators in December 1998. But Townsend's critique, Sulloway's reply, and the ten commentaries weren't published until February 2004, in an issue of *Politics and the Life Sciences* labeled September 2000. That issue of the journal also contains a thirty-five-page editorial by Gary Johnson, explaining the long delay in publication. What I will tell you here is based on Johnson's account.

In January 1999, Johnson reported, he received a letter from Sulloway. In it, Sulloway claimed that Townsend's manuscript was "defamatory in its present form" and demanded that it be revised. "It would be unfortunate," he told Johnson, "if your decision to publish Townsend's manuscript in its present form plunges you and your journal into serious legal difficulties." Just in case Johnson missed the point, Sulloway added this explanation: "Under the law, you cannot knowingly permit the publication of a pattern of defamatory claims without becoming a party to defamation yourself."[63]

Sulloway's demands went beyond a request that Townsend's article be expunged of defamatory material. He also said it would be "legally mandatory," if Johnson published a revised version of Townsend's article, to preface it with an editorial disclaimer. This disclaimer (for which Sulloway provided some sample wording) would say that the editor had decided to publish Townsend's paper in spite of its flaws, and would warn readers that Townsend's claims are not to be trusted because his evidence is "erroneous" and his paper contains "blatant errors of fact and interpretation."[64]

Again, Sulloway had underestimated his man. Johnson was not about to let Sulloway make his editorial decisions for him. On the other hand, nobody wants to be sued. Before he could publish Townsend's critique, Johnson decided, Townsend would have to revise it carefully, to make sure that it contained no defamatory remarks and that every factual statement was well documented. For his own good as well as Townsend's, Johnson explained, he wanted Townsend's critique to be as lawsuit-proof as possible.[65]

Townsend's re-revised manuscript was again sent out for peer review and again accepted. In July 2000, the final version was sent out to the commentators and to Sulloway.

"It was Sulloway, of course, who had demanded revisions in Townsend's manuscript," Johnson noted in his editorial. "However, the revisions Townsend made must not have been the revisions Sulloway had in mind." In fact, the final manuscript, though less sharply worded than the earlier version, was stronger and more convincing. Sulloway reacted as angrily to this manuscript as he had to the previous one, and again his attack was aimed, not at its author, but at the editor of the journal. "After receiving his copy of the revised Townsend manuscript," Johnson reported, "Sulloway made a variety of accusations against me." Sulloway's primary accusation was that Johnson had behaved improperly by allowing Townsend to make extensive changes to his manuscript after an earlier version had been sent out to the commentators. Johnson acknowledged that this was a departure from normal procedure, but pointed out that these were not normal circumstances. "Under normal circumstances," he explained, "participants in the peer commentary process do not threaten to bring suit if revisions are not made in the roundtable article."[66]

When Sulloway learned that Johnson was planning to go ahead with publication, he escalated his attack. He sent a letter to the president of Johnson's university, with copies to other prominent officials, saying that he was planning to file "formal charges of scientific misconduct against Gary Johnson with the American Political Science Association, the

Human Behavior and Evolution Society, members of Congress who have shown a concern about science fraud," and so on.[67] (Sulloway did not follow through on these threats. In May 2004, he explained to a journalist that it "wasn't worth the trouble."[68])

Johnson remained steadfast in his determination to publish, but the fight was long, wearisome, and costly. When the publisher of the journal got wind of the threat of litigation, he refused to print the issue in question unless both Sulloway and Townsend would agree in writing not to sue him, the printer, or the journal. (They would still be free to sue each other.) Townsend signed the release but Sulloway refused, so Johnson had to find another way to get the issue printed. He and his assistants ended up doing most of the work themselves.[69] That was one reason why the September 2000 issue of *Politics and the Life Sciences* didn't appear in print until February 2004.

The other reason was Johnson's decision, made late in the day, not to remain on the sidelines but to conduct his own investigation into Sulloway's research methods. As he explained in his editorial, he had started out with an "favorable predisposition toward *Born to Rebel*"; he approved of Sulloway's Darwinian approach. But when Sulloway finally submitted his reply to Townsend's revised critique, Johnson found it disappointing. Sulloway "oversimplifies some of the issues Townsend raises," Johnson said, "and he sidesteps or ignores others. In general, he seems to have used a 'dismissive onslaught' strategy. . . . The response to Townsend is dismissive and patronizing."[70]

The specific thing that caused Johnson to enter the fray was Sulloway's response to one small piece of Townsend's evidence. Townsend had obtained a copy of Sulloway's 1991 National Science Foundation grant proposal through the Freedom of Information Act. Both the proposal and *Born to Rebel* contain tables showing laterborn support for various scientific revolutions, but Townsend found that the numbers didn't agree: the ratios of laterborn support were considerably higher in *Born to Rebel*. In his reply to Townsend, Sulloway accounted for the discrepancies as follows: "It turns out that Townsend mistook relative risk ratios, which I provided in my 1991 grant proposal, for odds ratios, which I provided in my 1995 book." In a footnote he described Townsend's error as one of those "problems that can arise when unpublished documents and data are acquired by a nonprofessional who should have done the minimal amount of checking."[71]

Johnson, who is a professional, decided to do the minimal amount of checking. He examined Sulloway's NSF grant proposal. The table in the grant proposal, Johnson discovered, explicitly said that the numbers were odds ratios; the term "risk ratios" was used nowhere in the document. Having made this discovery, Johnson felt that he had to say something. If he hadn't—if he had allowed Sulloway to get the last word—readers would have come away believing that Townsend had made a stupid mistake, confusing odds ratios with risk ratios.[72]

In for a penny, in for a pound. Once aroused, Johnson was as tenacious as Townsend. He decided to look more closely at *Born to Rebel*. He soon discovered that attempting to find out how Sulloway had obtained the data in his graphs and tables was like being "involved in a shell game."[73]

One of the things Johnson looked at was Sulloway's claim about the religious martyrs killed during the Reformation. Sulloway classified the Protestant martyrs as rebels—which means, according to his theory, that they should be laterborns—and the Catholic martyrs as conservatives. He reported in *Born to Rebel* that "23 out of 24" Protestant martyrs had been laterborns (a list of their names was one of the things he had refused to send Townsend), whereas "most" of the Catholic martyrs (no numbers given) had been firstborns.[74]

Sulloway was talking about events that happened in the fifteenth century. In endnotes he listed some of the sources he used for obtaining information on the religious beliefs of these martyrs. But nowhere, Johnson discovered, did Sulloway say where he had found information on their birth order. And that was the tricky part, because good records weren't kept in those days. Dates of birth were often approximate; family arrangements were complicated by deaths, remarriages, step-siblings, adoptions, and illegitimate offspring. After a good deal of historical research, Johnson succeeded in obtaining birth order information on 28 Protestant martyrs and 22 Catholic martyrs.[75]

Both groups contained a preponderance of laterborns, because these people came from families with an average of seven children, of which only one was a firstborn. But Johnson found no difference between the (supposedly rebellious) Protestants and the (supposedly conservative) Catholics: 3 of the 28 Protestants and 2 of the 22 Catholics were firstborns. "It appears that there was no empirical basis," Johnson concluded, for Sulloway's statement that most Catholic martyrs were firstborns.[76]

According to a recent news article in the British journal *Nature*, Gary Johnson has submitted a formal request to the National Science Foundation, asking that an independent inquiry be made into the research methods used by Frank Sulloway in his book *Born to Rebel.* Johnson's request is based on the fact that Sulloway received a grant from the NSF to do the research for the book. "The evasiveness, the varying methodological accounts, the data discrepancies and the seemingly desperate attempts to interfere with publication together suggest that an independent review of Sulloway's research should be undertaken," Johnson explained to the journalist from *Nature.* Sulloway, for his part, accused Johnson of "unprofessional editorial tactics" and denied his allegations. As for the inquiry, "The only concern to me is the amount of time it takes to make all the data available," Sulloway told the journalist. "I'm just swamped with work."[77] An example of the kind of data that Sulloway would presumably be asked to provide is a list of the Protestant and Catholic martyrs he referred to in his book.

Other journalists have questioned Sulloway about the disputed issue of *Politics and the Life Sciences.* Here's an account written by a newspaper reporter in Berkeley, California, who interviewed Sulloway in person not long after the issue was published and recorded his reaction to it:

> Sulloway's intense focus becomes clear within minutes of meeting him. He is angry about what has happened and harbors a deep disdain for his critics, which he doesn't attempt to hide. They are unsophisticated detail freaks, he says, who are unable to grasp, replicate, or even understand the way he put his book together. He speaks of his detractors as if they were third-tier nuisances with insubstantial and irritating complaints, and says he is not alone in this thinking. He produces an e-mail from a colleague who calls Sulloway's critics a "confederacy of dunces." . . . This is a theme to which Sulloway and his supporters are sticking—they make much ado of credentials or lack thereof, noting that this is a case of nonpedigreed folks going after one of academia's brightest lights. "It's like being Tom Cruise or somebody else and people start going after you the way they go after stars in the tabloids," Sulloway says.[78]

I won't comment on Sulloway's similarity to Tom Cruise, only on his logic. To say that A is right and B is wrong because A has better credentials is an error in reasoning. The truth of a statement doesn't rest on who said it. As Johnson declared in a letter to Sulloway, "Unless science is to be a credentialed aristocracy, we must surely be open to participation by the uncredentialed and the unorthodox. The history of science seems to suggest that the work of amateurs deserves, if anything, special protection."[79]

A curious thing about this story is the fact that Sulloway is a laterborn.

According to his theory, it's supposed to be firstborns who are dominant and aggressive and who "employ their superior size and strength to defend their special status."[80]

Birth order effects are real; they affect behavior within the family. Siblings compete with each other for parental attention. Older ones are nurturant toward younger ones and boss them around. Parents treat firstborns differently from laterborns, and older children differently from younger ones, and the children are keenly aware of it. All these things go on within families and, for children who have siblings, are a deeply felt part of their early experiences at home. People remember them all their lives.

If these things don't have measurable effects on personality—if their effects can't be detected in the way kids behave on the playground or in the responses adults check off on personality tests—is it plausible to put the blame on within-the-family differences of the upper-versus-lower-bunk-bed sort? If the substantial, persistent differences between the family experiences of a firstborn and a laterborn don't leave visible marks on their personalities, is it likely that minor differences—due, say, to family members' reactions to the random differences between identical twins or to the fact that one of them made a mess of the mousse—are going to do the job? If personality isn't shaped by big things that happen to children at home, is it likely to be shaped by little things that happen to them at home?

I conclude that within-the-family differences in environment, of which the most conspicuous are the differences associated with ordinal position in the family, are a red herring. They are not the perpetrator we are looking for. They cannot account for the personality differences between ordinary siblings, much less the differences between identical twins.

That was my fourth red herring. Only one more to go, and I can eliminate it quickly—no need to give it a chapter of its own.

The fifth red herring is gene-environment correlations. Don't confuse them with gene-environment interactions; they're not the same. A gene-environment correlation occurs when a person's environment reflects, or is influenced by, the person's genes. As the behavioral geneticist Sandra Scarr put it, "Individuals make their own environments, based on their own heritable characteristics."[81] People's environments differ in part because their genes do.

Examples abound. Children born pretty or charming are given special attention by their parents and are treated well by other people too. Those who are hungry for knowledge are provided with books and taken to museums. Those who have an aptitude for schoolwork tend to choose studious friends and intellectually challenging activities. Some people are more likely than others to experience stressful life events, perhaps because they have a knack for putting themselves into situations (jobs, romantic relationships) that are likely to end badly. Like prettiness and academic aptitude, the tendency to experience stressful life events shows significant heritability.[82]

The correlation between genotype and environment sometimes comes about because of the way others react to an individual's heritable characteristics, sometimes because of the active role the individual plays in picking and choosing among the available options. The upshot is that environments are not shuffled and dealt out randomly: they are to some extent predictable on the basis of genotype. Children with different genotypes therefore grow up in different environments.

Gene-environment correlations produce what I call "indirect genetic effects": the effects of the effects of the genes.[83] Good-looking people and those who are big and strong get used to having their way and become more assertive. Children born bright and curious are attracted to intellectual activities and the result is that they get smarter. Those born with nasty dispositions evoke negative reactions from others and that makes them nastier still. Indirect effects of genes often, though not always, work in this vicious-circle fashion.

Standard behavioral genetic methods cannot distinguish between direct and indirect effects of genes; the data analyses lump them together. Therefore, "heritability" includes indirect effects of genes, as well as direct effects. This is the source of the critics' complaint that twin studies overestimate heritability: the observed similarities of identical twins may be partly due to indirect effects of genes. Identical twins are very similar in physical appearance, temperament, intelligence, aptitudes, and interests; and these similarities evoke similar reactions from other people and cause the twins themselves to make similar choices in deciding how to spend their time. If these reactions and choices have any systematic effects on the twins' personalities, the effects will contribute to the portion of the variance attributed to heritability, not to the unexplained variance.

Which means that, though gene-environment correlations may inflate heritability estimates, they can't be the solution to the mystery of individuality. They make identical twins more alike, not more different. Robert

Plomin made the same point in "Nonshared Environment a Decade Later." He and his coauthors asked whether gene-environment correlations could account for nonshared environment effects. "No," they said, "these can't account for why identical twins are different."[84]

And yet there are theories of personality development based on gene-environment correlations, proposed by eminent behavioral geneticists such as Sandra Scarr and Thomas Bouchard.[85] Another example is the theory proposed by the psychiatrist David Reiss in his book about the NEAD study. Reiss was unhappy with the results of the study and wanted to restore the family environment to what he felt was its rightful place. He thought maybe gene-environment correlations could do it. For example, he said,

> Heritable personality traits of adolescents may disrupt their relationships with their parents. These disrupted relationships may be a crucial step in the process whereby the personality traits evolve into serious antisocial behavior.[86]

A more straightforward explanation would be that the disrupted relationships and the serious antisocial behavior both result from the heritable personality traits. This interpretation fits the data just as well as the one Reiss suggested. But it doesn't matter for my purposes, because neither can account for the unexplained variance. The disrupted relationships are the indirect effects of genes, so they would contribute to genetic variance. To heritability.

What Reiss was doing was trying to explain how genes work. That's also what Sandra Scarr was trying to do, and Thomas Bouchard. Bouchard stated his purpose clearly in the subtitle of one of his articles: "How Genes Drive Experience and Shape Personality."

My purpose is different. I'm not interested in how genes shape personality: I'm interested in how the environment shapes personality. Here's what Bouchard said in that article about explaining the variation in personality that is *not* genetic: "How non-traumatic environmental determinants influence the normal range of variance in adult personality remains largely a mystery."[87]

Now I will start putting together the clues that point to the solution of the mystery.

5

The Person and the Situation

CLEARLY, THE PERPETRATOR I'm searching for is an elusive one. This perpetrator produces variation in personality above and beyond the variation produced by genes. It creates or widens personality differences even between identical twins who grow up together.

The perpetrator I'm searching for is a shaper of personality. To solve the mystery of individuality, I have to figure out how personality gets shaped. I'm proceeding on the premise that the shaping serves some purpose—that evolution provided humans with a certain amount of plasticity in behavior so they can profit from their experiences. People differ in personality, not just because they have different genes, but also because they have different experiences.

The way people profit from their experiences is through a process we call learning. Any theory that says that people's personalities are modified by their experiences is, implicitly or explicitly, a theory of learning. Thus, in order to figure out how personality is shaped by experience, it is necessary to have a clear idea of how people learn. In particular, since most of the shaping occurs in the first couple of decades of life, it is necessary to have a clear idea of how young people learn.

I've examined and eliminated five plausible suspects. Personality differences, as I showed in chapter 2, are not mainly due to differences in environment, nor to a combination of "nature" (genes) plus "nurture" (the part of the environment provided by parents). Nor, as I demonstrated in chapter 3, can they be explained in terms of gene-environment interactions. The remaining candidates were crossed off in chapter 4: environmental differences within the family and gene-environment correlations.

Five red herrings. None of them can be the solution to my mystery. All make predictions that are inconsistent with the evidence; none can explain the differences between identical twins. But there are plenty of fish in the sea. What about all the other theories of personality development?

Sorry, they won't work either. Before you dismiss that statement as sheer chutzpah, listen to my reason for making it. I can eliminate all the currently popular theories of personality development with a single flick of my hand, because they all rest on the same basic assumption about learning. The assumption is that learned behaviors or learned associations transfer readily and automatically from one situation to another. What all these theories have in common is the idea that children learn something in one environmental setting (usually the home), or with one social partner (usually the mother), and that this learning subsequently affects the way they behave, and the emotions they feel, in other places and with other people.

Those who make this assumption often place particular stress on very early experiences, the idea being that whatever is learned first will affect all subsequent experiences. Psychoanalytic theory is an obvious example and so is its grandchild, attachment theory. Modern attachment theorists believe that if you and your mother didn't happen to hit it off while you were an infant, you are doomed to plod through life with the self-fulfilling expectation that all your relationships will be disappointing. The first prominent behaviorist, John B. Watson, also placed much importance on learning in infancy, though he would have attributed your later disappointments to the reflexes that got conditioned during that time. Even Jean Piaget, the famous Swiss developmentalist and cognitive scientist, believed in the importance of early learning and its subsequent generalization. Here's a telling quote from Piaget:

> Day to day observation and psycho-analytic experience show that the first personal schemas are afterwards later generalised and applied to many other people. According as the first inter-individual experiences of the child who is just learning to speak are connected with a father who is understanding or dominating, loving or cruel, etc., the child will tend . . . to assimilate all other individuals to this father schema. On the other hand, the type of feelings he has for his mother will tend to make him love in a certain way, sometimes all through life, because here again he partially assimilates his successive loves to this first love which shapes his innermost feelings and behaviours.[1]

I am not, of course, the first to question this view of the role of early learning and generalization in personality development. In 1968, Walter Mischel—then a professor of psychology at Stanford, now at Columbia University—published a book that knocked personality psychology on its ear. The resulting uproar became known as "the person-situation controversy."

It was Mischel who drew my attention to Piaget's statement on the generalization of "first personal schemas." Mischel quoted the part that had to do with the father schema and then cited evidence showing that people's relationships with their fathers bore little or no resemblance to their relationships with other authority figures: "For example, attitude toward one's father correlated .03 with attitude toward one's boss."[2]

Other evidence that Mischel cited had to do with moral behavior and moral judgments. Children who learn not to lie or cheat at home may lie or cheat in the classroom or in games on the playground; children who are honest in the classroom may cheat on the playground. Whether children cheat when given the opportunity to do so bears little relation to what they say on paper-and-pencil tests of moral judgment. How they respond on a test of moral judgment depends in part on where they are when they take the test. "The data on moral behavior," Mischel concluded, "provide no support for the widespread psychodynamic belief in a unitary intrapsychic moral agency like the superego."[3]

Mischel's point can be stated more simply: people behave differently in different situations. This, he said, has serious implications for personality psychology.

> The intuitive conviction that persons do have consistent and widely generalized personality traits seems very compelling. . . . Obviously a person does not have to learn everything afresh in each new or slightly different situation, and his reactions to any novel situation are influenced by his prior experiences. The empirically established behavioral consistencies, however, do not seem large enough to warrant the belief in very broad generalized personality traits. . . . The conviction that highly generalized traits do exist may reflect in part (but not entirely) behavior consistencies that are *constructed* by observers, rather than actual consistency in the subject's behavior.[4]

Mischel was saying that the consistency of personality is an illusion. It's in the eye of the beholder, not in the head of the beholdee. There is such an illusion; I mentioned it in chapter 1: the fundamental attribution error. I gave the example of the subjects who believed that the graduate student who was nasty to them in the laboratory would also be nasty if they ran into her in the supermarket. The fundamental attribution error, I said, is a human universal. It's an illusion that everyone has, like the visual illusions you sometimes see on the back of cereal boxes—this one, for example:

All five spots are the same shade of gray, but we see the one on the pale background as dark, the one on the dark background as pale. As Steven Pinker remarked in *How the Mind Works*, our visual systems do not provide this illusion so that cereal manufacturers will have something to print on the back of the box. This illusion, and the others he discussed in his book, are the manifestations of mental mechanisms that serve a purpose. In this case the purpose is to identify objects. Is this a lump of coal or a lump of snow? The problem is that the amount of light reflected by an object depends on the overall illumination: "A photographer's light meter would show you that more light bounces off a lump of coal outdoors than off a snowball indoors." The visual system cleverly compensates for the overall illumination, with the result that we see the coal as black and the snowball as white whether we are indoors or out. The illusion is a product of the visual mechanism responsible for what cognitive scientists call "lightness constancy."

Lightness constancy occasionally causes us to make mistakes, but what it does under ordinary circumstances is to help us identify objects correctly. Because information from the senses is incomplete and imperfect, "the brain," Pinker explained, "must combine information from the senses with assumptions about the world to make an intelligent guess." Occasionally the world violates our assumptions and the result is an illusion, but most of the time our guesses are correct. That's why Pinker called them *intelligent* guesses.[5]

The fundamental attribution error is an illusion that results from what might be called "personality constancy." We are endowed with a mental mechanism that causes us to see a given individual's personality as relatively constant—more constant than a mechanical measuring device would indicate—whether we see this individual indoors or out, in a laboratory room or in the supermarket. The same way we attribute blackness to a lump of coal and whiteness to a snowball, we attribute friendliness to one person and nastiness to another.

The universality of the fundamental attribution error suggests that this bias helped, rather than hindered, our ancestors. Evidently it didn't lead them astray more often than not. The reason it didn't is that people are, at least to some extent, consistent in how they behave. There is such a thing as personality.

Walter Mischel didn't deny it. He just said that people are much less consistent than you have been led to believe.

Mischel comes from a school of psychology called cognitive behaviorism: behaviorism with some added frills. In other words, he's an environmentalist. His book—the one that shook up personality psychology—was published in 1968, a time when environmentalism was running rampant and there weren't any behavioral geneticists to kick around (if there were, they were keeping awfully quiet). Mischel knew nothing about the behavioral genetic evidence I told you about in chapter 2 because the studies hadn't been done yet.

In denying that people have consistent personalities, Mischel was denying not only that early learning generalizes but also that people have inborn predispositions to behave in certain ways—in other words, that there are genetic influences on personality. He was arguing against the view that "the same underlying disposition (or 'genotype')" may affect behavior in a variety of situations.[6]

As we now know, Mischel was wrong about there being no underlying dispositions. But he was right about the other things: that people behave differently in different situations and that "personal schemas" do not generalize to other persons.

The fact that people behave differently in different situations is one of the things I talked about (I devoted an entire chapter to it) in *The Nurture Assumption*.[7] But I never claimed that there was no correlation at all between the way an individual behaves in two different situations. Nor did Mischel make that claim. Mischel's point was simply that the correlation is low. My point was that it is *surprisingly* low, given the behavioral genetic evidence that genes account for about 45 percent of the variation in personality and social behavior.

Your genes you always have with you. They go with you wherever you go. People born with a predisposition to be agreeable or aggressive or shy will take these predispositions with them into a variety of social contexts. I touched on this in the previous chapter when I mentioned the study that found a correlation of .19 between children's obnoxious behavior with their parents and their obnoxious behavior with their peers.[8] I pointed out that the researchers hadn't considered the possibility that some children might inherit a predisposition to behave in a disagreeable or aggressive fashion wherever they go, and that this predisposition might account for the correlation between home behavior and playground behavior.

Behavioral geneticists can now look into such possibilities, thanks to a technique, developed within the past dozen years, called "multivariate genetic analysis." It enables them to assess the degree to which genetic and environmental influences each contribute to the correlations found between behavior in different contexts or at different times. Using this technique, researchers studying children's shy or inhibited behavior found that genetic influences account for almost the entire correlation between behavior in the laboratory and in the home. When a child behaves in an inhibited (or uninhibited) fashion both in the laboratory and at home, it's because he or she has a genetic predisposition to behave that way. The same is true of activity level—how physically active or inactive the child is. Genetic influences account for the entire correlation between activity level in the laboratory and in school.[9] The correlation between activity level in the laboratory and in school, incidentally, was .19.

Genetic influences also account for a major portion of the continuity in behavior or personality over long periods of time.[10] This finding has a very important implication. The fact that some personality characteristics show up early and persist through childhood and adulthood does not mean that environmental effects on personality must occur at an early age. The evidence suggests that these early-appearing and stable characteristics are due to inborn predispositions rather than to early experiences. This means that environmental influences on personality might occur at a later stage of development than many theorists have assumed.

The problem is not how to account for the continuities and consistencies in behavior: it's to explain why there isn't *more* continuity and consistency, in view of the .45 heritability of personality characteristics.

One answer is that genes can contribute, not only to stability, but also to change. Though the genome itself remains the same throughout life, some genes are turned on early while others (like the ones that determine breast size in women or baldness in men) don't begin to function until later in development.

Moreover, behavior in different contexts may be influenced by somewhat different suites of genes. The researchers who studied activity level found that genetic influences accounted not only for all the similarity in behavior between laboratory and school, but also for some of the differences. There were genetic influences that were specific to one setting or another, perhaps because the activity being measured was of a different sort—fidgeting in the lab, say, versus participation in active games on the school playground.[11]

But genetic influences account for only a minor portion of the differences in behavior from one setting to another. Mischel assumed that most of the differences result from learning and I agree with him on this. As he put it, "Individuals discriminate sharply between situations."[12] Those children who behaved in an obnoxious fashion with their parents but not with their peers might have learned that their parents would put up with it but their peers would not. Those children who behaved in an obnoxious fashion with their peers but not with their parents might have been big and strong enough to bully the other kids on the playground but not big and strong enough to bully their parents. In the previous chapter I described studies that showed that firstborns are more aggressive than laterborns at home but not at school. Children discriminate sharply between situations.

But what about babies? Ah, now we're getting to the nitty-gritty.

Generalization or discrimination? It's something you would have to decide if you were designing a baby. Since no two situations are ever exactly alike, learning would be impossible without *some* generalization. And repeating a previously learned behavior in a new (but similar) situation would presumably be easier than starting all over from scratch. On the other hand, repeating the previously learned behavior could be hazardous, if it turned out to be inappropriate in the new (though similar) situation. Thus, the designer of the baby has to balance the risks of overgeneralization against the inefficiencies of undergeneralization.

But undergeneralization is a serious disadvantage only if storage capacity is at a premium. If the baby's mind were unlimited in its storage capacity—in its ability to acquire and retain new patterns of behavior, properly labeled as to where and when they should be trotted out—then undergeneralization would appear to be the safer policy.

The evidence indicates that this is in fact the way the baby's mind was designed. A baby is far more likely to err by failing to generalize than by generalizing too freely.[13] Evolution provided the young of our species with a brain so large it can barely make it through the birth canal, and then shrugged her shoulders when the question came up about the inefficiencies of undergeneralization.

As demonstrated by the experiments of the developmentalist Carolyn Rovee-Collier and her colleagues, a young baby's initial inclination is to discriminate, rather than to generalize. Rovee-Collier begins her experiments by teaching a baby a simple trick. She ties one end of a ribbon to the baby's ankle, the other to a mobile suspended over the crib. When the baby kicks his foot, the mobile jiggles. Most babies are delighted to discover they can make the mobile jiggle; they show their enthusiasm by greatly increasing their rate of kicking the beribboned foot. Moreover, they will remember this trick several days later: if they're shown the mobile again, they will again kick the appropriate foot. But they will do this only if the experimental setup hasn't been changed. If the blue doodads hanging from the mobile have been replaced with red doodads, or if the crib has been rolled from the bedroom to the den, the baby will gaze cluelessly at the mobile, as though he had never seen such a thing in his life.[14]

Unexpected failures to generalize have been demonstrated in older babies, too. When babies first start to crawl at eight or nine months of age, they will attempt to crawl down slopes that are much too steep for them to negotiate. The developmentalist Karen Adolph trained babies by letting them crawl on an inclined plane—a carpet-covered walkway—that could be adjusted to different angles. When the walkway was too steep, the babies would tumble down it, landing safely but ignominiously on a cushioned surface at the bottom. After repeated experiences with the experimental setup, the babies learned which slopes they could crawl down without falling and which were too steep.

Then these babies learned to walk. Incredibly, there was no transfer at all from crawling to walking. In the first weeks of walking, the babies attempted to toddle down the same steep slopes that had caused them to plunge headlong as crawlers, with the same results.[15]

The studies of Rovee-Collier and Adolph have to do with motor learning. Their findings tell us something about the learning mechanism that enables babies to acquire physical skills. The mechanism evidently comes with a factory default setting: a bias against generalization. And yet we know perfectly well that generalization occurs. "Obviously," as Mischel observed, "a person does not have to learn everything afresh in each new or slightly different situation."[16] You walk into a dark hotel room and automatically grope for the light switch. You don't have to learn afresh, in every new room you enter, how to turn on the lights. The toddler who learns to drink from a cup at home doesn't have to relearn the skill in the day-care center.

So the question is not *whether* generalization occurs, but when and how it occurs. When do babies regard two situations as "same" and when do they regard them as "different"? How do their experiences teach them that two situations they initially regarded as different are in fact equivalent?

Rovee-Collier's experiments are again informative. To teach babies to generalize the foot-kicking trick from one mobile to another or from one setting to another, she discovered, all you have to do is to vary the training: train them with several different mobiles or in several different locations. When the training setup is varied in this way, the baby learns that the rule "kick your foot to make the mobile jiggle" holds true under a variety of conditions. Babies learn this readily but they don't come into the world already knowing it, even though it seems obvious to us that a trick that made a mobile jiggle in the bedroom should also make it jiggle in the den.

Interesting, but it still doesn't solve the problem. If varying the training setup teaches babies to generalize the foot-kicking trick, how come they don't learn that on their own, given that no two situations are ever exactly alike? Even if the same mobile is hanging overhead and the crib hasn't been moved, other things are bound to have changed. Maybe the first time the baby saw the mobile, sun was streaming through the window; the second time it was a rainy day. Why does a baby spontaneously generalize the foot-kicking trick from a brightly lit bedroom to a dimly lit bedroom, but not from the bedroom to the den?

Two situations are never exactly alike in every detail, and that is why, as Steven Pinker has pointed out, there must be an "innate similarity space."[17] Babies must be more tuned in to certain kinds of differences than to others. The innate similarity space determines whether an infant will initially regard a new situation as the same as a previous one or as different. Thus, to know how the baby will cut up the continuum of experience into different "situations," we have to know something about the baby's mind. As the psychologist Peter Gray put it, "You can't predict to what degree an individual will generalize from one stimulus to the next unless you understand something about the individual's mental concepts."[18] If the two stimuli evoke different mental concepts, generalization may not occur even if the stimuli are very similar in size, shape, and color. If the two stimuli evoke the *same* mental concept—which might mean only that the individual can't tell them apart—the individual is likely to respond in the same way to both. Babies can learn from experience that the same mental concept applies to two situations that initially occupied different positions in the innate similarity space.

The research on infant attachment provides some useful information about the baby's innate similarity space. I alluded to attachment theory earlier, when I made fun of the idea that your life is going to be blighted if you and your mother didn't happen to hit it off during the first twelve months of your life. Now I will take a more serious look at it.

According to the attachment theorists, a baby develops a mental concept—they call it a "working model"—of his relationship with his mother. The way the researchers assess the quality of this relationship is by putting a year-old infant and his mother into a unfamiliar laboratory room, having the mother leave the baby alone for a short time (most babies get upset at this point), and then watching what happens when the mother returns. According to attachment theory, a baby who has developed a "secure attachment" will greet his mother joyfully and will allow her to soothe away his tears. One whose attachment is insecure may ignore his mother, or keep on crying, or alternate between clinging to her and pushing her away. Attachment researchers have shown that a baby is more likely to behave in a securely attached fashion with his mother if she has taken good care of him, during the preceding months, by being responsive to his needs.[19]

There is nothing wrong with the attachment theorists' explanation of the baby's behavior; I think the baby really does form a mental model of his relationship with his mother and develop expectations about how she will behave. On the basis of his past experiences with her, he may regard her as someone he can rely upon to make him feel better when he is upset; alternatively, he may recognize that she is not useful under such circumstances. But—here's where I part company with the attachment theorists—his life is not going to be blighted if he comes to the latter conclusion, because his mother is not going to be the only person in his life and he doesn't expect people to be all alike. Babies who have received nothing but kindness from everyone they encountered during their first twelve months will nonetheless cry out in fear if a stranger tries to pick them up.

The fundamental attribution error shows that adults expect individuals to be consistent—more consistent than they really are. The work of the attachment theorists shows that babies have the same bias. The laboratory setting is brand new to a baby who participates in one of these studies—he's never been in this room before—and yet he expects his mother to behave the way she has behaved in more familiar settings. She may be wearing different clothing or a different hairstyle but she's still his mother, and the baby expects, on the basis of his prior experiences with her, that she either will or will not be helpful. But he doesn't generalize these expectations to other people, even if they're the same sex, age, and color as his mother. He doesn't reach up his arms to the stranger.

Researchers have found that the babies of mothers who are suffering from postpartum depression behave in a solemn, subdued fashion when they're with their mothers. When they're with other familiar caregivers, however, these babies behave normally: they are much livelier. The subdued behavior, according to the researchers, is "specific to their interactions with their depressed mothers."[20]

Whether behavior is generalized from one situation to another depends on whether the situations are regarded as the same or as different. For humans, probably the most salient cue to "same" or "different" is the cast of characters. A change in dramatis personae means that this must be a different play, with a different script.

Babies, as I said in chapter 1, are born with a tremendous interest in learning to tell people apart and in collecting information about them; the people-information acquisition device is ready to kick into action on the day it is delivered. A baby whose mother is depressed doesn't expect everyone to be depressed; one whose mother loves him doesn't expect everyone to love him. Babies can be securely attached to one caregiver and insecurely attached to another.[21]

Just as other developmentalists find weak correlations between a child's shyness or obnoxiousness in one setting and another, attachment researchers find weak correlations between the security of a toddler's attachment to his mother and his later success in other social arenas—friendships with peers, for instance.[22] My interpretation of all these correlations is the same: they result, not from generalization, but from genetic influences on the measured outcomes. The methods used by attachment researchers provide no controls (or inadequate controls) for genetic differences among their subjects. I take the correlations they find as evidence that characteristics the child is born with, including physical appearance, will help or hinder him in a variety of social situations. The cute face or ready smile that made his mother dote on him[23] will also stand him in good stead with other people, including peers.

Early experiences may have an effect on later behavior in another way—a way that doesn't fit the description of learning plus generalization. Early experiences, or the absence thereof, may affect the neurophysiological development of the brain. Since every kind of learning must have neurophysiological effects on the brain (strengthening synapses or whatever), you may be wondering how I could make a distinction between these two kinds of processes. Perhaps the best way to explain it is to give you some examples.

The first has to do with vision. Neuroscientists David Hubel and Torsten Wiesel won a Nobel Prize for their research, which showed that it is possible to produce permanent changes in the visual system of a cat by restricting its vision in various ways during a "critical period" in the early weeks of its life. Patterned stimulation to both eyes is required for normal development of the visual system. If a kitten is permitted to see out of only one eye during the critical period, vision in the occluded eye will be permanently impaired. The problem is not in the eye—it's in the brain. The brain area originally designated to serve the occluded eye has evidently been reassigned to other duties.[24]

A second example has to do with language. Babies who aren't exposed to a language—spoken or signed—during the first few years of life never become highly skilled communicators. Generally the way this happens is that a baby is born deaf and the parents either aren't aware of it or don't know what to do about it, so that the child's introduction to sign language (or to spoken language, if the hearing deficit is correctable) comes late. Deaf children who aren't exposed to sign language until school age never become proficient signers. The most eloquent users of sign language are the deaf offspring of deaf parents, who started learning it in infancy. In those rare and tragic cases where children have no opportunity to learn a language before they reach puberty, they never get the hang of it at all.[25]

My final example is attachment. There is some evidence that human babies who fail to form an attachment during the first two or three years of life may be permanently impaired in their ability to form close relationships. Under ordinary circumstances, all human babies become attached; that's why attachment theorists speak of secure versus insecure attachments, rather than attached versus unattached babies. Even babies who are abused by their mothers become attached to them, though there is a greater chance that the attachment will be insecure.[26] An unattached child is likely to be found only in the worst kind of institutional setting, where there is frequent turnover in caregivers. A recent study of some children who had spent their first two or three years in Romanian orphanages found that some—but not all—showed persistent abnormalities in social behavior. At age six these children tended to be indiscriminately friendly to all adults, even strangers, and they failed to look to their adoptive parents for reassurance at times when most children would do so. But, as I said, not all the orphanage children showed these symptoms. The researchers weren't sure why some children appeared to have recovered fully from their early deprivation. Perhaps they were genetically more resilient, or perhaps they had managed to find someone to become attached to in the orphanage. There is evidence that attachments to other children can serve, at least to some extent, as a substitute for an attachment to a caregiver.[27]

The same is true for monkeys. As I mentioned in chapter 3, baby rhesus monkeys that have been separated from their mothers develop into reasonably normal adults if they are raised with peers. However, researchers have found subtle differences between mother-reared and peer-reared monkeys.[28] Such differences do not surprise me; peer-rearing does not fall within the normal range of environments for a baby monkey. Because an infant mammal could never survive in the wild without a mother, its brain "expects" a mother to be present. The infant mammal's brain relies on the presence of a mother, the same way it relies on patterned visual stimulation, to fine-tune its development after birth.

But the developing brain isn't fussy. As long as the visual stimulation, or the mother, or the language, fall within the range normally encountered by the species, the fine-tuning proceeds according to plan. Only highly abnormal conditions—conditions of severe deprivation—cause permanent deficits. The environment needs only to provide the bare minimum; beyond that minimum, there is no evidence that variations in quality or quantity make a difference.[29] Babies who get to look at pretty pictures and intricate mobiles do not develop better visual systems than those reared in bare huts.

Nor is there evidence that these early experiences cause the brain to be permanently disposed to expect more of the same. Toddlers whose first language is Polish or Korean or sign language are not handicapped if they later discover that the language of their community is spoken English. The hearing children of deaf parents generally learn sign language first, but they soon become competent speakers of the language spoken outside the home. Which language is learned first doesn't matter in the long run, just as long as the child learns *some* language. Children are open to the possibility that the language used outside the home may differ from the language they learned from their parents.[30]

Attachment appears to work the same way. As long as the infant manages to form *some* attachment in the first few years of life, development proceeds according to plan. If the first relationship doesn't work out well, the child is open to the possibility that the next one will be better; he doesn't expect all people to behave like his mother. Isn't this the way you would design the baby, if it were up to you? If a child happens to have an abusive or neglectful mother but nonetheless manages to survive, why should the poor kid be burdened with additional handicaps? The goal, from an evolutionary viewpoint, is to minimize the damage caused by early adversity.

I said at the beginning of this chapter that all the currently popular theories of personality development are based on the assumption that children learn something in one environmental setting or with one social partner, and that this learning subsequently affects the way they behave in other places and with other people. What makes it hard to test this assumption is that genetic influences, too, can produce similarities of behavior across contexts. Thus, a convincing test would have to provide some way of eliminating or controlling for the misleading effects of genes.

I've already described two ways to do this. The first is to use behavioral genetic methods. The behavioral genetic evidence provides no support for the assumption that patterns of behavior learned at home affect behavior or personality outside the home. Nor does it confirm the predictions of attachment theory. Two people—even identical twins—who were cared for from birth by the same mother are no more alike in personality than two who had different mothers.

The second way is to do a birth order study. In the previous chapter I described the strengths of this method: the fact that there are no systematic genetic differences between firstborns and laterborns but there are systematic differences in their experiences at home. The evidence from birth order studies does not support the notion that patterns of behavior learned at home are generalized to other contexts: firstborn children are more aggressive at home but not on the playground. In adulthood there are no reliable differences between firstborns and laterborns in their scores on personality tests.

A third way is to look at the effects of context on a social behavior that is not influenced by genes. My favorite example is language. Though its acquisition is the product of a specialized mechanism in the human brain, once language is acquired it becomes a social behavior, sensitive to social context. Unlike most other social behaviors, however, it is free of genetic influence: differences in dialect are not due to differences in genes. Children are not born with a predisposition to speak English or Polish or Korean, or to use the accent of a particular region or social class. These things are entirely learned.

When we eliminate genetic influences by looking at language and accent, the apparent carryover of behavior from one context to another vanishes. A child who spoke Polish for the first few years of his life, and who continues to speak Polish at home with his parents, will speak unaccented English outside his home if he grows up in a neighborhood of native-born English-speakers.[31] The children of immigrants do not blend their two language contexts; they do not end up with some sort of a compromise. No trace of their parents' foreign accent leaks out into the language they use with their peers.[32]

That this phenomenon has something to do with the regulation of social behavior is shown by what happens if something goes wrong with the ability to respond normally to social inputs. Simon Baron-Cohen, the British cognitive scientist who studies autism, found that autistic children reared by immigrant parents do not lose their parents' foreign accents.[33]

The example of language also shows that consistencies in behavior across contexts are not invariably due to genetic influences. Most children who grow up in English-speaking countries speak English both at home and at school—not because they inherited a predisposition to speak that language but because experience has taught them that it works in a variety of contexts. Their behavior (speaking English) is similar in different contexts because their experiences (hearing people speak English, being understood when they speak English) have been similar in different contexts.

Some behaviors, such as speaking English, work in a variety of contexts. Others, such as being aggressive, work in some but not in others. The need to be aware of social context is as pressing in childhood as it is in adulthood. Nowadays many parents teach their children that it's good to express emotions. If you feel like crying, go ahead and cry. If you need a little loving, throw your arms around me. All very well and good at home, but if you take these behaviors outside with you, they could get you into trouble. The child who cries too much in school is likely to be teased or avoided. To say nothing of the one who throws his arms around people willy-nilly.

A fourth way to test the assumption that behaviors learned at home generalize to other contexts is to do an experiment.

Most research in developmental psychology is not experimental: it is observational. Typically, developmentalists make use of preexisting, spontaneous differences in child-rearing practices among the parents in their study. The problem is that a parent's child-rearing practices are not chosen at random. Parenting behavior is, in part, a response to the child's behavior, which is influenced by the child's genes. In part it is a function of the parent's own personality, which is influenced by the *parent's* genes.[34] Thus, families in which the parents use a harsh child-rearing style may differ genetically from those in which the parents use a more permissive style. They may also differ in other ways—in socioeconomic class, for instance.

A similar problem exists in medical research. Medical researchers know that studies in which subjects make their own decisions about treatments may produce misleading results. That's why the "gold standard" of medical research is the randomized control trial, in which subjects are randomly assigned to the experimental group or the control group.[35] Random assignment ensures that the only way the two groups of subjects differ systematically is in whether or not they are getting the treatment being tested. All the other relevant ways in which medical subjects can differ—how healthy they are to begin with, how cautious or impulsive in making health-related decisions, and so on—will average out in the two groups, if the N is sufficiently large. So the two groups will be approximately equal at the start of the experiment.

In developmental psychology, the equivalent of the randomized control trial is an intervention study. In a well-done study of this type, parents are randomly assigned to an intervention group or a control group. Those in the intervention group are taught better ways of dealing with their children—that is, ways that the researchers believe are better. Then the researchers look for effects of the changed parental behavior on the children's behavior.

If the intervention is successful in changing the way the parents behave at home, then the researchers are likely to find changes in the way the children behave at home. The question is, Will these changes in the children's behavior transfer to other settings? Will a child who is less troublesome at home also be less troublesome at school?

In my talk at the NICHD conference—the conference I told you about in chapter 3, the one in which the primatologist Stephen Suomi accused me of ignoring interactions—I went out on a limb. I said that my theory predicts that interventions designed to improve parents' child-rearing methods might change children's behavior at home but will not affect their behavior at school.[36]

No one stood up in the question period and told me I was wrong. Instead, three very nice interventionists came up to me afterwards and told me politely that there was lots of evidence that interventions aimed at parents can improve children's behavior in school.

In fact, one such study was presented at the conference that very afternoon, by Philip Cowan and Carolyn Pape Cowan, a husband-and-wife team at the University of California at Berkeley. Philip is the director of Berkeley's Institute of Human Development. The message the Cowans delivered to a receptive audience was that an intervention study can prove that parenting matters.[37]

To my regret, I was unable to attend the Cowans' presentation—I had to skip some of the sessions and spend the time resting in my hotel room—but afterwards I wrote to Philip Cowan in e-mail. I requested a copy of his talk and he promptly sent it to me. He also proved willing to answer my questions in e-mail. He was motivated, I believe, by a sincere desire to convince me of the error of my ways. Interventionists, I found, are a lot like the people who want to convert you to their religious beliefs so that you won't go to hell.

The paper Philip Cowan sent me began with an excellent critique of conventional methodology in developmental psychology, explaining why correlational data—even from studies that follow children over periods of years—are ambiguous and cannot be used as proof of parental influence. The best way to clear up the cause-or-effect ambiguities of correlational data, Cowan and Cowan advised, is to do an intervention study. Their own intervention—a four-month program of group counseling for the parents, designed to improve the marital relationship as well as the parent-child relationship—clearly demonstrated that parental behaviors play a role in child outcomes, they said. Their results showed that if you improve the parents' relationship with each other and with their child, you can improve the child's performance in school. The children had higher academic achievement and fewer behavior problems in kindergarten, and better adaptation to first grade.[38]

The words were impressive but I had trouble understanding their data. Cowan and Cowan used complex statistics—"latent variable path models"—to analyze their results. I looked for a straightforward comparison between the children in the experimental group and those in the control group and couldn't find one. So I asked Philip Cowan for a clarification:

> You said . . . "When parents shifted in these positive ways, their children did better in adjusting to the challenges of kindergarten." I'm not clear on what that means. Does it mean that positive effects of the intervention were found only for those children whose parents responded favorably to the intervention—only in those whose parents showed a measurable improvement in marital relations and/or parenting skills?[39]

Evidently I had interpreted the results correctly. In his reply, Cowan told me that this outcome is exactly what one should expect from an intervention aimed at improving parental behavior:

> Would we expect that all kids whose parents were in the intervention to benefit? No. Just the ones whose parents improved. That's what we expected and that's what we found.[40]

Hmm. So the parents who improved as a result of the intervention had kids who did better in kindergarten. Wait, hasn't this analysis turned your experiment into a correlational study? What you're doing is looking for parent-child correlations *within* the intervention group. In order to prove that the intervention had an effect on the children's behavior in school, don't you have to show that there's a difference between the children in the intervention and control groups? Isn't that the whole point of randomly dividing the subjects into two groups?

When I expressed these doubts to Philip Cowan, he understandably got a bit testy. "There are dozens of intervention studies that show effects of interventions with parents on children, with measures occurring outside the home," he said, naming several researchers. "None of them is cited in your work. This begins to raise skepticism about your openness to data that might not support your position."[41]

Ah. I am often accused of being unwilling to look at data that might contradict my position, but usually the accusers make vague reference to "dozens of studies" and then fail to name them. Philip Cowan had done me the favor of naming some of them.

To follow up on this I needed the kind of assistance that Brent Carradine provided to the detective in *The Daughter of Time*, so I got in touch with Joan Friebely. Joan did a thorough search of the intervention literature and sent me articles by all the researchers Cowan had named and by many others as well. Thanks to her efforts I have several thick folders full of intervention studies.

What a mess. In many of the studies there was no objective measure of the children's behavior outside the home; the success of the intervention was assessed by asking the parents who had received the counseling or training to judge their children's behavior. In some studies there was no control group. In others, the intervention took place at school as well as at home—teachers as well as parents were given training in how to deal with unruly behavior—so if the children behaved better in school you couldn't tell if it was due to a change in the parents' behavior or in the teachers'. I have made detailed criticisms of these studies elsewhere[42] and I'm not going to do that here, but there's one study in particular I'd like to tell you about, because the design was exemplary and the results were crystal clear.

The report, published in a peer-reviewed journal, is titled "Parenting through Change: An Effective Prevention Program for Single Mothers." The authors are Marion Forgatch—one of the researchers whose work Philip Cowan had advised me to look at—and David DeGarmo. The goal of the intervention was to reduce "coercive parenting" in the divorced mothers of young school-age sons; these mothers received group training sessions in "positive parenting," followed up by reminder phone calls from the interventionists. The children's behavior was assessed both at home and at school. There was a control group. Assessments at school were made by teachers who received no training.

To any casual reader of Forgatch and DeGarmo's article, the intervention appears to have been a resounding success. According to the authors' summary, it led to an improvement in parenting behavior: afterwards, the mothers in the intervention group engaged in less "coercive parenting" than those in the control group. Furthermore, "improved parenting practices correlated significantly with improvements in teacher-reported school adjustment," a result that led the researchers to conclude that "the intervention indirectly benefitted child outcomes through improved parenting practices."[43] This was exactly the result Philip Cowan had told me was to be expected from an intervention aimed at the parents, and it was based on the same statistical method he used: a path analysis.

But Forgatch and DeGarmo also provided a simpler statistic, the one I had been unable to find in the Cowans' paper: the results of a direct comparison between the children in the intervention and control groups. "Contrary to expectations," admitted Forgatch and DeGarmo, "there were no direct effects of the intervention on child adjustment." Based on assessments by the teachers, there were no significant differences in school behavior between children in the two groups. Those in the control group ended up as well-behaved and well-adjusted, on average, as those in the intervention group.[44] In other words, an intervention focused on improving the parents' behavior at home had failed to improve the children's behavior at school.

The strength of an intervention study is the random assignment of subjects to treatment and control groups. A path analysis can produce misleading results because it circumvents the rigorous control of randomization and looks within the groups of parents to identify which ones followed the advice given by the interventionists and which ones did not. The analysis showed that the children of the parents who complied with the interventionists' advice did better in school. But the parents who complied with the interventionists' advice were not selected randomly. Compliant parents may differ systematically from those who do not comply with an intervention.

I didn't know it at the time I was corresponding with Philip Cowan, but a similar error in data analysis also crops up in medical research. The path analysis introduces what medical epidemiologists call a "compliance-determined susceptibility bias." Here's an actual example. A randomized trial of a drug designed to reduce blood lipids showed that patients who faithfully took the drug had lower fatality rates than those who stopped taking it or took it irregularly. Sounds like a good drug, huh? The catch was that patients who faithfully took the *placebo* also had lower fatality rates. So it wasn't the drug: it was some other difference between the compliers and the noncompliers. People who comply and people who don't comply with doctors' instructions differ in personality and perhaps in intelligence as well. These differences cause them to do other things—other than taking or not taking the drug—that affect their life expectancy.[45]

Such differences in personality and intelligence are, in part, heritable. If the compliers differ in personality and intelligence from the noncompliers, their children will also tend to differ in these ways. And the ways in which they will tend to differ are precisely those that affect how well they will do in school. Parents who conscientiously follow the instructions of a Cowan or a Forgatch are likely, for genetic reasons alone, to have children who conscientiously follow the instructions of a teacher. Their children are likely to do well in school, with or without an intervention, just as the patients who complied with the drug regimen had lower fatality rates, with or without the drug.

Medical researchers deal with the problem of compliance bias by analyzing data on an "intention to treat" basis. This means that the division into treatment and control groups has to take place before the experiment begins, and the analysis of results has to compare the two groups as originally constituted. You can't allow patients to switch groups because that destroys the randomization. The path analysis used by Cowan and Cowan and by Forgatch and DeGarmo is the equivalent of allowing the parents to decide for themselves whether to be in the treatment group or the control group.

One of the researchers whose work Philip Cowan advised me to look at was Rex Forehand. Forehand is part of the old guard of the intervention field; he started running parent-training programs back in the 1970s. Cowan's tip led Joan and me to a review article coauthored by Forehand: an overview of the results of two decades of interventions aimed at changing parents' behavior. Forehand and his coauthor reported that parents found the training to be effective; their children behaved better at home. "However," the authors admitted, "research has been unable to show that child behavior is modified at school."[46]

Children's behavior at home is, in part, a response to the behavior of their parents. Anything that changes the behavior of the parents—a parent-training intervention, a divorce, a serious illness—can change the way the kids behave at home, no question about it. So perhaps I spoke too strongly when I said, in chapter 3, to run the other way if you see an advice-giver coming toward you. If you are having trouble getting your kid to listen to you, there are advice-givers who might be able to help. But beware of advice-givers who make more sweeping claims.

Because children discriminate sharply between situations, the way to improve their behavior in school is not by modifying their parents' behavior but by modifying their environment at school. School-based interventions, aimed at changing the behavior of whole classrooms of kids, can accomplish things such as reducing aggressiveness and bullying on the playground. Unfortunately, as Walter Mischel and I would predict, they produce no improvement in the way the children behave at home.[47]

As I said, all the currently popular theories of personality development are based on the assumption that learned behaviors or learned associations transfer readily and automatically from one situation to another—in particular, from the home to other social contexts. If this assumption is false, why do so many people believe it?

The most obvious explanation is that they've mistaken the effects of genes for the effects of learning. They've noticed that some children are aggressive or conscientious or timid both at home and in school, and attributed the consistencies in behavior to the generalization of behavior acquired at home. Evidence that most of these consistencies are due to genetic influences on behavior has turned up only recently—too recently to be incorporated into existing theories of personality development.

But there is another reason why theorists—even those who are well acquainted with the behavioral genetic evidence—make the erroneous assumption about learning and generalization. It's the fundamental attribution error. Psychologists, like other human beings, are prone to seeing a sample of someone's behavior as an indication of how that individual will behave in other situations. This bias makes developmentalists assume that they can find out what makes children tick by observing how they behave with their parents, or even by asking their parents. Their research methods rely heavily on observations of the children at home or in the presence of their parents, or questionnaires about the children's behavior filled out by their parents. Sometimes the questionnaires are filled out by the children themselves, but the researchers usually administer these tests in the chil-

Credit: © Bil Keane, Inc. King Features Syndicate

dren's homes. As Mischel pointed out, how children respond to a questionnaire depends in part on where they are when they check off their answers. Most developmentalists carry out their research in profound ignorance of the implications of the person-situation controversy. When they discover that mothers' judgments agree poorly, or don't agree at all, with judgments made by the children's teachers, the mothers' judgments may be dismissed as inaccurate, instead of being seen as evidence that children discriminate sharply between situations and behave differently in different settings.[48]

Like the rest of us, professors of psychology are predisposed to attribute a sample of behavior—even a hopelessly inadequate sample—to the enduring characteristics of the individual who is doing the behaving. But, as I pointed out in chapter 1, we humans were provided with no built-in explanation for these presumed enduring characteristics: the explanation is provided by the culture. When cultures change, so does the explanation. Alice James, in the nineteenth century, attributed her enduring characteristics to heredity; John Cheever, in the twentieth, attributed his to childhood experiences within his family.

Though talking about heredity is more acceptable now than it was in the 1960s and '70s, our culture still overwhelmingly favors environmental explanations of behavior.[49] The erroneous assumption I've been attacking in this chapter is the result of two biases working together: a built-in bias that causes us to expect consistencies of behavior across contexts, and a cultural bias that causes us to attribute the consistencies to learning.

These biases can explain, for example, the widespread belief that birth order has enduring effects on personality. Firstborns and laterborns do behave differently in the presence of their parents and siblings. When people notice these differences they assume, incorrectly, that they are good predictors of how firstborns and laterborns will behave in other contexts—that a firstborn who bosses around his younger siblings will be bossy in the workplace as well. Popular stereotypes of firstborns and laterborns are based on the way they behave in the context of their families. The reason we have these stereotypes is that our observations of firstborn and laterborn behavior are based, perforce, on people whose birth orders we know, which generally means people we've seen in a family context. The people we've seen only at work or in other public places have contributed little or no data to our stereotypes, because we are unlikely to know whether they are firstborns or laterborns.

The two biases also influence the work and the beliefs of professionals—clinical psychologists and psychiatrists—who administer psychotherapy.

Traditional psychotherapy, which seeks the source of patients' current unhappiness in the history of their early interactions with their parents and siblings, is like a factory that makes sausages out of sausages. By encouraging their patients to relive their childhood experiences with parents and siblings, the psychotherapists are tapping into the feelings associated with those relationships. What their patients say under these conditions is likely to reinforce the therapists' belief in the power of family relationships to shape (and perhaps to damage) a child's personality. Everything about traditional psychotherapy, including the homelike setting and the therapist's role as a substitute parent, is designed to put the patients back into the context of the family they grew up in and evoke the feelings and thoughts associated with that context.[50]

What's wrong with that? Nothing, I suppose, except that it doesn't work. Psychotherapy, like other forms of medical intervention, is now expected to be "evidence-based," and the evidence doesn't support the view that talking about childhood experiences has therapeutic value. Research has shown that the effective forms of therapy are those that focus on people's current problems, rather than their ancient history.[51] The basic premises of psychoanalysis—that every psychological disorder has its roots in the experiences of infancy and childhood, and that reconstructing these experiences is an essential part of psychotherapy—are being publicly questioned and sometimes publicly repudiated. Joel Paris, head of the Department of Psychiatry at McGill University, has done that in a book titled *Myths of Childhood*.[52] Alan Stone, a trained psychoanalyst and professor of psychiatry at Harvard, has changed the way he does psychotherapy and has given this explanation for the change:

> Our problem is that, in light of the scientific evidence now available to us, these basic premises [of psychoanalysis] may all be incorrect. Our critics may be right. Developmental experience may have very little to do with most forms of psychopathology, and we have no reason to assume that a careful historical reconstruction of these developmental events will have a therapeutic effect. . . . If there is no important connection between childhood events and adult psychopathology, then Freudian theories lose much of their explanatory power.[53]

Stone's new focus in psychotherapy is "almost entirely on the here and now, on problem-solving, and on helping patients find new strategies and new ways of interacting with the important people in their lives."[54] He means the important people in their *current* lives.

If you ever took a course in introductory psychology, it's likely that your textbook explained the term *generalization* by describing the famous experiment in which the behaviorist John B. Watson produced "conditioned fear" in an infant known as Little Albert. The story goes something like this. Watson made Albert afraid of a white rat—or, in some versions, a rabbit—by making a loud, unpleasant noise (produced by banging on a metal bar) whenever Albert reached for the animal, and the fear subsequently *generalized* to other furry things. The list of feared objects varies from one account to another, but it usually includes an assortment of animals and a Santa Claus beard, fleshed out with optional items such as Albert's mother's coat, a teddy bear, and the luxuriant hair on Watson's own head.

Everyone who has gone back to the original report of the Little Albert experiment—a 1920 paper by Watson and his graduate student Rosalie Rayner (soon to become his second wife)—has concluded that the stories in the textbooks are, to say the least, exaggerated. The Little Albert experiment involved one (1) child. The procedure was a shambles, the results were ambiguous, and the report was unclear. Albert was a stoic infant and a thumbsucker; in order to get any reaction at all from him, the experimenters had to yank his thumb out of his mouth. They didn't just condition him to fear a rat: they gave training trials with a dog and a rabbit as well. When they tested the infant in a different room he showed little or no reaction to the animals, so they gave additional training trials in that room, to "freshen the reaction." They did everything they could to frighten the child—when he failed to react to the sight of the rat they put it on his arm and then on his chest—but Albert's response to the animals continued to be ambivalent. He gurgled at the rat; he reached out and felt the rabbit's ear.[55]

Despite the fact that the Little Albert story has been repeatedly debunked,[56] and despite the fact that later researchers were unable to produce conditioned fear in other infants using Watson's method, the story persists; it continues to be cited as a textbook example of generalization. What few people realize is that the purpose of Watson and Rayner's experiment was not to extend Pavlov's work—they didn't even mention Pavlov—but to put Freud out of business. Watson didn't use the word *generalize*; he used the word *transfer*. Freud had talked about "transference" and "displacement," and Watson wanted to show that he could explain these things without invoking the unconscious or anything else in the Freudian armamentarium.[57] Watson and Rayner's article ended with a sneer at Freud:

> The Freudians twenty years from now, unless their hypotheses change, when they come to analyze Albert's fear of a seal skin coat—assuming that he comes to analysis at that age—will probably tease from him the recital of a dream which upon their analysis will show that Albert at three years of age attempted to play with the pubic hair of the mother and was scolded violently for it.[58]

Of course, Watson expected his readers to understand that it wasn't Albert's mother's pubic hair that caused the trouble: it was Watson himself, banging on a steel bar "four feet in length and three-fourths of an inch in diameter." I wonder what Freud would have made of *that.*

Watson thought he was pretty clever, but notice that he accepted two of the basic assumptions of Freudian theory: that personality is shaped by the experiences of infancy and early childhood (Little Albert was eleven months old at the start of the experiment) and that learned associations transfer readily from one stimulus to another. Watson's theory that it all boils down to conditioning didn't pan out, but the theorists who came after him were just as willing to accept his assumption that learning transfers or generalizes. Few bothered to state it out loud, fewer still to question it.

The reason why so many theorists believe in the importance of the early years and in the generalization of learning is that they're unaware that the continuities in behavior from the early years to adulthood, and from one situation to another, are due largely to genetic influences on behavior. They see an infant who is afraid of rats and rabbits turning into a timid child and later into a timid adult, and they attribute his timidity to something that happened to him in infancy. They are wrong; it was something that happened to him at conception. The timid infant who becomes a timid adult has, in all likelihood, inherited a predisposition to be timid.

My concern, however, is not with heredity; this chapter was about how young humans learn from their experiences. I've shown that the assumptions that underlie popular theories of personality development—that learned behaviors transfer readily from one situation to another, that children learn things at home which they automatically carry with them to other settings, that their experiences with their parents will color their subsequent interactions with other social partners—are incorrect. Generalization occurs (it has to), but it doesn't happen in this senseless, automatic way. Whether a learned behavior or emotion will be generalized from one situation to another depends on whether the situations are regarded as equivalent or as different. A child who initially regards two situations as different can learn through experience that in some relevant way they are equivalent. A baby learns very quickly that Mommy in a blue shirt and Mommy in a red shirt are in all important respects the same. But Mommy in a blue shirt and the babysitter in a blue shirt continue to be seen as different. Babies are predisposed from birth to make certain kinds of distinctions.

Over the past hundred years, a good deal has been written about personality development. Most of it was wrong. For far too long, psychologists have been constructing theories of personality on the same shaky foundation used by their predecessors. My purpose in this chapter was to clear away the rubble and get down to bedrock. Now I can start to build a new theory.

6

The Modular Mind

THERE IS ANOTHER Dr. Watson who is even more famous than the one who tormented Little Albert. He's the physician who serves as sidekick and chronicler to Sherlock Holmes. In a story called "The Five Orange Pips," Holmes said this to Watson:

> Now let us consider the situation and see what may be deduced from it. . . . I think that it is quite clear that there must be more than one of them. A single man could not have carried out [these] two deaths in such a way as to deceive a coroner's jury. There must have been several in it, and they must have been men of resource and determination.[1]

Holmes was using the word "deduced" loosely. To a philosopher the word has a specific meaning: reasoning from given premises to something that follows inexorably from those premises. An example is the old syllogism: All men are mortal, Socrates is a man, therefore Socrates is mortal. If the first two statements are true, then the third has to be true. Deduction is infallible.

But Sherlock Holmes wasn't infallible—he occasionally made mistakes—and the way he solved his mysteries was not deduction. Philosophers use the word "abduction" for the reasoning process Holmes actually used.[2] Abduction in the philosophers' sense (not to be confused with the way it is used by folks who believe they've been borrowed by extraterrestrials) means finding the hypothesis that provides the best explanation for the data. "Data! Data! Data!" Holmes exclaimed impatiently to Watson. "I can't make bricks without clay."[3]

The hypothesis that wins does so on the basis of probability, not infallibility. The less probable hypotheses are eliminated. This is how Sherlock

Holmes reasoned. Ideally, it is how scientists and medical diagnosticians reason. Ideally, it is how you and I reason. It can go wrong if there is an insufficiency of clay or if some hypotheses are given privileged status.

What Holmes abduced in the case of "The Five Orange Pips" is that sometimes the best hypothesis isn't the simplest. Sometimes there is more than one perpetrator.

A famous rule in science is called "Occam's razor": entities should not be multiplied needlessly. Much has been written about the harm done to psychology by Locke's blank slate and Rousseau's noble savage,[4] but what about the harm done by Occam's razor? The simplest explanation is not necessarily the correct one.

I didn't begin to see the solution to the mystery of individuality until four years after *The Nurture Assumption* was published. What got in my way was the confusion between socialization and personality development. Most psychologists, including those who study children and those who administer psychotherapy to adults, think of them as basically the same process—a learning process that has long-term effects on behavior. I thought so too. I was slow in realizing that there must be at least two processes, with different goals, and slower still (I'm no Sherlock Holmes!) in working out the implications. The goal of socialization is to fit children to their society. Socialization makes children more similar to their peers. But, as the behavioral genetic data showed, something other than genes makes children *differ* from one another in personality. Whatever it is, it can't be socialization.

"The mind," declared Steven Pinker in *How the Mind Works*, "is not a single organ but a system of organs, which we can think of as psychological faculties or mental modules." More than one psychological faculty is needed because a single general-purpose device—a jack of all trades—wouldn't do any jobs well. "The mind has to be built out of specialized parts," Pinker explained, "because it has to solve specialized problems." It was by a process of abduction that evolutionary psychologists came to this conclusion. "No single discovery proves the claim . . . but many lines of evidence converge on it." *How the Mind Works* is an enthralling introduction to those many lines of evidence.[5]

It has been said that research in psychology produces only two kinds of results. The first elicits the reaction "We already knew that, so why did you bother to do the research?"; the second, "That can't be true, so you must be wrong." The research that shows that the mind is a system of organs, not a single organ, is of the second kind. From inside it doesn't feel like a system of organs. We see one visual world out there—"So various, so beautiful, so new," as the poet Matthew Arnold described it.[6] We decide to do something—say, pick up a cup—and we do it. There is only one "me" picking up this cup. There is only one cup and it is in only one location at a particular point in time. It has a certain color, a certain shape, a certain weight.

But the same visual system that provides us with a picture of the various and beautiful world also provides the most convincing evidence that the mind is made up of a collection of specialized mechanisms or modules. The working parts of the visual system happen to be fairly well localized in the physical brain, which means that a minor brain injury (caused, perhaps, by a stroke) might knock out one module and leave others unharmed. Pinker has described some of the weird effects produced by such injuries:

> Selected aspects of visual experience are removed while others are left intact. Some patients see a complete world but pay attention to only half of it. . . . Other patients lose their sensation of color, but they do not see the world as an arty black-and-white movie. Surfaces look grimy and rat-colored to them. . . . Still others can see objects change their positions but cannot see them move. . . . Other patients cannot recognize the objects they see: their world is like handwriting they cannot decipher. They copy a bird faithfully but identify it as a tree stump. . . . Some patients can recognize inanimate objects but cannot recognize faces. The patient deduces that the visage in the mirror must be his, but does not viscerally recognize himself.[7]

There are separate modules in the visual system for seeing color, shape, and motion, but the conscious mind is not aware of them. We see the world as a seamless whole—so seamless that a person with a neurologically intact brain has trouble even imagining what it would be like to see an object change position without seeing it move.

The organs of the mind are hierarchically arranged. The visual system includes a mechanism that permits us to see the world in three dimensions. Several different lower-level modules feed into it. There is one that calculates the disparity between the views of the right eye and the left eye, one that uses shading (balls appear round, not flat, even in photographs), one that makes use of perspective (railroad tracks converge in the distance), and one that makes use of cues provided by the motion of your head or body.

The result is a unified perception of three-dimensionality. If one of the modules can't provide the necessary information, the others silently fill in for it. Multiple inputs yield a single output, and all this is going on behind your back, so to speak.

The combined information doesn't even have to come from the same modality. A perceptual system called "proprioception" makes use of sensory inputs from your joints and muscles to keep you informed about the position of the parts of your body even when your eyes are closed. But when you can see your arms and legs, the system makes use of the more precise (and usually more reliable) information provided by vision to update the perception. My husband demonstrated that in his dissertation research. Charles Harris had his subjects wear goggles that bend light in such a way that objects appear off to one side of where they really are. A subject who tries to reach for something while wearing these goggles misses by several inches at first. But after a brief period of practice she adapts to the displaced vision and is able to reach accurately again. Charlie showed that what changes during practice is the subject's perception of the position of her arm and hand: she comes to feel that her hand is where she sees it.[8]

It's a proprioceptive illusion, and it persists even after the subject can no longer see her hand. If you close your eyes after practicing with my husband's goggles, you will feel that your unseen hand is somewhere between where you saw it through the goggles and where it really is. Two modalities, vision and the joint and muscle sense, have provided conflicting information, and the proprioceptive system has taken the visual information into account in computing its output. The mental mechanism that performs these computations ordinarily goes unnoticed because, under ordinary conditions, it provides accurate results.

The concept of the modular mind is the outcome of a long series of discoveries. Much of the early evidence came from noticing what happens when something goes wrong with a particular mechanism, due either to neurological abnormalities or to experimental manipulations that feed abnormal inputs into a normal system (as in my husband's experiments with displaced vision). Such observations lead to new questions. "Scientists do not conduct research to find things whose existence they don't suspect," the evolutionary psychologists John Tooby and Leda Cosmides pointed out.[9] You may never suspect that your automobile has a device for determining the sequence in which the cylinders fire until something goes wrong with it.

Like the human mind—like almost any complicated machine—automobiles are modular. A brand new car will contain some modules "inherited" from earlier models and some that are recent innovations. Many of the mechanisms in the human mind are shared with other mammals or other primates, but some are recent innovations. Our species is a brand new model—less than 200,000 years old, an eyeblink in evolutionary time—and quite an innovative one. "Groundbreaking!" the critics might have raved, had there been any critics back then. "So various, so beautiful, so new!"

Sadly, the modules of the human mind, unlike those of the automobile, are not replaceable when something goes wrong with them—not *yet* replaceable, I should say. I can offer only my sympathy to the parents of children with the disorder called autism; autism is a tragedy for everyone involved. But it was partly through the study of autistic children that cognitive scientists and evolutionary psychologists like Simon Baron-Cohen came to appreciate some of the capabilities of neurologically normal children—capabilities that had gone unnoticed because they almost always work so reliably.

Autism has devastating effects on virtually every aspect of social behavior, including language; yet most nonsocial functions are spared. Baron-Cohen and his colleagues were the first to propose that the behavioral anomalies seen in children with autism are due to the malfunctioning of an organ of the brain called the "theory of mind" or "mindreading" mechanism. As I mentioned in chapter 1, Baron-Cohen believes that autistic people suffer from a disability he calls mindblindness. "Imagine what your world would be like," he suggests, "if you were aware of physical things but were blind to the existence of mental things"—things like thoughts, beliefs, knowledge, desires, and intentions. Say, for example, you see John walk into the bedroom, walk around, and then walk out. No doubt you could come up with a number of plausible explanations for John's behavior, such as: "Maybe John was **looking** for something he **wanted** to find, and he **thought** it was in the bedroom."[10] But if you were unable to guess about John's thoughts and motives, his behavior would be baffling.

For someone who is blind to the contents of other people's minds, there is no fundamental difference between a person and an object. Here is a classic description of an autistic child, written in 1943 by the child psychiatrist Leo Kanner:

> On a crowded beach he would walk straight toward his goal irrespective of whether this involved walking over newspapers, hands, feet, or

> torsos, much to the discomfiture of their owners. His mother was careful to point out that he did not intentionally deviate from his course in order to walk on others, but neither did he make the slightest attempt to avoid them. It was as if he did not distinguish people from things, or at least did not concern himself about the distinction.[11]

Autistic children don't try to draw another person's attention to something interesting by pointing at it; they don't check to see what another person is looking at. They don't play games of pretense; they don't recognize when other people are pretending. They don't engage in deception. They don't feel pride in meeting or exceeding other people's expectations; they don't administer praise. All these things require an awareness that other people have feelings, expectations, beliefs, and intentions.[12]

Baron-Cohen's theory is that neurologically normal people have a specialized mental mechanism dedicated to reading other people's minds, and that it evolved, through natural selection, to solve the particular adaptive problems of an intensely social lifestyle. Like Robin Dunbar, whose theory I described in chapter 1, Baron-Cohen believes that brains got bigger during hominid evolution mainly because of the need to process complex social information. Hominids who were able to understand the behavior of other hominids—to predict what they would do in a given situation, to outmaneuver them, perhaps to influence their behavior—were better able to function successfully in the network of social relationships that make up a primate group. They were better players in the game of "social chess," a game whose rules are immeasurably more intricate than those of real chess.[13] In real chess you know right from the start who your enemies are and what they intend to do, and nobody switches sides.

To show that mindreading depends on a specialized mechanism—that it isn't simply the result of a larger brain and an increase in general smartness—Baron-Cohen compared autistic children to normally developing children, to children with various types of mental retardation, and to blind children, testing them to see what each could and could not do. The tests showed very specific deficits in those with autism. Autistic children can do things that mentally retarded children cannot, and vice versa.

Baron-Cohen also compared neurologically normal children of different ages. The mindreading mechanism isn't ready to go at birth; it takes time, and no doubt some input from the environment, for it to develop. At the age of three, children can guess some of the contents of other people's minds by their facial expressions and where their eyes are pointing, but it

this is Sally
this is Anne
Sally puts her ball in the basket
Sally goes away
Anne moves the ball to her box
where will Sally look for her ball?

Credit: Axel Scheffler

isn't until they are about four that they can solve more difficult kinds of mindreading problems, such as the "Sally-Anne test," shown in the figure. The child watches Sally (played by a real person or a puppet) put the ball in the basket and leave the room. After she's gone, Anne takes the ball out of the basket and puts it in a box. Then Sally returns. The child is asked, "Where will Sally look for her ball?"

Normally developing three-year-olds flunk the Sally-Anne test and so do nearly all children with autism—even high-functioning ones, even in their teens.[14] They fail to take into account what Sally has seen and what she does and doesn't know; they say she'll look in the box because that's where *they* know the ball is. But nonautistic four-year-olds realize that Sally is unaware that the ball has been moved and correctly say that she'll look for it in the basket. The four-year-olds understand, not only that people have beliefs, but also that the beliefs may be untrue. One of the consequences of this advance in cognitive sophistication is that four-year-olds are capable of deliberate deception. How quickly innocence is lost!

The case for mindreading ability in nonhuman animals is still up in the air; cognitive scientists have yet to come to an agreement on whether our closest primate relative, the chimpanzee, has it. The brighter members of that species occasionally do things that are hard to interpret as anything other than a purposeful attempt to deceive.[15] On the other hand, chimpanzees flunk some pretty easy tests. For example, a tasty morsel is hidden in one of two opaque containers and then the animal is allowed to try to find it. A chimpanzee, it turns out, is not very good at using cues from a human to solve this problem. If the human looks at the correct container or even points at it, the chimpanzee might nonetheless choose the wrong one. Interestingly, the nonhuman animal that is best at using these cues to solve the two-containers problem is the dog. Wolves can't do it but dogs can—even kennel-raised dogs that have had little human contact. Evidently a skill at interpreting human social cues had survival value for the ancestors of the dog.[16]

What someone is looking at is a very useful clue to what they are thinking. The human mindreading mechanism proposed by Baron-Cohen receives information from a lower-level module he calls the "eye-direction detector." This device picks out eyes or eyelike stimuli from the visual array and ascertains where they are pointing—in particular, whether they are pointing at the self. If you see a pair of eyes and they are directed at you, your eye-direction detector signals (beep!) that someone or something is looking at you.

Perhaps only humans and dogs can tell which of two hiding places someone is looking at and use that information as a cue. But the ability to detect whether someone is looking at *you* has a long phylogenetic history—it goes way back. Animals that are preyed upon by other animals need to be aware of whether their predators have seen them. Being stared at is scary (hence the beep); it means you may have been marked as a target. A common response—observed in mammals, birds, and even reptiles—is to go still.

The sensitivity to eyes is present in humans from birth. I've already said that young infants look at faces; well, the part of the face they look at most is the eyes.[17] Eye contact—looking at someone who is looking at you—is physiologically arousing for babies, and they become uncomfortable if it goes on too long. (The same is true of adults, with one sweet exception: people who are madly in love can gaze into each other's eyes endlessly.) When I was introduced to my infant grandchildren, I knew enough to hold off gazing at them until they had had a chance to look me over without making eye contact.

It is characteristic of mental modules that they respond selectively to stimuli; that's one of their jobs. The language acquisition device pays close attention to spoken words but ignores sneezes, coughs, and the cat's meow. The eye-direction detector looks for eyes. In an earlier chapter I described an experiment in which rats made ill by X-rays learned to associate their illness with a taste but not with a light or a sound.[18] The responsible mechanism, designed to keep rats (and people) from eating food that previously made them ill, responds selectively to tastes.

But selectivity on the input side is not necessarily matched by selectivity on the output side. Like a subroutine in a computer program, a low-level mental module may serve more than one purpose; its output may be sent to two or three different higher-up mechanisms. Remember the eye-direction detector; I will put it to use again later on.

The evidence that the human mind contains specialized mechanisms, and that these mechanisms are processors of information, opened the door to further advances in cognitive science. "In this new phase of the cognitive revolution," John Tooby and Leda Cosmides predicted in 1995, "discovering and mapping the various functionally specialized modules of the human brain will be primary activities."[19]

In the absence of clear-cut examples of what happens when something goes wrong with one of these mechanisms, how do we go about discovering and mapping them? In *How the Mind Works*, Steven Pinker suggested one method; he called it "reverse-engineering."

> In forward-engineering, one designs a machine to do something; in reverse-engineering, one figures out what a machine was designed to do. . . . We all engage in reverse-engineering when we face an interesting new gadget. In rummaging through an antique store, we may find a contraption that is inscrutable until we figure out what it was designed to do. When we realize that it is an olive-pitter, we suddenly understand that the metal ring is designed to hold the olive, and the lever lowers an X-shaped blade through one end, pushing the pit out the other end. The shapes and arrangements of the springs, hinges, blades, levers, and rings all make sense in a satisfying rush of insight.[20]

But reverse-engineering has a serious drawback: it can be employed, as Pinker admitted, "only when one has a hint of what the device was designed to accomplish."[21] Fortunately, there is an alternative way to find out about mental mechanisms; perhaps we should call it "reverse reverse-engineering." One starts with the purpose—some job that the human mind might have been called upon to perform repeatedly during its evolutionary history—and then one figures out how a device to serve that purpose might be built. Then one can look for evidence that the human mind contains such a device. As Cosmides, Tooby, and their colleague Jerome Barkow put it,

> If one knows what adaptive functions the human mind was designed to accomplish, one can make many educated guesses about what design features it should have, and can then design experiments to test for them. This can allow one to discover new, previously unsuspected, psychological mechanisms.[22]

What I'm after in this case requires an understanding of the adaptive functions of the *immature* human mind. What does the child's mind need to accomplish while the child is growing up? To put it another way, what are the purposes of childhood? As Sherlock Holmes said to Dr. Watson, "I think that it is quite clear that there must be more than one of them."

Sherlock abduced, on the basis of the evidence available to him, that a single perpetrator was unlikely to be the solution to his mystery. So have I, though it took me a lot longer. A single-perpetrator explanation doesn't fit the evidence in this case any better than it did in Sherlock's. I have come to the conclusion that there are some previously unsuspected psychological mechanisms involved in children's social development. I posit three mechanisms, distinguishable by their different goals, by the different sorts of information they receive from the environment, and by the different ways they process that information. Only one of them can be held accountable for the differences between reared-together identical twins, but all three are needed to explain environmental effects on personality and behavior.

It was the trial-and-error process of natural selection that produced the design for the human mind. The design specs were worked out over eons of time: the two or three million years during which hominid head size was expanding and our remote ancestors were doing increasingly sophisticated things—using tools, making tools, acquiring language, creating art, developing cultures. The components of the mind of the modern human were road tested under rigorous conditions: the conditions that prevailed in the Paleolithic, prior to the end of the last ice age (around 10,000 B.C.) and the invention of agriculture. If the human mind hadn't passed that road test, we wouldn't be here. Our ancestors succeeded in becoming our ancestors because they had what it took to survive and reproduce. Along the way, millions of less successful hominids—the also-rans in the competition—bit the dust. We are the descendants of the winners.

To appreciate what it took to make a go of it back then, it helps to have an understanding of what "back then" was like. It wasn't like an endless camping trip, because there were no compasses, matches, sleeping bags, tents, metal knives or axes, pots or pans, bottles of water, chocolate bars, or cell phones. And it wasn't like the first part of Robinson Crusoe's sojourn on the island, before he met Friday, because our ancestors were hardly ever alone. Being alone was too dangerous for the members of a species as flimsy as ours. There was safety in numbers, so they traveled in groups. They wandered around looking for something to eat, fearful of predators, fearful of rival groups, fearful of straying too far from a source of water. The latter two concerns made them more or less territorial. They had to move fairly often—if you don't plant crops or raise domesticated animals, a small piece of land will soon be exhausted of its edibles—but most movement probably followed an annual circuit and the land they moved over was familiar.[23]

It's hard to imagine what it was like to raise a child under such conditions. A baby had to be carried everywhere for three or four years, until it could walk well enough to keep up with the group. Through rain and wind and darkness of night, you'd have to schlep this wet, dirty, hungry little creature wherever you went. It took tremendous effort just to keep a child alive, and yet our ancestors must have done it, because here we are. Some mental module provided them with enough motivation to see the job through. Anyone who thinks that humans don't have instincts needs to have his head examined.

Aside from the certainty that at least some children survived, we have no direct knowledge of what childhood was like in the Paleolithic. But anthropologists have studied societies that maintained a hunter-gatherer lifestyle into the twentieth century, and there is plenty of information on other traditional human societies—tribal and small village societies that, at the time of the anthropologists' visit, had had little or no exposure to Western culture. The commonalities among these societies serve as clues to ancient patterns.

Under ancestral conditions, the effort involved in rearing a new infant could jeopardize its mother's chances of survival and those of her previous children as well. Therefore, the first thing a baby had to do after drawing a breath was to win its mother's commitment. Should she keep it and rear it? If food or water was scarce, if her previous child wasn't old enough to be weaned, or if there was anything iffy about the newborn itself, the answer might be no. Such decisions could never have been easy; they were made with sadness and regret.[24]

Once the decision was made to keep the baby, the mother's commitment was wholehearted. The baby was carried everywhere, nursed whenever he whimpered. By night he slept by his mother's side. For three or four years the mother and the child were in almost constant physical contact.

Then his mother had another baby. If he hadn't already been weaned from the breast, weaning would come as an abrupt shock, without apology or explanation. The new baby was now the center of the mother's attention and her previous child, three or four years old, became a member of a coterie of children. He still knew who his parents were, of course, and would return to them at night and occasionally during the day for food or comfort, but decreasingly often as he grew older. Even at three or four, most of his daylight hours would be spent in the company of other children.

At the age when they graduate to the children's play group, children in traditional societies are about a year behind American babies in learning to talk. Mothers in these societies are very concerned about the physical well-being of their babies, but they don't talk to them much because they don't believe that babies can understand a word of what is said to them.[25] The children learn the local language the same way they learn the local rules of social behavior: from other children, a little older than themselves. Here's the German ethologist Irenäus Eibl-Eibesfeldt describing early childhood in the hunter-gatherer and tribal societies he studies:

> Three-year-old children are able to join in a play group, and it is in such play groups that children are truly raised. The older ones explain the rules of play and will admonish those who do not adhere to them, such as by taking something away from another or otherwise being aggressive. Thus the child's socialization occurs mainly within the play group. . . . Initially the older children behave very tolerantly toward the younger ones, although eventually they place definite limitations on behavior. By playing together in the children's group the members learn what aggravates others and which rules they must obey. This occurs in most cultures in which people live in small communities.[26]

Nowadays parenting is a job that lasts at least eighteen years and parents are held responsible for every aspect of their children's development. In the old days, parents had more worries about keeping their children nourished and healthy, but almost everything else was seen as the child's job. Children were expected to acquire the skills they would need in adulthood by observing adults or older children and eventually performing the tasks themselves. They were admonished for minor mistakes and beaten for major ones, but no explanations were given. Parents in traditional societies do not, as a rule, give long-winded lectures to their offspring. The adult's conversational partners are other adults; the child's are other children.[27]

But some things haven't changed. Modern children can't count on their families' remaining intact until they have made it through childhood and it was no better in the old days. An anthropologist who studied the Yanomamö (Amazonian Indians who live in the rainforests of Venezuela and Brazil) reported there was only a one-in-three chance that a child of ten would still be living with both parents. Though the rate of marital breakup was low compared to ours—about 20 percent—the death rate was considerably higher.[28] The Yanomamö get their meat from hunting but they also plant some crops; they lead a less precarious existence than people who rely entirely on foraging. In the Paleolithic, the chances that a child would still have both parents by the age of ten was probably less than one in three.

Children couldn't rely on their parents for companionship, teaching, or conversation, and they couldn't count on them to stick around for long. But the loss of one or both parents, though it lowered a child's chances of surviving, wasn't a death warrant because he was a member of a group. He was surrounded by other relatives who might be willing to look after him. Only if he lost his entire group did his chances plummet to zero. The survival of a small, peripatetic band of humans couldn't have been anything close to a sure thing in the Paleolithic, but it was a better bet than the survival of any particular individual.

Though the world held many dangers—predators, starvation, disease—the greatest threat to the survival of a hunter-gatherer group was probably the group next door. Group warfare is not a human invention; we share the willingness to engage in it with a variety of other creatures, including ants. That doesn't mean we inherited this propensity from ants; it evolved independently in the social insects. But we did inherit a taste for warfare from our primate ancestors. As Jane Goodall discovered, chimpanzees can be just as bloodthirsty as humans: they, too, engage in systematic efforts to wipe out other groups of their own species.[29] The main difference is that chimpanzees have to pick off their enemies one by one, whereas humans, with the aid of technology or cunning, can do it in one fell swoop.

According to the evolutionary psychologist Robin Dunbar, human hunter-gatherer and tribal societies are organized in tiers: "overnight groups" of 30 or 35 people, clans of about 150, and tribes of around 1,500 to 2,000.[30] The membership of overnight groups is unstable; their numbers vary according to local conditions and personal preferences. These groups remain in close contact with each other and people frequently switch from one to another, so within a clan everyone has a chance to get to know everyone. Contact is also maintained between clans, for the purposes of trade, finding marriage partners, and mutual defense. Between tribal groups, relationships are likely to be predominantly unfriendly. But war may also break out within a tribe, between clans. Someone might decide that he got cheated in a trade, or accuse another man of seducing his wife, and the matter could escalate, causing the tribal group to split up into feuding clans.

When a human group splits in two and the two new groups occupy adjacent territories, war between them is likely to be sporadic rather than continuous. There will be truces during which goods are traded and marriages arranged. Nonetheless, if the two groups remain distinct, cultural differences between them will inevitably emerge, due to what I call "group contrast effects."[31] These effects work in the opposite way to that of

Richard Dawkins' "memes." Cultural transmission by memes is analogous to genetic transmission by genes: bits of culture are passed from one generation to the next, with successful variations promulgating themselves and unsuccessful ones dying out. That's a reasonable description of what happens within a group, but to explain what happens *between* groups we need the concept of anti-memes.[32]

Anti-memes can come into play very quickly. In *The Nurture Assumption* I described an experiment in social psychology, done in Oklahoma in the 1950s, called the Robbers Cave study. Twenty-two boys, matched in every important demographic attribute, were divided into two groups and treated to a couple of weeks in a summer camp, in a wilderness area known as Robbers Cave. Hostility between the two groups broke out almost immediately and was quickly followed by the development of contrasting customs. The boys in one group gave up using naughty words and started saying prayers together, while those in the other group cursed like troopers and acted rough and tough.[33]

"Humans show a strong inclination to form such subgroups which eventually distinguish themselves from the others by dialect and other subgroup characteristics and go on to form new cultures," Eibl-Eibesfeldt observed. "To live in groups which demarcate themselves from others is a basic feature of human nature." Human groups demarcate themselves from one another by adopting different styles of dress, different norms of behavior, and different dialects. A stranger who dresses, behaves, or speaks differently is regarded with suspicion or hostility. "Xenophobia," lamented Eibl-Eibesfeldt, "is a universal quality."[34]

It's universal and it shows up early. Babies around the world begin to show a wariness of strangers at around six months of age. By then, in a typical hunter-gatherer or tribal society, they will have had a chance to meet most of the members of their clan and many of their tribe. An unfamiliar face alerts the baby: this person might be dangerous. If the stranger approaches too quickly and tries to pick up the baby, the baby will protest vigorously.[35]

But the appearance of a solitary stranger from another tribe would be a rarity in such a society. "To venture out of one's territory," explained evolutionary biologist Jared Diamond, "was equivalent to suicide." Diamond was describing tribal life in the interior highlands of New Guinea before the arrival of Europeans. Most New Guinea highlanders, he said, spent their lives within ten miles of where they were born.[36]

When human groups cease to have friendly contact with each other, cultural development proceeds independently. Each valley in New Guinea,

Diamond reported, had its own culture and its own language. When Europeans first ventured into the interior of New Guinea—an area about the size of Texas—they found it was a Tower of Babel: nearly a thousand different languages were spoken, most of them mutually unintelligible.[37]

Many tribal societies refer to themselves by a word that translates as "the people." The implication is that anyone who is not a member of their tribe is not a person. One Amazonian group, the Wari, go even further. Their language has a term that means "an edible thing" and they apply it to anyone who is not a Wari. My reaction, when I read about the Wari,[38] was indelicate, I'm afraid. Instead of going tsk-tsk, I wrote a little poem about them.

In the Wari dictionary
Food's defined as "not a Wari."
Their dinners are a lot of fun
For all but the un-Wari one.

You see, babies have good reason to be afraid of strangers.

I meant, of course, *adult* strangers. Babies are not afraid of other babies or of children—on the contrary, they are attracted to them. This means that babies not only distinguish familiar individuals from strangers: they also distinguish children from adults.

Months before they acquire the physical and social skills that will enable them to play with one another, babies show an interest in other babies.[39] Their interest increases as they get older. For a child, the sight or sound of other children is an irresistible invitation to come and play. This is true in all primate species. Young monkeys leave their mothers for sessions of rollicking play with their peers as soon as they can move around well on their own. One that is unable to find playmates in its own troop may go in search of them. The attraction of playmates transcends troop boundaries and even the boundaries between species: Goodall saw young chimpanzees playing with young baboons in Tanzania.[40]

Adults' quarrels can cause groups to split up, but children's desire for playmates—especially in places where there aren't many of them—can cause new groups to form. This, too, has been observed in chimpanzees. A young chimpanzee who hears other young chimpanzees playing in the distance will try to persuade his mother to move in that direction, and eventually she may give in to his pestering.[41]

Thus, children in ancestral times were not limited to the handful of playmates available in their overnight group: probably all the children in the clan played with each other at one time or another, and some friendships—especially among older children—might have transcended clan boundaries. Where life expectancy is short, the number of babies and children in a population far exceeds the number of adults,[42] so a clan of 150 or so would have contained plenty of children.

When they have a choice, children prefer to play with other children of their own sex and roughly their own age. Wherever there are enough children and adults don't interfere, children split up into sex-segregated groups. They do this in populous traditional societies and on school playgrounds in modern industrialized societies. But in places where there are fewer children—in sparsely settled neighborhoods in modern societies, for instance—they will play with whoever is available. Thus, neighborhood play groups often include both sexes and a range of ages.[43] It was probably much the same in the Paleolithic. When there weren't many children around, play groups would be mixed-sex and multi-age. When overnight groups coalesced into larger ones, the children might divide into three groups: younger kids, older girls, and older boys.

A child in a traditional society who enters the younger kids' play group will at first be watched over by an older child. Typically the one who is charged with this responsibility will be his next-older sibling, a child only three or four years older than himself. This is the very child whose place he usurped in their mother's arms, and yet the older sibling will show genuine concern for the younger one's well-being and will defend him against teasing or bullying by other children. In traditional societies (and in chimpanzee societies too), siblings are allies and generally remain so all their lives.[44]

But they do not remain playmates, because the age gap of three or four years will separate them before long. The older sibling will graduate to a group of older girls or boys and leave the younger one behind in the little kids' group. And then, at around fifteen or sixteen, the older one will become an adult.

In the majority of traditional human societies, males generally remain with the group they were born into, while females more often "marry out." They may be wooed away or the switch may be made involuntarily. A girl may be given in marriage to someone in another clan, or stolen in a raid by another tribe, and she may not see her parents and siblings again for a long time, if ever. It's less common today, but there are still places where a nubile young woman is regarded as something that can be bought, sold, stolen, or given to seal an alliance. The man who mistook his wife for a hat had a rare neurological disorder; the man who mistook his wife for a chattel is an anthropological commonplace.[45]

For boys there are other hazards: they are expected to participate in the defense of their group. A boy just past puberty may not be old enough to win a wife, but he is considered old enough to die for his group.[46]

Group warfare evolved in primates and in social insects because the winners of these wars left more descendants than the losers (or than those unwilling to fight at all). Nature has ways of motivating her creatures to do what she wants them to do. Nowadays one hears a lot about the horrors of war, but in the old days one heard mostly about its glories, perhaps because the stories were told mostly by the winners. An American who fought for the North in the Civil War—fought side by side with his comrades against an enemy whose faces they could see—described what it was like in an address he gave many years later. He described the excitement of a "fierce gallop against the enemy, with your blood up and a pace that left no time for fear." He described what it feels like when a soldier discovers he is "able to lift himself by the might of his own soul." He was wounded three times in the war and he wasn't sorry it was over, but he was glad to have had "the incommunicable experience of war . . . the passion of life at its top."[47]

Okay, what did children have to learn, back in the Paleolithic, to prepare themselves for adulthood? What did they have to do, or know, or know how to do, in order to be successful in their adult lives? By "successful" I mean in the ways that evolutionary psychologists talk about—ways that would increase their genetic contribution, or that of their close relatives, to future generations.

For social development, the learning tasks that have to be accomplished in childhood fall into three categories. The first involves managing relationships; the second, becoming socialized; and the third has to do with besting one's rivals—or at least not being bested by them—in Darwinian-style competition.

I'll start, as the baby does, with relationships. Before he can do anything else, the baby has to make his mother love him. Then he has to learn how to get along with a variety of other people: his father, his siblings, other children, other adults. He has to be able to tell these people apart, learn what to expect of each of them, and figure out how to behave with each. Crying may cause his mother to offer him milk and comfort, but it doesn't have that effect on other people and, once he's past a certain age, it may not work even on his mother.

As children get older, more people enter their lives and more decisions have to be made. To make wise choices in friendships, alliances, trading partners, and mates, children have to learn to size up people. They have to learn how to tell the trustworthy from the undependable. They have to know whom they can dominate and whom they had better defer to. These things all involve collecting information about people and dealing with them as individuals.[48]

The second category of learning tasks are those involved in socialization. This means learning the culture—adapting to one's group. It means acquiring the skills and knowledge, the language and customs, that people in one's society are expected to have. Children need to learn how to behave in a way that is deemed appropriate in their society.

Because the members of a tribe may not all know each other personally, having the right language and accent, the right customs, and the right clothing and hairstyle can be a matter of life or death. There is a good example in the Old Testament:

> And the Gileadites took the passages of Jordan before the Ephraimites: and it was so, that when those Ephraimites which were escaped said, Let me go over, that the men of Gilead said unto him, Art thou an Ephraimite? If he said, Nay; Then said they unto him, Say now Shibboleth: and he said Sibboleth: for he could not frame to pronounce it right. Then they took him, and slew him at the passages of Jordan: and there fell at that time of the Ephraimites forty and two thousand.[49]

Forty and two thousand might have been an exaggeration, but however many there were of them, they died because they spoke with the wrong accent.

Now for the third kind of learning task. Evolution is all about competition, and one of the purposes of childhood is to prepare children to compete successfully in adulthood. But humans have many ways of competing, and what works for one could be a disaster for another. Behaving aggressively, for example, can be a successful strategy for some people but not for others. Big, strong individuals versus puny ones, physically attractive individuals versus unattractive ones—they're going to have different sets of options. In order to succeed in adult life, children have to work out a long-term strategy of behavior that is tailored to their own particular assets and liabilities.

These three kinds of jobs—managing relationships, becoming socialized, and working out a long-term strategy for competing—are, I propose, the specialties of three separate departments of the mind. I will call them "systems," like the visual system, because each receives information from a number of hierarchically arranged, lower-level mechanisms. The three systems are products of evolution; they are organs of the mind. Like other essential organs, they are present in all physically normal humans, and (though the organs themselves will vary somewhat from one individual to another) their function is the same in everyone.

Leda Cosmides and John Tooby have explained how natural selection has produced a variety of complex mental mechanisms in our species:

> The statistically recurrent conditions encountered during hominid evolutionary history constituted a set of adaptive problems. These conditions selected for a set of cognitive mechanisms that were capable of solving the associated adaptive problems. . . . The more important the adaptive problem, the more intensely natural selection specializes and improves the performance of the mechanism for solving it. This is because different adaptive problems often require different solutions, and different solutions can, in most cases, be implemented only by different, functionally distinct mechanisms.[50]

My proposal is consistent with these principles.

In the next three chapters I will work out the design specs for the relationship system, the socialization system, and the system that specializes in competing. I'll explain how they differ and why we need all three to explain how the environment shapes personality. Why we need all three to explain how children learn, and what they learn, from their experiences with other people.

7

The Relationship System

SHERLOCK HOLMES concluded, in the case of "The Five Orange Pips," that the murders he was investigating must have been committed by more than one perpetrator. In fact, he told Dr. Watson, the responsible entity was a *group*: members of the secret society known as the Ku Klux Klan. Yes, it was a gang of sinister Americans. They had crossed the Atlantic in a ship named the *Lone Star* and were trying to regain possession of some incriminating documents that had been taken to England by the first victim.

Sherlock never nabbed the culprits. "Very long and very severe were the equinoctial gales that year," Dr. Watson recorded in his chronicle. The *Lone Star*, by then on its way back to America, was never seen again: only the shattered sternpost of a boat with the letters *L.S.* carved on it, spotted far out in the Atlantic.[1]

A convenient solution. An equinoctial gale can wipe out an entire group in a single blow: no need to convince a jury that each individual member was a co-conspirator in the crime.[2] The judicial systems of Great Britain and the United States were designed to assess the guilt or innocence of specific individuals, rather than groups. We hold each individual responsible for his or her own actions. If someone is convicted of a crime and it turns out to have been a case of "mistaken identity"—he was mistaken for the perpetrator—the conviction is rightly seen as a miscarriage of justice. It would be a miscarriage of justice even if the mistake was understandable: if, for instance, they were identical twins. Consider this case:

> On March 10, 1988, someone bit off half the ear of Officer David J. Storton. No one doubts who did it: either Shawn Blick, a twenty-one-year-old man living in Palo Alto, California, or Jonathan Blick, his identical twin brother. Both were scuffling with the officer, and one of

> them bit off part of his ear. . . . Officer Storton testified that one of the twins had short hair and the other long, and it was the long-haired man who bit him. Unfortunately, by the time the men surrendered three days later they sported identical crew cuts and weren't talking.

Their lawyers argued that neither twin could be convicted of biting off half the ear of Officer Storton.

> For each brother there is a reasonable doubt as to whether he did it, because it could have been the other. The argument is compelling because our sense of justice picks out the *individual* who did a deed, not the characteristics of that individual.[3]

Our minds go to a great deal of trouble to prevent us from making errors of mistaken identity. Officer Storton made an effort to distinguish the twins but unfortunately he chose a marker—hair length—that could easily be changed. He must have realized too late that he should have looked for something that couldn't be modified so readily, such as a scar or a mole.

There's a paradox here. We are willing to convict people of crimes only if we're certain, beyond a reasonable doubt, of their personal culpability; and yet for thousands of years the members of our species have been engaging in group warfare,[4] the goal of which is to kill off the members of other groups solely on the basis of their group membership. "Thou shalt not kill" is one of the Ten Commandments; yet hardly had the message been delivered than Joshua embarked upon his wholesale slaughter of the inhabitants of Jericho, Makkedah, Libnah, Lachish, Eglon, and Ai. It apparently never occurred to Joshua that God might have meant that he shouldn't kill *them*. On the contrary, he believed he was carrying out God's will.[5]

"Why," asked the psychologist William James in 1890, "are we unable to talk to a crowd as we talk to a single friend?"[6] Why do we shrug when we hear of hundreds of people killed in an earthquake but weep when we see a photo of one injured child? Why is it that getting to know and like someone doesn't necessarily cause us to think well of the group to which he or she belongs—a disjunction revealed by the ineffectiveness of the protest, "Some of my best friends are Jews"?

The answer is that there are multiple systems in the mind for processing information. We have, I propose, two different mental mechanisms designed to process and store information about people. One collects data on individuals, the other on groups or social categories—types or classes of people. Criminal justice and law enforcement are (or should be) based on information processed by the first mechanism; war and bigotry are outcomes of the second. These mechanisms belong to different mental systems. The one that specializes in individuals is part of the relationship system, the topic of this chapter.

The relationship system is the source of many of the things evolutionary psychologists love to write about, including mate selection and romantic love, reciprocal altruism, favoritism toward kin, dominance hierarchies, cheater detection, coalition formation, and gossip. It is responsible for the illusion called the fundamental attribution error. Its function is to furnish answers to evolutionarily important questions like these: Will this person help me if I am in need? Does this person repay favors? Can this person be relied upon to be a fair partner in trade? Is this person a close relative? Would this person have sex with me? Would this person be a good long-term mate? Can this person beat me up? Will this person take my side if someone else tries to beat me up? Does this person like me?

In the first chapter of this book I marveled at the vast storage capacity and tireless energy of what I named the people-information acquisition device. "Unlike the language acquisition device," I said, "which did its best work before your twelfth birthday and then rested on its laurels, your people-information acquisition device will keep chugging away all through your life." Perhaps I was a bit unfair to the language acquisition device: it's true that it did its *best* work before your twelfth birthday, but it hasn't closed up shop by any means. You can still learn new words.

Children start learning words around their first birthday. By the time they start school they know around 13,000 words, which averages out to a new word every two hours. Then, according to Steven Pinker, "the pace picks up, because new words rain down on them from both speech and print." A typical high school graduate has a vocabulary of about 60,000 words; double that number for readers of books like this one.[7] That's 120,000 words you have in your head!—more, I'd guess, than the number of people whose names or faces you recognize, but perhaps not vastly more.

Each word, and each person, has to be given its own mental storage space; it wouldn't do to mix up words, any more than it would do to mix up people. If it was Shawn who bit you, you don't want to punch Jonathan in the nose the next time you see him. If you want someone to hand you the hammer, you don't want to ask for the ax.

Words are stored in what Pinker calls a "mental lexicon." Each word has its own entry in the mental lexicon, just as in a real dictionary (except that they aren't in alphabetical order or in any fixed order at all). The mental entry for a word gives its meaning, pronunciation, and part of speech—noun, verb, and so on. Though we aren't ordinarily aware of knowing a word's part of speech, this largely unconscious knowledge is what enables us to put it together with other words to form grammatical sentences. Even very young children possess unconscious knowledge about parts of speech. When four-year-olds are shown a picture of a fictitious creature and told "This is a wug," they refer to a pair of the creatures as "wugs," showing that they classify the word as a noun and that they know how to form plurals of nouns. When shown a picture of "a man who knows how to rick," they say that yesterday he ricked, showing that they know how to form past tenses of verbs.[8]

Actually, there are two ways to form past tenses of verbs. As Pinker explained in his book *Words and Rules*, the two ways are by words and by rules. "Words" is how we have to do it for irregular verbs like *go–went*, *buy–bought*, and *hold–held*; each form of these verbs has its own separate listing in the mental lexicon. They have to be memorized one by one; there isn't any shortcut. What makes the job easier is that irregular verbs tend to be the ones used most often (this is true in all languages), and most of them are monosyllables.

The other way of forming past tenses, "rules," is illustrated by the children who said that yesterday the man ricked. Since there isn't such a verb, they couldn't have heard it before; and yet they knew how to form its past tense: just add *-ed*. Many of the errors young children make in speech are misapplications of general rules; sometimes they add *-ed* incorrectly and come out with words like "goed," "buyed," and "holded."

So here we have two separate mechanisms doing the same job—producing the same sort of output—and sometimes they give conflicting results. The mind solves such conflicts in different ways: sometimes by compromising, sometimes by giving one mechanism precedence over the other. In the case of verbs, the language system gives precedence to the list in the mental lexicon. First, look to see if the verb has a past tense listed there. If it doesn't, or if you can't find it quickly enough, go by the general rule. Can't find a past tense for "rick" in your lexicon? Okay, then add *-ed*. Children make errors for a while because the entries for *went*, *bought*, and *held* are not yet strong enough (they haven't been stamped in by enough repetition) to suppress the rule mechanism. The irregular past tense form doesn't pop up quickly enough to fill in the blank in the sentence.[9]

There is neurological evidence for these two systems, based in part on observations of patients with various types of brain injuries. Damage to the anterior portions of the language area (located around the Sylvian fissure) sometimes produces patients with a disability called agrammatism: they remember words (though not as well as people with neurologically intact brains do) but have great difficulty with grammatical suffixes and are almost incapable of thinking up a past tense for a made-up word like "rick." Damage to the posterior part of the language area, on the other hand, can produce a disability called anomia—difficulty in retrieving words. You know how frustrating it is when you can't think of someone's name and it's right on the tip of your tongue? Patients with anomia can't think of words like "clock":

> Of course, I know that. It's the thing you use, for counting, for telling the time, you know, one of those, it's a . . . I just can't think of it. Let me look in my notebook.[10]

But these patients know how to form plurals and past tenses. Sometimes they will make up a word if they can't think of the one they're looking for, and they'll put the correct suffixes on these made-up words: "I believe they're zandicks." "She wikses a zen from me." These patients commit the same kind of errors we hear from children: words like "holded" and "digged." Such errors also occur in the speech of people with Alzheimer's disease. A typical pattern in victims of Alzheimer's is that they can't think of words but, for a while, can still speak in grammatical sentences. They use fillers like "thing" and "you know" as substitutes for the missing words.[11]

With evidence from a variety of sources, Pinker supported his theory that the language system consists of two distinguishable components: a lexicon of memorized words plus a set of rules for combining and inflecting them. The part of this theory that is relevant here is the mental lexicon. I believe the evidence is equally good that the neurologically normal human mind contains a mental lexicon for people, with a separate entry for each individual we know anything about.[12] This lexicon is the product of the people-information acquisition device. Aided by the face-recognition module, which I mentioned earlier in the book, it distinguishes finely among individuals, just the way the language lexicon distinguishes finely among words.

One of the remarkable things about mental systems is that many of them provide their own incentives. That's part of their job: to motivate their owners to use them. Children are eager to learn the language; they don't have to be encouraged or rewarded. Nor do adults have to be paid for learning and using new words. But perhaps the urge to do so diminishes over the course of a lifetime. In contrast, the urge to collect and share information about people remains strong; grownups love to gossip, and to listen to gossip, just as much as kids do. It is this urge that makes people read biographies and novels and watch movies and plays, and that makes sports fans want to see the faces of the players and hear them interviewed. We follow the careers of famous people and are fascinated by revelations about their lives. We wouldn't think of voting for someone for president until we felt we knew a lot about him. Even though we will probably never meet him, we want to know: Can this person be relied upon to play fair?

In the Paleolithic, your life or the lives of your children might have hinged on the answer to such a question.

For hundreds of years, the writers of plays, operas, and novels have toyed with the idea of identity, particularly mistaken identity. A woman's husband disguises himself and pretends to be a stranger. She allows the stranger to seduce her. Has she betrayed her husband? Another scenario, this one from science fiction: a machine makes a replica of the husband that is accurate down to the last little molecule—it has his exact brain with all his memories and so on. If the woman has sex with the replica, has she betrayed her husband? The answer to the first question is no but the woman is nonetheless guilty; to the second it is yes but the woman cannot be blamed. There are two separate issues here: the identity of the seducer and what the woman thinks is the identity of the seducer. Put a mustache on a man or cut it off, dress him in mufti or in motley, have him speak with a British or Italian accent, and he will still be the same man. But a replica, however accurate and convincing, is a different man. We don't want Shawn sleeping with Jonathan's wife any more than we want him convicted of Jonathan's crimes.

But Jonathan's wife, if he has one, wouldn't want to sleep with Shawn. According to a twin study carried out by the behavioral geneticists David Lykken and Auke Tellegen, people who are married to one of a pair of identical twins feel, on average, only so-so about the other twin; only 13 percent of the men and 7 percent of the women think they could have fallen for their spouse's twin. The feeling, or lack thereof, is mutual: twins are generally not attracted to their co-twin's wife or husband.[13]

This, as Lykken and Tellegen pointed out, requires some explaining. Evolutionary psychologists sometimes give the impression that mate selection is pretty much cut and dried. First, eliminate Mom and Dad and other close relatives. Second, look for someone with youth and beauty (if you're a male) or high status (if you're a female) and rank your possible choices in order of desirability. Third, decide how high you can go on the desirability index—a judgment that entails some understanding of your own desirability. Shooting too high is a waste of energy and could prove embarrassing, so cross out the top three names on your list. Now flirt with the fourth, and if he or she is unreceptive, try the fifth.

Hold on, I've forgotten about similarity. At least in modern times, people tend to choose mates who are reasonably similar to themselves in characteristics such as physical attractiveness, height, education, intelligence, attitudes toward religion and politics, and (to a lesser extent) personality.[14] But if mate selection were simply a question of finding the person of the desired sex who is most like you, then the mates of identical twins would be more alike than the mates of fraternal twins, and they are not, Lykken and Tellegen discovered. The researchers concluded that the following model of mate selection would fit their data: eliminate half of the eligible population because they are too different from you or you have no hope of winning them, randomly select one from the remaining half, and fall madly in love with him or her. "The heart has its reasons that the reason knows not of," sighed Pascal.[15]

The point is that you don't fall madly in love with a class or group of individuals, or with everyone who meets your basic criteria. You fall in love (at least for a time) with a *particular individual*: your "one and only." It's called pair-bonding. Humans are not the only species that practice it, of course. Monogamy—or monogamy that lasts but a season or that admits a little playing around on the side—is fairly common in the animal kingdom. Its evolutionary purpose is clear: to motivate the male to help rear the young produced by the female. It's worth his trouble only if he has a reasonably good chance of being the biological father of her offspring.

The members of monogamous species, or quasi-monogamous species like ours, have to be able to identify their mates and not make errors of the "Oops, I thought you were my husband" sort. Pair-bonding is possible only if the members of the pair can reliably recognize each other. Birds that pair-bond (many birds do) have to be able to tell *their* male robin from all the other male robins, or *their* female goose from all the other female geese.

The same problem faces the members of species that rely on reciprocal altruism to get them through hard times—vampire bats, for example.

These bats live as long as eighteen years, and the ones that share a nesting site (not necessarily close relatives) get to know one another. They remember which of their buddies are indebted to them and which they are indebted to. After an unsuccessful night of hunting, they'll go for a handout to the bat that owes them a favor.[16]

The methods used to distinguish individuals vary from one species to another. Dogs are famous for their ability to tell humans apart on the basis of smell. But in case you wondered, even a dog probably couldn't have solved the problem of Shawn versus Jonathan. Identical twins, if they live in the same house and eat the same diet, smell alike to a dog.[17]

Although there is some evidence that human babies and their mothers can identify each other by smell,[18] and no question that we recognize familiar voices, humans rely principally on vision to distinguish one individual from another. Hence the importance of the face-recognition module. The neuroscientist Martha Farah and her colleagues have explored some of the ways that face recognition differs from ordinary vision—the kind of vision we use to identify an object. For example, recognizing an object is somewhat harder when it is upside down than when it is right side up, but recognizing a face is dramatically more difficult if it is upside down.[19] You can try it yourself: just turn the newspaper upside down and look at the photos.

Mechanisms of the mind do not necessarily correspond to specific areas in the brain; some are localized, others are spread around. The face-recognition module is localized. Brain-imaging studies have pinpointed a place in the brain that responds selectively to faces; it's called the fusiform face area and is located near the junction of the occipital and temporal lobes. Damage to this area, particularly on the right side of the brain, can produce the neurological disorder called prosopagnosia. People with this disorder don't recognize familiar faces—even their own face, seen in a mirror, looks like a stranger—and they can't learn to identify new ones.[20]

People with autism, too, are notoriously poor at recognizing faces. Brain-imaging evidence tells us why: their fusiform face area isn't working properly. Consequently they have to process faces as though they were objects. Because autistic people find it no more difficult to identify an upside-down face than an upside-down object, they are actually better than neurologically normal subjects at identifying faces shown upside down, though not nearly as good as the normal subjects when the faces are shown in their usual orientation.[21]

Another sign of malfunction of the face-recognition module is a failure to discriminate between familiar and unfamiliar faces, and this too is found in people with autism. Brain-imaging research has shown that a neurologically normal brain lights up in one way to a familiar face, in a different way to the face of a stranger. This difference in neural response is absent in four-year-old autistic children, but is present in normally developing babies as young as six months of age.[22] By six months, neurologically normal babies are also beginning to be wary of strangers, so this makes sense: their brain is discriminating between known and unknown. But oddly enough, the distinction is not a simply a matter of identifying a face as someone you know or failing to do so: there's apparently a brain device that signals (or fails to signal) familiarity and that operates independently, to some extent, of the one responsible for identification.

Malfunction of the familiarity device can have strange effects. A brain-injured patient may say that, yes, this person looks exactly like my wife, but she's not my wife—she's an impostor. The identification mechanism is working okay but the familiarity signal is missing. In other cases, the familiarity signal lights up when it shouldn't and patients become convinced that a stranger is a familiar person—that the patient in the next bed is really their mother masquerading as a stranger or inhabiting the stranger's body. In case you still enjoy learning new words, the first disorder is called the Capgras syndrome, the second, the Frégoli delusion.[23]

These are rare disorders. The familiarity signal usually works flawlessly, as parents discover when they put their young children on the lap of the department store Santa Claus. The children are not deceived by the name or the outfit; they know full well that this is a stranger.[24]

Even in the Paleolithic, face recognition alone wouldn't have been enough, because humans also need a way of identifying individuals to others. If you want to tell A what B is doing with C—and you do, you do!—it's awkward to have to identify B as "the guy with a big nose and a scar on his cheek." If you want to keep giving A updates on B's adventures, the description can be shortened to Bignose or Scarface, but what if B is just an ordinary-looking guy? If the exchange of social information is one of the purposes for which humans developed language, then people's names—some quick and reliable way of verbally identifying them—must have been among the very first items in the mental word lexicon.[25]

Perhaps they were also the first to be forgotten. You don't have to have anomia to experience the feeling of not being able to think of someone's name when it's right on the tip of your tongue: it happens to all of us, more frequently as we get older. Alzheimer's patients tend to forget proper nouns—names of people and places—before they forget common nouns. Injuries to the brain can sometimes produce the same effect: the loss of people and place names, while common nouns are spared. But less extensive injuries can sometimes lead to difficulties retrieving people's names *without* difficulties in retrieving names of places,[26] which suggests to me that the storage of people's names may be handled by a specialized mechanism—a name-storage device that works in a similar fashion to the face-recognition module. Perhaps the reason why names seem to be easier to forget is that the name-storage device has a much shorter evolutionary history. Natural selection hasn't had time to work out the bugs in the program.

On the other hand, it isn't only names we forget. Other kinds of failures in identifying people also occur. We see someone who looks familiar but we can't remember where we saw them before. Or we see someone at a distance and think it's someone we know, but when they get closer we discover we were mistaken. To account for such experiences, Andrew Young and his colleagues at Lancaster University proposed a model of memory storage for people information. They hypothesized that our minds contain a "person identity node" for each individual we know. Recognizing someone depends on the action of "recognition units" that indicate how closely the person's physical characteristics—face, hair, body build, voice, maybe even clothing—resemble those of a known individual. If the match is good, the person identity node for that individual is activated, which then gives us access to other information about him or her: name, occupation, and so on. But the links to the other information can fail to work. The person identity node, then, is a sort of junction where various kinds of information about a given individual are joined together, some of the joins being weaker (or more easily blocked) than others.[27]

Young's model of a device for storing people-information is based on nodes and links. I've used, and will continue to use, the more vivid image of a lexicon, or Rolodex, of people-information. But you shouldn't take this image literally: it's meant as a metaphor, not as a model. The node model is no doubt closer to the way the brain actually works; moreover, it correctly conveys the idea that there are many ways of getting to the information stored for a particular person: we can identify someone by name, by face, or by profession, and once we get to the right node we have access to other information about that person. The cards in a Rolodex, in contrast, are kept in alphabetical order, and if you don't happen to remember the person's name you're out of luck.

On the other hand, the lexicon image does a better job of conveying the idea of a vast collection of entries. We have thousands and thousands of mental storage sites for people-information. Each is associated with a particular individual; each contains (or is linked to) other information we have about that individual. Picture a mental lexicon with a page for each individual you know, with slots for the face, name, and whether he or she is a close relative; plus other information such as occupation; plus memories of the experiences you've had with him or her. There may also be an emotional marker, indicating how you feel about this person. The contents of some slots may be hard to read; other slots may never have been filled in. A page can be set up in the lexicon even if you've never set eyes (or ears) on the individual it refers to. You collect and store information on characters you read about in novels or hear about from other people. Folks you've never met may have a page in their lexicon for you! And they don't hesitate to tell you so, when you're finally introduced. "I've heard a lot about you," they say.

One more thing about the lexicon: each page also has slots for the person's group memberships and social categories. The first things we notice about people are their gender, age group, and race,[28] and these are duly listed on their page in the lexicon. The category information is analogous to the information about parts of speech in Pinker's word lexicon. Sometimes we treat words or people as unique individuals, as when we retrieve an irregular past tense; sometimes we treat them as members of a category, as when we add *-ed* to a verb. This chapter is about relationships; in relationships, people are treated as unique individuals. We will treat people as members of categories in the next chapter.

A word, according to Pinker, is an arbitrary sign that "works because a speaker and a listener can call upon identical entries in their mental dictionaries."[29] A name is an arbitrary word that refers to a particular individual: the speaker and the listener can use it to call upon corresponding entries in their mental lexicons of people. The virtue of a word is that its arbitrary association with a meaning permits us to exchange information with our conversational partners. The virtue of a name is that its arbitrary association with a person permits us to transmit information about that particular person.

Once we can do that, gossip becomes a commodity—a medium of

exchange. We can do a favor for A by conveying information about what B and C are doing. Watch out for D; he's stronger than he looks. Don't trust E; she tells lies. F has her eye on G. If J gets mad at you, you'll have K to contend with too. One of the reasons why *gossip* is a pejorative term is that much of the information passed along this way is unfavorable, which is why it is always a little unsettling to be told, "I've heard a lot about you."

The evolutionary purpose of the people lexicon is as clear as the evolutionary purpose of pair-bonding: to enable us to behave appropriately toward different individuals, depending on what we have learned about them. To enable us to tailor our behavior to the nature of the relationship we have with each. The baby lifts up its arms to its mother but not to the stranger, even if the stranger is the right age and sex. The child learns to avoid the bully but to seek out other kids in the neighborhood. People stop doing favors for people who never pay them back, unless they are close relatives.

"There is not just one 'social intelligence,' " explained the evolutionary developmental psychologists David Bjorklund and Anthony Pellegrini, "but a set of hierarchically arranged, relatively specific abilities that evolved to deal with the variety of social problems faced by our ancestors." Another evolutionary developmental psychologist, Daphne Bugental, has divided the problems of social life into several "domains" and proposed that humans are provided with specialized "regulatory mechanisms" to guide behavior in each domain.[30] These mechanisms may make use of the same kind of information and yet follow different rules. For example, what do we do with the information that someone is a close relative? The information is used in one way if it's a question of deciding whether or not to help them, in quite a different way if it's a question of whether or not to have sex with them.

So the relationship system contains many intricately connected parts. There's a people-information acquisition device that constructs and stores a lexicon of people and provides the motivation to collect the information. There are regulatory mechanisms that make use of the information stored in the lexicon to guide behavior in different domains of social life and that provide their own motivations, the sex drive being an obvious example. Other specialized modules deliver input to the relationship system; they include the face-recognition module, a device that assesses kinship, and the mindreading mechanism I described in the previous chapter. Whatever you are considering doing with another person—help them, mate with them, engage in trade with them, pick a fight with them—it is extremely useful to have an idea of what their intentions are and what they are thinking about you. Information provided by the mindreading mechanism is specific to a particular person (we understand that Anne may know where the ball is but that Sally may be ignorant of its whereabouts) and is stored on the appropriate page of the people lexicon. Or, if you prefer, linked to the appropriate person identity node.

The purpose of the relationship system is to guide the way we behave toward *specific individuals*. To show how it works I'll use as my example one particular kind of relationship: what Bugental calls the "hierarchical power domain."[31] These are relationships in which one individual dominates the other. What particularly interests me about dominance relationships is that they are an example of a process in which pairwise interactions between individuals give rise to a larger social structure—in this case, the dominance hierarchy or "pecking order."

Evolutionary biologists and network theorists refer to them as "self-organized systems." A school of fish, for instance, is a self-organized system. The school moves around in a coordinated way that makes it look as though it has a leader, but there is no leader. Each fish is simply doing what a fish of that species does: responding to environmental cues (moving toward food or away from danger) and, at the same time, taking account of the position of its neighbors. The pattern they form—so pleasing to the eye—results from the fact that the distance between them remains fairly constant as they swim this way and that. To maintain the pattern only two rules are needed: don't get too close and don't get too far away. The definitions of "too close" and "too far" are quite precise and vary by species.[32]

A school of fish is a social organization maintained by stereotyped behavior. Natural selection acts upon individual fish to produce the stereotyped behavior; in this way, evolution can produce patterns that are larger than the individual fish. Natural selection shapes the patterns by tuning the rules that produce the stereotyped behaviors. Evolutionary biologists call this "multilevel selection": the fitness of the individual fish depends not only on how well it does relative to other fish, but also on how well its school does relative to other schools.[33]

The individual fish in a school do not recognize one another; they do not need to. But the individual chickens in a pecking order do recognize one another. If you form a new flock by putting together ten unacquainted hens or roosters, a power struggle will begin immediately. A pair of birds will peck at each other, or threaten to do so, until one concedes defeat, thus establishing a dominant-submissive relationship between them. Once that has been established there is no longer any need to fight: the one with lower status simply gives way to the one with higher status, and peace reigns. The flock has become a smoothly functioning superorganism. Dominance hierarchies are beneficial not only to the winners (who thereafter get first access to food and mates) but also to the losers (who thereafter get beaten up less often and less severely). Both winners and losers get the advantages of being members of a group. An isolated bird is a sitting duck, so to speak, for predators.[34]

The pecking order in chickens depends on their recognizing each other and remembering their past encounters, but their memories are nowhere near as good as that of the proverbial elephant, the one who never forgets. Chickens get mixed up if their flock numbers more than ten (dominance hierarchies are unstable in larger flocks), and a flockmate that takes a vacation is soon forgotten. If you remove a chicken from the flock and put it back in a week, it will resume its place in the hierarchy, but after a three-week absence it will have to reestablish its rank all over again.[35] So a chicken's mental lexicon for chickens doesn't contain many pages and the ink fades quickly. But who would have expected a *chicken* to have a mechanism for recognizing individuals and behaving appropriately to them?

Now let's take another step downwards in brain size. How about paper wasps? Yes, paper wasps, which live in colonies and construct communal nests (those papery gray things you sometimes see attached to tree branches or the eaves of houses) have dominance hierarchies. Colonies are founded anew each spring by females that survive the winter; several females that overwinter in the same hideout will cooperate in starting a new colony. But the cooperation is at first of a belligerent sort: in the early days they interact aggressively with one another. Soon a dominance hierarchy emerges and there is a sharp reduction in fighting.

Among paper wasps, the payoff for being the alpha female is considerable: she gets to be the chief egg layer of the colony. The others lay an occasional egg, but Alpha tolerates no nonsense: if she spies an egg that isn't hers, she eats it. Before long the ovaries of the other wasps recede and they stop trying. They become workers in the nest, helping to rear Alpha's children. They stay because a paper wasp can't survive on its own and because there is always the possibility that Alpha might die and they can move up in the hierarchy (in which case their ovaries will grow back). Also, there is a good chance that Alpha is their sister, so the young they help to rear might be their nieces and nephews.[36]

Believe it or not, there is evidence that paper wasps are capable of some sort of limited recognition of individual nestmates.[37] But recognition, strictly speaking, isn't necessary: dominance hierarchies in this species may be established and maintained by means of feedback loops.

Many biological systems use feedback loops to accomplish a goal. The homeostatic mechanisms that control body temperature in warm-blooded creatures make use of negative feedback loops: too much of something triggers a process that reduces it. Too much warmth triggers reactions such as sweating that reduce body temperature. The two commandments of fish schools—don't get too close and don't get too far away—are negative feedback rules. But the commandment that formed the school in the first place—if you see a bunch of fish of your kind, join them—is a positive feedback rule. In positive feedback loops, the rich get richer: having a lot of something triggers a process that increases it.

Here's how positive feedback loops could produce dominance hierarchies in paper wasps. Assume that winning an aggressive encounter causes some change—hormonal, perhaps—in the winner. This change signals her status to potential rivals and thereby makes her more likely to prevail in future showdowns.[38] By behaving in a certain way and/or emitting the right kind of pheromones, she exudes the wasp equivalent of self-confidence. The wasps below her in the dominance hierarchy might be responding to these signals, rather than remembering what happened the last time they made the mistake of dissing Alpha.

Positive feedback loops of this sort are not restricted to species with wasp-size brains. They are observable in animals that are clearly capable of remembering every member of their group—wolves and monkeys, for example. According to the evolutionary biologist E. O. Wilson,

> The identity of the leading male in a wolf pack is unmistakable from the way he holds his head, ears, and tail, and the confident, face-forward manner in which he approaches other members of his group. He controls his subordinates in the great majority of encounters without any display of overt hostility. . . . Similarly, the dominant rhesus [monkey] male maintains an elaborate posture signifying his rank: head and tail up, testicles lowered, body movements slow and deliberate and accompanied by unhesitating but measured scrutiny of other monkeys that cross his field of view.[39]

The description rings true; we all know guys like that. There are positive feedback loops in humans, too.

The unhesitating scrutiny with which the alpha male looks at the other monkeys in his group is a mark of his status. In the hierarchical power domain, looking directly at another is a challenge. If two individuals—monkeys, apes, or humans—happen to make eye contact, the lower-ranked one indicates submission by looking down or away. If he maintains eye contact, he's responding to the challenge by issuing a challenge of his own.[40]

In the previous chapter I described a mental module that Simon Baron-Cohen called an "eye-direction detector" and which I will rename, for compactness, the "gaze detector." The gaze detector tells you where someone is looking—in particular, whether someone is looking at you. What you do with that information depends on what kind of relationship you have with the other person—or, to put it in Bugental's terms, which domain of social life is currently in play. In the hierarchical power domain, prolonged eye contact means "I challenge you." In the mating domain, it means "I love you." In the first case it can lead to a fight; in the second, to sex.

Briefer glances also have different meanings in the two domains. In the mating domain they are used in flirting.[41] In the hierarchical domain, they are a sign of what the ethologist Michael Chance has called the "attention structure" of a group. The alpha male in a primate group is not distinguished by how many glances he directs toward the others but by how many glances he receives: he receives by far the most. In general, high-ranked individuals are looked at more than those in lower ranks. Because the lower-ranked individual has to yield to a higher-ranked one, he has to keep track of where his superiors are and what they are doing. If these glances should happen to result in eye contact, he quickly averts his eyes.[42]

Rank in primate groups is not a simple matter; several factors are involved in determining an individual's status. Males and females generally have separate hierarchies, with all or most of the males able to dominate all or most of the females. Another important factor is kinship. An individual who has high-status relatives in the group can call on their help in a dispute with the members of other families.

It pays to belong to a powerful family. A recent study of baboons living in a game reserve in Botswana showed that these monkeys are keenly aware both of family connections and of power hierarchies within their troop. The researchers made auditory tapes of the baboons' noisy altercations and then pieced together sequences that sounded (to a baboon) as if one animal was asserting dominance and the other was yielding. The baboons who heard these phony sequences appeared to be more disturbed or puzzled (judging by how long they looked in the direction of the sounds) by sequences that involved status reversals—either a low-status animal getting the best of a high-status one from the same family, or an animal from a low-status family getting the best of one from a high-status family. But they were clearly more troubled by the latter type of reversal. The researchers concluded that baboons classify other baboons both by individual rank and by family, and that they understand that changes in the rank ordering of families are more disruptive.[43]

The results of this experiment also show that baboons can recognize individual members of their troop by the sound of their voices as well as by sight. Either form of recognition will lead them to the lexicon page for that particular baboon—a page that contains, not only information about their own kinship with that individual, but also information about its kinship with others in their troop.

Now we come to the chimpanzee. Dominance in this species depends not only on physical power and family connections, but also on alliances between nonrelatives. When two chimpanzees come to blows, explained the Dutch primatologist Frans de Waal,

> A third ape may decide to enter the conflict and side with one of them. The result is a coalition of two against one. In many cases the conflict extends still further, and larger coalitions are formed. . . . Chimpanzees act selectively when intervening in a conflict between other members of the group. All the group members have their own personal likes and dislikes which dictate how they act. The choices they make are biased choices, which generally remain constant over the years. This does not mean to say that relationships in the group do not change; indeed, this is the most fascinating aspect of chimpanzee coalitions. Why should C, who has supported A against B for years, gradually begin to support B against A?[44]

Something like that happened in the chimpanzee colony in the Arnhem Zoo in the Netherlands, where de Waal spent several years observing the primates. When he arrived at the zoo, the alpha male, A, was a dignified old chimpanzee named Yeroen, still physically powerful but beginning to show signs of age. B was Luit, a little younger but equally big and strong, and C was Nikkie, the youngest and most boisterous of the three, still gaining in size and strength.

For more than two years, A was the top banana. Then B began to challenge his supremacy. C sided with B and their coalition was successful in overthrowing A, so that both B and C became dominant over A. But now that A was acting submissive to C, C began a campaign against B and obtained A's cooperation. With A's backing, C toppled B and became the alpha male.

Such changes in status are accompanied by changes in behavior and demeanor. The alpha male looks very self-confident as long as he's the alpha male but, observed de Waal, "As soon as his position is seriously threatened, the self-confidence may disappear completely."[45] The other chimpanzees are well aware of what is going on. Each adult member of the colony has to know who's currently on top, who's plotting a coup, and who's supporting each contender. The pages in a chimpanzee's lexicon have to be kept up-to-date.

Earlier I said that the dominance hierarchy is the result of pairwise interactions between individuals. That is true despite the existence of coalitions of the sort de Waal described. Chimpanzee A may be dominant over B either because he is bigger and stronger or because he has the support of C. In either case the relationship between A and B is one of dominance and submission.

Dominance hierarchies have also been observed in groups of human children. The cross-cultural psychologist Carolyn Edwards studied the multi-age play groups of traditional small-village societies and reported,

> Older children respond to others younger and smaller than themselves by establishing dominance over them. . . . Accordingly, a pecking-order of size and strength consistently emerges in multi-age groups, certainly in the multi-age play group of siblings, half-siblings, and courtyard cousins found in most of our samples.[46]

In societies where children go to school and children's groups consist mostly of nonrelatives of roughly the same age, individuals who are taller or stronger than their agemates are likely to have higher status, especially in boys' groups. Researchers have studied children in nursery schools and found attention structures similar to those reported in other primates: high-status children are looked at more.[47]

But in humans—even in boys—the attention structure is not identical to the dominance hierarchy. The child with the highest position in the attention structure is not necessarily the largest or most aggressive; he or she may instead be an organizer or initiator—one who thinks up interesting games and persuades others to participate in them.[48] A child can have high status in a group without being at the top of the dominance hierarchy. In humans—I'll return to this point in a later chapter—status is complex and multidimensional.

The dominance hierarchy of a group depends on who's in it at the moment. If A is absent, the remaining members may simply move up a rung or, if coalitions are involved, there may be other repercussions: without A's support, B may lose his dominance over C. When a group splits up into two smaller groups or two groups coalesce, an individual's rank is likely to change. In ancestral times, when human families foraged together in small, temporary groups, a child's position in the dominance hierarchy might shift upwards or downwards whenever the adults decided to make a switch. A boy who could, for a while, dominate all the other boys in the play group might be quickly demoted when a family with a larger, stronger boy joined up. If children in ancestral times sooner or later became acquainted with all the other children in their clan, they must also have learned which ones they could dominate and which could dominate them.

As de Waal observed, the behaviors associated with being the alpha male depend on remaining the alpha male; the ex-alpha has lost, not only his status, but also his air of self-confidence. Whether one behaves in a dominant or submissive fashion depends on one's rank in a particular group at a particular time. That is why a child who has been dominated for years by an older sibling can become a dominant member of a group of agemates—or, for that matter, of any group that does not happen to include the older sibling.[49]

The relationship system is a discriminator, not a generalizer—a splitter, not a lumper.[50] Its purpose is to make fine distinctions among individuals, even between identical twins, so that the system's owner can behave appropriately toward each individual. Obligations must be repaid, duplicity remembered, compatible companions sought out, obnoxious ones avoided, those with higher status deferred to. Since information keeps coming in, the system has to distinguish between newer and older data and to favor the new: What have you done for me *lately*?

The information we collect on individuals is put to use in our dealings with them. Thus, parents behave differently toward each of their children. Thus, children behave differently toward older siblings than to younger ones, and differently toward peers than to siblings. Thus, a man's relationship with his boss is nothing like his relationship with his father. Thus, a woman who falls in love with a man is not sexually attracted to his identical twin.[51]

Humans build mental "working models," not just of their relationships with their parents, but for every individual with whom they interact. On the basis of a brief encounter, we create a new page in our lexicon, and whatever we have so far learned about that person is recorded there. The fundamental attribution error—our tendency to make a judgment about someone's personality on the basis of a small, perhaps atypical, sample of behavior—is a result of the way the lexicon works. Since its purpose is to tell us how to act if we should encounter this individual again, it makes the best guess on the basis of whatever information it has. The best guess is that this individual will behave in the future the way he or she behaved in the past.[52]

Managing relationships is Job 1 for a baby. The relationship system is ready to go, straight out of the starting gate. Human infants are prepared to begin assembling a lexicon of people as soon as they draw their first breath.

8

The Socialization System

ANIMALS ADAPTED by evolution to a group lifestyle are among the most successful on earth, but there is a drawback to this kind of adaptation: the members of these species generally can't survive on their own. Their lives, along with their chances of reproducing, are dependent on remaining members of the group. Hence the paper wasp at the bottom of the dominance hierarchy remains in the nest and the pecked-upon chicken remains in its flock.

In the old days, a human's life, too, depended on remaining a member of a group. But because human groups differ in culture, the behaviors necessary for group membership couldn't all be built in—much had to be learned. The baby's Job 2, therefore, is to learn how to behave in a way that is acceptable to the other members of his or her society. This is the process that developmentalists call "socialization." It consists of acquiring the social behaviors, customs, language, accent, attitudes, and morals deemed appropriate in a particular society.

Socialization makes children more alike—more similar in behavior to others of their age and gender. Therefore, socialization cannot solve the central mystery of this book: why people (even identical twins reared together) differ in personality and social behavior. But the socialization system is an essential part of the solution, because one of the things I have to explain is why children become both more alike and less alike while they are growing up. The ways in which they become more alike do not consist solely of language and customs. There is evidence that children become more alike even in the sorts of things that are measured on personality tests.

The evidence has to do with cultural differences in personality. Personality tests have been translated into many different languages and given to people all over the world. This research has shown that there are systematic differences in personality from one part of the world to another. The differences are smallish but they appear to be real—not due to problems in translation. Broadly speaking, Americans and Europeans tend to be more extraverted, more open to experience, and less agreeable and compliant than Asians and Africans. There are also differences within continents: between, say, Italians and Norwegians.

If there are differences between cultures, there must be similarities within them. Two people who grew up in the same culture are, on average, a bit more alike in personality and social behavior than two from different cultures.[1]

People from the same culture are also, on average, more alike in appearance and in the medical problems to which they are susceptible. Is it possible that some of the cultural differences in personality are genetic? The personality psychologist Robert McCrae has raised this question.[2] Answering it is not as straightforward as you might think, because the data from behavioral genetic studies are pretty much useless. Behavioral genetic methods can identify sources of variation only within the group of subjects who take part in a study, and the subjects in these studies almost always come from the same culture. Such studies can tell us about the role of genes in producing differences *within* a culture, but are uninformative about the role of genes in producing differences *between* cultures.

Fortunately, there are other ways to answer the question about cultural effects on personality. The best way to do it is to study immigrants. What happens when people move from one culture to another? The answer is that it depends on how old they were when they made the move.

McCrae himself provided some of the relevant data. He and his colleagues gave personality tests to Asian-Canadian college students, the offspring of Chinese parents from Hong Kong who had immigrated to Canada. Some of the students had been born in Hong Kong and had come to Canada with their parents; others had been born in Canada. The researchers found that the personalities of the subjects who had recently arrived in Canada were, on average, about the same as those of college-age people still living in Hong Kong. In contrast, the personalities of subjects who were born in Canada were about the same as those of other Canadian college students. Subjects who had arrived in Canada in childhood were somewhere in between the Hong Kong norm and the Canadian norm.[3]

So the personality differences between these cultures are not genetic. Nor are they transmitted from parents to children through training or imitation. The children reared in Canada by Hong Kong–born parents became Canadians. What influenced their personality was not their parents' culture but the culture of the society they grew up in.

Another study, by the Japanese social psychologist Yasuko Minoura, narrows down the time period during which the cultural environment exerts its effects. Minoura studied the children of Japanese executives who were assigned by their companies to temporary duties in the United States and who brought their families along. These children, transplanted to California, varied in how old they were when their parents made the move and in how long they remained there before returning to Japan. During their stay in California, the culture of their home remained steadfastly Japanese, because the parents knew they would be returning to Japan and made efforts to keep the children from becoming too Americanized. The success of these efforts depended on the children's age and on the length of their stay. Minoura found that children who arrived in California before the age of nine and who remained there for at least four years were likely to become completely assimilated and to adopt American patterns of social behavior. Many of these children experienced social difficulties with peers on their return to Japan. Those who were old enough to understand the source of their difficulties made efforts to change. Minoura puts an upper limit of fourteen or fifteen years on the possibility of returning to Japanese norms of social behavior, but above the age of twelve or thirteen the change had to be made consciously and involved considerable effort. Younger children adapted without conscious effort to the change in social norms.[4]

These two studies show that the culture does have effects—environmental effects—on personality and social behavior. But large, complex societies aren't culturally uniform: they contain subcultures. If there are personality differences between cultures, there may also be small personality differences between subcultures within a society. Siblings who grow up together belong (at least in childhood) to the same subculture: they share a neighborhood, social class, and ethnic group. I attribute the small shared environment effects that sometimes turn up in behavioral genetic studies to subcultural effects on personality.

Cultural and subcultural effects on personality are due to socialization; no one questions that. The disagreement is over *how* children are socialized. The conventional theory is that they're socialized by their parents, but the conventional theory is not supported by the evidence.

Nor does it make sense from an evolutionary point of view. The evolutionary purpose of childhood is to prepare for adulthood—an adulthood that is unlikely to be spent in the parental home. People outside the immediate family, being less motivated by kinship, are going to be less tolerant of deviant behavior. The child has to learn to behave in a manner that is acceptable, not just to his or her parents, but to other people as well. That's why getting socialized is the child's Job 2.

The mental machinery I described in the previous chapter won't serve this purpose. For Job 2, the child needs different equipment. The socialization system I propose has ancient roots: it is the descendant of the system that makes fish swim in schools and birds of a feather flock together. The human version of the device is more elaborate—some new bells and whistles have been added—but it provides the same motive: to go where my group goes, to do what my group does.

Consider the challenge facing the child. She has to learn how to behave appropriately for her society—how to behave in a way that won't get her laughed at, picked on, or shunned. What makes it difficult is that the people in her society don't all behave alike. Aside from the striking individual differences, there are also systematic differences in behavior between people in different social categories. Within every society, males behave differently from females and children behave differently from adults. These two age categories, children and adults, were probably enough in hunter-gatherer times, but most contemporary societies provide at least one more, for adolescents. There may also be distinctions based on other factors, such as social class. Adolescents behave neither like adults nor like children. Princes behave differently from peons.

The behavioral differences between social categories mean that the child can't learn how to behave properly simply by imitating her mother, because she's a child and her mother is an adult. She can pretend to be an adult while playing a game, but a child who behaved like an adult in other circumstances would be considered silly or impertinent. Though children can learn skills such as cooking, weaving, and fishing by imitating the actions of adults, it won't work for social behavior.

It won't work even for language. In many societies, children are expected to use a somewhat different language—different verb forms—in talking to their parents than their parents use in talking to them. The parents in traditional French families, for instance, use the *tu* form in addressing their children but expect their children to reply in the *vous* form. Moreover, in many societies (including those in which one of the forms of "you" has disappeared), children use a somewhat different vocabulary in conversing with other children than when talking to adults. The language of the play group is likely to be peppered with dirty words—words the children didn't learn from their parents and wouldn't dare use in their presence.[5]

So how does a child go about learning to behave like a child—more precisely, like a female child or a male child? Through a cognitive process that requires specialized mental equipment. The system I described in the previous chapter maintains a lexicon of people-information and avoids mixing together data from different individuals. In contrast, the system I will describe in this chapter combines data and does statistics on them: it computes averages.

The first step for the child is to figure out the social categories that exist in his or her society. This task is equivalent to that of learning other kinds of categories: for example, *chairs* and *fish*. Like *chairs* and *fish*, categories of people have fuzzy boundaries. Is a three-legged stool a chair? Is a seahorse a fish? Is this person a boy or a man? Traditional societies often provide rites of passage to sharpen the boundaries between age categories, but industrialized societies seem to manage pretty well without them. What we haven't gotten used to yet is the blurring of the boundary between *males* and *females*.

An interesting thing about fuzzy mental categories is that, although they tend to be hazy around the edges, they're clear at the center. We have an image of what the ideal or prototypical member of each category should be, and it's somewhere in the middle.[6] When I say "man," you probably don't think of an eighteen-year-old or an eighty-year-old and you probably don't picture him wearing a dress. When I say "bird," you think of a robin or sparrow, not an ostrich or vulture. The prototypical chair has four legs, a seat, and a back.

Computer graphic programs can be used to blend together two or more photographs of women's faces, producing a picture that is the average of the individual photos. Psychologists have asked subjects to judge the attractiveness of these blends. The journal article reporting the results of the first experiment of this kind, by the psychologists Judith Langlois and Lori Roggman, was titled "Attractive Faces Are Only Average." The subjects judged an artificial face, created by blending sixteen real faces together, as more attractive than any of the real ones. Using photos of men's faces yielded similar results.[7]

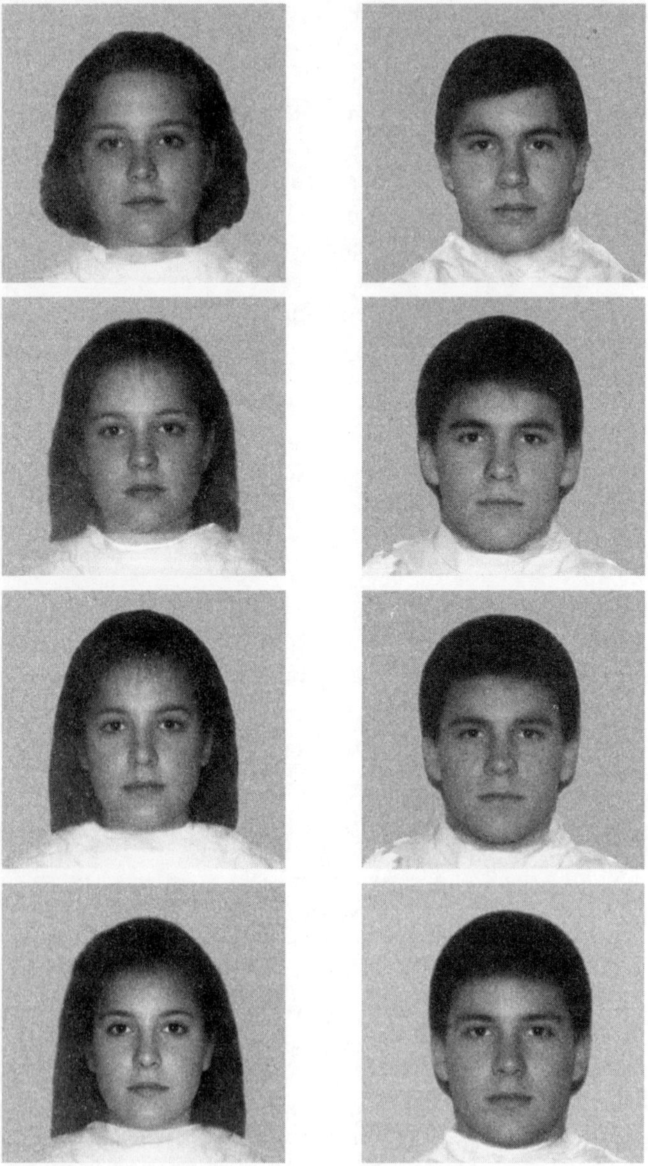

Averaged faces, produced by blending together (from top to bottom) photos of four, eight, sixteen, and thirty-two different individuals. *(Courtesy of Judith H. Langlois, University of Texas.)*

Evolutionary psychologists have explained these findings in terms of an evolved preference for healthy partners. Since health problems before or after birth can produce asymmetries and irregularities, the symmetry and regularity of the averaged face are signals of good health.[8] I have no doubt that signals of good health are perceived as attractive, but I don't think that averaged faces are attractive simply because they look healthy. Something else is coming into play here: the categorization mechanism. One of the psychological effects of categorization is that we tend to see the average member of a category not only as more typical but also as more attractive. This is true not just in judging people's faces; it also holds for birds, dogs, and wristwatches. Subjects in these experiments say that an average-looking dog or wristwatch is more attractive than an unusual-looking one.[9]

And yet unusual-looking watches are sold, basset hounds and shih tzus become cherished pets, and unusual-looking men and women find mates. Some of the most beautiful people in the world have faces that are neither average nor symmetrical. Judging artificial, blended faces is different from judging real ones, and the reason, I propose, is that different mental mechanisms are involved. Judgments of blended faces or the faces of strangers are the province of the categorization mechanism; people who don't have a page in your people-information lexicon are seen simply as anonymous representatives of their social category. But when the face belongs to someone you know, the relationship system speaks up and offers its opinion.

Categorization has its strongest effects on reactions to strangers. Once you know someone, your opinion of her attractiveness doesn't depend on her symmetry; nor can it be accurately predicted on the basis of judgments made by people who don't know her. Your opinion of someone's attractiveness, once you've gotten to know her, is strongly influenced by whether or not you like her.[10] The relationship system sees a familiar face and immediately turns to the proper page in the people-information lexicon. The categorization mechanism, which seeks averageness, is overruled. That wasn't a lady I saw you with last night: that was your wife.

Daniel Schacter, a Harvard psychology professor whose specialty is memory, once played a round of golf with a man with amnesia. Frederick, as Schacter calls him, was in his mid-fifties; he had been an enthusiastic golfer for many years. Though his memory disorder was severe, he had by no means lost everything; indeed, Schacter's first impression was that there was nothing wrong with him. Frederick could converse in a normal fashion and remembered how to do most things. In particular, he remembered the words, rules, and physical skills of the game of golf. He still knew how to swing a golf club, which club to use for long shots or short ones, and the meaning of words like *birdie* and *par*. He still knew that the golfer whose ball lands closest to the hole marks its position with a coin and lets the other player putt first. But by the time it was Frederick's turn to putt, he had forgotten that the coin on the green was his. He had forgotten that he placed it there.

With occasional reminders from Schacter, Frederick played a pretty decent round of golf. So Schacter invited him to come back for another round on another day.

> When I picked up Frederick at his home to play our second round, about a week later, he warned me that he was not a very good player, that he had not been out on a golf course for several months, and that he might be a bit nervous since this was the first time he had ever played with me. I did not have the heart to tell him the truth.[11]

All memories are not alike; nor are all memory disorders. What Frederick had lost was his ability to form new memories of a sort called "episodic"—explicit memories of actual events, which can be consciously recalled and put into words. What he had retained was his semantic memories (factual knowledge, like the meaning of *birdie*) and his implicit or procedural memories (how to play golf). You may have episodic memories of being taught to play golf by your father, but your knowledge of how to play golf is procedural. Sad to say, you may lose your explicit memories of your father sooner than your implicit memories of how to play golf.

We know that these memory systems are located in different areas of the brain, because brain injuries or diseases can wipe them out selectively, depending on where the damage is. The hippocampus and adjacent areas are involved in the formation of new explicit memories (episodic or semantic), which are then stored in the cortex, chiefly in the temporal and parietal lobes. These brain areas tend to be among the first ones damaged by Alzheimer's disease.[12] Mildly affected Alzheimer's victims forget words; as the disease progresses they may fail to recognize the faces of their spouses or children. Newer memories tend to be lost before older ones. My mother, during her long, slow decline due to Alzheimer's disease, mistook my brother for her father. She didn't remember having a son that old—probably didn't remember having a son at all—but for a while she still remembered having a father. And my brother's face still turned on a familiarity signal in her failing brain.

Parkinson's disease has distinctly different effects: it damages the basal ganglia and the areas in the frontal lobes to which they are connected by neural pathways. These brain areas are involved in procedural memories. People afflicted with this disorder may lose, not only physical skills like the ability to swing a golf club, but also other kinds of procedural knowledge such as the rules of grammar—how to form the past tense of a verb, for instance. In the previous chapter I told you about the two systems Steven Pinker described for language: one based on words, the other on rules. Alzheimer's victims tend to lose the words, Parkinson's victims the rules.[13]

Our memory for words is explicit memory; our memory for rules is implicit, procedural. Amnesiacs who can no longer form new explicit memories can still acquire new procedural knowledge. A person with a damaged hippocampus can still be taught to play golf, though he will not remember who taught it to him or when he learned it.[14]

Categorical knowledge is based on implicit memory, not explicit. Amnesiacs like Frederick can learn artificial categories, such as random-dot patterns that look somewhat alike; they can tell you whether a new pattern is or is not in the category. People with intact brains acquire categorical knowledge without realizing they're doing it. Babies have the ability to acquire procedural and categorical knowledge before they are capable of long-term storage of episodic memories. Those babies who, in chapter 5, learned to kick one foot to make a mobile jiggle were demonstrating procedural knowledge.[15]

Babies make categorical distinctions between men and women and between children and adults before they have words for the categories.[16] They are prepared to acquire knowledge about these social categories and other social categories they may encounter later—racial categories, for instance. This knowledge is acquired implicitly, mostly without conscious awareness. Though no one sees anything wrong with implicit knowledge about chairs, fish, dogs, wristwatches, or verbs, implicit knowledge about social categories of people is frowned upon and given a pejorative name: stereotypes.

Forming stereotypes, learning categories, and figuring out the rules of grammar all depend on storing up and putting together data from multiple observations—something the mind does automatically, without any orders from the captain. But once it's there, the rule or stereotype can often be fished up by the conscious mind. Even if you never thought about it before, you could probably tell me the rule for forming the past tense of a regular verb. Novelists and playwrights make use of the availability of social stereotypes, especially for their minor characters, and so did Sherlock Holmes. The great detective was a master of disguise but he didn't disguise himself as a particular person: he disguised himself as a particular *type* of person—a stereotype. Here's a passage from a story called *The Sign of Four*, narrated by the faithful Dr. Watson:

> A heavy step was heard ascending the stair, with a great wheezing and rattling as from a man who was sorely put to it for breath. Once or twice he stopped, as though the climb were too much for him, but at last he made his way to our door and entered. His appearance corresponded to the sounds which we had heard. He was an aged man, clad in seafaring garb, with an old pea-jacket buttoned up to his throat. His back was bowed, his knees were shaky, and his breathing was painfully asthmatic. As he leaned upon a thick oaken cudgel his shoulders heaved in the effort to draw the air into his lungs. He had a colored scarf round his chin, and I could see little of his face save a pair of keen dark eyes, overhung by bushy white brows and long gray side-whiskers.[17]

Watson was fooled: it was Sherlock Holmes himself. The disguise was aimed squarely at the social category "aged man," with a few extra touches to provide the seafaring theme. The ancient mariner—minus, of course, the albatross.

The construction of stereotypes begins early. The mommies and daddies young children pretend to be in their imaginative games are stereotypical adults, not real ones. Their real mommies and daddies are sometimes perplexed when, for example, a four-year-old girl whose own mother is a physician insists that girls can become nurses but only boys can become doctors.[18] This anecdote was reported some years ago, at a time when female physicians were still uncommon. The little girl is a grownup now and no doubt her stereotypes have changed. But no doubt she still has stereotypes.

Research on adults has shown that people who deny being prejudiced may have negative stereotypes of other races. However, this research almost always involves showing subjects pictures (or giving them ethnically identifiable names) of *strangers*. If you have no other information about a person, the categorization mechanism kicks in, and it does its work largely on an unconscious level.[19] But once you have established a page in your people-information lexicon for a particular individual, the relationship system clamors to be heard. Now you have two different systems telling you things about the same individual.

One of the clues that two different systems are involved in regulating behavior is that they occasionally issue conflicting orders. The conflicts between the categorization mechanism and the relationship system are palpable, familiar, and sometimes dramatic. I love Juliet but Juliet is a Capulet. I hate Jews but some of my best friends are Jews. Boys are yucky but after school I play with Andrew.

Remember the study in which subjects judged a so-called grad student to have a friendly or unfriendly personality after having a brief discussion with her? The subjects made the judgment on the basis of how the young woman had behaved during the discussion, even if they knew that she had been instructed to behave that way.[20] I said it made sense for the subjects to do that because they had nothing else to go on. But they did have something else to go on: they knew her (supposed) occupation, her gender, her approximate age, and her apparent race. The reason they didn't use that categorical information to judge her personality is that she was no longer a stranger. She was someone they had talked to face-to-face, someone they now knew as an individual, someone who had been assigned a page in their people-information lexicon. To judge her personality they used the other information on the page, not the information about her occupation, age, gender, or race.

Memories of how a given individual behaved on a given occasion are explicit—readily recalled a day later, readily put into words and passed on in the form of gossip. The relationship system tends to take up an inordinately large share of the conscious mind. Though the categorization mechanism does most of its work silently, it is more robust, more impervious to damage. An amnesiac who has forgotten having met you yesterday may still know how to use words like *fish*, *chair*, *man*, *woman*, *girl*, and *boy*.

According to the social psychologist Susan Fiske, "Culture consists mostly of practices, skills, and motives whose cognitive representation is primarily procedural, not explicit semantic knowledge."[21] In other words, socialization consists largely of implicit, rather than explicit, learning. An important aspect of this learning is storing up information about the behavior of the members of various social categories.

Then the stored-up information is averaged. The categorization mechanism creates prototypes by looking for central tendencies and ignoring what statisticians call "outliers."[22] The socialization system makes use of these prototypes. Children become socialized, I propose, not by imitating specific people in their lives, but by tailoring their behavior to that of the appropriate prototype.

The ability to collect data and calculate central tendencies is not unique to our species; even birds can do it. Researchers observed collared flycatchers peering into the nests of other birds of the same species and wondered why. Turned out the birds were collecting "public information" on how the other collared flycatchers in the neighborhood were doing in terms of reproductive success. They use the information in selecting a nesting site for the following year. The researchers discovered that the birds take into account both the number and the condition of the fledglings in nearby nests. Birds "know what's going on in their own area," one researcher explained. Knowing what's going on involves, in this case, collecting data by observing a number of different nests and averaging the data.[23]

The birds collected public information and averaged it because it was in their best interests to do so. If they considered only a single nest—if their choice was based solely on their own reproductive success—they might make the wrong decision. Perhaps they were lucky this year. But if most of the other birds in the neighborhood also did well, that information is far more likely to be a reliable indicator of the quality of the nesting site. The more data one collects, the more accurate and useful the results are likely to be, if one has the ability to calculate central tendencies.

The child's situation is similar to the bird's. Taking a single individual as her model is risky; what if she inadvertently chooses an atypical example, an outlier? It is far safer to collect as much information as her environment provides, average the data, and use the prototype as her model. I'm not saying that this is what children *always* do; there may be times when they imitate specific people. But that is not how they become socialized. The way children become socialized is by constructing prototypes and using the prototypes as models. The cognitive processes involved—category formation, averaging, and the acquisition of procedural knowledge—are largely implicit. These things could all be done by someone like Frederick, someone with no ability to form new episodic memories.

This theory explains why socialization affects personality and social behavior on a society-wide (or neighborhood-wide) level. It explains why children who are reared in atypical homes may nonetheless become acceptable members of their society. It explains why siblings are no more alike in personality (once genetic similarities are taken into account) than pairs reared in separate homes. The child may have an older sibling of the same sex, and may associate with that sibling outside the home, but the sibling provides only a single data point, which is washed out by the much larger amount of data provided by people outside the family.[24]

However, all members of a social category might not contribute equally to the data. Higher-status members of a group—those who rank higher in the attention structure—are looked at more, which means they have more opportunities to contribute data. The effect would be to shift the prototype in the direction of the higher-status members.[25] Rather than being the mathematical average of the group, the prototype might be a little above average.

I've left out a step. Before children can tailor their behavior to the appropriate prototype, they have to figure out which one is appropriate. They therefore need to know, not only which social categories exist in their society and how the prototypical member of each category behaves, but also which category they themselves belong in. Now we come to the parts of the socialization system that are uniquely human—the bells and whistles I promised you.

The problem that humans have to face is that a given individual can be categorized in different ways, and the categorization will depend on social context—on the situation. But let me begin with a simple case: a female child who categorizes herself as a girl. This "self-categorization," as the Australian social psychologist John Turner calls it, causes her to favor her own social category over others and to use this social category to set the standards for her own behavior.[26] What she uses as her model, according to my theory, is a prototype based on her processing of public information about her own social category.

Like many other mental mechanisms, the socialization system provides not only the abilities but also the motivation to use them. Thus, socialization is *self*-socialization, not something imposed on the child by an outside force. Not, for instance, due to "peer pressure."[27] Rewards or punishments from peers or parents are not ordinarily required, because children *want* to be like others of their age and gender. Hence the plea, familiar to all parents, "But all the other kids are doing it." Parents have a standard response: "If all the other kids threw themselves off a cliff, would you do it too?" The question generally receives, by way of a reply, a deep sigh of exasperation. But the parent has a point. Bison in herds sometimes do throw themselves off cliffs (though lemmings, I understand, do not).

Children differ from bison not so much in their motivation to do what the herd does but in the complexity and flexibility of their concept of the herd. A female child does not invariably categorize herself as a girl. Depending on circumstances, she might identify herself as a fourth grader, one of the subset of good or poor students in her class, a black or white or Mexican or Chinese child, a member of a sports team or chorus, a member of her family, or simply as a child. Her behavior will be adjusted accordingly. On the school playground, where girls and boys form separate groups, she will classify herself as a girl and act girlish. In her neighborhood, where there are fewer children and boys and girls play together, she will classify herself as a child and the girlishness will be greatly reduced.[28]

Anthropologists who have studied hunter-gatherer societies report similar observations. The surviving hunter-gatherer groups tend to be small and there usually aren't enough children to divide up by sex, so girls and boys play together and there are few sex differences in behavior. But in nearby agricultural societies, where there are enough girls and boys to form separate play groups, the differences are very noticeable. Sex differences in behavior are partly biological—the same differences show up all over the world—but the inborn differences are minimized when girls and boys form a single group. When they split up into separate groups, the inborn differences are exaggerated by group contrast effects (the "anti-meme" effects I described in chapter 6). These behavioral differences have proven to be resistant both to the efforts of contemporary American parents to treat their sons and daughters alike and to the reduction of gender differences in the adult society.[29]

When a person switches from one self-categorization to another, the prototype to which she tailors her behavior will also change. This, then, is one of the reasons why people behave differently in different social contexts. It also explains some of the changes that occur as children grow up. When their self-categorization shifts from "child" to "teenager," their behavior is modified accordingly, because a different prototype has become their standard. Later, when they marry, get a job, or have a baby, their self-categorization changes again, to "grownup." One of the reasons why people become more like their parents as they get older—especially when they become parents themselves—is that now they are members of the same social category.[30]

Self-categorizations are exquisitely sensitive to social context and can change at the drop of a hat. Girls and boys in a school lunchroom or playground ordinarily categorize themselves as girls and boys, but the presence of a mean or bossy teacher can cause them to unite in a common cause and to classify themselves simply as children.[31] After the terrorist attacks of September 11, 2001, Democrats and Republicans classified themselves, for a while, simply as Americans.

As that last example illustrates, humans can identify even with groups (such as Democrats and Republicans) composed chiefly of strangers. They can identify with groups even if they don't know who is in them. The social psychologist Henri Tajfel told some boys, supposedly on the basis of a test, that they were "overestimators" and others that they were "underestimators." That's all it took to evoke what Tajfel called "groupness" in the boys. When they were given the opportunity to award monetary payments to other members of the overestimator and underestimator groups (identified by group but not by name), they not only awarded more to the members of their own group: they also made sure to *underpay* the members of the other group.[32] The boys who participated in this study all went to the same school, but none of them knew which of their classmates were overestimators and which were underestimators. There was no opportunity for the relationship system to put in its two cents. Social categorization operates independently of the relationship system, just as the system for generating the past tense of a regular verb operates independently of the system for retrieving the past tense of an irregular verb.

Though a word like "overestimators" can create a brand new social category, categories don't require names. Babies, as I said, show awareness of social categories before they've had time to learn any words. Chimpanzees, too, are aware of social categories—at least the two basic ones, "us" and "them." Jane Goodall described what happened when the chimpanzee troop she was watching split up into two groups of unequal size. The more numerous group went to war against the smaller one, systematically picking off its members one by one and fatally injuring them, until the smaller group was wiped out.[33] The fact that the members of these groups were familiar to one another—they had played together in their youth—was not enough to avert the outcome. When push came to shove, groupness overrode the relationship system.

For a chimpanzee, familiarity is not sufficient to evoke groupness but it is necessary. A chimpanzee can never regard a stranger as one of *us*: an unfamiliar chimpanzee is automatically regarded as one of *them*. Only humans are capable of expanding the social category with which they identify beyond the circle of their close acquaintances, even beyond the circle of their tribe. The biblical story of the Good Samaritan illustrates what can happen when a human being categorizes himself simply as a human being.

What's unique about human groups is that they no longer have to be real groups: they can be virtual groups. The group has become a concept, an abstract category like *chair* or *verb*. The members of a social category do not have to gather together in one place; a little girl can identify herself as a girl and form a mental prototype of a girl even though she may never have seen an actual group of girls (girls usually play in pairs). Nor is personal contact required. A child can identify with a social category even if its members reject her. She can identify with a social category even if nobody but herself believes she belongs in it. Occasionally, despite the best efforts of their parents, children identify with a gender category that doesn't correspond to their biological sex, or doesn't correspond to the gender category to which they've been assigned by well-meaning but misguided physicians.[34]

Brain size ballooned during hominid evolution. The result was a primate, *Homo sapiens*, that could form a concept of a group and apply the motivations and emotions originally associated with actual groups to the conceptual group. These new cognitive abilities enabled humans to form larger groups without a loss of groupness. The size of the group was now, in effect, unlimited, because its members didn't have to be personally acquainted with one another.

Natural selection acts on individuals, not on groups. But, as I said in the previous chapter when I was talking about schools of fish, evolution can produce patterns on the group level by tuning the characteristics of the individuals that make up the group. The fitness of a group-adapted individual depends not only on how it does relative to other individuals within its group, but also on how its group does relative to other groups. In species that go in for group-against-group warfare, such as chimpanzees, humans, and ants, bigger groups are capable of wiping out smaller ones. Hence individuals adapted to living in larger groups have an evolutionary edge. As E. O. Wilson observed, the ability to form larger groups can give individuals who inherit this ability a "decisive advantage" over their competitors.[35] This decisive advantage may be the reason why we are still here and all the other hominid species—our family tree produced a fair number of them—are gone.

"I'm not that good at relationships," confessed the private investigator Kinsey Millhone in *"N" Is for Noose.*[36] She was explaining why her marriages never work out and why she doesn't want to marry, or even live with, her current lover. As I mentioned at the beginning of the book, Kinsey and I differ in this respect: I have no problem with relationships. I am on good terms with all the members of my family and have a number of friends who are dear to me. But as a child I flunked socialization.

The mental organs I describe in this book are part of human nature. Every normal human brain comes equipped with them, just as every normal human body comes equipped with arms and legs. But arms and legs vary from one individual to another—some people can lift heavier weights or run faster—and there are individual differences in mental organs too: differences, for example, in the strengths of the motivations they provide. There are people with an unusually powerful sex drive, people who would rather eat than do anything else, and people with a strong urge to nurture small creatures. There are those who are good at relationships and those who aren't.

My Achilles' heel is the socialization system. Like "Z," the ant played by Woody Allen in the movie *Antz*, I am deficient in the motivation to affiliate with a group and to conform to the group's standards. Here's Z:

> I was not cut out to be a worker, I'll tell you right now. I, I feel physically inadequate. I—my whole life, I've never—I've *never* been able to lift more than ten times my own body weight.

Wouldn't you think that Woody Allen, of all people, would have heard of Ernst and Angst? Apparently not. Z's explanation for why he lacked the urge to dig tunnels was based on birth order:

> I think everything must go back to the fact that I had a very anxious childhood. You know, my, my mother never had time for me. You know, when you're—when you're the middle child in a family of five million, you don't get any attention.

I had a pretty anxious childhood too, even though I was a firstborn. You know, I was—I was rejected by my, my peers. But I think my motivational deficiencies were the cause, rather than the result, of the rejection. Not only did I fail to figure out why the other kids my age didn't accept me: I didn't even *try* to figure it out. I remember a day when a girl in my class—a popular girl who was visiting my house because her mother was my mother's best friend—took me aside and gave me a lecture on what I should do to make myself more acceptable. It included some guidance on how to dress properly, a topic I have always found extremely boring. In fact, I found the whole lecture boring and mystifying, and paid no attention to it. It was only years later that I realized it was meant as a kindness: my classmate had been trying to help me.

I am not totally lacking in the motivation to conform; it's just weak. I did eventually become more or less socialized, though I suspect in my case it was more a matter of learning how *not* to behave in order to avoid social punishment. But I've never been interested in joining clubs and I belong to no organized religion. I was kicked out of graduate school at Harvard because, the letter from the Department of Psychology informed me, they doubted I would ever fit their "stereotype of what an experimental psychologist should be." They were right: I'm no good at fitting stereotypes.

A child whose socialization system is doing its job well will score high in what developmentalists call "group acceptance." But this child may not be particularly good at managing personal relationships. Research has shown that children who rate high on acceptance by their peer group do not necessarily have successful friendships, and that children who are poorly accepted may nonetheless be good at making and keeping friends.[37] Even during the years when none of my classmates would talk to me, I did have one close friend; she lived next door and was three grades behind me in school.

Group acceptance and success in friendships are largely, but not completely, unrelated. I wouldn't expect them to be completely unrelated because some qualities—an attractive appearance, an amiable disposition, intelligence, imagination—stand a child in good stead in every domain of social life. But researchers have found that acceptance and friendship make independent contributions to children's satisfaction with their lives and have distinguishable implications for adult outcomes. A longitudinal study showed that group acceptance or rejection in childhood was a fairly good predictor of "overall life status" in adulthood, but that success in friendships was not. Doing well in childhood friendships had "unique predictive implications only for positive relationships with family members."[38] Having good relationships in childhood means you're good at relationships. It doesn't mean you're good at anything else.

My description of the socialization system is still not enough to explain how children get socialized. Okay, children form social categories, figure out which one they belong in, and tailor their behavior to that of the prototype for their category. But how do the other kids in their category get socialized? They can't just be copying one another, because we know that cultures do get passed down from one generation to another. There has to be some input from the older generation.

To explain how cultures are passed down, I'll again use my favorite example, language. Acquiring the local language and accent is part of socialization, and once they're acquired they become social behaviors, sensitive to context. Also, as I mentioned in an earlier chapter, which language or accent someone uses is determined entirely by the environment; genes play no role. If children speak the same language or use the same accent as their parents, we know it isn't due to heredity. Whereas if they hold the same political attitudes as their parents, or have the same positive or negative feelings about going to church or reading books, these similarities can be partly inherited. The heritability of attitude to the death penalty is .50; to organized religion, .46; and to reading books, .37.[39]

Here's how it works for language. In modern societies most children learn the local language at home from their parents. When the child starts school or goes outside to play, she finds that the language she learned at home is also spoken outside the home, so she keeps using it. The result is that the language of the child matches that of her parents: the parents have succeeded in passing on their language to their child. But it works this way only if the parents speak the same language as the other parents in the community. If the child's parents happen to speak a different language at home, she will first acquire her parents' language and then find, when she goes outside, that the people out there speak a different language. In this case the child will learn the language used outside the home—the language of her peers—and will soon begin to favor it over the one she learned from her parents. The children of immigrants often forget how to speak the language of their parents, unless they have an opportunity to use it outside the home. They will speak the language of their community without an accent. That is, they will speak it with the same accent as their peers.[40]

Other aspects of socialization are passed on in the same way. The child learns things from her parents and siblings and takes them with her when she starts to play with children outside her family. If what she learned agrees with what she finds out there—if the other children are following the same customs or expressing the same attitudes—then she will retain what she learned at home. If they don't agree, if she finds herself out of step with the others, she will change. The socialization system (if it is working properly) will signal a discrepancy between her behavior and that of the prototype for her social category, and will motivate her to reduce that discrepancy.

In traditional societies, children don't actually learn much from their parents; they are socialized mainly in the children's play group. Play groups pass on languages and customs the same way they pass on children's games: the younger children learn the vocabulary and rules from the older ones. The games, language, and customs can remain unchanged for hundreds of years, while generations of children enter the group, learn the rules from the older children, and pass them down in turn to younger children before graduating from the group. The children's culture matches the parents' culture because the children and the parents were socialized in the same way, by the same groups, whose membership changed over the years but whose games and culture remained constant.[41]

Even in a complex, industrialized society, some aspects of the culture can remain relatively constant for generations. It will depend in part on how homogeneous the society is. In a homogeneous society, what one child learns at home is likely to agree quite well with what her peers learned at home, so what she brings to the peer group is fine—she needn't change. In most parts of the United States, nearly everyone speaks English, and generation after generation of children learn English at home and continue to speak English in adulthood. The parents assume, and most developmentalists do too, that the children speak English in adulthood because that's what their parents taught them. They have no observations to tell them that this assumption is incorrect.

Nonetheless, they are correct in assuming that parents have the power to determine their children's language and accent. The way parents exert this power is by deciding where their children will grow up and which schools they will attend. One of the reasons upper-class British parents send their children to boarding schools like Eton and Harrow is so they will acquire the proper accent.[42] Britain's former prime minister Margaret Thatcher, whose father was a grocer, acquired her plummy accent by winning a scholarship to a fancy private school. Children who go to these schools don't just acquire an accent: they acquire an upper-class culture as well. The language and culture are passed on by the students in these schools in the same way that children's games are passed on by the play groups in tribal societies.

Many people explain their actions or beliefs by saying "I was raised that way," by which they mean that they got their attitudes toward honesty, hard work, or whatever, from their parents. It's true that they might have first heard these principles expressed by their parents, but they retained them because they agreed with what they encountered outside the home. They agreed because their schoolmates were hearing the same views expressed by *their* parents. Someone who says "I was raised that way" is implying that there was something unusual about the way she was raised, but the actions or beliefs in question are almost always commonplace within the subculture to which the speaker belongs. In the pages of the *New York Times*, the daughter of a Nobel Prize–winner in physics attributed her success to her father's advice to "maintain the highest standards"; the son of a Korean Airlines executive attributed his success to having learned from his father "that with hard work and perseverance you can overcome a lot of things."[43]

People have a tendency to attribute their actions to what they remember, and—thanks to the way the relationship system hogs the conscious mind—they remember their parents. But culture consists largely of behaviors, attitudes, and knowledge acquired through implicit learning. Your memories therefore cannot be relied upon to give you accurate information about how you were socialized. What the conscious mind does, when it lacks an explanation for something, is to use whatever material it has and make up a plausible story.[44]

Many developmentalists believe they can improve children's behavior outside the home—make them less aggressive or more amenable to instruction—by modifying the parents' child-rearing methods. Such interventions, I concluded in chapter 5, may improve children's behavior at home but are ineffective in improving their behavior in school. The socialization system can explain why some kinds of interventions succeed and others fail.

I'll again use my favorite example, language. This is a story of two men who spent their lives pursuing an improbable goal: they wanted to change people's language. As far as I know, they never met; but these two Eastern European Jews were born within a few hundred miles and a few hundred days of each other. Eliezer Ben-Yehuda was born in Lithuania in 1858; Ludwik Lejzer Zamenhof was born in Poland in 1859. Ben-Yehuda's ambition was to revive Hebrew as a spoken language so that Jews from all different countries would have a common language in which to converse. Zamenhof's ambition was even loftier: he wanted a common language for everyone on earth. Since no existing language was good enough for his purpose, he created one. He named it Esperanto.

Zamenhof succeeded in recruiting a remarkable number of people to his cause. There are hundreds of thousands of Esperanto users in the world; they belong to Esperanto clubs and publish Esperanto magazines. Some users even teach the language to their children.[45] And yet, as an intervention, the Esperanto movement failed. There are few, if any, native speakers of Esperanto; it remains a second (or, more commonly, third or fourth) language for the dedicated adults who speak or write it.

Ben-Yehuda's task was not a whole lot easier than Zamenhof's. Reviving a dead language—Hebrew hadn't been used for ordinary conversation for two thousand years—required almost as many arbitrary decisions, and almost as much creativity, as constructing one from scratch. Jews in different parts of the world had different ways of pronouncing Hebrew words; Ben-Yehuda decided which pronunciations to use. A greater challenge was the vocabulary, or lack thereof. Many of the nouns and verbs needed to get along in the modern world didn't exist in ancient Hebrew. Ben-Yehuda had to invent them.

He married a woman who shared his ideals; they moved to Jerusalem and had a child—a boy who became the first native speaker of Hebrew in two thousand years. The child learned Hebrew because he had no choice: it was the only language his mother and father spoke in his presence. Ben-Yehuda was fanatical about preventing his son from hearing other languages. On one occasion he erupted in anger when he caught his wife singing a lullaby to the child in her native Russian.[46]

So the boy spoke Hebrew. But what good did that do, when their neighbors all spoke other languages? Whom could the child talk to, other than his parents and, later, his younger brothers and sisters?

There was only one solution to the problem, and Ben-Yehuda knew what it was: Hebrew would have to become the language used in the schools. He accepted a position as a schoolteacher, with the provision that he would be permitted to teach in Hebrew. The Jerusalem school in which he taught became the first in which Hebrew was used (for some subjects, at least) as the language of instruction.

But it was an uphill battle; Ben-Yehuda didn't win it in his lifetime. Hebrew as a spoken language didn't make much headway until a generation later, when a wave of idealistic new immigrants arrived in Palestine and formed little communities. The communities created schools, and the children who went to these schools were taught in Hebrew. Hebrew became the children's "native language," though it wasn't the native language of their parents, because it was the language they used with one another. The interventionists who succeeded were not those who made Hebrew the language of the home but those who made it the language of the school.[47]

This example shows how much power parents can have when they get together with other like-minded parents. It works for other aspects of socialization as well. The Amish and the Hutterites prevent their children from being assimilated into the majority culture by sending their children to schools they run themselves—schools in which all the students are offspring of Amish or Hutterite parents.

Ordinary run-of-the-mill American parents do the same sort of thing (though with less dramatic results) when they decide to live in a certain neighborhood or to send their children to a certain school. In many cases, these decisions are based on the feeling that they have something in common with the other people in the neighborhood or with the other parents whose children go to the school. Thus, Republicans and Democrats tend to rear their children in places where the majority of their neighbors belong to their political party. College-educated parents rear their children in neighborhoods where most of the parents are college educated. And parents who think religion is important send their children to religious schools.

Attitudes toward intellectual activities and academic achievement are part of socialization. Different subcultures within our society—different socioeconomic classes or racial or ethnic groups—have different attitudes regarding the importance of education; their members tend to choose different leisure-time activities. Even within a single classroom, kids may split up into subgroups with contrasting attitudes toward schoolwork. This is the anti-meme effect I've mentioned before.

A difference in attitudes towards intellectual pursuits can have important repercussions. Time spent doing schoolwork—or reading books, going to museums, or performing chemistry experiments—is time well spent, because these things can increase a child's IQ. A child who enjoys such activities or considers them important is likely to end up with a higher IQ than one who turns up her nose at them.[48]

Some neighborhoods or subcultures foster more positive attitudes toward academic and intellectual achievement than others. In the mythical town of Lake Wobegon, everyone believes in the value of hard work, nobody sneers at good students, and all the children are above average.[49]

The socialization system makes children more alike in the ways that are affected by socialization, and IQ is one of the things affected, in this indirect way, by socialization. So two children who grow up in the same neighborhood or go to the same school will, on average, be more alike in IQ than two who grow up in different neighborhoods or go to different schools. This means that in a behavioral genetic study, especially if an effort is made to include subjects from more than one subculture or socioeconomic class, there may be a measurable effect of shared environment on IQ. Twins reared together are a little more alike in IQ than those separated in infancy and reared in separate homes.[50]

The socialization system is responsible for some of the strongest emotions we feel, and some of the nastiest. In human warfare, as in ant warfare and chimpanzee warfare, it is standard practice for the victors to show no mercy to the losers. The losers are "them" and are treated accordingly. Simply being told that he's an overestimator can make a schoolboy feel favorably disposed to other overestimators and mildly hostile to underestimators.

Two famous and never-to-be-repeated experiments in social psychology demonstrate how easy it is for social categorization to lead to hostility and thence to violence. The two groups of eleven-year-old boys at the Robbers Cave summer camp went to war against each other. They got into fistfights, raided each others' cabins (where they stole or destroyed each other's property), and filled socks with stones to prepare for retaliatory raids. The subjects in the second study were male college students, prescreened to make sure they were all in good mental health, and then randomly divided into two groups: "prisoners" and "guards." Within a few days, the guards were mistreating the prisoners and finding loathsome ways to humiliate them. The experiment had to be brought to a halt before its scheduled completion date.[51]

The power of groupness was brought home to me while I was watching a golf game on television. Golf is a game that ordinarily pits individual against individual, and one of the pleasures for the viewer is the opportunity to get to know the players: people from all over the world, varying in color, language, accent, body type, age, personality, and skill, all competing with one another for trophies and ridiculously large sums of money. All wanting very much to win.

But once in a while golf is played as a team sport. The Presidents Cup competition in November 2003 pitted a team of twelve American golfers against an "International Team" of twelve golfers from six different countries. On the final day of the tournament, with the score very close, a player for the International Team, Nick Price, missed a putt. If he had made it, his team would have won; as it was, the tournament ended in a tie. Price was so upset when his ball rolled by the cup that he broke his putter over his knee.

I have often seen golfers miss crucial putts in ordinary tournaments, and sometimes they let their disappointment show, but I had never before seen anyone break a golf club. And Nick Price is normally an easygoing guy who never loses his cool. But team play evokes stronger emotions than tournaments in which individuals are competing only for themselves.[52] The emotions are evoked even if the team is a short-lived, artificial construct composed of twelve golfers from six different countries, some of whom hardly knew each other before the competition began.

Far back in our evolutionary history, "us" was a real group in which all the members knew one another and most of them were related. The strong emotions associated with groupness were inherited from those ancestors. They served the same purpose, and were passed down in the same way, as the instinct that impels a bee to give up its life to defend its hive.

The mental system that enables children to adapt to their culture works differently from the one used for managing personal relationships; the two systems rely on different kinds of memory. Socialization is a robust form of learning that is carried out at a level not fully accessible to the conscious mind. Important things go on during childhood that we are not aware of at the time and cannot remember afterwards.

I said at the beginning of this chapter that the socialization system can't explain personality differences because it makes people within a culture (or people in a given social category within a culture) more alike in behavior. But just as we have to take account of the effects of genetic effects on personality before we can get a clear picture of environmental effects, we also have to take account of the effects of the relationship system and the socialization system before we can get a clear picture of what the third system does.

The reason why it has been so difficult to distinguish the effects of these three systems from one another and from the effects of genes is that they often combine to produce a single output. Several different visual mechanisms can combine to produce a unified perception of three-dimensionality; likewise, several different mental mechanisms can simultaneously influence social behavior—for example, emotional expressiveness. Whether, at a given point in time, you bottle up your emotions or blow your cool depends in part on your innate predispositions. It also depends on the culture you were reared in: in some societies, people are expected to keep a stiff upper lip. It also depends on whether you are talking to your father or your boss, and whether you are on your own or are a member of a group. It also depends on a long-term process of personality development, which is the subject of the next chapter.

What I've been doing all this time is paring away the alternatives. Uncovering and eliminating suspects that left confusing clues. Peeling off masks. Now at last I'm ready to identify the perpetrator, the mental system responsible for human individuality.

9

The Status System

HEEDING OCCAM'S advice about not multiplying entities, many scientists have spent their careers trying to force ten pounds of data into five-pound theories. They would have done better to listen to Einstein, who gave similar advice but phrased it in a wiser way. Make things as simple as you can, he said, but *no simpler.*

There is good evidence for the existence of both the systems I described in the previous two chapters, but neither can solve the central mystery of this book: why identical twins who grow up in the same home differ so much in personality. The socialization system makes reared-together twins more alike in behavior and personality. The relationship system produces no long-term effects on personality—only short-term adjustments that enable people to behave appropriately with a variety of social partners. To solve the mystery we need a third entity, which I will call the status system.[1]

The purpose of this system is the baby's Job 3: to compete successfully. I'm talking now about competition within the group—classic Darwinian competition. To compete with one's groupmates is to strive for status; the goal is to be better than one's groupmates. "Humans everywhere pursue status," observed the evolutionary psychologist Donald Symons, and for good Darwinian reasons: higher-status individuals have access to more of the world's goodies.[2]

But in humans, striving for status is a complicated matter. There are no straightforward rules for how to go about it; no single set of tactics is going to work for everyone. The status system's assignment is to work out a long-term strategy of behavior that is tailor-made for the individual in whose head it resides.

Mental organs are specialized collectors of data; each is tuned to respond selectively to certain kinds of cues. The relationship system and the socialization system both collect information about other people. The status system has a more difficult job: it specializes in collecting information about the self. One of the important things that children have to learn while they are growing up is what sort of people they are. Are they big or small, strong or weak, fast or slow, smart or dumb, pretty or plain? Without this information they would have no basis for deciding whether to try to dominate others or yield without a fight, to make suggestions or follow the suggestions of others, to turn down potential mates in hopes of doing better or take whatever comes along.

During childhood and adolescence, young humans collect information on how they compare with the others who will be their rivals in adulthood. Armed with this information, they make long-term modifications in their behavior. It is the status system that enables them to do this.

One way to tell mental organs apart is by the motives they provide. The socialization system makes you want to be like others of your kind; the status system makes you want to be *better* than others of your kind. If you think these two motives can't coexist, your mind must have crossed you off its mailing list.

In an experiment carried out more than half a century ago by the social psychologist Solomon Asch (have you noticed how many of the landmark experiments I've described in this book were the work of social psychologists?), a subject was given a simple task: judge the length of a line by comparing it to three other lines. He was required to do this in a group of six or seven others, and they all had to announce their answers out loud. You may have heard of this experiment; if so, you will know that the other "subjects" were not what they appeared to be. They were confederates of the experimenter, trained to give wrong answers (the same wrong answers) without cracking a smile—without even looking at the real subject, the victim of this ruse.

Asch's experiment is sometimes called a study of "group pressure," but no pressure was exerted by the others; they remained impassive. The pressure to conform to the group's consensus came from within the subject. In fact, the subjects did *not* conform most of the time: they yielded to the group's unanimous opinion, and consequently gave wrong answers, on only about a third of the trials on average. But the subjects' comments afterwards made it clear that all had felt themselves to be in a quandary.

They all experienced an inner conflict in which their desire not to be different vied with their desire to be correct.[3]

Two mental systems—one providing the motivation to conform, the other, to be better (in this case, more accurate) than the others—were issuing contradictory instructions. "Behavior is the outcome of an internal struggle among many mental modules," said Steven Pinker in *How the Mind Works*, "and it is played out on the chessboard of opportunities and constraints defined by other people's behavior."[4] Usually the internal struggle is carried on quietly, but sometimes the noise of the clash is loud enough to reach the conscious mind. Sometimes it's loud enough to keep you up at night.

If the motives to conform and to compete are provided by built-in equipment, no external rewards or punishments should be required. But without rewards and punishments, how do you know whether your efforts to achieve these goals are succeeding? The answer is that feedback is required from the environment—social feedback. Deviating from group norms reduces one's acceptability to the group; thus, the socialization system can use information about group acceptance to keep track of how well it is doing its job. The status system requires a different kind of information. As the evolutionary psychologists Lee Kirkpatrick and Bruce Ellis have pointed out, winning acceptance by a group and achieving high status within the group are by no means the same thing and may even work in opposition to each other: "It may be 'lonely at the top' because intense status-striving can undermine social inclusion." Kirkpatrick and Ellis proposed that humans are equipped with a set of "sociometers" to monitor success and failure in various domains of social life. This set includes a device that keeps its owner apprised of group acceptance and another that supplies information about status.[5]

Supporting evidence comes from a study in which college students were provided with two different kinds of (fictitious) social feedback: feedback about group acceptance or rejection, and feedback about their ability to influence the other members of the group. The researchers found that the two types of feedback had independent effects on the self-esteem of the subjects. One can feel good about one's acceptability as a member of a group at the same time one feels rotten about one's status within the group. Or vice versa.[6]

The existence of these two separable kinds of self-esteem solves one of the puzzles of the playground: why bullies don't feel bad about themselves. Because big, tough kids who push other kids around are generally disliked, many developmentalists have assumed that they must have low self-esteem. But they don't. Nor do aggressive adults lack self-esteem.[7] Aggressive people may get negative feedback on group acceptance, but they make up for it by getting positive feedback on their rank in the pecking order. Most self-esteem tests lump together the effects of these two kinds of feedback.

Kirkpatrick and his colleagues unlumped them. They gave their subjects (college students again) two different self-esteem tests: one to assess the degree to which the subjects felt socially accepted, the other to assess the degree to which they felt superior to others. Then each subject was given a chance to administer a mildly aggressive punishment to a nonexistent person who had supposedly given him a bad grade on an essay. (The punishment involved eating food spiked with hot sauce in a fictitious taste test. The subject could specify the amount of hot sauce the grader of his essay would have to consume.)

The results again supported the distinction between status and acceptance. Subjects who felt superior to others—high in status—were more aggressive than average. Subjects who felt socially accepted were *less* aggressive than average. As Kirkpatrick and his colleagues pointed out, aggression is a useful tactic only for those who can carry it off—those who have confidence in their ability to overpower their rivals. On the other hand, aggression can incur heavy costs for those who rate themselves high on social acceptance: it can tarnish their reputation as reliable, cooperative members of the group.[8]

Status within a human group isn't a simple matter of ups and downs: it is multidimensional and dependent on context. A child who has high status on the playground because of his size or strength may have low status in the classroom because he can't answer the teacher's questions. Researchers have assessed children's self-perceived status in the various arenas in which they compete by measuring their "academic self-esteem," "athletic self-esteem," and so on.

The measurement of academic self-esteem gives us another way to look at what happens when the status system is pitted against the socialization system. A child of above-average academic ability will generally have above-average academic self-esteem. But if we put this child in a highly selective school where she is only an average student, her academic self-esteem will drop.[9] So, does this lead to a poorer academic outcome? No, because something else is going on as well: the child is getting socialized. She's conforming to the norms of her group. A quarter century of research has shown that children learn more in schools and classrooms that have a relatively high concentration of able students.[10] The reason is that attitudes toward academic achievement and intellectual activities are part of the culture that the child absorbs through socialization.

The internal struggle between the status system and the socialization system can itself be influenced by socialization. Cross-cultural psychologists divide the world's cultures into two types, called individualist (or competitive) and collectivist (or cooperative).[11] In individualist, competitive societies like ours, people strive mightily for status; in collectivist, cooperative societies, conformity is felt to be the greater good. Asch's experiment on group conformity has been carried out in a number of different countries and the results back up this distinction: conformity is higher in collectivist cultures. Interestingly, conformity within the United States has gone down since Asch carried out his experiments in the 1950s; fewer subjects now yield to the group's consensus. Evidently American culture has grown increasingly individualistic over the years.[12]

Children assimilate these cultural values because the feedback they receive for cooperating or competing differs in different societies. But even in societies in which personal achievement receives no praise, people vary in what they think they are good at. Even in societies that emphasize conformity, the world's goodies are not handed out in a strictly equitable fashion. In fact, most collectivist societies permit polygyny (or used to, before the missionaries got there). Depending on his wealth or prestige, a man might have two wives, or one wife, or none.

I've given you evidence that the socialization system and the status system provide different motives and respond to different kinds of feedback. Now it's time to examine the status system more closely and figure out how it works. I said at the beginning of this chapter that children have to learn, while they are growing up, what sort of people they are: big or small, strong or weak, fast or slow, smart or dumb, pretty or plain. The question is, how do children find out whether they are big, strong, smart, or pretty? What they need is information on how they compare with others like themselves, others of their sex and approximate age.

Children are motivated to seek out others of their sex and approximate age; they are motivated to collect this kind of information. These assertions are by no means novel; they are the basis of social comparison theory, formulated in 1954 by yet another eminent social psychologist, Leon Festinger. One of the tenets of social comparison theory is the "similarity hypothesis": people prefer to compare themselves with others who are similar to themselves, which means others in their own social category.[13]

All over the world, children's preferred playmates are other children of the same sex and approximate age. According to the anthropologist Beatrice Whiting and the cross-cultural psychologist Carolyn Edwards,

> In interaction with same-sex children who are close in age, a child can compare her appearance, behavior, and likes and dislikes with those of the companion. These experiences teach understanding of the self, as well as understanding of the behavior of others who are perceived as similar in salient attributes of gender.[14]

During middle childhood—what Freud called the "latency period"—girls and boys spontaneously separate into single-sex groups. As developmentalists have observed, boys' groups tend to be larger (girls often split up into pairs or trios) and more hierarchical, or at least more overtly hierarchical. Boys appear to be more concerned about competition and status and their play is rougher.[15] One of the reasons boys and girls form separate play groups is that boys go in for a lot of rough-and-tumble play and most girls don't like it. This activity, also called "play fighting," can be seen in the young of most mammalian species, from puppies to chimpanzees. In virtually every species, the males do more of it than the females.

In virtually every species, males are more aggressive than females. But rough-and-tumble play shouldn't be confused with aggression. Though occasionally it does escalate into real aggression, children recognize the difference and get angry if the boundary is crossed. After a bout of rough-and-tumble play, children continue to play together; after an aggressive encounter they go their separate ways.[16]

Children also engage in a lot of active play that isn't rough-and-tumble, but this kind of play reaches a peak around age four or five and then gradually declines during middle childhood. In contrast, rough-and-tumble play is less common during the preschool years and increases in frequency until just before puberty. This distinctive pattern has led the evolutionary developmental psychologists Anthony Pellegrini and Peter Smith to propose that it has a specific purpose: "We postulate that R & T may serve a social function in peer groups, for boys especially, by assisting in the establishing and maintaining of dominance relationships." In play, stronger children hold back in an effort to avoid hurting their friends, but nonetheless, the researchers report, "many children say they can determine their own as well as peers' strength from these encounters."[17]

Although rough-and-tumble play is seen less often during adolescence, it tends to be more serious: more prevalent in teenagers who also engage in real aggression and more likely to escalate. Its purpose is the same but now the stakes are higher. A researcher who studied the playground tussles of twelve- and thirteen-year-old boys reported, "Once a weaker boy has registered distress the [friendship] bond can be maintained by the fight taking a more playful form, but if he does not do so at the start of the fight, the stronger boy may increase the intensity of the fight until he does."[18]

Notice how the stronger boy lets up as soon as the weaker one cries uncle. When I said that this chapter is about classic Darwinian competition, the words "nature red in tooth and claw" may have popped into your head. But the sort of competition that is more apt to turn bloody is competition between groups, not within them. Within-group homicide does occur but it is not routine. Because the members of group-adapted species need their groupmates (and may be related to them), aggression within the group tends to be muted, tamped down. The members of most group-adapted species—no doubt our own included—have instincts that serve this purpose. The weaker individual demonstrates by its behavior that it accepts its lower status and the demonstration has a pacific effect on the stronger one. The subordinate wolf or dog rolls over and exposes its tender underbelly to the dominant one. Within the group—between two animals that know each other—this seemingly suicidal behavior averts, rather than invites, aggression.[19] The goal of the stronger one is to dominate, not to kill.

Ask a four-year-old boy who is the toughest or the smartest in his nursery school class and the answer you will probably get is "Me!"[20] The status sociometer arrives from the factory with a default setting of alpha. Even after many years of use, it is still apt to register high. The tendency for people to overestimate themselves—in toughness, smartness, looks, honesty, niceness, driving ability, you name it—has been demonstrated again and again. The exceptions are people suffering from depression. But depressed people don't actually *under*estimate themselves: they estimate themselves pretty accurately, which turns out not to be such a good idea.[21]

It wouldn't do, however, to run around with one's sociometer forever fixed at the factory default. A 97-pound weakling who goes around trying to dominate everyone he meets is likely to lead a life that is nasty, brutish, and short. An individual has to learn that there are areas of endeavor in which he might be able to compete successfully and others in which it is best to cut his losses and concede defeat. Childhood is the time to find these things out: a time when a mistake is less likely to have irrevocable consequences.

The very same four-year-old boy who told you that he is the toughest in his nursery school class tells a different story by his behavior: he averts his eyes and yields possession of toys when challenged by a bigger, stronger classmate. Dominant-submissive relationships are clearly visible in behavior at this age; and yet the child has little or no idea of his status in the group as a whole.[22] Dominance and submission are the outcome of pairwise interactions between individuals and are handled by the relationship system, which (as I said in chapter 7) is ready to go from birth. A dominance hierarchy is the larger, group-wide structure that results from these interactions. Awareness of such structures and understanding of one's own position in them requires a higher level of cognitive sophistication. The status system is the slowest of the three systems to develop.

By kindergarten age—five or six—boys have a much better idea of their toughness relative to other boys, and by first grade they are fairly accurate (though still overly optimistic) in their self-assessment. They can also, by first grade, do a pretty good job of ranking their classmates in toughness. Ranking themselves and others in smartness takes a little longer, because the necessary information is harder to come by. But by second or third grade, they can do this too.[23] I'm focusing here on toughness and aggressiveness because a lot of research has been done on these things and because they are obviously pertinent to Darwinian fitness, especially in males.

Whether aggressiveness will be a successful behavioral strategy for a particular male depends in part on his genetic endowment, in part on environmental factors that his genes cannot foresee. An individual's physical size and strength are affected, not only by genes, but also by things like malnutrition, parasites, illnesses, and injuries, which would have taken a heavier toll under ancestral conditions than they do today. Moreover, bigness and toughness are not absolutes: they depend on how you compare with the competition. The luck of the draw could give you Woody Allen or it could give you Shaquille O'Neal. A kid who ranks alpha in his play group might be beta, gamma, or omega in another group. Culture matters, too. Aggressiveness works better in some cultures than in others.

In earlier chapters I described evidence showing that children's experiences at home do not affect their aggressiveness outside the home. Firstborns who dominate their younger siblings are no more aggressive than laterborns when they're with their peers. Kids who are well-behaved in the presence of their parents may be bullies on the playground. My conclusion was that children's experiences at home have only short-term, context-specific effects on their behavior. Now the question is whether children's experiences *outside* the home have long-term consequences. In order to convince you that the status system has the power I attribute to it, I need to provide evidence that children's experiences with their peers (in this case, experiences related to aggressiveness and dominance) do in fact have long-term effects on personality.

One way to do that would be to show that having high or low social status in childhood has effects on adult personality. Do the social experiences associated with being bigger, stronger, or more physically mature than others of his age have lasting effects on a boy's personality? There is plenty of evidence for a connection between physical size or strength, status, and personality in adulthood (tall or muscular men tend to have higher status and to be more competitive and aggressive),[24] but what I need now is a link between physical size or strength in *childhood* and personality in adulthood.

That link is provided by longitudinal studies of height. The starting point is the well-established finding that tall men, on average, earn higher salaries than short men. The difference isn't negligible: it amounts to around eight hundred dollars per inch in annual income.[25] Though evolutionary psychologists are not surprised by this finding, economists find it puzzling. The salaried workers in question are not playing basketball; they're not even changing lightbulbs. Mostly they're just sitting behind a desk. Why would it be worth it to an employer to pay a higher salary to a tall guy if all he's going to do is sit behind a desk?

Recently three economists—Nicola Persico, Andrew Postlewaite, and Dan Silverman—attempted to answer that question. They were lucky enough to have access to two large databases of information on almost 4,500 white American and British males, including the subjects' salary and height in adulthood (around age thirty), height at age sixteen, and, for about half of the subjects, height at ages seven and eleven. There was also a good deal of background information on the subjects.

The economists analyzed the data till smoke started coming out of their computers, but they didn't find the answer to the question of why tall guys get paid more. What they found instead was another puzzle. Employers, they discovered, are not paying for height per se—that is, they are not paying for adult height. What matters in terms of salary is not height in adulthood but height in adolescence. Though a man who is taller than average in adulthood is also likely to have been taller than average in adolescence, the rank ordering of individuals can change, and this enabled the economists to statistically separate the effects of height at different ages. They found that the men with the fattest paychecks were not necessarily those who were tallest at age thirty: they were those who had been tallest at age sixteen. As for height at ages seven and eleven, it made little difference once height at age sixteen was statistically controlled.[26]

The economists tested several hypotheses that might explain what they called the "teen height premium." Differences in childhood health didn't account for it; nor was it a function of the socioeconomic status of the subjects' parents. Of the factors they looked at, the one that mattered most—it accounted for about a third of the teen height premium—was participation in extracurricular activities in high school, especially participation in sports. Notice that participation in sports requires strength as well as size, and that high school athletes generally have high status among their peers.

The economists' conclusion was that employers aren't paying a premium just to have tall employees. Employers are paying for something else—something associated with being tall in adolescence and with being good at sports, something that must persist into adulthood. What could it be?

The answer, had the economists known where to look for it, was provided by a much older, much smaller study done—no, not by a social psychologist, but by a developmentalist. Her name was Mary Cover Jones and her research was published in 1957. As far as I know it has never been replicated—except, in an indirect way, by the three economists.

Jones studied two types of subjects: teenage boys who were maturing slowly (in the bottom 20 percent for their age in terms of bone maturity) and teenage boys who were maturing rapidly (top 20 percent). These boys differed considerably in size; the gap was widest at age fourteen, when the early maturers averaged a whopping eight inches taller and thirty-four pounds heavier than the slow maturers.

The marked differences in size, strength, and success in sports (which Jones mentioned in passing) were accompanied, in adolescence, by differences in personality and social behavior. In ratings by trained observers, the early maturers scored higher on "behavior items suggesting a large component of self-acceptance": they were poised, relaxed, and matter-of-fact. In contrast, the slow maturers were eager, talkative, and tense, and more likely to have mannerisms that Jones described as "affected" and "attention-seeking." Boys who are small for their age tend to be pushed around a lot by their peers; other researchers have found that such boys have more than their share of mental health disturbances.[27]

The slow maturers eventually caught up in size; in their early thirties, when Jones revisited them, the two groups of subjects differed by an average of only half an inch. They were also about equal in educational attainment. But the early maturers were more likely to have achieved what Jones called "status-conferring" positions in their careers, and there were still significant differences in personality (as measured now by standard personality tests) between the groups: the early maturers scored higher on personality characteristics associated with dominance.[28]

Jones's study and the one by the three economists fit together like Lego blocks. Qualities such as tallness, strength, and athletic ability give a boy high status in his adolescent peer group,[29] and having high status in adolescence has lasting effects on his personality. It makes him more sure of himself, more dominant, more competitive, more of a leader. These personality characteristics impress employers and they also impress voters. In presidential elections in the United States, the taller candidate usually wins.[30]

The finding that height in adolescence matters more than height in childhood implies that personality can still be modified as late as age sixteen. This is consistent with the results of the study of personality development across the life course, which I mentioned in chapter 1, and suggests that the status system does its work at a more leisurely pace than the socialization system. Sixteen is not too late for a boy to develop a self-assured personality, but it is too late for the son of a Japanese executive who has lived for several years in the United States to return to Japanese norms of social behavior, and it is too late for a new immigrant to learn to speak the language of his new country without an accent.[31] Each system has its own developmental timetable.

Personality can change during childhood and adolescence as a result of experiences. Theorists who believe that children's personalities are shaped early, presumably by experiences at home, have been misled by the continuities they see in personality: the timid child who becomes a timid adult, the conscientious child who becomes a conscientious adult. Such continuities are due mainly to genetic influences on these traits.[32]

Status within the group is important for females too, but it doesn't depend on their size or strength. A woman's status is determined in part by her beauty. Of course, beauty isn't the only thing that counts—nor are size and strength the only things that count for men—but these are characteristics that have been studied.

Beauty is a woman's bargaining chip in the mating game; a good-looking woman has a better chance of pairing up with a high-status mate. Having a high-status mate had evolutionarily relevant advantages for ancestral women. (I won't elaborate, since so much has already been written on this topic.[33])

To make a wise decision in the mating game, a woman has to have a reasonably accurate idea of her own value in the mating market. If she overestimates herself, she might turn down offers that might not come her way again; if she underestimates herself, she might be too quick to say yes to the first guy who asks her. The evolutionary psychologist Robin Dunbar noted that women who marry men of higher social status tend to marry at a younger age,[34] which suggests that women who haven't yet found their prince may be holding out just in case he shows up later. But meanwhile the clock keeps ticking. Shakespeare, who understood so much about human nature, was aware of this dilemma. In *As You Like It*, a character tries to persuade a young woman named Phoebe to accept the advances of a low-status suitor by telling her that she is not very good-looking and hence has limited appeal: "Sell when you can: you are not for all markets."[35]

You see, there is a problem here, and Shakespeare recognized it. How does Phoebe know how good-looking she is? They had mirrors in Shakespeare's time, but even a mirror can't give a girl the information she needs. A boy can assess his size, strength, and speed relative to other boys by playing competitive games with them, but how does a girl figure out how pretty she is relative to other girls?

What's true for beauty is true for most of the qualities that affect people's status and their desirability in the mating market. Size, strength, and speed turn out to be the exceptions rather than the rule. How would you know, if you were a child, whether you were well or poorly endowed with things like sense of humor and the ability to plan ahead? How would you know, if you lived in the days before schools existed, how smart you were? How would you find out how good you were going to be at tasks such as settling disputes, figuring out how to get somewhere and how to get back, or identifying edible plants? What you need is knowledge of how you compare with others, but in the absence of objective criteria, comparing yourself with others is difficult to do with any degree of accuracy.

But other people can do it much more accurately. Other people can see you far more clearly than you see yourself. What matters in determining status in the group and desirability in the mating market is not how you see yourself but how other people see you—how they rate you in comparison with others in your age group. To guide you in picking a strategy that will serve you well in your adult life, the best information you can get is knowledge of how other people see you.

Once again I find wisdom in the words of a social psychologist from an earlier era. Here's what George Herbert Mead said in 1934:

> The individual experiences himself as such, not directly, but only indirectly, from the particular standpoints of other individual members of the same social group, or from the generalized standpoint of the social group as a whole to which he belongs.[36]

Sociologist Gary Fine put it more succinctly: "The other is the mirror by which individuals learn of their selves."[37] What Fine meant by "the other" was what Mead called the "generalized other." The added together or averaged other.

So the status system, too, collects data and does statistics on them. What matters is not what your parents tell you (they might think you're gorgeous but so what?), or what your brother tells you (he's just teasing), or what your best friend tells you.[38] What matters is how you're seen by the "generalized other." It matters because it's more accurate and hence has more predictive value than the opinion of any single individual.

Of course, children have no way of knowing that the best thing to do is to figure out how other people see them and add up the data. But they don't have to know it: they have a mental organ that does it for them. Mental organs, like physical ones, are the result of natural selection operating over thousands of generations, and natural selection is wiser than any child. Leda Cosmides and John Tooby explained how evolution—which is incapable of foreseeing the future but has a great deal of information about what happened in the past—can produce such devices:

> Natural selection does not work by inference or simulation. It takes the real problem, runs the experiment, and retains those design features that lead to the best available outcomes. Natural selection "counts up" the

> results of alternative designs operating in the real world, over millions of individuals, over thousands of generations, and weights alternatives by the statistical distribution of their consequences. In this sense, it is omniscient—it is not limited to what could be validly deduced by one individual, based on a short period of experience, it is not limited to what is locally perceivable, and it is not confused by spurious local correlations. It uses the statistical foundations of the actual lives of organisms, in the actual range of environments they encounter, under the statistical regularities they experience and, using alternative developmental programs leading to alternative designs, tests for the best solution.[39]

So natural selection can ask, "What kind of information, available to a child, is the best basis for forming long-term patterns of behavior?", run the experiment, and come up with the answer. Natural selection can ask, "Which is better, to have children's personalities shaped by their experiences within the family or by their experiences outside the family?", run the experiment, and come up with the answer. The mental organ with the design specs that enabled it to outperform the other candidates for the job was one that wouldn't be hijacked by random events or misleading experiences, but would collect as much relevant data as it could, for as long a period as it could afford to, because ugly ducklings sometimes do turn into swans. Being favored by a parent tells a child nothing that will be useful to her later on, but being given special treatment by many different people is informative. Being dominated by an older sibling conveys no useful information to a child, but being dominated by children of his own age is informative. Being beaten up once by a bully is a random event; being pushed around for years by many different adversaries is informative.

In the trial-and-error experiment that produced our species, a device that made long-term modifications of behavior on the basis of random events would have easily been beaten out by one that looked for systematic trends. Likewise, a device that made long-term modifications on the basis of experiences with parents or siblings would have been beaten out by one that used data with better predictive value: data collected in the arena in which the child will compete in adulthood.

Most animals, including humans, distinguish between relatives and nonrelatives; they favor relatives when it comes to sharing and nonrelatives when it comes to mating. If the relative–nonrelative distinction has already been made, why not use it to put a lower value on input coming from parents and siblings? This is only a suggestion; perhaps all that happens is that input from parents and siblings is outnumbered and outweighed by input coming from other sources. But there's no theoretical reason why the system couldn't distinguish between the various sources of input and rely more on some sources than on others.

The mental system I am proposing is tuned to receive certain kinds of signals from the environment: signals that help the individual work out a strategy of behavior that can be tried out in childhood and perhaps discarded if the results are disappointing or a more promising strategy becomes available later. This system requires a lot of brain power and takes a long time to complete its development, but human children are well provided with both.

Good-looking people receive better treatment in infancy, childhood, and adulthood. They are given more attention and get more respect from everyone—parents, teachers, peers, and employers—which means that there is widespread agreement on who is good-looking and who is not, and an equally widespread tendency to judge books by their covers.[40] No, it's not fair, but evolution cares not a whit for fairness.

As you might expect, good-looking people tend to be more assertive and sure of themselves. The female subjects in one experiment were treated rudely and made to wait while a researcher left the room in the middle of a fake interview. The less attractive women sat and waited for an average of nine minutes before raising a protest; the more attractive women started to complain after three minutes and twenty seconds. What produces the assertiveness is not the good looks themselves but the social effects of being good-looking. In childhood and adolescence, pretty girls have higher status among their peers; in fact, the effects for girls of being pretty are similar to those for boys of being tall and strong.[41]

The question is, how do children find out about their status, when it's not simply a matter of who can dominate whom? In an earlier chapter I told you about attention structure: the high-status members of a group—children or adults, humans or apes—get looked at more often than those of lower status. I also told you about the eye-direction detector, a mental module that Simon Baron-Cohen included in his model of a mechanism for reading other people's minds. The gaze detector, as I call it, gives a little beep whenever it notices that someone is looking at its owner.[42]

Being looked at by others makes a person more self-confident and more likely to speak out in a group. Researchers in a media lab in Canada were testing video conferencing equipment that enabled each participant in a group discussion to see images of the other participants. The researchers manipulated the images so that sometimes they appeared to be looking directly at a given participant—the subject—and sometimes they appeared to be looking elsewhere. The more gazes a subject received from these images, the more he or she contributed to the discussion. The timing of the gazes didn't matter much; nor did their source. It was the sheer number of gazes the subject received.[43] A simple counting device, working below the level of consciousness, determines whether you will sit through a meeting with your mouth shut or blurt out something you may later regret.

The counting device is one of the components of the status system; it counts eye-gazes the way a voting machine counts votes, and for much the same reason. This device is not new; vote-counting, like averaging, has been observed in nonhuman animals. Two British biologists recently presented evidence for what they called "group decision-making in animals." Animal groups, they reasoned, are generally better off making decisions on a democratic basis, rather than following a leader, because the group as a whole is likely to have more and better information than any single animal within it. So decisions such as when to move and which way to go may be made by a majority-rules rule—in other words, by counting votes. African buffalo do this by tallying eye-gazes: the herd moves in the direction in which the majority of the adults are looking.[44]

Counting the eye-gazes they receive is one way that children and adults can assess their status; this is one of the cues the status system is sensitive to. But eye-gazes are not enough. Human social life is complex; status is multidimensional; the strategies available to children are limitless. They need information of a more subtle and detailed sort, information that cannot be conveyed by a simple vote-count.

What children need, ideally, is information on how they are seen by other people—what the "generalized other" thinks of them. They need a way of peering into other people's minds and finding out what these people think of them.

We already know that normally developing children—children not afflicted with the disorder called autism—can do some mindreading. By the age of four, a child can figure out that if Anne hid the ball when Sally wasn't looking, then Sally doesn't know where the ball is. By around this age a child can also figure out that lying about what he did or didn't do can put false information about his activities into another person's mind, which means he knows that one of the things that other people can think about is *him*.[45]

Part of our ability to read other people's minds—a very important part—is the ability to discern what other people think of us. It develops slowly, never becomes highly accurate, and some are better at it than others, but most adolescents and adults have a reasonably good idea of how others are reacting to them. We can usually tell whether someone we're talking to likes us or not, respects us or not, and does or does not find us sexually attractive.

True, other people sometimes send out misleading signals. But the very fact that the signals are misleading shows that we must have a way of receiving and interpreting them. The signals come in a variety of forms: eye-gazes, facial expressions, body language, actions, and words. It is not unusual for mental organs to combine information coming in through different modalities; the mechanism that tells us where things are located in three-dimensional space can make use of vision, hearing, and/or touch.

Earlier I mentioned a set of mental devices called sociometers. The theorists who thought up these devices gave them a simple job: all they have to do is indicate, with a thumbs-up or thumbs-down signal, how a particular aspect of social life is going. The device I'm now proposing as a component of the status system is much fancier than a sociometer; it collects and processes information of a richer sort and issues more detailed reports. It can handle the thumbs-up/thumbs-down business—so it is, among other things, a sociometer—but it does harder jobs as well.

Here's how I think it works. The status system, designed to collect and store information about the self, makes clever use of features of the relationship system (the system designed to collect information about other people). The activities of the two systems dovetail like this: while *your* relationship system is gathering information about me and storing it on the page assigned to me in your people-information lexicon, *my* status system is trying to figure out what you've got recorded on that page. *You* keep the information you've learned about me separate—you don't mix it together with information about other people—but *I* take the information I've gotten about myself from my page in your lexicon and put it together with similar information I've gotten from other people's lexicons. What I need is a picture of myself from the point of view of the "generalized other."

Did that sound impossibly complicated? It will make more sense, I think, if I go through the series of steps by which evolution could have produced the mental system I'm proposing. It started back when animals became able to recognize and remember specific individuals of their species—their mates, their offspring, their adversaries in one-on-one dominance contests. Once that ability existed, another step became possible: now the animal could collect information on specific individuals and store this information in a mental lexicon. A useful ability for any social species.

The next innovation probably occurred fairly recently: during the six million years of evolution that separate our line of descent from the chimpanzee's. What happened was that hominids gradually developed the ability to read each others' minds. They got better and better at mindreading. This was undeniably a handy ability to have, but for a long time the information was used only by the relationship system.

Okay, now we have a mindreading mechanism plus a mental lexicon containing people-information. Put 'em together and what've you got? The logical next step: the ability to read what someone else has recorded about you on the page assigned to you in their mental lexicon. How handy is *that*?

I'm proposing a device that figures out what other people are thinking of you and how they regard you, and that puts together information collected from many different sources to give you a picture of yourself. Unfortunately the device doesn't work perfectly—the picture is blurry—which is why the poet Robert Burns demanded his money back. "Oh wad some power the giftie gie us, to see oursels as ithers see us!" he memorably complained. The power is natural selection, and it did its best to gie us that giftie but was forced to make compromises. The reason we can't read the page as accurately as we would like (or as accurately as we *think* we would like) is that the mind in which that page resides doesn't want us to. It is to my advantage to know what you are thinking about me, but it may be to *your* advantage to keep me from knowing it.[46]

The picture may be blurry but it's nuanced and multidimensional. The status system uses this information to work out a long-term strategy of behavior tailored specifically for its owner. Using data collected in childhood and adolescence—How many people can beat me up? How often do other people look at me? Do people trust me to give good advice?—the status system shapes and modifies personality in a way that takes account of the individual's preexisting characteristics and the opportunities afforded by the environment. It places a bet—the stakes are high and sometimes it loses—that this is the best way to go, the best thing to do, to maximize the chances of success in the adult world.

The system I'm proposing wouldn't work very well without the mindreading mechanism. It could rely on counting eye-gazes and the number of times its owner wins or loses dominance contests, but it's hardly worth making long-term modifications of behavior on such a basis. Therefore I don't expect animals that lack a mindreading mechanism to have a mental organ analogous to the human status system. I'm predicting, in other words, that nonhuman animals—even chimpanzees—lack a mental system that makes "personality" modifiable by experiences such as having high or low status in the juvenile group. In nonhuman primates, the behaviors associated with being an alpha male may be context dependent; being at the top for a while may have no lasting consequences. That may sound unlikely to you but it makes perfectly good sense for a nonhuman. After all, an animal's status in its dominance hierarchy is subject to radical changes—gradual or abrupt—over the course of its lifetime, and the animal has to accustom itself, slowly or rapidly, to these changes. According to the primatologist Frans de Waal, when an alpha male chimpanzee is deposed he immediately loses his air of lordly self-confidence.[47]

Humans, too, have to accustom themselves to changes in status. So why did evolution provide our species with a system that shapes personality on the basis of childhood and adolescent experiences? The answer is that there came a point in hominid evolution when it became advantageous to be able to modify patterns of social behavior on a long-term basis. That point was reached when the mindreading mechanism was able to provide more subtle and multidimensional information than could be conveyed by eye-gazes or the outcomes of dominance contests, when individuals were able to make more subtle and multidimensional adjustments in their behavior, and when longer preparation was needed to fill specialized niches within the group.

I have described a mental system that shapes or modifies personality in a way that takes account of the individual's size, strength, beauty, and so on. The existence of such a system has previously been suggested by others;[48] what I've done is to show how it might work. The system I'm proposing is built out of components for which there is already good evidence and for which analogs exist in mental systems serving other functions, such as language.

Now for the big question. Can this mental system be the perpetrator I'm looking for? Can it be responsible for the personality differences between identical twins?

In the mystery *Five Red Herrings*, the detective Peter Wimsey eliminated five likely looking suspects. Then he was faced with a obstacle: the sixth suspect had what appeared to be an unassailable alibi. Before Wimsey could solve the mystery, he had to break down that alibi. He had to show that the sixth suspect could, in fact, have committed the crime.

There's an obstacle in my case, too. The status system I've described is capable of shaping personality in a way that takes account of an individual's size, strength, beauty, and so on. The problem is that identical twins are very much alike in size, strength, beauty, and so on. Therefore, other people will react to them in much the same way. The twins will have similar social experiences and will receive similar social feedback. Of course, they won't have *identical* experiences, but their experiences should be more similar than those of two people who aren't identical twins. And if their experiences are similar, the status system should make them *more* alike, rather than *less* alike!

But the problem, like the sixth suspect's alibi, turns out not to be one. No, I'm not going to deny that the social experiences of identical twins are more similar than those of two people who aren't twins—I admitted it a long time ago, when I was talking about the equally-similar-environments assumption in chapter 2. Nevertheless, the status system could still be the perpetrator we've been looking for. This is going to take some explaining, but I will be quicker about it than Peter Wimsey was.

To begin with, let's look closely at the way behavioral geneticists apportion the variance in personality. Identical twins (who share 100 percent of their genes) are more similar in personality than fraternal twins (who share only 50 percent). Behavioral geneticists use this greater similarity as one way to estimate heritability—the amount of variance accounted for by differences and similarities in genes.

If personality is affected by social experiences, and if social experiences are in part the result of highly heritable characteristics such as size, strength, and beauty, then it's true that the social experiences of twins are likely to make them more alike in personality. But this greater similarity is going to be included—wrongly, in the view of the critics of behavioral genetics—in the estimate of *genetic* effects on personality. That's why estimates of the heritability of personality may be a little inflated; perhaps "true" heritability—the direct results of the actions of genes—is only .30 or .35, rather than .45. The behavioral genetic methods currently in use don't permit researchers to distinguish between the direct effects of genes and the indirect effects, the effects of being treated in a certain way because of one's inherited characteristics. It's a serious flaw, according to the critics of behavioral genetics.

But, as I said in chapter 2, it's no skin off my nose. On the contrary: it makes things easier for me. I'm interested in the personality *differences* between identical twins. The fact that they are treated more similarly by others cannot account for their differences: it can account only for their similarities, and their similarities are attributed to heritability. My interest is in the portion of the variance *not* attributed to heritability. The alleged flaw in behavioral genetic methods—the overestimation of heritability—actually simplifies my job, because the portion of the variance I'm interested in, the unexplained variance, has already had the effects of the more similar treatment of identical twins subtracted out of it.

To the extent that people's social experiences are correlated with their genetic similarities or differences, the results of such experiences don't contribute to the unexplained variance: they contribute to heritability. To the extent the unexplained variance in personality results from people's social experiences, the experiences in question must be uncorrelated with their genes. I am looking, therefore, for experiences that are *not* the result of inherited characteristics. Variations in genes make people differ from one another but something else makes them differ still more, so that even two people who have identical genes differ noticeably in personality. Can the status system—a system that shapes personality on the basis of self-knowledge obtained through a complex kind of social feedback—supply the something else?

Yes, I believe it can, for three reasons. The first has to do with the way another mental system works: the relationship system. These two systems collaborate in producing differences between identical twins. The relationship system, you'll recall, enables us us to identify particular individuals and to distinguish one from another. It motivates us to find and remember differences even between two people who look very much alike (including pairs who aren't twins, like the golfers Nick Price and Nick Faldo, whom I used to mix up when I first started watching golf tournaments). If you have a pair of identical twins among your close friends or family, I'll bet you can tell them apart, though you may not be able to say exactly how you do it. Doesn't matter how you do it: what matters is that once you've learned to distinguish them, your relationship system can set up separate pages for each of them in your mental lexicon of people-information, and you can begin storing data for each twin separately. Donald (not George) owes you a favor. Shawn (not Jonathan) bit you in the ear.

The consequence is that when Donald tries to read what you've recorded about him on his page in your lexicon, he will see something different from what George sees. Shawn will see something different from what Jonathan sees. They *don't* get the same social feedback because your relationship system has discriminated between them. The relationship system is far more interested in the differences between people—the things that make each one unique—than in their similarities.

The second reason has to do with the nature of status. Within a group of boys, only one can be the toughest. Within a group of girls, only one can be the prettiest. If a group contains a pair of identical twins—even if they're both very tough or very pretty—one will inevitably be second best and the other will rank higher in the attention structure. The twin who receives more gazes will tend to speak out more in the group and will consequently receive yet more gazes, so that what might have started out as a tiny difference will widen. Questions or comments from the other members of the group will tend to be addressed to the more outspoken twin, and he or she may become the spokesperson for the pair.

I opened this book with a description of Ladan and Laleh, the conjoined twins who died during surgery to separate them. Ladan was the one who explained to journalists, "We are two completely separate individuals who are stuck to each other." She was the more outspoken of the two—the one who was described by a close acquaintance as "very friendly."[49]

The third reason has to do with the nature of social feedback. The status system's purpose is to enable children to find out about themselves, so that they can adjust their social behavior accordingly. The input collected by this system comes in the form of social cues, information provided by other people. No other kind of information could do the job required of it. But social cues can be ambiguous, and other people have their own agendas. The result is that this system could have effects that are completely unrelated to genes. Does everyone defer to you because you're big and strong or because you have a big strong brother who is quick to come to your defense? Is everyone nice to you because you're beautiful or because your father is the village headman? If the social cues are the same, the status system will treat these alternatives as equivalent.

In these cases, the alternatives *are* in some sense equivalent. But social cues that you repeatedly receive from others in your group may be based on things that shouldn't have any evolutionary significance at all, because they're random. You tripped and fell at a dinner party and landed in the salmon mousse. You shot an arrow into the air and it chanced to hit a bird. You made an offhand remark that was interpreted as a prediction and the prediction happened to come true. Incidents like these can give an individual a reputation that can persist for years, spread and perpetuated through gossip.

The incidents may be random but their consequences are not. The status system is designed not to be hijacked by random events and to look for consistencies and trends, but a random event can cause everyone in your group to think you're wise or clumsy or funny or brave, and to go on thinking that for years. I acknowledged a long time ago (in chapter 2) the undeniable fact that a random event can change the course of a person's life. I gave the example of how writing a classified ad for a dog set me on a path that led to my becoming a writer of books. Some random events are isolated occurrences—they happen once and then they are over—but others have repercussions that echo through the years. It is this second kind of random event—the kind that has long-term effects on a person's experiences—that can produce long-term changes in personality. What shapes personality is not the event itself but the persisting experiences that follow from the event. The outcome, which may also appear to be random, is actually the result of an orderly process. Helping a friend write a classified ad for her dog was an unimportant event in my life, but the repercussions turned out to be important: my friend recorded "has a way with words" on the Judy Harris page of her people-information lexicon. A few months later, when she again needed help in writing something, she thought of me.[50]

I conclude that the status system can indeed be the perpetrator we've been looking for. It is capable of producing personality differences that are unrelated to differences in genes. It is capable of producing personality differences between identical twins.

The unpredictable zigs and zags in development called developmental noise produce little physical differences between identical twins, including physical differences in their brains. Some of the behavioral differences between twins are the result of this developmental noise. The close associates of identical twins notice these differences and record them in their people-information lexicons. One of the reasons identical twins don't receive identical social feedback is that they aren't exactly alike, due to developmental noise.

Among the people who notice and respond to the differences between identical twins are the twins' parents. This has led some researchers to claim that they've found new evidence for parental influence on children's personalities. The researchers found differences in parental treatment toward identical twins that were correlated with differences in the twins' behavior, and they interpreted these correlations as evidence of a causal relationship, the parents' behavior being the cause and the children's the effect. The idea is that they've controlled for genetic effects on behavior by using identical twins. Therefore, the researchers reason, any differences between the twins must be due to environmental differences, and if they can demonstrate an environmental difference that involves parental treatment, that must be the environmental difference that matters. At the very least, it must be *one* of the environmental differences that matter.[51]

Sorry, but it still won't work. The researchers have controlled for genetic effects but they haven't controlled for child-to-parent effects: the fact that parental treatment is in part a response to the child's behavior. If twins behave differently, the parents might be *responding* to these differences, rather than causing them. The behavioral differences may actually be due to developmental noise or to environmental factors the researchers haven't considered.

There is simply too much other evidence that parental influence is ineffective in shaping children's personalities. If the little differences in the way parents treat identical twins are responsible for the behavioral differences between them, how come the much bigger differences in parental treatment experienced by ordinary siblings who differ in birth order don't have measurable effects on their personalities? If, as one group of researchers claimed, greater maternal warmth expressed toward one twin can produce differences between the twins in their ability to pay attention in school,[52] how come intervention programs that increase maternal warmth have no effects on children's behavior in school?

There is no question that greater maternal warmth can improve the mother-child relationship. The relationship system adjusts behavior toward a particular person in order to take account of what it has learned about that person. But the relationship system doesn't make long-term modifications of behavior. A parent's effects on a child's behavior are context specific: specific to the relationship itself or to the setting in which the parent and the child have interacted. The context specificity of learned behavior is not apparent to the naked eye; it's hard to see because children's genes influence their behavior in every context. Their behavior in every context may also be influenced by biological factors that are not genetic—biological factors that are due to developmental noise, or to illnesses or injuries, and that may differ even for identical twins.

Parents do have some power to produce long-term effects on their children's behavior, but their power is indirect: it comes by way of the socialization system. It resides in their ability to determine where and by whom their children will be socialized. The parents decide which society to live in, which culture their children will grow up in, where they will go to school. To some extent, they can even determine which group or groups within the society their children will become members of.

Parents do not, however, have the power to influence the personality development of their children via the status system. This system either discounts information obtained from close relatives or averages it together with so much other information that it doesn't have much impact. The way you are regarded by the "generalized other" is unlikely to be the same as the way you are regarded by your mother. Mother doesn't always know best.

I have sketched out the plans for a system that is capable of producing what looks like randomness on the basis of systematic information collected over a long period of time. Now I am going to suggest that the apparent randomness it produces may not be an accident: it may be one of the things this system was designed to do, or it may be a side effect that proved to have unforeseen benefits. Evolution may have given us a mental organ that widens the behavioral and personality differences among us because variation is itself advantageous.[53]

In a previous chapter I mentioned self-organized systems or groups. Here is a good definition of self-organization from a recent book on the topic:

> Self-organization is a process in which pattern at the global level of a system emerges solely from numerous interactions among the lower-level components of the system. Moreover, the rules specifying interactions among the system's components are executed using only local information, without reference to the global pattern. In short, the pattern is an emergent property of the system, rather than a property imposed on the system by an external ordering influence.[54]

The pattern is determined by the rules that specify how the components of the system interact. If the system is biological, the rules are tuned by natural selection. Through the trial and error of natural selection, rules evolve that produce global patterns that are beneficial to the system, or to its owner (if the system is an organ), or to its components (if the system is a group of animals).

Many self-organized systems use rules involving positive feedback. Fish that swim in schools and birds that fly in flocks are attracted to others of their species; these animals follow a rule of the form "I go where you go" or "I do what you do."

But there are also systems that depend primarily on negative feedback rules: "I *don't* do what you do" or "I do what you *don't* do." An example is the olfactory system, which enables mammals to detect thousands of different odors. The olfactory system is constructed on a "one neuron, one olfactory receptor" principle. Each neuron has a single olfactory receptor, which determines its response profile. The negative feedback rule responsible for this arrangement has the following effect: in a given neuron, the production of a protein by a particular olfactory gene (or part of a gene) ensures that no other olfactory genes will produce their proteins in that neuron.[55] It's like a worker telling another worker, "I can handle this job. You go somewhere else and do something else."

I used the word *worker* on purpose, because the most impressive example of a self-organized biological system is a colony of ants. Look at the ant, the Bible advises us, but phrases the advice in a needlessly insulting way: "Go to the ant, thou sluggard; consider her ways."[56] If you have gotten this far, thou reader, you are no sluggard and have no reason to feel inferior to the ant. On the other hand, the ant does what she does with a lot less equipment than you have at your disposal. Her brain is no bigger than a grain of salt.

And yet ants vie with humans in their domination of the earth. Though they are very small, they are so numerous and so widespread that the biomass of ants is approximately equal to the biomass of humans. The secret of the ants' success is their ability to form complex social groups called colonies. What the Bible really should have advised us to do is to look at the ant colony, not at the individual ant. As the myrmecologists Bert Hölldobler and E. O. Wilson observed, "One ant alone is a disappointment; it is really no ant at all."[57]

In the movie *Antz*, Woody Allen played a worker ant who wasn't happy with his lot.

> It's this whole gung-ho, superorganism thing that—that, you know, I can't get. I try, but I don't get it. I mean, what is it? I'm supposed to do

> everything for the colony? And—and what about my needs? What about me?

There, in a nutshell, is the evolutionary dilemma of the group-adapted animal: Should I try to maximize my success at the expense of my groupmates, or should I put my efforts into supporting and defending the group? My goal is to put as many of my genes as possible into the next generation, but if the group ceases to exist, my offspring will have no chance of surviving.

It's a real dilemma for a human but not for an ant, due to the peculiarities of reproduction in the order Hymenoptera (the ants, bees, and wasps). In these insects, sex is determined in a way that seems bizarre to us mammals: fertilized eggs develop into females, unfertilized eggs into males. Males consequently have only one set of chromosomes; females have two. The result, in an ant colony founded by a single queen who mated with a single male, is that the queen's daughters are more closely related to each other than are full siblings in a species such as ours. Two female workers in an ant nest (all the workers are females) share three-quarters of their genes. In terms of genetic similarity, they are midway between human siblings and identical twins.[58]

This means that a female ant shares more genes with her sisters than she would with her own offspring, if she had any. In order to maximize the number of her genes in future generations, therefore, what an ant should do is help her mother produce more sisters. And that is what she does. The social system of the ant colony—an egg-laying queen supported by workers that do not reproduce—has been so successful that it has evolved independently a dozen times in the order Hymenoptera.[59]

The ant's tiny brain gives her instructions that cause her to spend her life working to maintain, defend, and if possible expand the colony. An individual ant—the one Hölldobler and Wilson described as a disappointment—will unhesitatingly give up her life to benefit her sisters. Workers whose job it is to go out of the nest and forage for food have a death rate of 6 percent per hour.[60]

What has made the social insects so successful is the division of labor. All ants practice division of reproductive labor: only the queen reproduces. Most ants also divide up other kinds of labor. There are lots of jobs to do in an ant nest—digging tunnels, clearing away debris, caring for eggs and larvae, defending the nest against intruders, foraging for food. In some species, ants take on inside jobs (such as caring for larvae) when they are young and then graduate to outside jobs as they get older. In other species, an individual ant may spend her entire life working at a single job. In either case, the choice of the job is determined not by the ant's genes but by environmental factors, because the ants in a nest are basically all alike genetically. Here's the puzzle of the ants' nest: they have almost identical genes and yet they do different jobs!

As the Bible pointed out, ants do their jobs with "no guide, overseer, or ruler"; their queen is neither a despot nor an organizer but merely an egg-laying machine. So how do the different jobs get distributed? How does the colony manage to function in such a way that all the important jobs get done? The answer: through positive and negative feedback. Ants respond to signals from other ants and from the environment. If ants foraging outside the nest come across a rich source of food—what we beleaguered humans call a "picnic"—they recruit other ants to come and help them carry the booty home. That's positive feedback. If the nest has been damaged by a heavy rain, the ants give up foraging for a while and concentrate on nest repair. That job works on negative feedback, like a thermostat: once the nest has been repaired, the stimulus for repairing it disappears and the ants can do something else.[61]

What got me interested in the parallels between ant societies and human societies was a recent article in the journal *Science* titled "Social Insect Networks." Its author, the biologist Jennifer Fewell, uses the word "networks" to describe the simple interactions among the members of an insect colony that have global effects on the colony. Self-organization in insect colonies, Fewell explains, can produce emergent properties that make the whole greater than the sum of its parts—properties such as mass actions, social hierarchies, and the division of labor. Division of labor—Fewell calls it "divergence"—is produced by negative feedback in which the performance of a task by one individual reduces the chances that another individual will do it, because it no longer needs to be done. But to produce *stable* division of labor, positive feedback is needed as well:

> Most divergence models also include a positive feedback loop, in which performance of the behavior increases the probability that the individual will perform the behavior again. This self-reinforcement generates divergence even with initially small random differences in behavior and produces a faster and more stable system of divergence. . . . Division of labor also appears frequently within [other] social species, including humans. As an example, we can imagine an apartment where housemates share tasks. Used dishes pile up in the sink, produc-

> ing a continuously increasing stimulus. The dishes go unnoticed until the threshold of the one most sensitive to them is met, and he or she washes them. This removes the dishes as a stimulus, further reducing the likelihood that the other group members will ever wash them. The result is a dishwashing specialist (much to his/her dismay), and a set of nondishwashers.[62]

If that describes you, aren't you glad to know that it's not your housemates' fault that you ended up with the job of dishwasher? Nor, for that matter, is it your fault. It's an emergent property of the system. Blame the system.

Geneticists used to think that much of the variation within species, as well as the differences between species, was due to differences in genes. Now it appears that much of the variation, both within and between species, is due instead to differences in gene *expression.* When a gene is expressed, or turned on, it means that it is used as a template to produce a particular protein. Genes are turned on and off during the course of the lifespan; they are expressed in some cells and not in others. A given gene, present in both of two individuals, may be expressed in one and not in the other.[63]

The expression of genes can be influenced by environmental factors—in other words, by experience. Researchers studying honeybees have found differences in gene expression between "nurse" bees, which take care of the eggs and larvae, and bees that go out of the nest to forage for nectar and pollen. Worker bees usually start out as nurses and then, when they get older, switch to foraging. This change in jobs, researchers have found, is accompanied by changes in the expression of certain genes in the bee's tiny brain.

Are the changes in gene expression the *cause* or the *result* of the job change? The answer, it turns out, is both. If all the older bees in a hive are removed, the young bees that remain will divide up the duties: some will become foragers and the rest will remain nurses. The same differences in gene expression between the brains of nurses and foragers were found even when they were all the same age. Switching to foraging at a younger-than-usual age caused the foraging genes in their brains to turn on.[64]

What this means is that the dishwashing specialist and the nondishwasher may be expressing different genes in their brains, even if they were born with exactly the same genes.

Division of labor is an emergent property of human groups; no doubt it always has been. As the British evolutionary biologist Matt Ridley has suggested, it was one of the things that made our species a blockbuster success.

> In human society, the advantages of society are those provided by the division of labour. Because each person is a specialist of some sort—usually from an early enough age to have become good at their chosen trade while still mentally malleable—the sums of all our efforts are greater than they would be if each of us had to be a jack of all trades.[65]

Does that remind you of something? That's right, the mind. Or, for that matter, the body. Or, for that matter, the car. They're all modular—made up of an assortment of devices that were each designed to do a specific job. Ridley likens the division of labor in human societies to the organs of the body. "The division of labour is what makes a body worth inventing," he says. "Each organ, each muscle, each tooth, each nerve and each bone plays its separate part in the whole enterprise."[66]

Ridley doesn't claim credit for the idea that a society is greater than the sum of its parts because each part can specialize in something: he credits the Scottish philosopher and economist Adam Smith, who said much the same thing back in 1776. But Adam Smith, writing a century before Darwin, didn't know about evolution through natural selection. Or did he? He certainly seems to have had some of the relevant ideas. He attributed division of labor not to the individual's desire to benefit his society but to his desire to benefit himself:

> It is not from the benevolence of the butcher, the brewer, or the baker, that we expect our dinner, but from their regard to their own interest. We address ourselves, not to their humanity but to their self-love, and never talk to them of our own necessities but of their advantages.[67]

Smith also suggested how the division of labor might come about through self-interest: in "a tribe of hunters," one who proves adept at making arrows can do better by trading his arrows for meat than by going out to hunt for it himself.[68]

Humans are motivated by self-interest because, unlike ants, they live in groups that do not consist entirely of close relatives. That's one of the things that made our species such a blockbuster success—our ability to form big, inclusive groups that aren't necessarily based on kinship. But the consequence is the dilemma I mentioned when I was talking about ants: whether to try to maximize one's success at the expense of one's groupmates or to put one's efforts into supporting and defending the group. It is a true dilemma for humans (though it isn't for ants), and different humans solve it in different ways. Some are willing to fight and die to defend their group. Then there's Woody Allen, who doesn't even want to *work* for his group, much less die for it. "It's not that I'm afraid to die," he explained. "I just don't want to be there when it happens."[69]

When people work or die for their group, the motivation to do so has been provided by the socialization system—an ancient system that dates from the time when all the members of the group were close relatives. The motives provided by the status system, in contrast, are entirely those of self-interest. It is this self-interest that produces divergence in human groups. The status system doesn't give a damn about the group's welfare; it asks, "How can *I* best compete?" To find the best answer requires self-knowledge, so the status system searches for self-knowledge in the social cues provided by others. It then uses this information to plot a long-term strategy that will involve direct competition only in those arenas of endeavor in which the individual has a hope of succeeding and, if possible, avoid competition in other arenas. The result is that individuals seek unoccupied niches; they specialize in different things. I cannot better Adam Smith's description of the long-term outcome of this process:

> The difference of natural talents in different men is, in reality, much less than we are aware of; and the very different genius which appears to distinguish men of different professions, when grown up to maturity, is not upon many occasions so much the cause, as the effect of the division of labour. The difference between the most dissimilar characters, between a philosopher and a common street porter, for example, seems to arise not so much from nature, as from habit, custom, and education. When they came into the world, and for the first six or eight years of their existence, they were perhaps, very much alike, and neither their parents nor playfellows could perceive any remarkable difference. About that age, or soon after, they come to be employed in very different occupations. The difference of talents comes then to be taken notice of, and widens by degrees.[70]

Accidentally or on purpose (so to speak), evolution provided a primate with a mental organ that has the effect of increasing behavioral diversity.

The result was a species, *Homo sapiens*, that is well suited, not just to living in groups, but to living in *large* groups. The most obvious advantage this gives us is that large groups are capable of wiping out smaller ones. That's another thing we share with ants.

In some circumstances and for some behaviors, it is advantageous to minimize behavioral differences within a group. That's what socialization does. For example, communication within the group works best if everyone speaks the same language and has the same accent. The better communication benefits both the individual and the group.

In other circumstances or for other behaviors, it is advantageous for individuals to maximize the behavioral differences between them. Differences in personality, when they aren't genetic, are at first the result of behaving differently; later they become the cause of behaving differently—of following divergent paths in adult life. The reason that the differences persist may be that different genes have been turned on, or cranked up, in the brain.

As a consequence of the way the status system operates, even identical twins will develop different personalities. It doesn't matter whether they grow up in the same home or in different homes, whether they belong to the same group or different groups. In either case their close associates are going to see them as distinct individuals. Once their associates see them as distinct individuals, it doesn't even matter that they are twins. A person is seen as an individual whether he or she is one of a pair of twins, a set of siblings, or a group of friends. We see people as unique individuals because the relationship system goes to pains to distinguish them. Human differences in personality, to the extent that they are not biological, are the outcome of a collaboration between the relationship system in your head and the status system in mine.

The collaboration between the relationship system and the status system doesn't just make twins different: it makes everyone different. And it doesn't make twins differ only from each other: it makes each twin differ from everyone else—everyone in their group, everyone of their age and sex. The others with whom they will have to compete in adulthood.

10

Denouement

AT THE END of a classic British mystery novel there is usually a scene in which the detective assembles all the characters in the library of a stately mansion and ties up the loose ends, explaining how the perpetrator did it and why the clues make perfect sense when put together the right way. In the American mystery novels featuring the private investigator Nero Wolfe, this scene takes place in Wolfe's spacious office on the ground floor of a three-story brownstone in Manhattan. Nero Wolfe seldom leaves his house, so he arranges for all the suspects, plus a police officer or two, to come to his office. Then he asks some questions, makes some deductions—that is, abductions—and pretty soon everything is all wrapped up. The perpetrator picks from the standard menu of emotions—denial, anger, grief, resignation—and may try to make a break for it, but is quickly collared by the cops and marched off in handcuffs.[1]

I'm writing this in my office, considerably smaller and more cluttered than Nero Wolfe's, on the ground floor of a two-story house in suburban New Jersey, and wondering whether the cops brought enough handcuffs, because there are three perpetrators in this case. Three mental organs or systems. All three affect social behavior; all three collect information that comes from other people. Though only one, the status system, can actually be held responsible for producing personality differences between identical twins, it couldn't have done the deed without the help of the relationship system. Together, the three systems left such a welter of confusing clues that it was impossible to solve the mystery without figuring out the modus operandi of all of them.

The three systems work in different ways (see the table on the next two pages for a summary). They collect different kinds of information from the environment and process the data differently. They provide different moti-

	Relationship System	Socialization System	Status System
Goal	To establish and maintain favorable relationships.	To be a member of a group.	To be better than one's rivals.
Motivations provided	To acquire knowledge about other people. To share that knowledge with others.	To affiliate with a group. To be accepted by its members. To conform to the group's norms. To defend the group.	To compete. To improve one's status. To acquire self-knowledge by comparing oneself with others.
Emotions	Love, hatred, dependency, trust, aggressiveness, lust, jealousy, etc.	Hostility toward other groups, group pride or patriotism, unhappiness at being excluded.	Ambition, envy, triumph, conceit. Embarrassment, anger, or unhappiness at losing status.
Typical behaviors	Infant attachment behaviors, making friends, dominance contests, courtship, trading favors, gossiping.	Adopting the behaviors, language, accent, dress, and attitudes of one's groupmates. Fighting for one's group.	Matching oneself against one's peers. Competing in contests one might win and avoiding contests one is likely to lose.
Typical errors	The fundamental attribution error. Believing and passing on unreliable gossip.	Underestimating within-group variation. Automatically regarding one's group as good and other groups as bad.	Overestimating oneself and underestimating one's rivals.
Important components	A mental lexicon of people-information. A face-recognition module. A mind-reading mechanism. A relationship sociometer.	A categorization module. A calculator of central tendencies. A group-acceptance sociometer.	A mindreading mechanism. An eye-gaze detector. A sociometer that gives detailed, multidimensional information about status.
Data collected	Information about specific people, based on personal experience or hearsay.	Information about the members of social categories.	Information about how one compares with others in one's social category.

	Relationship System	**Socialization System**	**Status System**
How data are processed	Information about each individual is stored separately.	Information about the members of social categories is averaged to form prototypes.	Information obtained from different individuals is combined. Eye-gazes are counted. Hierarchies are assessed.
Level of consciousness	Fully available to consciousness.	Most of the work done by this system is not available to the conscious mind.	Though some work (e.g., eye-gaze counting) may be done unconsciously, most is available to consciousness.
Developmental timetable	Ready to go at birth and remains active throughout the lifespan.	Working by age three. Socialization appears to be largely complete by adolescence. Affiliation with new groups is possible throughout the lifespan, but fervor may decline in the later years.	Competitiveness is evident in three-year-olds, but other components of this system develop slowly. Changes in strategy are common during adolescence and still possible in adulthood.

vations and different emotions. Disagreements sometimes arise. Occasions in which two mental mechanisms issue contradictory commands—"the human heart in conflict with itself," as the novelist William Faulkner put it—are a familiar part of human life.[2]

My goal was to explain the variation in personality—the big and little differences among individuals—that cannot be attributed to variations in their genes. The behavioral geneticists had shown that this variation was not due to differences among the homes in which the individuals grew up, because the amount of variation between two people was about the same, whether they grew up in the same home or in different homes. I looked at one plausible explanation after another, including gene-environment interactions and environmental differences within the family, but they all proved to be red herrings. So I had to come up with a theory that hadn't been considered previously.

Or hadn't been considered lately. Here is a statement made in 1799 by the American political philosopher Thomas Jefferson:

> I consider man as formed for society, and endowed by nature with those dispositions which fit him for society.[3]

Jefferson got it right. Humans are formed for society—they are a group-adapted species with a highly active social life—and they are endowed by nature with abilities and motivations that fit them for that life. Isn't it interesting that Jefferson said "endowed by nature" sixty years before Darwin explained how nature did it?

I came across that quote only yesterday, so I can't claim it was Thomas Jefferson who inspired me to think up a theory in which humans are endowed by nature with a number of dispositions that fit them for society. My inspiration came from more recent sources, especially Steven Pinker's work on language and Simon Baron-Cohen's work on the mindreading mechanism. These theorists first showed that using language and reading other people's minds are special abilities that have mental systems of their own. Then they took the systems apart and figured out how they work, using evidence of many different kinds.[4]

The disposition to acquire a language is one of the things that fit humans for society. So is the disposition to figure out what other people are thinking. Three other things that fit humans for society are their disposition to form and maintain personal relationships, their disposition to adjust their behavior to the norms and customs of their society, and their disposition to compete with the other members of their society and, if possible, outdo them in some way.

Here's how I think the perpetrators do their work. Here's how babies develop, how they become socialized, and how each one acquires a unique personality.

From birth, babies are tuned in to auditory stimuli that sound like words and to visual stimuli that look like faces. They study the faces of the people they encounter and quickly learn to recognize the ones who keep turning up. Before they are halfway through their first year, they are behaving differently—and appropriately—with the various people in their lives. With a depressed person the baby is subdued, with a cheerful person the baby is lively. From Mommy, the baby expects food and comfort; from older siblings the baby looks for entertainment. These different responses to different people are superimposed upon, or averaged in with, underlying behavioral predispositions. A baby born with a stolid temperament will be less lively with every social partner than one born with an exuberant temperament. We know next to nothing about how genes produce such effects.

At one year of age, the relationship system is operating on all cylinders—the baby's mind already contains an extensive people-information lexicon—and the language system is just beginning to roll. The socialization system has made a start at categorizing people and at calculating central tendencies (prototypes) for the members of these social categories, but at this point babies still have no idea which category they themselves belong in.

They start to figure it out when they're around two years old. By age three, children know that they are children, not grownups, and they know whether they are girls or boys. Once they've categorized themselves, children begin to conform to the norms of their own social category and to favor that category over others. But self-categorization depends on context. A child may categorize herself with the girls (versus the boys) in some situations, with the children (versus the adults) in others, and as a member of her race or religion or team in still others. Part of getting older is the need to adapt to changes in self-categorization. When an individual stops categorizing herself as a child and starts categorizing herself as a teenager, she has to adjust her behavior to a whole new set of norms. Later, when she starts categorizing herself as a grownup, the norms will change again, to the immense relief of her parents.

The effect of socialization is that children become more similar to their same-sex peers in behavior—some kinds of behavior, at least. That is why behavioral geneticists occasionally find nongenetic similarities between twins or siblings—similarities that can be attributed to "shared environment." The environment they share is a culture or subculture: the culture of the neighborhood, school, social class, or ethnic group that siblings who grow up together have in common. Small subcultural effects are sometimes found for personality and intelligence; larger effects are found for things like delinquency and accents. Siblings almost always speak with the same accent, and it doesn't necessarily match that of their parents.[5]

I have been quoted as saying that children are socialized by their peers.

In a sense that is correct, but they aren't socialized by *interactions* with their peers or by *relationships* with their peers. What causes them to become more like their same-sex peers is their identification with a particular social category and their own effort (motivated by the socialization system) to tailor their behavior to that of the prototypical member of that social category. Interaction with peers gives them useful feedback on how well they are doing the tailoring, but if need be they can do these things without any interaction at all.

Social categorization defines for children who their allies are and also who their rivals are. They want to be part of a group and to do what the other members do, but at the same time they want to be *better* than the other members of their group—they seek high status. The existence of these two conflicting motives is a clue that more than one mental system is involved. The motivation to compete is provided by the status system. Little boys vie for status by trying out for the position of alpha male. In play they get an idea of how strong they are relative to other boys their age.

But humans compete in many arenas; information obtained solely through contests of strength is not enough. One reason the status system is slow to get moving is that much of its input is provided by the mindreading mechanism, which is capable of doing some impressive things by the age of four but takes many more years to become good at its job. Though the mindreading mechanism evolved to serve the relationship system and continues to do so, it also provides important information to the status system: information on how the self is regarded by other people. Information on how the self compares, in the eyes of other people, with other girls or boys or other children or teenagers—the others with whom the self is vying for status.

The information keeps coming in. At least through adolescence and probably well into adulthood, people are capable of modifying their behavioral strategies on the basis of new information. I can't outdo my rivals by overpowering them? Then let me try something else. Maybe I can be the funniest, or the smartest, or the one who is best at identifying plants or hitting a golf ball. I can't be the prettiest? Then maybe I can be the nicest, and if that doesn't work either, maybe I should try being the nastiest. Humans have many ways of finding something to be good at, but the limits put on them by their genes and their environment make some choices impractical, and some individuals are constrained to pick from a smaller menu than others. Shakespeare's Richard III is physically deformed and Shakespeare has him explain himself like this: "Therefore, since I cannot prove a lover . . . I am determined to prove a villain."[6]

Peers are as important for the status system as they are for the socialization system, but for different reasons. To the status system, the child's same-sex peers are his rivals, and one of the things he has to do is figure out how he compares with them. But the information that tells him how he compares with them needn't come only from peers: it can come from anyone in his community, the more information the better. I suspect that information provided by close relatives is discounted because it is likely to be inaccurate and biased, but even if it is given equal weight it isn't going to count for much in the long run, because as children get older they spend more and more of their time with nonrelatives.

Personality varies in part because people have different genes, in part because even people with the same genes have slightly different brains, in part because even people with the same genes have different social experiences, and in part because variation and division of labor are emergent properties of human groups.

Identical twins have different social experiences because the members of their community see them as unique individuals. They may differ initially only because of developmental noise, but people who know them pick up on these little differences and use them to distinguish the twins. That's one of the jobs of the relationship system: to keep individuals straight, to tell them apart. If I'm mad at Shawn I don't want to make the mistake of punching Jonathan in the nose, so I keep a separate page in my people-information lexicon for each of them. The status system in Shawn's mind tries to read what my lexicon says about Shawn, and the status system in Jonathan's mind tries to read what my lexicon says about Jonathan. Since I hold different opinions of Shawn and Jonathan, their status systems will receive different input. They'll receive different input from everyone who knows them. The self-knowledge Shawn acquires will differ from the self-knowledge Jonathan acquires.

Division of labor is an emergent property in human groups, just as it is in ant nests. While the socialization system is motivating the child to conform—"I do what the others do"—the status system is motivating the child to find something to be best in, perhaps something no one else is doing—"I do what they *don't* do."

All these things create or widen behavioral differences between identical twins. Such differences, if they are persistent, are both the cause and the result of differences in the brain. Behaving differently causes different synapses to form and different genes to be expressed, and these changes in the brain cause the behaviors to persist.

Each of the three systems I have described gives people a way of adjusting to or making use of a particular aspect of their social environment. Nature—that is, evolution—has endowed humans with dispositions which fit them for society. These dispositions enable people to behave appropriately in different social contexts and with different social partners. People make long-term adjustments in behavior that adapt them to their culture; thus they become more alike in some ways. People also find different ways of competing with their rivals; thus they become less alike in other ways. The result is that no two people have the same personality. No two are alike.

Nero Wolfe relies on the members of the local constabulary to haul the perpetrators off to jail, but otherwise he has little use for them. Like most fictional detectives who are not themselves cops, he harbors a fine disdain for the people who are officially charged by the society with the duty of identifying and nabbing perpetrators. He sees cops as close-minded, unidirectional in their thinking, and prone to settling prematurely on the easiest solution and confining their investigation to attempts to prove it.

Admittedly, I have done my share of throwing brickbats at the professionals, but I don't want to leave you with the impression that I think most of them are clueless. On the contrary, the professionals have provided every single one of the clues. The clues, however, came from many different sources—not just from evolutionary psychology and behavioral genetics but from social psychology, developmental psychology, psycholinguistics, neurophysiology, anthropology, primatology, and entomology. The academic world, like the human mind, is made up of specialists. I've found that the most important advantage in not being a member of that world is the freedom not to specialize. Specialists view their field through a magnifying glass: they see very small details in a very small area. There are occasions when a jack of all trades like me can come in handy.

It is not specialization per se, however, that has caused so many academic psychologists to waste their time (and ours) chasing red herrings. It's mostly that they don't know enough about one particular area: behavioral genetics. Academics who are not themselves behavioral geneticists are apt to turn up their noses at it. This has been true since the late 1940s, when it became socially unacceptable even to hint that some of the differences among people might have a genetic basis. Despite the fact that the word "genes" can now be spoken aloud in polite company, most academic psychologists remain willfully ignorant of the methods and findings of behavioral genetics. They reveal their ignorance every time they open their mouths to say something about the length and width of a rectangle.

It is impossible to figure out what the environment does without taking into account what the genes do. It's like trying to figure out how much you've earned by looking at how much money you have at the end of the year, without considering your assets and debts at the beginning of the year. All research that looks at individual differences has to have some way of controlling for the effects of genes—otherwise the results are meaningless. Regrettably, most research on individual differences does not meet this standard. People take such research seriously because the results confirm what they already believe and because there is so much of it. But no matter how high you pile it, worthless research is still worthless research. And theories based on worthless research are worthless theories.

Let me give you an example. In 1991, two developmentalists and an anthropologist—Jay Belsky, Laurence Steinberg, and Patricia Draper—proposed an "evolutionary theory" of female mating strategy.[7] They reasoned that there is no one best mating strategy for human females, and that evolution has therefore endowed females with two alternative strategies, short-term and long-term. Which one will a given individual adopt? According to this theory, it depends on the family environment she experienced in infancy and early childhood. Girls who spent those early years in stressful environments—homes without fathers, or homes in which the parents got along poorly—will tend to adopt a short-term mating strategy: reach sexual maturity early, find a guy, jump into bed with him, kiss him good-bye, and find another guy. Girls reared in homes with nice, steady dads, on the other hand, will tend to adopt a long-term mating strategy: mature late, be choosy about whom to have sex with, find a guy just like dear old Dad, and stick with him.

Many evolutionary psychologists found this theory appealing, especially the part about the effects of a fatherless home. The reasoning made sense to them. If you live in an environment where security is nonexistent, why waste time waiting for it? Reproduce while you can. It's a theory that seemed to explain how girls adapt to the harsh or benign realities of their environment, and there were plenty of data to support it. Girls reared in fatherless or troubled homes do reach puberty earlier, on average. They do have sex earlier. They do have more sexual partners and more broken relationships.[8]

The believers in this theory were willing to admit that genetic factors play a role in determining rate of sexual maturation and age at puberty; it has long been known that women who matured early are likely to have daughters who mature early. The believers were also willing to admit that girls who mature early are more likely to have sex early. But it couldn't just be heredity, they reasoned, because the "effects" of a fatherless or troubled home were still detectable even after researchers controlled for the age at which the subjects' mothers reached puberty.[9]

But girls inherit behavioral predispositions, as well as physical traits, from their mothers. And what about their fathers? Don't girls inherit anything from their fathers?

Certainly they do. A group of medical geneticists recently identified a gene that girls inherit from their fathers (it's on the X chromosome) and that has psychological and physical effects on both sexes. Males who inherit a particular variant of this gene tend to be impulsive and aggressive and are more likely to have troubled relationships—hence, more likely to sire children who grow up fatherless. Females who inherit this gene variant tend to reach sexual maturity earlier, begin having sex earlier, and have more sexual partners. The researchers who did this study looked at only a single gene; there must be other genes involved as well. But the study showed that genetic explanations of the "father absence effect" are plausible.[10]

The problem with the "evolutionary theory" of female mating strategy proposed by Belsky, Steinberg, and Draper is that it was based on the wrong kind of research. Individual differences in girls' physical maturation and sexual activity were attributed to their home environment in early childhood, but the method used by the researchers provided no way of establishing that the differences they found were indeed due to the home environment and not to genetic differences among their subjects. The researchers should have looked at pairs of twins or siblings reared in the same home, to see if the home environment had similar effects on both siblings. They didn't do this; they looked at only one subject per home. It was a behavioral geneticist, David Rowe, who finally did the right kind of research. Rowe found that environmental factors do play a small role in the age of onset of sexual activity, but his evidence suggests that these factors operate during the teen years, not in early childhood, and involve cultural or subcultural influences—the environment shared by siblings *outside* the home.[11]

This was not the only case in which lack of knowledge of behavioral genetics, and the seductive use of the word "evolutionary," led evolutionary psychologists astray. Another example is the birth order theory presented by Frank Sulloway in his book *Born to Rebel*. Sulloway claimed that his explanation of the personality differences between siblings was an evolutionary theory and many evolutionary psychologists embraced it. They accepted his misinterpretation of the behavioral genetic evidence—the notion that growing up together makes siblings less alike—because they liked his Darwinian-sounding story of why siblings become less alike: it's because they compete with each other. But the evidence I told you about in chapter 4 shows that growing up together is not responsible for sibling differences; nor is competing with each other. Environmental effects on personality are about the same in magnitude, whether siblings grow up together or apart and whether they compete or cooperate.

As you know, I'm not a behavioral geneticist myself; my interest is in the environment, not in genes. But I have come to the conclusion that current theories of environment are wrong, and that most of them are wrong because the theorists have not paid adequate attention to genetic factors. They have failed to use research methods capable of assessing the contributions of genes, and they have failed to understand—or even to attempt to understand—the results of research that did use such methods.

Since the late 1940s, theorists and researchers in most areas of psychology have persistently underestimated the influence of genes on behavior. When they see children with the same faults and virtues as their parents, they attribute the similarities to what the children learned from their parents. When they see children displaying the same faults and virtues at school as they do at home, they attribute the similarities to generalization—a carryover of learned behavior from the home to the school. They are wrong on both counts. Genetic influences on behavior account for most behavioral similarities between parents and children and for most of the behavioral similarities across social contexts (cultural or subcultural effects account for the remainder). Genetic influences also account for most of the continuity in personality between early childhood and adulthood. When traits show up early and persist into adulthood, it's because of heredity, not early environment.

Don't worry, there's still plenty of room for environmental effects on behavior. Evolution provided the members of our species with a mind prepared from birth to collect specific kinds of information from the environment. The question is not whether young humans are responsive to their environment—of course they are! The question is, what kinds of information do they collect and what do they do with it? My answer is that they collect information of a pertinent sort, as close as possible to the time when they will be needing it (so that the information is up-to-date), and they use it in ways that make evolutionary sense. To assume that children are fashioned in such a way that their adult behavior is contingent on their experiences with their parents in the first few years of life is not just to underrate them but to underrate evolution itself. The reason why evolutionary psychologists fall prey to such ideas is that they, too, find it hard to put aside their faith in the nurture assumption.

Why are parents so convinced of their importance in their children's lives? Why do they believe their child's future success or failure depends on what they do today at home? I've thought about this question for a long time and still haven't settled on a conclusion, but here are my top three hypotheses.

First, it may result from a set of closely related illusions that social psychologists lump together under the term "self-serving bias." Most people overestimate their own importance and their ability to control the way things turn out, not just in child-rearing but in everything they do. Also, people are more likely to feel that they were responsible for good outcomes than for poor ones. Thus, if parents think their children are turning out well—and most parents do seem to think so—they are likely to give themselves the credit. Another manifestation of the self-serving bias is a tendency to feel a sense of uniqueness, at least in regard to one's virtues. So parents whose children are turning out well are likely to attribute that outcome to child-rearing skills or practices they regard as unique and original, though in fact they may be doing exactly what Mr. and Mrs. Jones next door are doing.[12]

A second hypothesis is that the parents' conviction of their own importance in their children's lives is a concomitant of the package of parenting instincts with which evolution provided us. Hominid babies whose parents took good care of them were more likely to survive than those whose parents were negligent, and the surviving babies inherited the mental mechanisms that impelled their parents to provide that care. The instinct to take good care of our children is built in, but the justification for that care—the feeling of parental importance—needn't be built in. The conscious mind has a habit of concocting after-the-fact explanations for things we do for reasons the conscious mind knows nothing about.[13]

My third hypothesis is that the feeling of parental power is a peculiarity of our culture. The flip side of parental power is parental culpability—the idea that if anything goes wrong with the kid it's the parents' fault. It was Sigmund Freud who made that idea part of European and American culture. But Freud did most of his writing in the early part of the twentieth century, and the idea of parental culpability didn't take off until the late 1940s, after World War II. Two things gave it the nudge it needed: genetic explanations of behavior became unacceptable when people became aware of what the Nazis had done and the reasons they gave for doing it, and palatable versions of Freudian theory worked their way into books of advice to parents. In the United States, the leading promulgator was the advice-giving pediatrician Benjamin Spock.[14]

These two cultural influences working together produced a seismic shift in the child-rearing philosophy of ordinary middle-class parents. When I was a little kid, back in the early 1940s, the view was that troublesome kids were "born that way." I was a troublesome kid and my parents got sympathy, not blame; they felt unlucky rather than guilty. Only a decade later, guilt had become part of the job description of parenting. As the Danish sociologist Lars Dencik observed, "The guilty conscience, which accuses us of not paying sufficient attention to the interests of the child, and which nowadays so plagues parents and other caregivers, is in fact a very new and rather unique feeling in our modern epoch."[15]

In middle-class homes in North America and Western Europe, the modern epoch began shortly after the end of World War II and was accompanied by a new set of cultural myths. Just as people in traditional cultures attribute a child's faults to something the mother ate or looked at while she was pregnant, or to a hex laid on by a jealous neighbor or a punishment sent by the gods, people in our culture attribute a child's faults to something the parents did wrong after the child was born.

New myths can supplant old ones. The fact that almost everyone in a society believes something doesn't make it true. Was Richard III a villain, as Shakespeare depicted him and as he was believed to be for four hundred years, or was he an honorable man, as detective Alan Grant insisted in *The Daughter of Time*? I don't know, but the answer cannot be decided by a popular vote.

Even people who aren't parents themselves give their own parents the credit and blame for how they turned out. The classic case is the poet Philip Larkin, who famously griped, "They fuck you up, your mum and dad." Though he admitted that he shared most of his faults with his parents, he never entertained the thought that he might have inherited them.[16]

Of course, Larkin too was a product of his culture. But there's more to it than cultural myths. Introspection—conscious thoughts about our-

Credit: Non Sequitur © 2000 Wiley Miller. Dist. by Universal Press Syndicate. Reprinted with permission. All rights reserved.

selves—play a role in our theories of why we are the way we are. Freud couldn't have succeeded as he did if his theory hadn't struck a chord in those who read or heard about it. Something in what Freud said rang true. I believe it was the picture he painted of a complex mind made up of components that struggle with one another and that sometimes operate below the level of consciousness. The man was none too scrupulous in his use of evidence, and on the whole he did far more harm than good, but he happened to get some things right. Though Freud wasn't the first to speak of innate drives and unconscious processes, he was the one who brought them to people's attention.[17]

But it wasn't the unconscious mind that provided most of the support for Freud's theory. On the contrary, his greatest ally was the *conscious* mind. In the first chapter of this book I mentioned Robin Dunbar's study of conversation. Dunbar and his students listened in on people's conversations and found that two-thirds of their conversation time was spent on "matters of social import. Who is doing what with whom."[18] The people carrying on these conversations weren't actively engaged in any work-related tasks; if they had been, no doubt more of their talk would have been about the work at hand. Furthermore, people don't say everything that pops into their heads. But surely what they're talking about gives us some indication of what's in their conscious minds at the moment, and what they're talking about a lot of the time is other people. They're transmitting and receiving information of the type that is stored in the people-information lexicon, part of the relationship system. If a large share of our conversational material is generated by the relationship system, this implies that the relationship system also takes up a large share of our conscious thoughts and, therefore, of our accessible memories.

Though Freud talked a lot about the unconscious, his theory is almost entirely about relationships, and the relationship system does most of its work right out in the open. The motives that so engrossed him, sex and aggression, are provided by mechanisms that serve the relationship system and are readily accessible to the conscious mind. The conversation Freud elicited from his subjects (I hesitate to call them his patients, since he didn't seem to regard them that way himself[19]) was all about relationships. It is not surprising that relationships with parents should figure prominently in one's memories of childhood, or that Mom's and Dad's pages in one's people-information lexicon should be very full.

In contrast to the relationship system, the socialization system does most of its work underground, at a level not easily accessible to consciousness. We do not know how we got socialized because we weren't thinking about it when it happened. In fact, the socialization system I have described bears a resemblance to Freud's superego, and the two serve similar functions. But in attributing the formation of the superego to identification with the same-sex parent, Freud was demonstrably wrong. The idea that the child learns how to behave by identifying with the same-sex parent is one of the few aspects of Freudian theory that generates testable predictions, and research has not supported the predictions. Boys growing up without a father are no less masculine than those in two-parent homes. Children in two-parent homes do not resemble their same-sex parent in degree of masculinity or femininity. In fact, the evidence suggests (according to two developmentalists who looked at a good deal of it) that "a boy resembles other children's fathers [in behavior] as much as he does his own."[20]

Freud's notion that young children learn how to behave by identifying with their parents may have been based on what he knew about the children of his neighbors and colleagues in late-nineteenth-century Vienna, as well as on his own memories of childhood. These children were too young to go to school and perhaps had less contact with peers than children do nowadays. Many of them seem to have been firstborns or only children, so they also lacked siblings. Children will imitate whoever is around, and these children had a very limited choice of models. In *The Nurture Assumption*, I described a child who was reared with a young chimpanzee and who imitated the chimpanzee.[21] A child without siblings whose parents have neglected to provide him with a chimpanzee will imitate, for want of an alternative, a grownup. Hence we have the photos in child development textbooks of little boys pretending to shave or little girls pretending to cook. But children soon learn that behaving like grownups doesn't work very well, even at home. They may *pretend* to be grownups in their imaginative games, but from an early age children recognize the difference between real life and play-acting. Anyway, the grownups they pretend to be are not their parents: they're prototypes, generated by the central-tendencies calculator of the socialization system—as much like other children's parents as their own.

The third mental organ I have proposed, the status system, has no counterpart in Freudian theory. Freud attributed motives such as striving for status to the sex drive and I strongly disagree, even though access to desirable sexual partners is one of the things that status can buy. The desire for status begins early and lasts a lifetime. Old people in nursing homes, well past the point when Viagra can do them any good, still care about their status. In my view, status is an end in itself for humans. The fact that it buys access to desirable sexual partners in adulthood is no doubt one of the evolutionary reasons we are endowed with this motive, but evolution's reasons shouldn't be confused with people's motivations. Status also buys access to desirable things to eat and drink, but the drive to gain status isn't a side effect of hunger or thirst. If anything, hunger and thirst are likely to interfere with the quest for status. Sex can too. Ask Bill Clinton.

Like the relationship system, the status system does much of its work at a level that is accessible to the conscious mind. Freud thought he needed to explain why some things go on below the level of consciousness, but modern psychologists and philosophers have turned the question around: Why does *anything* have to be conscious? That's the philosophers' version of the question and I leave it to them. The psychologists' version is narrower but has the virtue of being at least potentially answerable: Why are some functions carried on right out in the open while others remain underground? For my purposes, the question can be narrowed still more: Given the limited workspace in the conscious mind, why is so much of that valuable space assigned to the relationship system and the status system?

One reason, I believe, has to do with language. Before we can put anything—a thought, a feeling, a bit of information—into words, it has to be accessible to the conscious mind. If consciousness gives us the ability to communicate in words, then it also makes it possible for us to gossip. Thus, consciousness serves the relationship system by enabling it to collect (and trade with others) information of the sort that is stored in the people-information lexicon. It serves the status system in a similar way. One of the ways we acquire information about ourselves is through verbal communication.

Both systems make use of the mindreading mechanism; indeed, the status system couldn't get along without it. This suggests another reason for granting these two systems the gift of consciousness. The evolutionary psychologist Nicholas Humphrey has hypothesized that consciousness enables us to reflect upon ourselves, and that this is what makes it possible to look into other people's minds. Humphrey's point is that we wouldn't be able to understand what other people are thinking unless we had the ability to introspect on our own mental processes.[22]

A final reason has to do with memory—in particular, with the distinction (explained in chapter 8) between explicit and procedural memory. Explicit memories, by definition, are available to the conscious mind; procedural memories generally are not. Memories for specific events are explicit; procedural memories are not about specific events but about things that happen over and over again. An explicit memory captures what was unique about a particular event; a procedural memory captures what a series of events had in common.[23] The relationship system requires explicit memory because the relevant experiences aren't necessarily things that happen over and over again—they may happen only once. The status system makes use of both explicit and procedural memory.

Explicit memory has other functions as well; it is not used solely for social purposes or for things that happen only once. Factual knowledge (semantic memory) is also accessible to the conscious mind and is therefore explicit. There are mental systems I haven't talked about in this book; they do other jobs and collect other kinds of information, such as the fact that a certain plant is poisonous or the location of the nearest source of water. That kind of knowledge, too, can be received in the form of verbal messages and profitably shared with other people.

My solution to the mystery is that three perpetrators are involved: three mental systems that go about their business in different ways. Together, these three can answer the hows, whys, whens, and wheres of personality development. They can explain why children, while they are growing up, become more like their peers in some ways and less like them in other ways, why they are motivated both to conform and to compete, and why they behave differently with different people and in different situations. My three-systems theory accounts for the behavioral genetic findings and for observations made by social psychologists. It is consistent with the increasingly prevalent view, proposed by evolutionary psychologists and supported by neurophysiological data, that the human mind is a toolbox of specialized devices.

But have I proved it? At the beginning of the book I quoted a famous saying by Sherlock Holmes: "When you have excluded the impossible, whatever remains, however improbable, must be the truth." But what if there were other alternatives that Sherlock hadn't excluded because they hadn't occurred to him? In science, all one can say is that one's theory accounts for more of the evidence, or accounts for it in a more intellectually satisfying way, than the other theories currently available.

An intellectually satisfying theory is one that follows Einstein's rule: make things as simple as you can, but no simpler. I will be the first to admit that my theory of personality development isn't simple. The problem is that none of the simpler theories work. I spent half the book showing that none of the simpler theories work.

Though it's possible that a new simple theory will suddenly appear on the horizon and turn out to be the winner, at this point it seems unlikely. More likely, I'm afraid, is that my theory will ultimately be beaten out by one that is even more complex. Biological processes have turned out to be fancier and messier than anyone imagined, and the brain is a hodgepodge of biological processes. Both as a theorist and as a writer, I like to make things clear and elegant, but this inevitably means leaving out exceptions and glossing over complications. For example, I spoke of the fusiform face area of the brain as an area that specializes in the recognition of faces, but neuroscientists have found that this area may also be involved in expertise in other kinds of recognition, where the expert's job is to discriminate among large numbers of similar items, such as postage stamps for stamp collectors or birds for ornithologists.[24]

More important, I've depicted the three systems as neatly separate and distinguishable, but the truth is unlikely to be that neat. The systems may overlap or share facilities; the borders between them may be hazy rather than sharp. Does the mind really make a distinction between dominating one rival (the relationship system) and being top man on the totem pole in a group of three (the status system)? And is the relationship system really just one system? Some evolutionary psychologists prefer to think that relationships are managed by a bunch of separate modules: one for mating, one for friendships, one for partnerships in reciprocal trade, one for parent-child relationships, and so on. I've depicted it as a single system because all these types of relationships rely on recognition and memory of individuals, and because the drive to acquire people-information appears to be much like the drive to learn words: we needn't have a specific purpose in mind in order to want to acquire the information. Maybe it will come in handy someday for some purpose or other; maybe it won't. When we meet new people, we generally don't know whether they will become friends, lovers, trading partners, or what; but that doesn't prevent us from starting to collect information about them. And if someone who once was a friend becomes a lover, we needn't start all over from scratch finding out what he or she is like. What we learned about this person when we were friends will still be available to us and will probably still be useful.

On the other hand, once we do have a particular kind of relationship with a person, we are likely to be more interested in obtaining some kinds of information than others, and we will use the information in different ways. The knowledge that someone is a close relative will be used in one way if we're thinking about mating, in another way if we're thinking about sharing. In the table on pages 242–43, I assigned the relationship system a single sociometer, which gives a thumbs-up or thumbs-down signal depending on whether the relationship currently in the spotlight is going well or poorly. But one sociometer might not be enough: separate gadgets might be needed for the various kinds of relationships. A mating sociometer, designed to tell us whether another person is willing to jump into bed with us, wouldn't be very useful for judging whether someone trusts us as a trading partner.[25]

If you think my theory is unnecessarily complex, just wait till you see what the theories will be like fifty years from now.

"Scientists do not conduct research to find things whose existence they don't suspect," the evolutionary psychologists John Tooby and Leda Cosmides noted.[26] It is my hope that this book will inspire scientists to conduct research on three mental systems whose existence they might not have suspected, or suspected only vaguely.

Perhaps I might make some suggestions. Brain-imaging studies have proved very useful in research on how the mind works: the activation of different mental processes lights up the brain in different ways. This technique provides one way to test my theory. What happens in the brain when, for example, people are given different kinds of feedback regarding social success or failure? In a recent experiment, subjects were given information that made them think they were being excluded from a group. Brain scans done immediately afterwards showed activation of two areas in the brain (the anterior cingulate cortex and the right ventral prefrontal cortex) that are also activated by physical pain; the conclusion was that being excluded hurts.[27] Well, a demotion in status also hurts, as does finding out that someone you like doesn't like you. But perhaps these things hurt in different ways. My theory predicts that feedback on group acceptance, on status, and on success or failure in a relationship should produce somewhat different responses in the brain.

A second method that has been useful in the search for mental mechanisms is the examination of individuals whose brains aren't working in the usual fashion, due to inborn abnormalities or to damage. The subjects who gave Baron-Cohen the idea for his model of a mindreading mechanism were children with autism. Such children lack the ability to read people's minds.

Unfortunately, the disabilities of children with autism cannot be used to distinguish the three systems I have proposed because the deficits are too pervasive; all three systems appear to be disrupted. Autism affects every aspect of social life. Children with this disorder aren't interested in people and don't form normal relationships. They don't conform and they don't compete. The neurological abnormalities that produce such devastating effects must be widespread.

What about more limited social disabilities? Are there people with malfunctioning relationship systems whose socialization and status systems are working okay? People who don't get socialized but who are good at competing? Yes, certainly. Researchers have found and reported such disparities and I've mentioned them here and there: for instance, the fact that children who are poorly accepted by their peer group may nonetheless be good at making and keeping friends, and vice versa. Folklore supports such distinctions. Sayings like "There's honor among thieves" imply that people who feel no need to conform to the norms of their society may nonetheless have successful relationships.

My theory doesn't predict, however, that these three areas of social life will be completely uncorrelated. Some weaknesses—a problem with language, say, or below-average skill at mindreading—can adversely affect the functioning of two or more systems at once. Other characteristics, such as physical appearance, can have widespread effects on social success or failure. Good-looking people are likely to be high in status and also high in group acceptance.

Because there are many ways to go about it, I think it will be relatively easy to obtain evidence of the existence of the three systems I have described. What will be more difficult is finding ways to test my solution to the mystery this book is about—the mystery of the unexplained variance in personality, exemplified by the personality differences between reared-together identical twins. To the extent that these differences are environmental in origin, and not the result of developmental noise, I attribute them to the workings of the status system.

The difficulties involved in testing this theory are illustrated by a true story about a pair of identical twins. Conrad and Perry McKinney, age fifty-six, were featured in an article in the *Boston Globe* titled "Two Lives, Two Paths." Born and reared in New Hampshire, the twins did everything together in their early years. They attended the same schools, sat in the same classrooms. Academically they were average students, but they were troublemakers. Eventually their teachers got fed up with their shenanigans and the twins were separated: Perry was held back in fifth grade, Conrad was promoted to sixth. That, according to the *Globe* reporter, was where their paths diverged. Conrad went on to graduate from high school; Perry dropped out in eleventh grade. Today, Conrad is a successful businessman—as it happens, he runs a private detective agency. Perry . . . well, Perry is a homeless alcoholic "who sleeps amid trash under a bridge," by the Piscataqua River in New Hampshire.[28]

This story shows, first of all, why ethical considerations make it impossible to test my theory by doing an experiment. We cannot tinker with the lives and futures of human beings. Testing my theory will therefore have to rely on "natural" experiments, provided by the world. The cruel experiment the world performed on Conrad and Perry produced results that were consistent with my theory. The theory predicts that if you change the way the community sees a child, and the change is substantial and persistent, the result will be a change in the child's personality. When a child is made to repeat a grade in school, it's a public event that changes the way the community sees him. Thereafter, when the child looks into his classmates' minds to find out what they think of him, he reads things like "dummy" and "loser."

But natural experiments tend to lack scientific rigor. When the decision was made to hold one twin back, did the teachers flip a coin and it came up Perry? Unlikely. More likely, they chose Perry because he was already doing a little less well in his schoolwork than Conrad, or acting a little more troublesome. It's even possible that Perry was already showing early signs of a mental illness that would worsen over the years.

Though identical twins are genetically identical (or nearly so), they have slightly different brains due to developmental noise or to minor injuries or infections. These little neurophysiological differences can result in differences in behavior, which means that if we find a behavioral difference between identical twins, it's usually impossible to tell whether it's due to the twins' experiences or to a preexisting difference in their brains. If people treat them differently and they behave differently, is the difference in how they're treated a cause or an effect of the difference in behavior? Even longitudinal studies can't answer this question. Researchers may find that differential treatment by teachers or peers at Time 1 is correlated with a difference in the twins' behavior at Time 2. But the teachers or peers might be reacting to a difference in behavior that already existed at Time 1, though it might not yet have been apparent to the researchers. The fact that some behavioral problems and mental illnesses show up in a mild form in the early years and worsen as time goes on doesn't prove that the worsening is due to the child's experiences: neurophysiology can work that way too.

Another problem in interpreting the story of Conrad and Perry is that being left back in school affects many aspects of a child's life, not just one. The status system, which keeps its owner informed about what others think of him, might not have been the only perpetrator involved in Perry's long, slow slide: the socialization system could also have played a role. Left-back kids, though they're bigger than most of their classmates and hence rank high in the pecking order, tend to be poorly accepted. Kids who are rejected by their peers often get together and form groups of their own—

in many cases, antisocial groups. The *Globe* reporter mentioned that after Perry was left back he "began to accumulate a circle of friends who were rowdier and more risk-taking" than Conrad's friends.[29] This means that socialization by a delinquent peer group could be one of the reasons why Perry ended up the way he did. As it happened, the poor guy didn't have any luck in relationships, either. His wife died suddenly at the age of twenty-nine from an aneurysm. So all three systems may have conspired to put Perry under the bridge.

In chapter 4, I pointed out that birth order studies are a handy way to test the theory that within-the-family environmental differences are responsible for sibling differences in personality. The virtue of this method is that (as far as we know) there are no systematic biological differences, due either to genes or to developmental noise, between firstborns and laterborns. Thus, birth order studies give us a way of controlling for biological differences while varying within-the-family environment. The cause-or-effect problem is solved, in this case, by a very common natural experiment: siblings born one at a time, in random order. If the birth order theorists had turned out to be right—if systematic differences in adult personality between firstborns and laterborns had been found—we would know that these differences must be an effect and not a cause of the environmental differences.

Now I'm looking for a way to control for biological differences while varying *outside*-the-family environment, and it's a good deal harder to find one. Environmental differences that are unrelated to biological differences tend to be idiosyncratic and nonsystematic, and thus not very useful to researchers. So far, the best I've been able to do was to find characteristics such as height and strength that are linked to systematic differences in outside-the-family experiences but that presumably are not genetically associated with particular personality characteristics. "Presumably" is the caveat here. Though theoretically unlikely,[30] it is not impossible that people who inherit genes that make them tall or strong may also tend to inherit genes that make them aggressive. Another possibility is that developmental noise may affect these physical and psychological characteristics in similar ways.

Though my theory is, in principle, testable, these methodological and ethical problems are not going to be easy to solve. Researchers are not likely to come up with a quick and easy way to test the theory. But perhaps it can offer them something better: a new approach, a new way of looking at personality development and social behavior. A viewpoint that can make existing research more understandable and suggest more productive strategies for future research.

You know by now, because I've belabored the point, that research on human behavior is useless if the method doesn't provide a way of controlling for the effects of genes. The behavioral geneticists have been saying that for years. I agree with them completely, but it's only a start. The research method also has to be sensitive to the effects of context, because people behave differently in different contexts and with different social partners. Ideally, the research method should not only control for the effects of genes but also assess the role they play in the carryover of behavior from one context to another.

But controlling for genes and for context is still not enough. The confusion between the effects of the socialization system and those of the status system—between the processes that enable children to adapt to their culture and those that cause each child to develop a unique personality—has long been an impediment to progress. So has the belief that successful relationships are the be-all and end-all of the child's life. I predict that researchers will make more progress if they attempt to distinguish the effects of the three systems I've described, rather than use methods that jumble them together. It was only when I started thinking of three separate systems, providing different motives and collecting different kinds of information from the environment, that I began to understand how evolution could have produced a bunch of conforming individualists like us. What a piece of work is the human being!

One of my goals in writing this book was to give you a healthy skepticism in regard to research. Researchers are human; they make mistakes; they have their own hopes and needs, their own beliefs. Doing research is a lot of work and is seldom carried out for the sake of pure curiosity. The researcher is earning a living, burnishing a reputation, trying to prove a pet theory (or disprove a competing one), or all of the above.

Some years ago, students taking a college course in experimental psychology were given the assignment of testing maze learning in rats. The students were told that the rats they would be testing were the products of selective breeding: some of the rats were bred to be quick at learning mazes, others were bred to be slow. Half the students were each given five "maze-bright" rats to test; the others received five "maze-dull" ones.

The students ran their rats in the maze, recorded the data, and tallied their results. According to the reports the students handed in, the "maze-bright" rats learned the maze significantly faster than the "maze-dull" ones. These rats made fewer errors, ran at a speedier pace, and were less likely to stall at the starting gate.

The truth is that the rats all came from the same genetic stock and were handed out randomly to the students. The "maze-bright" rats did better because the students who ran them in the maze expected them to do better. Since the rats had no way of knowing how well they were expected to do, the expectation must have exerted its effects on the students. Without realizing it, they must somehow have tipped the scales in favor of the results they were expecting to get. It's called "unconscious experimenter bias."[31]

How does it work? One possibility in this case is that the students might have treated the rats differently, depending on their expectations for them. Perhaps the students were more favorably inclined toward the "maze-bright" rats and handled them more gently, with the result that these rats were less scared. Bias could also have been introduced in the process of recording data and even in correcting errors. If a student inadvertently wrote down a wrong number, she might have been more likely to notice the error and correct it if it disagreed with her expectations.

There's no end of ways in which a researcher's expectations, or hopes, can influence the outcome of a study. As medical researchers have discovered, the only sure way to avoid experimenter bias is to use strict double-or triple-blinding. The physicians who examine the patients, and the statisticians who analyze the results, aren't supposed to know whether a given patient received the drug or the placebo.

Someone who thinks up a new theory is the last person who should be trusted with the job of testing it. A new theory should be tested by independent researchers who aren't cronies of the theorist and who don't have an axe to grind.[32] It's division of labor again: proposing theories and doing research to test them are jobs that should be carried out by different entities.

"A good theory should go in advance of the evidence," the evolutionary psychologist Geoffrey Miller said in a recent interview. "It should stick its neck out and say, this is how I think the world is, and leave it to other people to test it."[33]

Making a virtue of necessity, I will leave it to other people to test my theory.

Notes

CHAPTER 1: AN APPRECIATION OF DIFFERENCES

1. Reuters, December 12, 2002: "Adult conjoined twins may get surgery" (http://www.cnn.com/); J. Wong and K. Espina, July 8, 2003: "Iranian twins die after historic surgery" (http://dailynews.att.net/); W. Arnold, July 8, 2003: "Iranian twins die after separation surgery" (http://www.nytimes.com/).
2. Lykken and Tellegen, 1993.
3. Dyson, 2002.
4. Arthur Conan Doyle, "The Beryl Coronet" (1892), in Doyle, 1994, p. 274.
5. Grafton, 1989, p. 3.
6. Tey, 1951/1977, p. 7.
7. Tey, 1951/1977, p. 88. I know it's presumptuous to compare myself to fictional detectives such as Alan Grant and Kinsey Millhone. But after I finished writing this book, I discovered that someone else had made a similar comparison: I've been called "the Miss Marple of developmental psychology." See Wesseling, 2004.
8. Arthur Conan Doyle, "A Scandal in Bohemia" (1892), in Doyle, 1994, p. 11.
9. Pinker, 1997.
10. Pinker, 2002, p. 1.
11. Napolitan and Goethals, 1979.
12. Gilbert and Malone, 1995.
13. Myers, 2002.
14. Buss, 1995.
15. Hamilton, 1964. See Dawkins, 1989.
16. Searby and Jouventin, 2003.
17. Trivers, 1971.
18. Wilkinson, 1990.
19. Ridley, 1996.
20. Garcia and Koelling, 1966; Garcia, McGowan, and Green, 1972.
21. Quoted in Seligman and Hager, 1972, p. 15.

22. Pinker, 1994, p. 18.
23. Pinker, 1997, p. 403.
24. Carpenter, 1975; DeCasper and Fifer, 1980.
25. Dunbar, 1996, p. 62.
26. Dunbar, 1996.
27. Murphy, 1976, cited in Lykken, 1995.
28. Sacks, 1985.
29. Farah, 1992.
30. Pliny the Elder (1st century A.D.), *Natural History*, Book VII.
31. Tey, 1951/1977, p. 83.
32. Bellew, ca. 1955, p. 16.
33. *Macbeth*, act 1, scene 4.
34. Gladwell, 2000, p. 39.
35. Dunbar, 1996, pp. 4, 79.
36. Pinker, 2003.
37. Allport and Odbert, 1936.
38. D. E. Brown, 1991.
39. Muhle, Trentacoste, and Rapin (2004) give a concordance rate of 60 percent for classical autism in identical twins. If autism is defined more broadly, to include related syndromes such as Asperger's, concordance increases to 92 percent.
40. Dawson, Carver, Meltzoff, Panagiotides, McPartland, and Webb, 2002.
41. Baron-Cohen, 1995; see also Frith and Frith, 2001.
42. Barkow, 1992.
43. Gray, 1999, p. 563.
44. Caspi and Roberts, 2001.
45. McCrae and Costa, 1999.
46. Kagan, 1998b, p. 36.
47. Personality correlations: Bouchard, Lykken, McGue, Segal, and Tellegen, 1990; depression: Plomin, DeFries, McClearn, and Rutter, 1997; schizophrenia: Gottesman, 2001.
48. Sayers, 1931/1968.
49. Staples, 2003.

CHAPTER 2: THAT DAMN RECTANGLE

1. Harris, 1998a, p. 48.
2. E.g., Gladwell, 1998.
3. Cheever, 1991. Cheever's mother supported their family by running a gift shop; he described his father as an "unemployed shoe salesman" (p. 215).
4. E.g., Harris and Liebert, 1991.
5. My epiphany is described in Harris, 1998a, pp. 264–265. The textbook I was working on at the time was never completed; I backed out of the project when I realized I could no longer give the publishers what they were expecting.

6. Sayers, 1931/1968.
7. To calculate the variance, subtract the mean (average) score from each individual score and square each of these deviations from the mean. The variance is the mean of these squared deviations.
8. More precisely, heritability is defined as the proportion of the variance in the measured outcome—the variance in a personality trait, for example—that can be attributed to variations in genes.
9. Bouchard and Loehlin, 2001.
10. Falbo and Polit, 1986.
11. Minor differences between children who did or did not go to day-care centers have turned up in some studies, but the differences have not been consistent from one study to the next. Some studies (e.g., NICHD Early Child Care Research Network, 2003; Sagi, Koren-Karie, Gini, Ziv, and Joels, 2002) show negative effects, while others (e.g., Andersson, 1992; Harrison and Ungerer, 2002) show positive effects. Similar inconsistencies are found in the research on the only child.
12. Golombok, Cook, Bish, and Murray, 1995; Golombok, MacCullum, Goodman, and Rutter, 2002; van Balen, 1998.
13. Begley, 1998, p. 56
14. Vandermeer, 2004, p. 473.
15. Ehrlich, 2000.
16. Bouchard and Loehlin, 2001; Lake, Eaves, Maes, Heath, and Martin, 2000.
17. E.g., Hoffman, 1991
18. Eisenberg, Cumberland, and Spinrad, 1998.
19. Feinstein, 1985, p. 409.
20. Feinstein, 1985, p. 408.
21. Estimates of the proportion of the variance attributable to shared environment cannot go below zero, which is one reason why they are seldom *exactly* zero. Any imprecision in the estimate will put it above zero, since it can't wobble in the other direction.
22. E.g., Bateson, 2002, p. 2212.
23. Heritability does not have to be squared to get the proportion of the variance accounted for. Heritability *is* the estimated proportion of variance accounted for by variations in genes.
24. Laleh and Ladan Bijani: see chapter 1. Chang and Eng: Ehrlich, 2000.
25. E.g., Greenspan, 1997; Joseph, 2002.
26. E.g., Kamin, 1974.
27. Reiss, 2000.
28. A correlation shouldn't be confused with a percentage. A correlation of .50 between identical twins doesn't mean that half of the twins are exactly alike and the other half are entirely different. It means that, on average, identical twins are fairly similar to each other in personality, but not extremely similar.
29. Twins: Bouchard, Lykken, McGue, Segal, and Tellegen, 1990; Plomin, DeFries, McClearn, and Rutter, 1997. Adoptive siblings: Bouchard and Loehlin, 2001.

30. Note that correlations can be either positive or negative, whereas heritability can only be a positive number (or zero). If adoptive siblings were less alike in personality than two adoptees picked at random, then the correlation for adoptive siblings would be negative.
31. Reiss, 2000, p. 142.
32. Plomin and Daniels, 1987.
33. Pinker, 2002.
34. Steinmetz, Herzog, Huang, and Hackländer, 1994.
35. Diabetes: Bach, 2002. Ear infections: Casselbrant, Mandel, Fall et al., 1999.
36. Andreasen, 1999; Bach, 2002.
37. Kondo, Schutte, Richardson et al., 2002.
38. Pinker, 2002.
39. Dickens, 1860–1861, chapter 9.
40. See Harris, 1998a, chapter 8; Harris, 2004a.
41. Caspi and Roberts, 2001.

CHAPTER 3: MONKEY BUSINESS

1. Harris, 1995.
2. J. R. Harris, "Don't Blame Your Parents: The Nurture Assumption on Trial." Paper presented at the annual meeting of the American Psychological Association, San Francisco, August 15, 1998 (available on the Gifts of Speech website, http://gos.sbc.edu/).
3. APA *Monitor*, December 1998.
4. Phone conversation with M. Bristol-Power, May 16, 2002.
5. E.g., Suzuki, Griffiths, Miller, and Lewontin, 1989. My thanks to Kevin Rich, the artist who made these drawings.
6. Maccoby, 2002, p. 42.
7. Maccoby, 2002, p. 42.
8. Plomin and Daniels, 1987.
9. Rare in nature: Rowe, 2001. Mutant fruit flies: Suzuki et al., 1989.
10. Caspi, Sugden, Moffitt et al., 2003.
11. Criminal behavior: Mednick, Gabrielli, and Hutchings, 1987. Schizophrenia: Tienari, Wynne, Moring et al., 1994.
12. IQ: Capron and Duyme, 1989. Criminal behavior: Gottfredson and Hirschi, 1990. Schizophrenia: Andreasen, 1999. Neighborhoods: Sampson, Morenoff, and Gannon-Rowley, 2002; see also Harris, 1998a, pp. 297–299.
13. S. J. Suomi, "Parents, Peers, and the Process of Socialization in Primates." Paper presented at the NICHD conference on Parenting and the Child's World, Bethesda, MD, August 2, 1999.
14. Harris, 1998a, p. 153.
15. McCrae and Costa, 1988; Myers, 1992.
16. Collins, Maccoby, Steinberg, Hetherington, and Bornstein, 2000; Rowe, 1994.
17. Harris, 1998a. For my reply to Collins et al. (2000), and to a similar article by Vandell (2000), see Harris, 2000b.

18. Collins et al., 2000, p. 224.
19. Suomi, 1997. The title of the book and the names of the editors are given incorrectly in the reference list of Collins et al., 2000.
20. Tey, 1951/1977, p. 84.
21. Suomi, 1999.
22. E-mail from W. A. Collins, February 18, 2000.
23. E-mail from S. J. Suomi, March 1, 2000.
24. E-mail from S. J. Suomi, March 1, 2000.
25. Suomi, 1987, pp. 405, 406.
26. Suomi, 1987, p. 414.
27. Suomi, 1991, p. 48.
28. Suomi, 1987, pp. 408, 410, 412, 413; Suomi, 1991, pp. 50, 51, 52, 54.
29. E-mail from E. E. Maccoby, July 17, 2000.
30. In the last few years, several papers by Suomi and his colleagues have been published that contain terms like "rearing condition" in their titles (e.g., Bastian, Sponberg, Suomi, and Higley, 2003). The studies described in these papers involve differences between peer-reared and mother-reared monkeys, not differences between monkeys reared by good versus bad mothers. Although I accept that peer-rearing—an unnatural condition that could never occur in the wild—might have deleterious long-term effects on a monkey's social development, there is another possible explanation for the subtle deficits found in these animals: nutritional deficiencies. The mother-reared animals are breast-fed; the peer-reared animals are bottle-fed. A study from Suomi's own laboratory (Champoux, Hibbeln, Shannon et al., 2002) showed that standard commercial monkey formula lacks certain fatty acids that are important in brain development, and that baby monkeys bottle-fed on the standard formula had weaker "orienting and motor skills" (p. 273). Adult humans who are deficient in these nutrients were found to have higher levels of a hormone associated with fear and anxiety (Hibbeln, Bissette, Umhau, and George, 2004).
31. Suomi, 2002.
32. Maestripieri, 2003, p. 321.
33. Maestripieri, 2003, p. 322.
34. Kagan, 1994.
35. Begley, 1998, p. 56.
36. Kagan, 1994; Arcus, 1991.
37. Arcus, 2001, pp. 48, 50, 52–55. See also Kagan, 2003. In this article on biological and environmental influences on temperament and personality, Kagan doesn't mention Arcus's research at all. "It has proven difficult," he reports, "to demonstrate that experiences of the infant years determine profiles during childhood or adolescence" (p. 12).
38. Rowe, 2002b.
39. Bouchard and Loehlin, 2001.
40. Quartz and Sejnowski, 2002, p. 129.
41. E-mails from T. J. Sejnowski, June 18 and June 20, 2003.
42. K. Wright, 1997, p. 78.

43. B. Harris, 1979.
44. Bellew, ca. 1955, p. 16.
45. Collins, Maccoby, Steinberg, Hetherington, and Bornstein, 2001.
46. Downloaded December 19, 2004, from http://www.psych.umn.edu/courses/psy1001/study/Wk6and7LrnObj.pdf.
47. Collins et al., 2000, p. 228.
48. Maccoby, 2002, p. 42.
49. Letter from D. Alexander, December 1, 1999.
50. National Institute of Child Health and Human Development, 2001, pp. 9, 14 (also available on the NICHD website, http://www.nichd.nih.gov/publications/pubs/parenting/index.cfm).
51. Maccoby, 1992, p. 1008; see Harris, 1998a, pp. 8–9.
52. Kagan and Moss, 1962.
53. McCrae and Costa, 1994, made this discovery.
54. Kagan and Moss, 1983.
55. E-mail from G. Fein, June 29, 1996.
56. Waring, 1996, p. 76.
57. F. Farley, quoted in Begley, 1998, p. 54.
58. Caspi, Sugden, Moffitt et al., 2003.
59. Caspi, McClay, Moffitt et al., 2002.
60. The criteria used by the researchers to categorize a subject as maltreated were not given in the report published in *Science* but are available online (http://www.sciencemag.org/cgi/content/full/297/5582/851/DC1). A subject was classified as "maltreated" if he was exposed to one unfavorable experience in childhood, and as "severely maltreated" if he was exposed to two or more unfavorable experiences. The unfavorable experiences included: two or more changes in primary caregiver before the age of ten; a mother who was observed to behave in an unhelpful or indifferent manner to the child at age three; and parents whose responses to a questionnaire on their child-rearing methods were in the top 10 percent in regard to harshness of discipline.
61. Knutson, 1995.

CHAPTER 4: BIRTH ORDER AND OTHER ENVIRONMENTAL DIFFERENCES WITHIN THE FAMILY

1. Rowe, *The Limits of Family Influence*, 1994. David Rowe, whose earlier article titled "As the Twig Is Bent?" (1990) was an important influence on my thinking, died in 2003, at the age of fifty-three, of liver cancer. His death was a personal loss (David was an e-mail friend and colleague) as well as a great loss to science.
2. Plomin and Daniels, 1987, p. 1.
3. Plomin, Asbury, and Dunn, 2001.
4. Turkheimer and Waldron, 2000, p. 78.
5. Harris, 1998a, p. 27.

6. Stattin and Kerr, 2000.
7. Reiss, 2000, pp. 406–407.
8. Quoted in A. M. Paul, 1998, p. 46.
9. Plomin et al., 2001, p. 231.
10. D. Grady (2003, September 13), "Surgeons meet conjoined twins: One quiet, the other with a grin." *New York Times* (http://www.nytimes.com/2003/09/13/nyregion/13TWIN.html).
11. There is an exception to the rule that differences between firstborns and laterborns are nonbiological. Blanchard (2001) has reported that the incidence of homosexuality is higher among laterborn males with older brothers than among firstborn males or laterborn males with older sisters. Blanchard believes that this effect is due to biological factors in the prenatal environment: he hypothesizes that the mother's immune system becomes sensitized to an antigen produced by male fetuses and produces antibodies to it.
12. The concept of dethronement comes from Alfred Adler (1927).
13. Cheever, 1991, pp. 106–107.
14. Daly and Wilson, 1988.
15. Daly and Wilson, 1988; R. Wright, 1994.
16. Trivers, 1985, p. 156.
17. Eibl-Eibesfeldt, 1989; LeVine and LeVine, 1963; Romney and Romney, 1963.
18. Jenkins, Rasbash, and O'Connor, 2003.
19. British parents: Dunn and Plomin, 1990, p. 75. Americans: McHale, Crouter, McGuire, and Updegraff, 1995.
20. Ernst and Angst, 1983; Hoffman, 1991.
21. Sulloway, 1996, pp. xiv, 79. (Italics omitted.)
22. Sulloway, 1996, pp. xv, 60.
23. E.g., Dick and Rose, 2002, p. 70; Plomin, 1989, p. 109.
24. Adoptive siblings: Bouchard and Loehlin, 2001. Twins: Bouchard, Lykken, McGue, Segal, and Tellegen, 1990.
25. McCartney, M. J. Harris, and Bernieri, 1990.
26. Quoted in Boynton, 1996, p. 74. (Italics omitted.)
27. Plomin and Caspi, 1999, p. 254; Schachter and Stone, 1985; Simonoff, Pickles, Hervas, Silberg, Rutter, and Eaves, 1998; Spinath and Angleitner, 1998.
28. E.g., E. M. Miller, 1997.
29. Segal, 1999, p. 54.
30. Sulloway, 1996, p. 373.
31. Dawkins, 1989; Hamilton, 1964.
32. Kin recognition: Pfennig and Sherman, 1995. Polygamous communities: Jankowiak and Diderich, 2000. Twin competition and grief: Segal, 1999, 2002; Segal and Hershberger, 1999.
33. Sulloway, 1996, p. xv.
34. Trivers, 1985, p. 156.
35. Ernst and Angst, 1983.

36. Sulloway, 1996, p. 21.
37. Edwards, 1992, p. 302.
38. Goodall, 1986, pp. 173, 116.
39. Shatz and Gelman, 1973.
40. Dunn, 1985.
41. Dishion, Duncan, Eddy, Fagot, and Fetrow, 1994.
42. Abramovitch, Corter, Pepler, and Stanhope, 1986, p. 228.
43. Deater-Deckard and Plomin, 1999. The sibling pairs in this study were identified as older child, younger child, rather than firstborn, laterborn. However, by a conservative estimate, at least 80 percent of the older siblings in this study were in fact firstborns (e-mail from K. Deater-Deckard, September 9, 2003).
44. Siblings who fight: East and Rook, 1992; Stocker and Dunn, 1990. Only children: Falbo and Polit, 1986.
45. Turkheimer and Waldron, 2000; Reiss, 2000, p. 407.
46. Sulloway, 1999, p. 192.
47. Sulloway, 1996, p. 474, n. 78; 1999, p. 192. For a reply to these criticisms, see Jefferson, Herbst, and McCrae, 1998.
48. Sulloway, 1996, p. xiii.
49. Behavior with peers: Abramovitch et al., 1986; Deater-Deckard and Plomin, 1999. Academic achievement: Blake, 1989; Ernst and Angst, 1983; McCall, 1992.
50. Paulhus, Trapnell, and Chen, 1999.
51. Drugs and sex: Ernst and Angst, 1983; Rodgers and Rowe, 1988. Delinquency: Plomin and Caspi, 1999; Rowe, 1994. Early maturing girls: Stattin and Magnusson, 1990; D. M. Wilson, Killen, Hayward et al., 1994.
52. Falbo, 1997, p. 939.
53. Ernst and Angst, 1983; Sulloway, 1996, p. 73.
54. My effort to replicate Sulloway's meta-analysis is described in appendix 1 of *The Nurture Assumption*; my tally was posted in August 2000 on *The Nurture Assumption* website (http://xchar.home.att.net/tna/birth-order/). For a more detailed review, see J. R. Harris (2002), "The Mystery of *Born to Rebel*: Sulloway's Re-Analysis of Old Birth Order Data" (http://xchar.home.att.net/tna/birth-order/methods.htm).
55. Science reviewer: Modell, 1997. J. Angst is quoted in Horgan, 1999, p. 192.
56. The results of Sulloway's meta-analysis of Ernst and Angst's data were first published in the journal *Psychological Inquiry*, in a short commentary (Sulloway, 1995) on a target article by Buss (1995). No list of the 196 findings was included. Commentaries are handled differently from regular journal articles; they are not ordinarily subjected to peer review. A commentary I wrote for the same journal (Harris, 1998b) was accepted without peer review.
57. Park, 2000, p. 27; Townsend, 2000a/2004, pp. 144, 143. Sulloway's letters to Townsend are quoted in Townsend, p. 144, and in Goldsmith, 2004, p. 14.
58. Townsend, 2000a/2004, pp. 147–153. In March 2004, after Townsend's lists of studies and findings from Ernst and Angst (1983) were published, Sulloway

posted a list of his own on his website (http://www.sulloway.org/metaanalysis.html). What he posted, however, was not the long-awaited list of 196 findings (72 positives, 110 nulls, and 14 negatives) reported on pp. 72–73 of *Born to Rebel*. Instead there are 230 "scorable outcomes" based on "more than a nine hundred individual findings [*sic*]." These outcomes include "57 full confirmations, 42 partial confirmations, 112 nulls, 17 partially opposed outcomes, and 2 fully opposed outcomes" (downloaded September 28, 2004). The original 196 findings are presumably included in this list but perhaps re-coded in a different way; they are not identifiable. See Johnson, 2000/2004, p. 226.

59. Sulloway, 1996, pp. 39–41, 332. See Townsend, 2000a/2004, p. 140, for a list of the points that have changed.
60. Goldsmith, 2004, p. 18; Townsend, 2000b/2004.
61. Johnson, 2000/2004.
62. Harris, 2000/2004.
63. Sulloway's letter is quoted in Johnson, 2000/2004, pp. 212–213. (Johnson's italics omitted.)
64. Quoted in Johnson, 2000/2004, p. 213. Sulloway supplied Johnson with the wording for a lengthy "editorial forewarning," which Johnson has printed not above Townsend's article but in his editorial explaining the delay in publication.
65. Johnson, 2000/2004, pp. 217–218, 222.
66. Johnson, 2000/2004, pp. 218–219, 222. I've mentioned only one of Sulloway's accusations; for the others, see Johnson.
67. Sulloway's letter to the president of Lake Superior State University is quoted in Johnson, 2000/2004, p. 222.
68. Ritter, 2004, p. 17.
69. Johnson, 2000/2004, p. 223.
70. Johnson, 2000/2004, pp. 223–224.
71. Townsend, 2000a/2004, p. 142; Sulloway, 2000/2004, p. 183; p. 198, n. 2.
72. Johnson, 2000/2004, pp. 224–225. The use of odds ratios instead of risk ratios has been criticized by medical researchers (e.g., Davies, Crombie, and Tavakoli, 1998; Deeks, 1998) because odds ratios can give a misleadingly inflated impression of effect sizes. For example, Sulloway (1996, p. 51) reported that in one sample 54 out of 63 laterborns and 9 out of 20 firstborns supported liberal theories. The risk ratio is (54/63)/(9/20) =.86/.45 = 1.91; thus the "risk" of supporting a liberal theory was about twice as high for the laterborns in the sample. But Sulloway instead computed the odds ratio: (54/9)/(9/11) = 6.00/.82 = 7.32, which, he said, "equals 7.3 to 1 in favor of laterborn adoption."
73. Johnson, 2000/2004, p. 228.
74. Sulloway, 1996, pp. 266–267.
75. Johnson, 2000/2004, pp. 233–235.
76. Johnson, 2000/2004, p. 239. (Italics omitted.)
77. Dalton, 2004, p. 889. On April 26, 2005, I received a letter from Sulloway, informing me that "The Inspector General's Office at the National Science Foundation has conducted an inquiry into Johnson's allegations and rejected

them." It is unclear, however, what kind of inquiry NSF conducted. According to Johnson, "No one from NSF ever contacted me about my data or anything else that related to the controversy" (e-mail, May 13, 2005).

78. Goldsmith, 2004, p. 18.
79. Quoted in Johnson, 2000/2004, p. 216.
80. Sulloway, 1996, p. xiv.
81. Scarr, 1992, p. 17.
82. Plomin and Caspi, 1999.
83. Harris, 1998a, pp. 30–31.
84. Plomin et al., 2001, p. 226.
85. Scarr, 1992; Bouchard, 1997.
86. Reiss, 2000, p. 65.
87. Bouchard, 1997, p. 61.

CHAPTER 5: THE PERSON AND THE SITUATION

1. Piaget, 1951/1962, p. 207.
2. Mischel, 1968/1996, p. 22.
3. Mischel, 1968/1996, p. 26.
4. Mischel, 1968/1996, pp. 42–43.
5. Pinker, 1997, pp. 7, 458.
6. Mischel, 1968/1996, p. 38.
7. Harris, 1998a, chapter 4.
8. Dishion, Duncan, Eddy, Fagot, and Fetrow, 1994.
9. Multivariate genetic analysis: Saudino, 1997. Shyness: Cherny, Fulker, Corley, Plomin, and DeFries, 1994. Activity level: Schmitz, Saudino, Plomin, Fulker, and DeFries, 1996.
10. Caspi and Roberts, 2001.
11. Schmitz et al., 1996.
12. Mischel, 1968/1996, p. 28.
13. Spelke, 1994.
14. Rovee-Collier, 1993.
15. Adolph, 1997. See also Adolph, 2000.
16. Mischel, 1968/1996, p. 43.
17. Pinker, 1994, p. 417. Pinker attributes the concept of similarity space to the philosopher W. V. O. Quine.
18. Gray, 1999, p. 138.
19. Bretherton, 1985; De Wolff and van IJzendoorn, 1997.
20. Pelaez-Nogueras, Field, Cigales, Gonzalez, and Clasky, 1994.
21. Fox, Kimmerly, and Schafer, 1991; Goossens and van IJzendoorn, 1990.
22. Sroufe, Egeland, and Carlson, 1999.
23. Langlois, Ritter, Casey, and Sawin (1995) found that mothers of cute babies pay their babies more attention and play with them more than do mothers of unattractive babies.

24. Bruer, 1999; Mitchell, 1980.
25. Grimshaw, Adelstein, Bryden, and MacKinnon, 1998; Newport, 2002; Senghas, Kita, and Özyürek, 2004.
26. Schneider-Rosen, Braunwald, Carlson, and Cicchetti, 1985.
27. Orphanage children: Rutter, O'Connor, and the English and Romanian Adoptees Study Team, 2004. Attachments to other children: A. Freud and Dann, 1951/1967; see Harris, 1998a, pp. 153–158.
28. E.g., Fahlke, Lorenz, Long, Champoux, Suomi, and Higley, 2000. As I mentioned in note 30 to chapter 3, there is an alternative explanation for these differences. The peer-reared monkeys were bottle-fed. The formula they were given may have been deficient in certain nutrients necessary for optimal brain development.
29. Bruer, 1999.
30. Mayberry, 1976; Mayberry, Lock, and Kazmi, 2002; Winitz, Gillespie, and Starcev, 1995.
31. Winitz et al., 1995.
32. I am speaking here of children who grow up in neighborhoods where almost everyone is a native-born English speaker. Children who grow up in ethnic neighborhoods, where many of the inhabitants are immigrants from the same country, may speak with a "foreign" accent all their lives or may combine their two languages, if that's the way the other children in their neighborhood speak. Evidence I presented in *The Nurture Assumption* (chapter 9) indicates that what matters is how their peers speak, not how the adults speak.
33. Baron-Cohen, 1999; Baron-Cohen and Staunton, 1994.
34. The child's genes: Reiss, 2000. The parent's personality: Rowe, 2002b.
35. The best-known case involves hormone replacement therapy for postmenopausal women. Observational studies had found it to be beneficial; a randomized control trial yielded different results. See Kolata, 2003.
36. J. R. Harris, "Beyond the Nurture Assumption: Testing Hypotheses About the Child's Environment." Paper presented at the conference on parenting, National Institute of Child Health and Human Development, Bethesda, MD, August 2, 1999.
37. P. A. Cowan and C. P. Cowan, "What an Intervention Design Reveals About How Parents Affect Their Children's Academic Achievement and Social Competence." Paper presented at the conference on parenting, August 2, 1999 (see previous note).
38. Cowan and Cowan, 2002.
39. E-mail to P. Cowan, September 24, 1999.
40. E-mail from P. Cowan, October 9, 1999. (Original was in all capitals.)
41. E-mail from P. Cowan, October 14, 1999.
42. Harris, 2000a; Harris, 2000b; Harris, 2002.
43. Forgatch and DeGarmo, 1999, p. 711.
44. Forgatch and DeGarmo, 1999, p. 718.
45. Feinstein, 1985, p. 303.

46. Wierson and Forehand, 1994, p. 148. Other researchers (e.g., Magnuson and Duncan, 2002; White, Taylor, and Moss, 1992) have also come to the conclusion that interventions aimed at improving parents' behavior are ineffective in improving children's adaptation to school. In one report (Zaslow, Tout, Smith, and Moore, 1998) children whose mothers received an intervention actually did *worse* than those in the control group. Occasional negative outcomes are to be expected if the true effect is zero.
47. Barkley, Shelton, Crosswait et al., 2000; Grossman, Neckerman, Koepsell et al., 1997.
48. E.g., Kagan, 1994.
49. Pinker, 2002.
50. I thank David M. Goldberg, a cognitive behavioral therapist, for pointing this out to me.
51. DeRubeis and Crits-Christoph, 1998.
52. Paris, 2000.
53. Stone, 1997, p. 39.
54. Stone, 1997, p. 39.
55. Watson and Rayner, 1920/2000, p. 315.
56. B. Harris, 1979; Hulbert, 2003; D. B. Paul and Blumenthal, 1989.
57. Rilling, 2000.
58. Watson and Rayner, 1920/2000, p. 317.

CHAPTER 6: THE MODULAR MIND

1. Arthur Conan Doyle, "The Five Orange Pips" (1891), in Doyle, 1994, pp. 118–120.
2. Josephson and Josephson, 1994.
3. Arthur Conan Doyle, "The Adventure of the Copper Beeches" (1892), in Doyle, 1994, p. 286.
4. Pinker, 2002.
5. Pinker, 1997, pp. 27, 30, 31. See also Barkow, Cosmides, and Tooby, 1992.
6. Matthew Arnold, "Dover Beach," 1867.
7. Pinker, 1997, p. 19.
8. C. S. Harris, 1963, 1965.
9. Tooby and Cosmides, 1995, p. xii.
10. Baron-Cohen, 1995, p. 1.
11. L. Kanner, quoted in Baron-Cohen, 1995, p. 61.
12. Baron-Cohen, 1995; Frith and Frith, 1999, 2001.
13. Baron-Cohen credits the idea of "social chess" to the evolutionary psychologist Nicholas Humphrey.
14. Frith and Frith, 1999.
15. Baron-Cohen, 1995; Frith and Frith, 1999; Goodall, 1986; Povinelli and Vonk, 2004.
16. Hare, Brown, Williamson, and Tomasello, 2002.

17. Baron-Cohen, 1995.
18. Garcia and Koelling, 1966.
19. Tooby and Cosmides, 1995, p. xv.
20. Pinker, 1997, pp. 21–22.
21. Pinker, 1997, p. 42.
22. Cosmides, Tooby, and Barkow, 1992, p. 10.
23. Eibl-Eibesfeldt, 1989.
24. Eibl-Eibesfeldt, 1989.
25. Pinker, 1994.
26. Eibl-Eibesfeldt, 1989, pp. 600–601.
27. LeVine and LeVine, 1963; McDonald, Sigman, Espinosa, and Neumann, 1994; Rogoff, Mistry, Göncü, and Mosier, 1993.
28. Chagnon, 1992.
29. Goodall, 1986.
30. Dunbar, 1996.
31. Harris, 1995, p. 470; 1998a, p. 132.
32. Dawkins, 1989; Harris, 1999.
33. Sherif, Harvey, White, Hood, and Sherif, 1961.
34. Eibl-Eibesfeldt, 1995, pp. 260–261; 1989, p. 289.
35. Eibl-Eibesfeldt, 1989, 1995.
36. J. Diamond, 1992, p. 229.
37. J. Diamond, 1992.
38. Pinker, 1997, p. 51. See also Pinker, 2002, p. 320.
39. Eckerman and Didow, 1988.
40. Edwards, 1992; Fagen, 1993; Goodall, 1986; Napier and Napier, 1985.
41. Goodall, 1986.
42. Chagnon, 1992.
43. Edwards, 1992; Maccoby, 1990; Maccoby and Jacklin, 1987; Schlegel and Barry, 1991; Schofield, 1981; Thorne, 1993.
44. Eibl-Eibesfeldt, 1989; Whiting and Edwards, 1988; Goodall, 1986.
45. Sacks, 1985; M. Wilson and Daly, 1992.
46. Chagnon, 1992; Eibl-Eibesfeldt, 1989.
47. Oliver Wendell Holmes, Jr., in a speech he gave in 1895, quoted in Langton, 2003, p. 313.
48. Buss, 1995.
49. Judges 12:5–6.
50. Cosmides and Tooby, 1994, pp. 87–89.

CHAPTER 7: THE RELATIONSHIP SYSTEM

1. Arthur Conan Doyle, "The Five Orange Pips" (1891), in Doyle, 1994, p. 125.
2. Agatha Christie solved this problem in a different way in *Murder on the Orient Express*. The twelve people who conspired to commit the murder got off scot free.

3. Pinker, 1997, p. 117.
4. J. Diamond, 1992; Keeley, 1996.
5. Joshua 6–12, in the Old Testament.
6. James, 1890, p. 387.
7. Pinker, 1999, p. 3; Bloom, 2000.
8. Pinker, 1999, pp. 22, 14.
9. Pinker, 1999, p. 197.
10. Pinker, 1999, p. 249.
11. Pinker, 1999, pp. 250, 252.
12. See Pinker, 1994, p. 420.
13. Lykken and Tellegen, 1993.
14. Buss, 1994; Lykken and Tellegen, 1993.
15. Blaise Pascal, quoted in Lykken and Tellegen, 1993, p. 56.
16. Ridley, 1996.
17. Hepper, 1988.
18. Cernoch and Porter, 1985; Fleming, Corter, Surbey, Franks, and Steiner, 1995.
19. Farah, 1992; Farah, Wilson, Drain, and Tanaka, 1998.
20. Cohen and Tong, 2001; Dawson, Carver, Meltzoff et al., 2002; Farah, 1992.
21. Dawson et al., 2002.
22. Dawson et al., 2002.
23. Schacter, 2001.
24. McNeil, 2003.
25. There are societies in which it is considered rude to use people's names in conversation, but these societies provide other unambiguous ways of identifying individuals. See Chagnon, 1983.
26. Schacter, 2001.
27. Young, Hay, and Ellis, 1985; see also Schacter, 2001.
28. Fiske, 1992.
29. Pinker, 1999, p. 3.
30. Bjorklund and Pellegrini, 2002, p. 193; Bugental, 2000.
31. Bugental, 2000.
32. Camazine, Deneubourg, Franks, Sneyd, Theraulaz, and Bonabeau, 2001.
33. Camazine et al., 2001; Hemelrijk, 2002; Keller, 1999; Seeley, 1997; D. S. Wilson, 2002; E. O. Wilson, 1975.
34. E. O. Wilson, 1975.
35. E. O. Wilson, 1975.
36. Camazine et al., 2001.
37. Tibbetts, 2002.
38. Camazine et al., 2001.
39. E. O. Wilson, 1975, p. 280.
40. Abramovitch, 1976; Eibl-Eibesfeldt, 1989.
41. Baron-Cohen, 1995; Eibl-Eibesfeldt, 1989.
42. Chance, 1967/1976; Pitcairn, 1976.
43. Bergman, Beehner, Cheney, and Seyfarth, 2003.
44. de Waal, 1989, pp. 42–44.

45. de Waal, 1989, p. 62.
46. Edwards, 1992, p. 303.
47. Higher status: Pellegrini and Smith, 1998. Attention structures: Hold, 1976.
48. Abramovitch, 1976; Hold, 1976.
49. Abramovitch, Corter, Pepler, and Stanhope, 1986.
50. There is a limit to the relationship system's tendency to split rather than lump. If it were a *really* compulsive splitter, it would not only discriminate Individual A from Individual B: it would also discriminate Individual A in Situation 1 at Time 1 from Individual A in Situation 2 at Time 2 (see Bloom, 2004, pp. 38–39). Though it is capable of doing that if it has to, its initial tendency is to lump together all the information about a given individual.
51. Parents' differential behavior and children's behavior to siblings versus peers: see chapter 4. Father versus boss: see chapter 5. Attraction to identical twin: Lykken and Tellegen, 1993.
52. Myers, 2002.

CHAPTER 8: THE SOCIALIZATION SYSTEM

1. Allik and McCrae, 2004.
2. McCrae, 2004.
3. McCrae, Yik, Trapnell, Bond, and Paulhus, 1998.
4. Minoura, 1992. Haidt (2001) has proposed that moral judgments are acquired in much the same way (through exposure to peers), and over the same age range, as the patterns of social behavior described by Minoura.
5. Fine, 1986; LeVine and LeVine, 1963.
6. Fiske and Taylor, 1991; Pinker, 1997; Rosch, 1978.
7. Langlois and Roggman, 1990.
8. E.g., Buss, 1994, p. 54.
9. Faces: Rubenstein, Kalakanis, and Langlois, 1999. Dogs and watches: Halberstadt and Rhodes, 2000.
10. Kniffin and Wilson, 2004.
11. Schacter, 1996, p. 137.
12. Ullman, Corkin, Coppola et al., 1997.
13. Pinker, 1999; Ullman et al., 1997.
14. Schacter, 1996; Ullman et al., 1997. Sherry and Schacter (1987) proposed that these two independent memory systems evolved because the functions they perform are incompatible; hence, one system couldn't do both jobs.
15. Dot patterns: Knowlton and Squire, 1993. Learning without awareness: Lewicki, Hill, and Czyzewska, 1992. Categorization in babies: Eimas and Quinn, 1994. Kicking: Rovee-Collier, 1993.
16. Leinbach and Fagot, 1993; Brooks and Lewis, 1976.
17. Doyle, 1890/1975, pp. 209–210.
18. Girls can only become nurses: Maccoby and Jacklin, 1974, p. 364. Swim, 1994, has shown that stereotypes of men and women tend to be fairly accurate; her subjects (college students) didn't overestimate sex differences.

19. Greenwald and Banaji, 1995; Kunda and Thagard, 1996.
20. Napolitan and Goethals, 1979.
21. S. Fiske, quoted in Snibbe, 2003, p. 31.
22. Rubenstein et al., 1999; J. D. Smith, 2002.
23. Doligez, Danchin, and Clobert, 2002; Withgott, 2002, p. 1107.
24. The fact that a single data point has little impact on an average is also the reason why stereotypes are so resistant to change.
25. Barkow, 1976.
26. Turner, 1987.
27. See *The Nurture Assumption*, pp. 280–281.
28. Maccoby, 1990; Thorne, 1993.
29. Hunter-gatherers: Draper, 1997; Draper and Cashdan, 1988; Morelli, 1997. Contemporary Americans: Serbin, Powlishta, and Gulko, 1993.
30. Genetic influences also play a role in parent-child similarities in adulthood. Adult offspring may use a child-rearing style similar to that of their parents because child-rearing styles are in part a function of heritable personality characteristics (Rowe, 2002b).
31. Thorne, 1993.
32. Tajfel, 1970.
33. Goodall, 1986.
34. Bradley and Zucker, 1990; Colapinto, 2000; M. Diamond, 1997.
35. E. O. Wilson, 1975, p. 117.
36. Grafton, 1998, p. 5.
37. Parker and Asher, 1993a; Vandell and Hembree, 1994.
38. Parker and Asher, 1993b; Vandell and Hembree, 1994; Bagwell, Newcomb, and Bukowski, 1998, p. 150.
39. Olson, Vernon, J. A. Harris, and Jang, 2001; Tesser, 1993.
40. Bickerton, 1983; Harris, 1998a; Pinker, 2002. I am assuming that the parents immigrated before the children were born or while they were still quite young. People who immigrate in adolescence usually retain a foreign accent (Pinker, 1994). So do autistic children reared by immigrant parents (Baron-Cohen, 1999).
41. Socialized in the play group: Eibl-Eibesfeldt, 1989. Children's games: Opie and Opie, 1969. In the same way: Harris, 1998a.
42. Glyn, 1970.
43. C. C. Cranston, "Sons and daughters of the successful," *New York Times*, June 27, 2003 (http://www.nytimes.com/2003/06/27/opinion/L27NEPO.html); S. S. Lee, quoted in E. Tahmincioglu, "The boss: Digging in to find success," *New York Times*, November 28, 2004 (http://www.nytimes.com/2004/11/28/business/yourmoney/28boss.html?8dpc).
44. Schacter, 1996.
45. Janton, 1993.
46. Fellman, 1998.
47. Fellman, 1998; Harshav, 1993.

48. Neisser, Boodoo, Bouchard et al., 1996.
49. Garrison Keillor, on his radio show "Prairie Home Companion."
50. Shared environment and IQ: Capron and Duyme, 1989; Stoolmiller, 1999. Twins reared together or apart: Bouchard, Lykken, McGue, Segal, and Tellegen, 1990.
51. Sherif, Harvey, White, Hood, and Sherif, 1961; Zimbardo, 1972/1993.
52. The other team event in golf is the Ryder Cup competition, held in alternate years. According to C. Brown (2004), "No other event in golf stirs up similar passions."

CHAPTER 9: THE STATUS SYSTEM

1. In an article written before I had all the details of this theory worked out (Harris, 2004b), I referred to the third system as the "behavioral strategy system." I've also considered calling it the "competition system."
2. Symons, 1992, p. 153.
3. Asch, 1952.
4. Pinker, 1997, p. 42.
5. Kirkpatrick and Ellis, 2001, p. 432. They were building on the work of Leary and his colleagues (Leary, 1999; Leary, Tambor, Terdal, and Downs, 1995), who first proposed the idea of a sociometer and who gave it that name.
6. Leary, Cottrell, and Phillips, 2001.
7. Playground bullies: Olweus, 1995; Juvonen, Graham, and Schuster, 2003. Aggressive adults: Baumeister, Smart, and Boden, 1996.
8. Kirkpatrick, Waugh, Valencia, and Webster, 2002.
9. Marsh and Hau, 2003.
10. Rutter, 1983; Boozer and Cacciola, 2001.
11. Triandis, 1995; Bonda, 1997.
12. Bond and Smith, 1996.
13. Festinger, 1954; Wood, 1989.
14. Whiting and Edwards, 1988, pp. 231–232.
15. Maccoby, 1995.
16. Bjorklund and Pellegrini, 2002.
17. Pellegrini and Smith, 1998, p. 587.
18. S. Neill, quoted in Pellegrini and Smith, 1998, p. 588.
19. E. O. Wilson, 1975.
20. Omark and Edelman, 1976.
21. Taylor and Brown, 1988; Myers, 2002.
22. Omark and Edelman, 1976.
23. Omark and Edelman, 1976; Stipek, 1992.
24. Child, 1950; Ellis, 1992; Judge and Cable, 2004; Sheldon, 1942.
25. Judge and Cable, 2004; Persico, Postlewaite, and Silverman, 2004.
26. Persico et al., 2004
27. Behavioral differences: M. C. Jones, 1957, p. 116. Small boys: Richman, Gordon,

Tegtmeyer, Crouthamel, and Post, 1986; Steinhausen, Dörr, Kannenberg, and Malin, 2000; Weisfeld and Billings, 1988.

28. M. C. Jones, 1957, p. 122.
29. Savin-Williams, 1979.
30. Persico et al., 2004. The rule that the taller candidate gets more votes held true in the 2000 election, when Al Gore, the taller candidate, won the popular vote; but not in 2004, when the majority voted for George W. Bush, the shorter candidate. No one, as far as I know, has compared political candidates on the basis of their height at age sixteen. It would be interesting to see if adolescent height proved a better predictor of election outcomes than adult height.
31. Personality across the life course: Caspi and Roberts, 2001. Offspring of Japanese executives: Minoura, 1992 (see chapter 8). Accents of immigrants: Pinker, 1994.
32. Theorists misled by continuities: e.g., Kagan, 1998a. Genetic influences: Caspi and Roberts, 2001.
33. See Buss, 1994; Cronin, 1991; G. F. Miller, 2000; Pinker, 1997.
34. Dunbar, 1996, p. 185.
35. Shakespeare, *As You Like It*, act 3, scene 5.
36. Mead, 1934, p. 138.
37. Fine, 1981, p. 31.
38. The title of a recent book sums it up nicely: *You Have to Say I'm Pretty, You're My Mother* (Pierson and Cohen, 2003).
39. Cosmides and Tooby, 1994, pp. 93–94.
40. Langlois, Kalakanis, Rubenstein, Larson, Hallam, and Smoot, 2000.
41. Fake interview: Jackson and Huston, 1975. Good looks in adulthood: Buss, 1994; Campbell, Kleim, and Olson, 1986; Etcoff, 1999. In childhood: P. A. Adler, Kless, and Adler, 1992.
42. Baron-Cohen, 1995.
43. Vertegaal and Ding, 2002.
44. Conradt and Roper, 2003.
45. Frith and Frith, 1999.
46. A further step is now possible. One of the things humans do is to try to present themselves—by adopting certain behaviors, a certain style of dress, and so on—in a way that will cause other people to form a certain picture of them. Self-presentation, as it's called, is very interesting but beyond the scope of this book. See Goffman, 1959.
47. de Waal, 1989.
48. Tooby and Cosmides, 1990; Buss, 1995; Bouchard and Loehlin, 2001; Pinker, 2002.
49. J. Wong and K. Espina, 2003, July 8. "Iranian twins die after historic surgery." Reuters (http://dailynews.att.net/).
50. This incident also demonstrates that calling it a people-information *lexicon* is somewhat misleading. It's really more like a computerized database. We don't have to go through the whole lexicon page by page to find a writer, a redhead,

or someone who grew up in Arkansas. We can go directly to the appropriate page or pages, in much the way we use Google to find things on the Web.

51. Caspi, Moffitt, Morgan et al., 2004.
52. Tully, Arseneault, Caspi, Moffitt, and Morgan, 2004.
53. That variation might itself be advantageous, both to the individual and to the group, has often been suggested by evolutionary biologists and psychologists. Some examples: Dall, Houston, and McNamara, 2004; Gadagkar, 2004; J. C. Jones, Myerscough, Graham, and Oldroyd, 2004; E. M. Miller, 1997.
54. Camazine, Deneubourg, Franks, Sneyd, Theraulaz, and Bonabeau, 2001, p. 8. (Italics omitted.)
55. Lewcock and Reed, 2003.
56. Proverbs 6:6.
57. Hölldobler and Wilson, 1994, p. 107.
58. Cronin, 1991.
59. Hölldobler and Wilson, 1994.
60. Hölldobler and Wilson, 1994.
61. Gordon, 1999.
62. Fewell, 2003, p. 1869.
63. Ridley, 2003; Yan, Yuan, Velculescu, Vogelstein, and Kinzler, 2002.
64. Whitfield, Cziko, and Robinson, 2003.
65. Ridley, 1996, p. 41; Ridley, 2003.
66. Ridley, 1996, pp. 41–42.
67. A. Smith, 1776/1904, book 1, chapter 2, part 1.
68. A. Smith, 1776/1904, book 1, chapter 2, part 2.
69. Allen, 1975, p. 99.
70. A. Smith, 1776/1904, book 1, chapter 2, part 3.

CHAPTER 10: DENOUEMENT

1. Rex Stout, e.g., *Murder by the Book*, 1951.
2. Faulkner's Nobel Prize address, Stockholm, December 10, 1950.
3. Thomas Jefferson, in a letter to William G. Munford, June 18, 1799. Quoted in *Time*, July 5, 2004, p. 79.
4. Pinker, 1994, 1999; Baron-Cohen, 1995.
5. Two siblings may speak with different accents if they are immigrants and one arrived in childhood and the other in adolescence (see Pinker, 1994, p. 291). They may also speak differently if they differ in sex: in some parts of the world, boys' groups and girls' groups adopt somewhat different accents.
6. *The Tragedy of King Richard III*, act 1, scene 1.
7. Belsky, Steinberg, and Draper, 1991.
8. Chisholm, 1999; Ellis, McFadyen-Ketchum, Dodge, Pettit, and Bates, 1999; Kim and Smith, 1999.
9. Bjorklund and Pellegrini, 2002, p. 284.
10. Comings, Muhleman, Johnson, and MacMurray, 2002, p. 1046.

11. Rowe, 2000, 2002a.
12. Myers, 2002.
13. Pinker, 1997.
14. Dolnick, 1998.
15. Dencik, 1989, p. 156.
16. Larkin, "This Be the Verse," 1989, p. 140 (originally published in 1974).
17. Crews, 1996; Dolnick, 1998; Esterson, 1993.
18. Dunbar, 1996, p. 4.
19. Dolnick, 1998.
20. Stevens, Golombok, Beveridge, and the ALSPAC Study Team, 2002; Stevenson and Black, 1988; Maccoby and Jacklin, 1974, p. 363.
21. Kellogg and Kellogg, 1933. See *The Nurture Assumption*, pp. 98–100.
22. Humphrey, 2004. See also Pinker, 1997, pp. 131–136.
23. Sherry and Schacter, 1987.
24. Insel and Fernald, 2004.
25. You might be wondering whether a separate sociometer would be needed for each of the hundreds of relationships that people have. I think not. That information could be stored on the appropriate page of the people-information lexicon. The sociometer is needed only to keep the information updated.
26. Tooby and Cosmides, 1995, p. xii.
27. Eisenberger, Lieberman, and Williams, 2003.
28. Farragher, 1998.
29. Farragher, 1998.
30. As Tooby and Cosmides (1990) pointed out, sexual recombination scrambles the genes in each generation; it is therefore unlikely that genes that affect physical size and strength and genes that affect personality will remain linked together generation after generation. However, it is possible that some genes may have effects both on physical attributes and on personality.
31. Rosenthal, 2002.
32. McDonagh, 2000.
33. G. F. Miller, quoted in Angier, 2000.

References

Abramovitch, R. (1976). The relation of attention and proximity to rank in preschool children. In Chance, M. R. A., and Larsen, R. R., eds., *The social structure of attention* (153–176). London: Wiley.

Abramovitch, R., Corter, C., Pepler, D. J., and Stanhope, L. (1986). Sibling and peer interaction: A final follow-up and a comparison. *Child Development* 57, 217–229.

Adler, A. (1927). *Understanding human nature.* New York: Greenberg.

Adler, P. A., Kless, S. J., and Adler, P. (1992). Socialization to gender roles: Popularity among elementary school boys and girls. *Sociology of Education* 65, 169–187.

Adolph, K. E. (1997). Learning in the development of infant locomotion. *Monographs of the Society for Research in Child Development* 62, no. 3 (serial no. 251).

Adolph, K. E. (2000). Specificity of learning: Why infants fall over a veritable cliff. *Psychological Science* 11, 290–295.

Allen, W. (1975). *Without feathers.* New York: Random House.

Allik, J., and McCrae, R. R. (2004). Toward a geography of personality traits. *Journal of Cross-Cultural Psychology* 35, 13–28.

Allport, G. W., and Odbert, H. S. (1936). Trait-names: A psycho-lexical study. *Psychological Monographs* 47, no. 211 (whole issue).

Andersson, B.-E. (1992). Effects of day-care on cognitive and socioemotional competence of thirteen-year-old Swedish schoolchildren. *Child Development* 63, 20–36.

Andreasen, N. C. (1999, Feb. 25). Understanding the causes of schizophrenia. *New England Journal of Medicine* 340, 645–647.

Angier, N. (2000, May 30). A conversation with Geoffrey Miller: Author offers theory of gray matter of love. *New York Times*, F2.

Arcus, D. M. (1991). Experiential modification of temperamental bias in inhibited and uninhibited children. Unpublished doctoral dissertation, Harvard University.

Arcus, D. M. (2001). Inhibited and uninhibited children: Biology in the social context. In T. D. Wachs and G. A. Kohnstamm, eds., *Temperament in context* (43–60). Mahwah, NJ: Erlbaum.

Asch, S. E. (1952). *Social psychology*. Englewood Cliffs, NJ: Prentice-Hall.

Bach, J. F. (2002, Sept. 19). The effect of infections on susceptibility to autoimmune and allergic diseases. *New England Journal of Medicine* 347, 911–920.

Bagwell, C. L., Newcomb, A. F., and Bukowski, W. M. (1998). Preadolescent friendship and peer rejection as predictors of adult adjustment. *Child Development* 69, 140–153.

Barkley, R. A., Shelton, T. L., Crosswait, C., Moorehouse, M., Fletcher, K., Barrett, S., Jenkins, L., and Metevia, L. (2000). Multi-method psycho-educational intervention for preschool children with disruptive behavior: Preliminary results at post-treatment. *Journal of Child Psychology and Psychiatry* 41, 319–332.

Barkow, J. H. (1976). Attention structure and the evolution of human psychological characteristics. In Chance, M. R. A., and Larsen, R. R., eds., *The social structure of attention* (203–219). London: Wiley.

Barkow, J. H. (1992). Beneath new culture is old psychology: Gossip and social stratification. In J. H. Barkow, L. Cosmides, and J. Tooby, eds., *The adapted mind: Evolutionary psychology and the generation of culture* (627–637). New York: Oxford University Press.

Barkow, J. H., Cosmides, L., and Tooby, J., eds. (1992). *The adapted mind: Evolutionary psychology and the generation of culture*. New York: Oxford University Press.

Baron-Cohen, S. (1995). *Mindblindness: An essay on autism and theory of mind*. Cambridge, MA: MIT Press.

Baron-Cohen, S. (1999, Apr. 22). Peering into a child's priorities (review of *The Nurture Assumption*). *Nature* 398, 675–677.

Baron-Cohen, S., and Staunton, R. (1994). Do children with autism acquire the phonology of their peers? An examination of group identification through the window of bilingualism. *First Language* 14, 241–248.

Bastian, M. L., Sponberg, A. C., Suomi, S. J., and Higley, J. D. (2003). Long-term effects of infant rearing condition on the acquisition of dominance rank in juvenile and adult rhesus macaques (*Macaca mulatta*). *Developmental Psychobiology* 42, 44–51.

Bateson, P. (2002, Sept. 27). The corpse of a wearisome debate. *Science* 297, 2212–2213.

Baumeister, R. F., Smart, L., and Boden, J. M. (1996). Relation of threatened egotism to violence and aggression: The dark side of self-esteem. *Psychological Review* 103, 5–33.

Begley, S. (1998, Sept. 7). The parent trap. *Newsweek*, 52–59.

Bellew, G. (ca. 1955). *The kings and queens of Britain*. London: Pitkin Pictorials.

Belsky, J., Steinberg, L., and Draper, P. (1991). Childhood experience, interpersonal development, and reproductive strategy: An evolutionary theory of socialization. *Child Development* 62, 647–670.

Bergman, T. J., Beehner, J. C., Cheney, D. L, and Seyfarth, R. M. (2003, Nov. 14). Hierarchical classification by rank and kinship in baboons. *Science* 302, 1234–1236.

Bickerton, D. (1983, July). Creole languages. *Scientific American* 249, 116–122.

Bjorklund, D. F., and Pellegrini, A. D. (2002). *The origins of human nature: Evolutionary developmental psychology*. Washington, DC: American Psychological Association.

Blake, J. (1989, July 7). Number of siblings and educational attainment. *Science* 245, 32–36.

Blanchard, R. (2001). Fraternal birth order and the maternal immune hypothesis of male homosexuality. *Hormones and Behavior* 40, 105–114.

Bloom, P. (2000). *How children learn the meanings of words.* Cambridge, MA: MIT Press.

Bloom, P. (2004). *Descartes' baby: How the science of child development explains what makes us human.* New York: Basic Books.

Bond, R., and Smith, P. B. (1996). Culture and conformity: A meta-analysis of studies using Asch's (1952b, 1956) line judgment task. *Psychological Bulletin* 119, 111–137.

Bonda, B. D. (1997). Cooperation and competition in peaceful societies. *Psychological Bulletin* 121, 299–320.

Boozer, M., and Cacciola, S. E. (2001). *Inside the 'black box' of Project Star: Estimation of peer effects using experimental data.* Center Discussion Paper no. 832, Economic Growth Center, Yale University (http://papers.ssrn.com/sol3/papers.cfm?abstract_id=277009).

Bouchard, T. J., Jr. (1997). Experience Producing Drive Theory: How genes drive experience and shape personality. *Acta Paediatrica* 86, suppl. no. 422, 60–64.

Bouchard, T. J., Jr., and Loehlin, J. (2001). Genes, evolution, and personality. *Behavior Genetics* 31, 243–273.

Bouchard, T. J., Jr., Lykken, D. T., McGue, M., Segal, N. L., and Tellegen, A. (1990, Oct. 12). Sources of human psychological differences: The Minnesota study of twins reared apart. *Science* 250, 223–228.

Boynton, R. S. (1996, Oct. 7). The birth of an idea. *The New Yorker,* 72–81.

Bradley, S. J., and Zucker, K. J. (1990). Gender identity disorder and psychosexual problems in children and adolescents. *Canadian Journal of Psychiatry* 35, 477–486.

Bretherton, I. (1985). Attachment theory: Restrospect and prospect. In I. Bretherton and E. Waters, eds., Growing points of attachment theory and research (3–35). *Monographs of the Society for Research in Child Development* 50, nos. 1–2, (serial no. 209).

Brooks, J., and Lewis, M. (1976). Infants' responses to strangers: Midget, adult, and child. *Child Development* 47, 323–332.

Brown, C. (2004, Sept. 15). "It may not be Red Sox–Yankees, but Ryder Cup rivalry is real." *New York Times* (http://www.nytimes.com/2004/09/15/sports/golf/15golf.html).

Brown, D. E. (1991). *Human universals.* New York: McGraw-Hill.

Bruer, J. T. (1999). *The myth of the first three years.* New York: Free Press.

Bugental, D. B. (2000). Acquisition of the algorithms of social life: A domain-based approach. *Psychological Bulletin* 126, 187–219.

Buss, D. M. (1994). *The evolution of desire.* New York: Basic Books.

Buss, D. M. (1995). Evolutionary psychology: A new paradigm for psychological science. *Psychological Inquiry* 6, 1–30.

Camazine, S., Deneubourg, J.-L., Franks, N. R., Sneyd, J., Theraulaz, G., and Bonabeau, E. (2001). *Self-organization in biological systems*. Princeton, NJ: Princeton University Press.

Campbell, K. E., Kleim, D. M., and Olson, K. R. (1986). Gender, physical attractiveness, and assertiveness. *Journal of Social Psychology* 126, 697–698.

Capron, C., and Duyme, M. (1989). Assessment of the effects of socio-economic status on IQ in a full cross-fostering study. *Nature* 340, 552–554.

Carpenter, G. (1975). Mother's face and the newborn. In R. Lewin, ed., *Child alive*. Garden City, NY: Doubleday.

Caspi, A., McClay, J., Moffitt, T. E., et al. (2002, Aug. 2). Role of genotype in the cycle of violence in maltreated children. *Science* 297, 851–854.

Caspi, A., Moffitt, T. E., Morgan, J., et al. (2004). Maternal expressed emotion predicts children's antisocial behavior problems: Using monozygotic-twin differences to identify environmental effects on behavioral development. *Developmental Psychology* 40, 149–161.

Caspi, A., and Roberts, B. W. (2001). Personality development across the life course: The argument for change and continuity. *Psychological Inquiry* 12, 49–66.

Caspi, A., Sugden, K., Moffitt, T. E., et al. (2003, July 18). Influence of life stress on depression: Moderation by a polymorphism in the 5-HTT gene. *Science* 301, 386–389.

Casselbrant, M.L., Mandel, E. M., Fall, P. A., Rockette, H. E., Kurs-Lasky M., Bluestone, C. D., and Ferrell R. E. (1999, Dec. 8). The heritability of otitis media: A twin and triplet study. *Journal of the American Medical Association* 282, 2167–2169.

Cernoch, J. M., and Porter, R. H. (1985). Recognition of maternal axillary odors by infants. *Child Development* 56, 1593–1598.

Chagnon, N. A. (1983). *Yanomamö: The fierce people*. 3rd ed. New York: Holt, Rinehart and Winston.

Chagnon, N. A. (1992). *Yanomamö: The last days of Eden*. San Diego, CA: Harcourt Brace Jovanovich.

Champoux, M., Hibbeln, J. R., Shannon, C., Majchrzak, S., Suomi, S. J., Salem, N., Jr. and Higley, J. D. (2002). Fatty acid formula supplementation and neuromotor development in rhesus monkey neonates. *Pediatric Research* 51, 273–281.

Chance, M. R. A. (1976). Attention structure as the basis of primate rank orders. In Chance, M. R. A., and Larsen, R. R. eds., *The social structure of attention* (11–28). London: Wiley. Originally published in 1967.

Cheever, John (1991). *The journals of John Cheever*. New York: Knopf.

Cherny, S. S., Fulker, D. W., Corley, R., Plomin, R., and DeFries, J. C. (1994). Continuity and change in infant shyness from 14 to 20 months. *Behavior Genetics* 24, 365–380.

Child, I. L. (1950). The relation of somatotype to self-ratings on Sheldon's temperamental traits. *Journal of Personality* 18, 440–453.

Chisholm, J. S. (1999). Attachment and time preference: Relations between early stress and sexual behavior in a sample of American university women. *Human Nature* 10, 51–83.

Cohen, J. D., and Tong, F. (2001, Sept. 28). The face of controversy. *Science* 293, 2405–2407.

Colapinto, J. (2000). *As nature made him: The boy who was raised as a girl.* New York: HarperCollins.

Collins, W. A., Maccoby, E. E., Steinberg, L., Hetherington, E. M., and Bornstein, M. H. (2000). Contemporary research on parenting: The case for nature *and* nurture. *American Psychologist* 55, 218–232.

Collins, W. A., Maccoby, E. E., Steinberg, L., Hetherington, E. M., and Bornstein, M. H. (2001). Toward nature *with* nurture. *American Psychologist* 56, 171–173.

Comings, D. E., Muhleman, D., Johnson, J. P., and MacMurray, J. P. (2002). Parent-daughter transmission of the androgen receptor gene as an explanation of the effect of father absence on age at menarche. *Child Development* 73, 1046–1051.

Conradt, L., and Roper, T. J. (2003, Jan. 9). Group decision-making in animals. *Nature* 421, 155–158.

Cosmides, L., and Tooby, J. (1994). Origins of domain specificity: The evolution of functional organization. In L. A. Hirschfeld and S. A. Gelman, eds., *Mapping the mind: Domain specificity in cognition and culture* (85–116). Cambridge, England: Cambridge University Press.

Cosmides, L., Tooby, J., and Barkow, J. H. (1992). Introduction: Evolutionary psychology and conceptual integration. In J. H. Barkow, L. Cosmides, and J. Tooby, eds., *The adapted mind: Evolutionary psychology and the generation of culture* (3–15). New York: Oxford University Press.

Cowan, P. A., and Cowan, C. P. (2002). What an intervention design reveals about how parents affect their children's academic achievement and behavior problems. In J. G. Borkowski, S. L. Ramey, and M. Bristol-Power, eds., *Parenting and the child's world: Influences on academic, intellectual, and social-emotional development* (75–97). Mahwah, NJ: Erlbaum.

Crews, F. (1996). The verdict on Freud. *Psychological Science* 7, 63–68.

Cronin, H. (1991). *The ant and the peacock.* Cambridge, England: Cambridge University Press.

Dall, S. R. X., Houston, A. I., and McNamara, J. M. (2004). The behavioural ecology of personality: Consistent individual differences from an adaptive perspective. *Ecology Letters* 7, 734–739.

Dalton, R. (2004, Oct. 21). Quarrel over book leads to call for misconduct inquiry. *Nature* 431, 889.

Daly, M., and Wilson, M. (1988, Oct. 28). Evolutionary social psychology and family homicide. *Science* 242, 519–524.

Davies, H. T. O., Crombie, I. K., and Tavakoli, M. (1998, Mar. 28). When can odds ratios mislead? *British Medical Journal* 316, 989–991.

Dawkins, R. (1989). *The selfish gene.* 2nd ed. New York: Oxford University Press.

Dawson, G., Carver, L., Meltzoff, A. N., Panagiotides, H., McPartland, J., and

Webb, S. J. (2002). Neural correlates of face and object recognition in young children with autism spectrum disorder, developmental delay, and typical development. *Child Development* 73, 700–717.

Deater-Deckard, K., and Plomin, R. (1999). An adoption study of the etiology of teacher and parent reports of externalizing behavior problems in middle childhood. *Child Development* 70, 144–154.

DeCasper, A. J., and Fifer, W. P. (1980, June 6). Of human bonding: Newborns prefer their mother's voice. *Science* 208, 1174–1176.

Deeks J. (1998, Oct. 24). Odds ratios should be used only in case-control studies and logistic regression analyses. *British Medical Journal* 317, 1155–1156.

Dencik, L. (1989). Growing up in the post-modern age: On the child's situation in the modern family, and on the position of the family in the modern welfare state. *Acta Sociologica* 32, 155–180.

DeRubeis, R. J., and Crits-Christoph, P. (1998). Empirically supported individual and group psychological treatments for adult mental disorders. *Journal of Consulting and Clinical Psychology* 66, 37–52.

de Waal, F. (1989). *Chimpanzee politics: Power and sex among apes*. Paperback ed. Baltimore: Johns Hopkins University Press.

De Wolff, M., and van IJzendoorn, M. H. (1997). Sensitivity and attachment: A meta-analysis on parental antecedents of infant attachment. *Child Development* 68, 571–591.

Diamond, J. (1992). *The third chimpanzee*. New York: HarperCollins.

Diamond, M. (1997). Sexual identity and sexual orientation in children with traumatized or ambiguous genitalia. *Journal of Sex Research* 34, 199–211.

Dick, D. M., and Rose, R. J. (2002). Behavior genetics: What's new? What's next? *Current Directions in Psychological Science* 11, 70–74.

Dickens, C. (1860–1861). *Great expectations*. (Available on several sites on the World Wide Web.)

Dishion, T. J., Duncan, T. E., Eddy, J. M., Fagot, B. I., and Fetrow, R. (1994). The world of parents and peers: Coercive exchanges and children's social adaptation. *Social Development* 3, 255–268.

Doligez, B., Danchin, E., and Clobert, J. (2002, Aug. 16). Public information and breeding habitat selection in a wild bird population. *Science* 297, 1168–1170.

Dolnick, E. (1998). *Madness on the couch: Blaming the victim in the heyday of psychoanalysis*. New York: Simon & Schuster.

Doyle, A. C. (1975). The sign of four. In *A Study in Scarlet and The Sign of Four*. New York: Berkley Prime Crime. Originally published in 1890.

Doyle, A. C. (1994). *The Adventures of Sherlock Holmes*. New York: Berkley Prime Crime. Stories originally published in the 1890s.

Draper, P. (1997). Institutional, evolutionary, and demographic contexts of gender roles: A case study of !Kung bushmen. In M. E. Morbeck, A. Galloway, and A. L. Zihlman, eds., *The evolving female: A life-history perspective* (220–232). Princeton, NJ: Princeton University Press.

Draper, P., and Cashdan, E. (1988). Technological change and child behavior among the !Kung. *Ethnology* 27, 339–365.

Dunbar, R. (1996). *Grooming, gossip, and the evolution of language*. Cambridge, MA: Harvard University Press.

Dunn, J. (1985). *Sisters and brothers.* Cambridge, MA: Harvard University Press.

Dunn, J., and Plomin, R. (1990). *Separate lives: Why siblings are so different*. New York: Basic Books.

Dyson, F. (2002, Jan. 24). Why am I me? *Edge: The World Question Center* (http://www.edge.org/q2002/q_dyson.html).

East, P. L., and Rook, K. S. (1992). Compensatory patterns of support among children's peer relationships: A test using school friends, nonschool friends, and siblings. *Developmental Psychology* 28, 163–172.

Eckerman, C. O., and Didow, S. M. (1988). Lessons drawn from observing young peers together. *Acta Paediatrica Scandinavica* 77, 55–70.

Edwards, C. P. (1992). Cross-cultural perspectives on family-peer relations. In R. D. Parke and G. W. Ladd, eds., *Family-peer relationships: Modes of linkage* (285–316). Hillsdale, NJ: Erlbaum.

Ehrlich, P. R. (2000, Sept. 22). The tangled skeins of nature and nurture in human evolution. *The Chronicle of Higher Education* (http://chronicle.com/free/v47/i04/04b00701.htm).

Eibl-Eibesfeldt, I. (1989). *Human ethology*. Hawthorne, NY: Aldine de Gruyter.

Eibl-Eibesfeldt, I. (1995). The evolution of familiality and its consequences. *Futura* 10, no. 4, 253–264.

Eimas, P. D., and Quinn, P. C. (1994). Studies on the formation of perceptually based basic-level categories in young infants. *Child Development* 65, 903–917.

Eisenberg, N., Cumberland, A., and Spinrad, T. L. (1998). Parental socialization of emotion. *Psychological Inquiry* 9, 241–273.

Eisenberger, N. I., Lieberman, M. D., and Williams, K. D. (2003, Oct. 10). Does rejection hurt? An fMRI study of social exclusion. *Science* 302, 290–292.

Ellis, B. J. (1992). The evolution of sexual attraction. In J. H. Barkow, L. Cosmides, and J. Tooby, eds., *The adapted mind: Evolutionary psychology and the generation of culture* (267–288). New York: Oxford University Press.

Ellis, B. J., McFadyen-Ketchum, S., Dodge, K. A., Pettit, G. S., and Bates, J. E. (1999). Quality of early family relationships and individual differences in the timing of pubertal maturation in girls: A longitudinal test of an evolutionary model. *Journal of Personality and Social Psychology* 77, 387–401.

Ernst, C., and Angst, J. (1983). *Birth order: Its influence on personality.* Berlin, Germany: Springer-Verlag.

Esterson, A. (1993). *Seductive mirage: An exploration of the work of Sigmund Freud*. Chicago, IL: Open Court.

Etcoff, N. L. (1999). *Survival of the prettiest: The science of beauty*. New York: Doubleday.

Fagen, R. (1993). Primate juveniles and primate play. In M. E. Pereira and L. A. Fairbanks eds., *Juvenile primates* (182–192). New York: Oxford University Press.

Fahlke, C., Lorenz, J. G., Long, J., Champoux, M., Suomi, S., and Higley, J. D. (2000). Rearing experiences and stress-induced plasma cortisol as early risk factors for excessive alcohol consumption in nonhuman primates. *Alcoholism: Clinical and Experimental Research* 24, 644–650.

Falbo, T. (1997). To rebel or not to rebel? Is this the birth order question? *Contemporary Psychology* 42, 938–939.

Falbo, T., and Polit, D. F. (1986). Quantitative research of the only child literature: Research evidence and theory development. *Psychological Bulletin* 100, 176–189.

Farah, M. J. (1992). Is an object an object an object? Cognitive and neuropsychological investigations of domain specificity in visual object recognition. *Current Directions in Psychological Science* 1, 164–169.

Farah, M. J., Wilson, K. D., Drain, M., and Tanaka, J. N. (1998). What is "special" about face perception? *Psychological Review* 105, 482–498.

Farragher, T. (1998, Aug. 30). Two lives, two paths: For twins, one succeeds while one goes homeless. *Boston Globe*, A1.

Feinstein, A. R. (1985). *Clinical epidemiology: The architecture of clinical research.* Philadelphia: W. B. Saunders.

Fellman, J. (1998). Eliezer Ben-Yehuda and the Revival of Hebrew (http://www.us-israel.org/jsource/biography/ben_yehuda.html).

Festinger, L. (1954). A theory of social comparison processes. *Human Relations* 7, 117–140.

Fewell, J. H. (2003, Sept. 26). Social insect networks. *Science* 301, 1867–1870.

Fine, G. A. (1981). Friends, impression management, and preadolescent behavior. In S. R. Asher and J. M. Gottman, eds., *The development of children's friendships* (29–52). Cambridge, England: Cambridge University Press.

Fine, G. A. (1986). The dirty play of little boys. *Society/Transaction* 24, 63–67.

Fiske, S. T. (1992). Thinking is for doing: Portraits of social cognition from daguerreotype to laserphoto. *Journal of Personality and Social Psychology* 63, 877–889.

Fiske, S. T., and Taylor, S. E. (1991). *Social cognition.* 2nd ed. New York: McGraw-Hill.

Fleming, A., Corter, C., Surbey, M., Franks, P., and Steiner, M. (1995). Postpartum factors related to mother's recognition of newborn infant odours. *Journal of Reproductive and Infant Psychology* 13, 197–210.

Forgatch, M. S. and DeGarmo, D. S. (1999). Parenting through change: An effective prevention program for single mothers. *Journal of Consulting and Clinical Psychology* 67, 711–724.

Fox, N. A., Kimmerly, N. L., and Schafer, W. D. (1991). Attachment to mother/attachment to father: A meta-analysis. *Child Development* 62, 210–225.

Freud, A., and Dann, S. (1967). An experiment in group upbringing. In Brackbill, Y., and Thompson, G. G., eds., *Behavior in infancy and early childhood* (494–514). New York: Free Press. Originally published in 1951.

Frith, C. D., and Frith, U. (1999, Nov. 26). Interacting minds—A biological basis. *Science* 286, 1692–1695.

Frith, U., and Frith, C. (2001). The biological basis of social interaction. *Current Directions in Psychological Science* 10, 151–155.

Gadagkar, R. (2004, Dec. 3). Sex . . . only if really necessary in a female monarchy. *Science* 306, 1694–1695.

Garcia, J., and Koelling, R. A. (1966). Relation of cue to consequence in avoidance learning. *Psychonomic Science* 4, 123–124.

Garcia, J., McGowan, B. K., and Green, K. F. (1972). Biological constraints on conditioning. In M. E. P. Seligman and J. L. Hager, eds., *Biological boundaries of learning* (21–43). New York: Appleton-Century-Crofts.

Gilbert, D. T., and Malone, P. S. (1995). The correspondence bias. *Psychological Bulletin* 117, 21–38.

Gladwell, M. (1998, Aug. 17). Do parents matter? *The New Yorker*, 54–64.

Gladwell, M. (2000). *The tipping point: How little things can make a big difference.* Boston: Little, Brown.

Glyn, A. (1970). *The British: Portrait of a people.* New York: G. P. Putnam's Sons.

Goffman, E. (1959). *The presentation of self in everyday life.* Garden City, NY: Doubleday Anchor.

Goldsmith, S. (2004, Apr. 28). Frank's War: How a Berkeley scholar's groundbreaking research sparked one of the nastier academic debates in recent memory. *East Bay Express*, 1, 13–23 (http://www.eastbayexpress.com/issues/2004-04-28/feature.html).

Golombok, S., Cook, R., Bish, A., and Murray, C. (1995). Families created by the new reproductive technologies: Quality of parenting and social and emotional development of the children. *Child Development* 66, 285–298.

Golombok, S., MacCullum, F., Goodman, E., and Rutter, M. (2002). Families with children conceived by donor insemination: A follow-up at age twelve. *Child Development* 73, 952–968.

Goodall, J. (1986). *The chimpanzees of Gombe: Patterns of behavior.* Cambridge, MA: Harvard University Press.

Goossens, F. A., and van IJzendoorn, M. H. (1990). Quality of infants' attachments to professional caregivers: Relation to infant–parent attachment and day-care characteristics. *Child Development* 61, 550–567.

Gordon, D. M. (1999). *Ants at work: How an insect society is organized.* New York: Free Press.

Gottesman, I. I. (2001). Psychopathology through a life span–genetic prism. *American Psychologist* 56, 867–878.

Gottfredson, M. R., and Hirschi, T. (1990). *A general theory of crime.* Stanford, CA: Stanford University Press.

Grafton, S. (1989). *"F" is for fugitive.* New York: Bantam Books.

Grafton, S. (1998). *"N" is for noose.* New York: Fawcett Crest.

Gray, P. (1999). *Psychology.* 3rd ed. New York: Worth.

Greenspan, S. I. (1997, Nov. 21). Twin studies, heritability, and intelligence. *Science* 278, 1384–1385.

Greenwald, A. G., and Banaji, M. R. (1995). Implicit social cognition: Attitudes, self-esteem, and stereotypes. *Psychological Review* 102, 4–27.

Grimshaw, G. M., Adelstein, A., Bryden, M., and MacKinnon, G. E. (1998). First-language acquisition in adolescence: Evidence for a critical period for verbal language development. *Brain and Language* 63, 237–255.

Grossman, D. C., Neckerman, H. J., Koepsell, T. D., et al. (1997, May 28). Effectiveness of a violence prevention curriculum among children in elementary school: A randomized controlled trial. *Journal of the American Medical Association* 277, 1605–1611.

Haidt, J. (2001). The emotional dog and its rational tail: A social intuitionist approach to moral judgment. *Psychological Review* 108, 814–834.

Halberstadt, J., and Rhodes, G. (2000). The attractiveness of nonface averages: Implications for an evolutionary explanation of the attractiveness of average faces. *Psychological Science* 11, 285–289.

Hamilton, W. D. (1964). The genetical evolution of social behaviour (I and II). *Journal of Theoretical Biology* 7, 1–52.

Hare, B., Brown, M., Williamson, C., and Tomasello, M. (2002, Nov. 22). The domestication of social cognition in dogs. *Science* 298, 1634–1636.

Harris, B. (1979). Whatever happened to Little Albert? *American Psychologist* 34, 151–160.

Harris, C. S. (1963, May 17). Adaptation to displaced vision: Visual, motor, or proprioceptive change? *Science* 140, 812–813.

Harris, C. S. (1965). Perceptual adaptation to inverted, reversed, and displaced vision. *Psychological Review* 72, 419–444.

Harris, J. R. (1995). Where is the child's environment? A group socialization theory of development. *Psychological Review* 102, 458–489.

Harris, J. R. (1998a). *The nurture assumption*. New York: Free Press.

Harris, J. R. (1998b). The trouble with assumptions (commentary on target article by Eisenberg, Cumberland, and Spinrad). *Psychological Inquiry* 9, 294–297.

Harris, J. R. (1999, June 29). Children don't do things half way. Online interview on *Edge* (http://www.edge.org/documents/archive/edge58.html).

Harris, J. R. (2000a). Research on child development: What we can learn from medical research. Paper presented at a meeting of the Children's Roundtable, Brookings Institution, Washington, DC, Sept. 28 (http://xchar.home.att.net/tna/brooking.htm).

Harris, J. R. (2000b). Socialization, personality development, and the child's environments: Comment on Vandell (2000). *Developmental Psychology* 36, 711–723.

Harris, J. R. (2000, appeared in print in 2004). Personality and birth order: Explaining the differences between siblings (commentary on target article by Townsend). *Politics and the Life Sciences* 19, 160–163.

Harris, J. R. (2002). Beyond the nurture assumption: Testing hypotheses about the child's environment. In J. G. Borkowski, S. L. Ramey, and M. Bristol-Power, eds., *Parenting and the child's world: Influences on academic, intellectual, and social-emotional development* (3–20). Mahwah, NJ: Erlbaum.

Harris, J. R. (2004a). The gift of solitude. In J. Brockman, ed., *Curious minds: How a child becomes a scientist* (227–236). New York: Pantheon.

Harris, J. R. (2004b). Social behavior and personality development: The role of experiences with siblings and with peers. In B. J. Ellis and D. F. Bjorklund, eds., *Origins of the social mind: Evolutionary psychology and child development* (245–270). New York: Guilford.

Harris, J. R., and Liebert, R. M. (1991). *The child: A contemporary view of development*, 3rd ed. Englewood Cliffs, NJ: Prentice Hall.

Harrison, L. J., and Ungerer, J. A. (2002). Maternal employment and infant-mother attachment security at 12 months postpartum. *Developmental Psychology* 38, 758–773.

Harshav, B. (1993). *Language in time of revolution*. Berkeley, CA: University of California Press.

Hemelrijk, C. K. (2002). Self-organization and natural selection in the evolution of complex despotic societies. *Biological Bulletin* 202, 283–289.

Hepper, P. G. (1988). The discrimination of human odour by the dog. *Perception* 17, 549–554.

Hibbeln, J. R., Bissette, G., Umhau, J. C., and George, D. T. (2004). Omega-3 status and cerebrospinal fluid corticotrophin releasing hormone in perpetrators of domestic violence. *Biological Psychiatry* 56, 895–897.

Hoffman, L. W. (1991). The influence of the family environment on personality: Accounting for sibling differences. *Psychological Bulletin* 110, 187–203.

Hold, B. C. L. (1976). Attention structure and rank specific behaviour in preschool children. In Chance, M. R. A., and Larsen, R. R., eds., *The social structure of attention* (177–201). London: Wiley.

Hölldobler, B., and Wilson, E. O. (1994). *Journey to the ants: A story of scientific exploration*. Cambridge, MA: Harvard University Press.

Horgan, J. (1999). *The undiscovered mind: How the human brain defies replication, medication, and explanation*. New York: Free Press.

Hulbert, A. (2003). *Raising America: Experts, parents, and a century of advice about children*. New York: Knopf.

Humphrey, N. (2004). A self worth having. Online essay on *Edge* (http://www.edge.org/3rd_culture/humphrey04/humphrey04_index.html).

Insel, T. R., and Fernald, R. D. (2004). How the brain processes social information: Searching for the social brain. *Annual Review of Neuroscience* 27, 697–722.

Jackson, D. J., and Huston, T. L. (1975). Physical attractiveness and assertiveness. *Journal of Social Psychology* 96, 79–84.

James, W. (1890). *The principles of psychology*. Vol. 2. New York: Henry Holt.

Jankowiak, W., and Diderich, M. (2000). Sibling solidarity in a polygamous community in the USA: Unpacking inclusive fitness. *Evolution and Human Behavior* 21, 125–139.

Janton, P. (1993). *Esperanto: Language, literature, and community*. Ed. and trans. H. Tonkin. Albany: State University of New York Press.

Jefferson, T., Jr., Herbst, J. H., and McCrae, R. R. (1998). Associations between birth order and personality traits: Evidence from self-report and observer ratings. *Journal of Research in Personality* 32, 498–509

Jenkins, J. J., Rasbash, J., and O'Connor, T. G. (2003). The role of the shared family context in differential parenting. *Developmental Psychology* 39, 99–113.

Johnson, G. J. (2000, appeared in print in 2004). Science, Sulloway, and birth order: An ordeal and an assesssment. *Politics and the Life Sciences* 19, 221–245.

Jones, J. C., Myerscough, M. R., Graham, S., and Oldroyd, B. P. (2004, July 16).

Honey bee nest thermoregulation: Diversity promotes stability. *Science* 305, 402–404.

Jones, M. C. (1957). The later careers of boys who were early or late maturing. *Child Development* 28, 113–128.

Joseph, J. (2002). Twin studies in psychiatry and psychology: Science or pseudoscience? *Psychiatric Quarterly* 73, 71–82.

Josephson, J. R., and Josephson, S. G., eds. (1994). *Abductive inference: Computation, philosophy, technology*. New York: Cambridge University Press.

Judge, T. A., and Cable, D. M. (2004). The effect of physical height on workplace success and income: Preliminary test of a theoretical model. *Journal of Applied Psychology* 89, 428–441.

Juvonen, J., Graham, S., and Schuster, M. A. (2003, Dec.). Bullying among young adolescents: The strong, the weak, and the troubled. *Pediatrics* 112, 1231–1237.

Kagan, J., with Snidman, N., Arcus, D., and Reznick, J. S. (1994). *Galen's prophecy: Temperament in human nature*. New York: Basic Books.

Kagan, J. (1998a, Sept. 13). A parent's influence is peerless: 'Nurture Assumption' ignores more theory than it proposes. *Boston Globe*, E3.

Kagan, J. (1998b). *Three seductive ideas*. Cambridge, MA: Harvard University Press.

Kagan, J. (2003). Biology, context, and developmental inquiry. *Annual Review of Psychology* 54, 1–23.

Kagan, J., and Moss, H. A. (1962). *From birth to maturity: A study in psychological development*. New York: Wiley.

Kagan, J., and Moss, H. A. (1983). *From birth to maturity: A study in psychological development*. 2nd ed. New Haven: Yale University Press.

Kamin, L. (1974). *The science and politics of IQ*. Mahwah, NJ: Erlbaum.

Keeley, L. H. (1996). *War before civilization*. New York: Oxford University Press.

Keller, L., ed. (1999). *Levels of selection in evolution*. Princeton, NJ: Princeton University Press.

Kellogg, W. N., and Kellogg, L. A. (1933). *The ape and the child: A study of environmental influence upon early behavior*. New York: McGraw-Hill.

Kim, K., and Smith, P. K. (1999). Family relations in early childhood and reproductive development. *Journal of Reproductive and Infant Psychology* 17, 133–148.

Kirkpatrick, L. A., and Ellis, B. J. (2001). An evolutionary-psychological approach to self-esteem: Multiple domains and multiple functions. In G. J. O. Fletcher and M. S. Clark, eds., *Blackwell handbook of social psychology: Interpersonal processes* (411–436). Malden, MA: Blackwell.

Kirkpatrick, L. A., Waugh, C. E., Valencia, A., and Webster, G. D. (2002). The functional domain specificity of self-esteem and the differential prediction of aggression. *Journal of Personality and Social Psychology* 82, 756–767.

Kniffin, K. M., and Wilson, D. S. (2004). The effect of nonphysical traits on the perception of physical attractiveness: Three naturalistic studies. *Evolution and Human Behavior* 25, 88–101.

Knowlton, B. J., and Squire, L. R. (1993, Dec. 10). The learning of categories: Parallel brain systems for item memory and category knowledge. *Science* 262, 1747–1749.

Knutson, J. F. (1995). Psychological characteristics of maltreated children: Putative risk factors and consequences. *Annual Review of Psychology* 46, 401–431.

Kolata, G. (2003, Apr. 22). Hormone studies: What went wrong. *New York Times*, F1, F6.

Kondo, S., Schutte, B. C., Richardson, R. J., et al. (2002, Oct.). Mutations in IRF6 cause Van der Woude and popliteal pterygium syndromes. *Nature Genetics* 32, 285–289.

Kunda, Z., and Thagard, P. (1996). Forming impressions from stereotypes, traits, and behaviors: A parallel-constraint-satisfaction theory. *Psychological Review* 103, 284–308.

Lake, R. I. E., Eaves, L. J., Maes, H. H. M., Heath, A. C., and Martin, N. G. (2000). Further evidence against the environmental transmission of individual differences in neuroticism from a collaborative study of 45,850 twins and relatives on two continents. *Behavioral Genetics* 30, 223–233.

Langlois, J. H., Kalakanis, L., Rubenstein, A. J., Larson, A., Hallam, M., and Smoot, M. (2000). Maxims or myths of beauty? A meta-analytic and theoretical review. *Psychological Bulletin* 126, 390–423.

Langlois, J. H., Ritter, J. M., Casey, R. J., and Sawin, D. B. (1995). Infant attractiveness predicts maternal behaviors and attitudes. *Developmental Psychology*, 31, 464–472.

Langlois, J. H., and Roggman, L. A. (1990). Attractive faces are only average. *Psychological Science* 1, 115–121.

Langton, J. (2003). *The deserter: Murder at Gettysburg*. New York: St. Martin's.

Larkin, P. (1989). *Collected poems*. Ed. A. Thwaite. New York: Farrar, Straus and Giroux.

Leary, M. R. (1999). Making sense of self-esteem. *Current Directions in Psychological Science* 8, 32–35.

Leary, M. R., Cottrell, C. A., and Phillips, M. (2001). Deconfounding the effects of dominance and social acceptance on self-esteem. *Journal of Personality and Social Psychology* 81, 898–909.

Leary, M. R., Tambor, E. S., Terdal, S. K., and Downs, D. L. (1995). Self-esteem as an interpersonal monitor: The sociometer hypothesis. *Journal of Personality and Social Psychology* 68, 518–530.

Leinbach, M. D., and Fagot, B. I. (1993). Categorical habituation to male and female faces: Gender schematic processing in infancy. *Infant Behavior and Development* 16, 317–332.

LeVine, R. A., and LeVine, B. B. (1963). Nyansongo: A Gusii Community in Kenya. In B. B. Whiting, ed., *Six cultures: Studies of child-rearing* (15–202). New York: Wiley.

Lewcock, J. W., and Reed, R. R. (2003, Dec. 19). ORs rule the roost in the olfactory system. *Science* 302, 2078–2079.

Lewicki, P., Hill, T., and Czyzewska, M. (1992). Nonconscious acquisition of information. *American Psychologist* 47, 796–801.

Lykken, D. T. (1995). *The antisocial personalities*. Hillsdale, NJ: Erlbaum.

Lykken, D. T., and Tellegen, A. (1993). Is human mating adventitious or the result of lawful choice? A twin study of mate selection. *Journal of Personality and Social Psychology* 65, 56–68.

Maccoby, E. E. (1990). Gender and relationships: A developmental account. *American Psychologist* 45, 513–520.

Maccoby, E. E. (1992). The role of parents in the socialization of children: An historical overview. *Developmental Psychology* 28, 1006–1017.

Maccoby, E. E. (1995). The two sexes and their social systems. In P. Moen, G. H. Elder, Jr., and K. Lüscher, eds., *Examining lives in context: Perspectives on the ecology of human development* (347–364). Washington, DC: American Psychological Association.

Maccoby, E. E. (2002). Parenting effects: Issues and controversies. In J. G. Borkowski, S. L. Ramey, and M. Bristol-Power, eds., *Parenting and the child's world: Influences on academic, intellectual, and social-emotional development* (35–46). Mahwah, NJ: Erlbaum.

Maccoby, E. E., and Jacklin, C. N. (1974). *The psychology of sex differences*. Stanford, CA: Stanford University Press.

Maccoby, E. E., and Jacklin, C. N. (1987). Gender segregation in childhood. *Advances in Child Development and Behavior* 20, 239–287.

Maestripieri, D. (2003). Similarities in affiliation and aggression between cross-fostered rhesus macaque females and their biological mothers. *Developmental Psychobiology* 43, 321–327.

Magnuson, K., and Duncan, G. J. (2002). Family investments in children's potential: Resources and behaviors that promote children's success. Paper presented at the conference of the Joint Center for Poverty Research, Chicago, IL, Sept. 19–20 (http://www.jcpr.org/conferences/SRI_2002/magnuson_duncan.pdf).

Marsh, H. W., and Hau, K.-T. (2003). Big-fish-little-pond effect on academic self-concept: A cross-cultural (26-country) test of the negative effects of academically selective schools. *American Psychologist* 58, 364–376.

Mayberry, R. I. (1976). An assessment of some oral and manual-language skills of hearing children of deaf parents. *American Annals of the Deaf* 121, 507–512.

Mayberry, R. I., Lock, E., and Kazmi, H. (2002, May 2). Linguistic ability and early language exposure. *Nature* 417, 38.

McCall, R. B. (1992). Academic underachievers. *Current Directions in Psychological Science* 3, 15–19.

McCartney, K., Harris, M. J., and Bernieri, F. (1990). Growing up and growing apart: A developmental meta-analysis of twin studies. *Psychological Bulletin* 107, 226–237.

McCrae, R. R. (2004). Human nature and culture: A trait perspective. *Journal of Research on Personality* 38, 3–14.

McCrae, R. R., and Costa, P. T., Jr. (1988). Recalled parent-child relations and adult personality. *Journal of Personality* 56, 417–434.

McCrae, R. R., and Costa, P. T., Jr. (1994). The paradox of parental influence: Understanding retrospective studies of parent-child relations and adult personality. In C. Perris, W. A. Arrindell, and M. Eisemann, eds., *Parenting and psychopathology* (107–125). New York: Wiley.

McCrae, R. R., and Costa, P. T., Jr. (1999). A five-factor theory of personality. In L. A. Pervin and O. P. John, eds., *Handbook of personality psychology*. 2nd ed. (139–153). New York: Guilford.

McCrae, R. R., Yik, M. S. M., Trapnell, P. D., Bond, M. H., and Paulhus, D. L. (1998). Interpreting personality profiles across cultures: Bilingual, acculturation, and peer rating studies of Chinese undergraduates. *Journal of Personality and Social Psychology* 74, 1041–1055.

McDonagh, J. (2000). Science without a degree of objectivity is dead. *American Psychologist* 55, 678.

McDonald, M. A., Sigman, M., Espinosa, M. P., and Neumann, C. G. (1994). Impact of a temporary food shortage on children and their mothers. *Child Development* 65, 404–415.

McHale, S. M., Crouter, A. C., McGuire, S. A., and Updegraff, K. A. (1995). Congruence between mothers' and fathers' differential treatment of siblings: Links with family relations and children's well-being. *Child Development* 66, 116–128.

McNeil, D. G., Jr. (2003, Dec. 16). There is no joy in Toyville: Mighty Santa's striking out. *New York Times*, F5.

Mead, G. H. (1934). *Mind, self, and society from the standpoint of a social behaviorist*. Ed. C. W. Morris. Chicago: University of Chicago Press (http://spartan.ac.brocku.ca/~lward/Mead/pubs2/mindself/Mead_1934_18.html).

Mednick, S. A., Gabrielli, W. F., Jr., and Hutchings, B. (1987). Genetic factors in the etiology of criminal behavior. In S. A. Mednick, T. E. Moffitt, and S. A. Stack, eds., *The causes of crime: New biological approaches* (74–91). Cambridge, England: Cambridge University Press.

Miller, E. M. (1997). Could nonshared environmental variance have evolved to assure diversification through randomness? *Evolution and Human Behavior* 18, 195–221.

Miller, G. F. (2000). *The mating mind: How sexual choice shaped the evolution of human nature*. New York: Doubleday.

Minoura, Y. (1992). A sensitive period for the incorporation of a cultural meaning system: A study of Japanese children growing up in the United States. *Ethos* 20, 304–339.

Mischel, W. (1996). *Personality and assessment*. Mahwah, NJ: Erlbaum. Originally published in 1968.

Mitchell, D. E. (1980). The influence of early visual experience on visual perception. In C. S. Harris, ed., *Visual coding and adaptability* (1–50). Hillsdale, NJ: Erlbaum.

Modell, J. (1997, Jan. 31). Family niche and intellectual bent (review of *Born to Rebel*). *Science* 275, 624–625.

Morelli, G. A. (1997). Growing up female in a farmer community and a forager community. In M. E. Morbeck, A. Galloway, and A. L. Zihlman, eds., *The evolving female: A life-history perspective* (209–219). Princeton, NJ: Princeton University Press.

Muhle, R., Trentacoste, S.V., and Rapin, I. (2004). The genetics of autism. *Pediatrics* 113, e472–e486.

Myers, D. G. (1992). *The pursuit of happiness: Who is happy and why?* New York: Avon.

Myers, D. G. (2002). *Intuition: Its powers and perils.* New Haven, CT: Yale University Press.

Napier, J. R., and Napier, P. H. (1985). *The natural history of the primates.* Cambridge, MA: MIT Press.

Napolitan, D. A., and Goethals, G. R. (1979). The attribution of friendliness. *Journal of Experimental Social Psychology* 15, 106–116.

National Institute of Child Health and Human Development (2001). *Adventures in parenting.* U.S. Department of Health and Human Services.

Neisser, U., Boodoo, G., Bouchard, T. J., et al. (1996). Intelligence: Knowns and unknowns. *American Psychologist* 51, 77–101.

Newport, E. L. (2002). Critical periods in language development. In L. Nadel, ed., *Encyclopedia of cognitive science* (737–740). London: Macmillan.

NICHD Early Child Care Research Network (2003). Does amount of time spent in child care predict socioemotional adjustment during the transition to kindergarten? *Child Development* 74, 976–1005.

Olson, J. M., Vernon, P. A., Harris, J. A., and Jang, K. L. (2001). The heritability of attitudes: A study of twins. *Journal of Personality and Social Psychology* 80, 845–860.

Olweus, D. (1995). Bullying or peer abuse at school: Facts and intervention. *Current Directions in Psychological Science* 4, 196–200.

Omark, D. R., and Edelman, M. S. (1976). The development of attention structure in young children. In Chance, M. R. A., and Larsen, R. R., eds., *The social structure of attention* (119–151). London: Wiley.

Opie, I., and Opie, P. (1969). *Children's games in street and playground.* London: Oxford University Press.

Paris, J. (2000). *Myths of childhood.* Philadelphia, PA: Brunner/Mazel.

Park, R. (2000). *Voodoo science: The road from foolishness to fraud.* New York: Oxford University Press.

Parker, J. G., and Asher, S. R. (1993a). Beyond group acceptance: Friendship and friendship quality as distinct dimensions of children's peer adjustment. In D. Perlman and W. H. Jones, eds., *Advances in personal relationships: Vol. 4* (261–294). London: Jessica Kingsley Publishers.

Parker, J. G., and Asher, S. R. (1993b). Friendship and friendship quality in middle childhood: Links with peer group acceptance and feelings of loneliness and social dissatisfaction. *Developmental Psychology* 29, 611–621.

Paul, A. M. (1998, Jan./Feb.). Kid stuff: Do parents really matter? *Psychology Today* 31, 46–49, 78.

Paul, D. B., and Blumenthal, A. L. (1989). On the trail of Little Albert. *Psychological Record* 39, 547–553.

Paulhus, D. L., Trapnell, P. D., and Chen, D. (1999). Birth order effects on personality and achievement within families. *Psychological Science* 10, 482–488.

Pelaez-Nogueras, M., Field, T., Cigales, M., Gonzalez, A., and Clasky, S. (1994).

Infants of depressed mothers show less "depressed" behavior with their nursery teachers. *Infant Mental Health Journal* 15, 358–367.

Pellegrini, A. D., and Smith, P. K. (1998). Physical activity play: The nature and function of a neglected aspect of play. *Child Development* 69, 577–598.

Persico, N., Postlewaite, A., and Silverman, D. (2004). The effect of adolescent experience on labor market outcomes: The case of height. *Journal of Political Economy* 112, 1019–1053.

Pfennig, D. W., and Sherman, P. W. (1995, June). Kin recognition. *Scientific American* 272, 98–103.

Piaget, J. (1962). *Play, dreams, and imitation in childhood.* Trans. C. Gattegno and F. M. Hodgson. New York: W. W. Norton. English translation originally published in 1951.

Pierson, S., and Cohen, P. (2003). *You have to say I'm pretty, you're my mother.* New York: Simon & Schuster.

Pinker, S. (1994). *The language instinct.* New York: HarperCollins.

Pinker, S. (1997). *How the mind works.* New York: W. W. Norton.

Pinker, S. (1999). *Words and rules: The ingredients of language.* New York: Basic Books.

Pinker, S. (2002). *The blank slate.* New York: Viking.

Pinker, S. (2003). Language as an adaptation to the cognitive niche. In M. H. Christiansen and S. Kirby, eds., *Language evolution: The states of the art* (16–37). Oxford, England: Oxford University Press.

Pitcairn, T. K. (1976). Attention and social structure in *Macaca fascicularis.* In Chance, M. R. A., and Larsen, R. R., eds., *The social structure of attention* (51–81). London: Wiley.

Plomin, R. (1989). Environments and genes: Determinants of behavior. *American Psychologist* 44, 105–111.

Plomin, R., Asbury, K., and Dunn, J. (2001). Why are children in the same family so different? Nonshared environment a decade later. *Canadian Journal of Psychiatry* 46, 225–233.

Plomin, R., and Caspi, A. (1999). Behavioral genetics and personality. In L. A. Pervin and O. P. John, eds., *Handbook of personality: Theory and research.* 2nd ed. (251–276). New York: Guilford.

Plomin, R., and Daniels, D. (1987). Why are children in the same family so different from one another? *Behavioral and Brain Sciences* 10, 1–16.

Plomin, R., DeFries, J. C., McClearn, G. E., and Rutter, M. (1997). *Behavioral genetics.* 3rd ed. New York: W. H. Freeman.

Povinelli, D. J., and Vonk, J. (2004). We don't need a microscope to explore the chimpanzee's mind. *Mind and Language* 19, 1–28.

Quartz, S. R., and Sejnowski, T. J. (2002). *Liars, lovers, and heroes: What the new brain science reveals about how we become who we are.* New York: William Morrow.

Reiss, D., with Neiderhiser, J. M., Hetherington, E. M., and Plomin, R. (2000). *The relationship code: Deciphering genetic and social influences on adolescent development.* Cambridge, MA: Harvard University Press.

Richman, R. A., Gordon, M., Tegtmeyer, P., Crouthamel, C., and Post, E. M. (1986). Academic and emotional difficulties associated with short stature. In B. Stabler and L. E. Underwood, eds., *Slow grows the child: Psychosocial aspects of growth delay* (13–26). Hillsdale, NJ: Erlbaum.

Ridley, M. (1996). *The origins of virtue*. New York: Viking.

Ridley, M. (2003). *Nature via nurture: Genes, experience, and what makes us human.* New York: HarperCollins.

Rilling, M. (2000). John Watson's paradoxical struggle to explain Freud. *American Psychologist* 55, 301–312.

Ritter, J. (2004, May 20). Rebelling against birth order. *Chicago Sun-Times*, 16–17 (http://www.suntimes.com/output/lifestyles/cst-nws-insight20.html).

Rodgers, J. L., and Rowe, D. C. (1988). Influence of siblings on adolescent sexual behavior. *Developmental Psychology* 24, 722–728.

Rogoff, B., Mistry, J., Göncü, A., and Mosier, C. (1993). Guided participation in cultural activity by toddlers and caregivers. *Monographs of the Society for Research in Child Development* 58, no. 8 (serial no. 236).

Romney, K., and Romney, R. (1963). The Mixtecans of Juxtlahuaca, Mexico. In B. B. Whiting, ed., *Six cultures: Studies of child-rearing* (541–691). New York: Wiley.

Rosch, E. (1978). Principles of categorization. In E. Rosch and B. B. Lloyd, eds., *Cognition and categorization* (27–47). Hillsdale, NJ: Erlbaum.

Rosenthal, R. (2002). Covert communication in classrooms, clinics, courtrooms, and cubicles. *American Psychologist* 57, 839–849.

Rovee-Collier, C. (1993). The capacity for long-term memory in infancy. *Current Directions in Psychological Science* 2, 130–135.

Rowe, D. C. (1990). As the twig is bent? The myth of child-rearing influences on personality development. *Journal of Counseling and Development* 68, 606–611.

Rowe, D. C. (1994). *The limits of family influence: Genes, experience, and behavior.* New York: Guilford.

Rowe, D. C. (2000). Evolutionary ecology embraces early experience. *Evolution and Human Behavior* 21, 352–364.

Rowe, D. C. (2001). The nurture assumption persists. *American Psychologist* 56, 168–169.

Rowe, D. C. (2002a). On genetic variation in menarche and age at first sexual intercourse: A critique of the Belsky-Draper hypothesis. *Evolution and Human Behavior* 23, 365–372.

Rowe, D. C. (2002b). What twin and adoption studies reveal about parenting. In J. G. Borkowski, S. L. Ramey, and M. Bristol-Power, eds., *Parenting and the child's world: Influences on academic, intellectual, and social-emotional development* (21–34). Mahwah, NJ: Erlbaum.

Rubenstein, A. J., Kalakanis, L., and Langlois, J. H. (1999). Infant preferences for attractive faces: A cognitive explanation. *Developmental Psychology* 35, 848–855.

Rutter, M. (1983). School effects on pupil progress: Research findings and policy implications. *Child Development* 54, 1–29.

Rutter, M., O'Connor, T. G., and the English and Romanian Adoptees Study Team (2004). Are there biological programming effects for psychological development? Findings from a study of Romanian adoptees. *Developmental Psychology* 40, 81–94.

Sacks, O. W. (1985). *The man who mistook his wife for a hat and other clinical tales.* New York: Summit Books.

Sagi, A., Koren-Karie, N., Gini, M., Ziv, Y., and Joels, T. (2002). Shedding further light on the effects of various types and quality of early child care on infant-mother attachment relationship: The Haifa Study of Early Child Care. *Child Development* 73, 1166–1186.

Sampson, R. J., Morenoff, J. D., and Gannon-Rowley, T. (2002). Assessing "neighborhood effects": Social processes and new directions in research. *Annual Review of Sociology* 28, 443–478.

Saudino, K. J. (1997). Moving beyond the heritability question: New directions in behavioral genetic studies of personality. *Current Directions in Psychological Science* 6, 86–90.

Savin-Williams, R. C. (1979). Dominance hierarchies in groups of early adolescents. *Child Development* 50, 923–935.

Sayers, D. (1968). *Five red herrings.* New York: Avon. Originally published in 1931.

Scarr, S. (1992). Developmental theories for the 1990s: Development and individual differences. *Child Development* 63, 1–19.

Schachter, F. F., and Stone, R. K. (1985). Difficult sibling, easy sibling: Temperament and the within-family environment. *Child Development* 56, 1335–1344.

Schacter, D. L. (1996). *Searching for memory: The brain, the mind, and the past.* New York: Basic Books.

Schacter, D. L. (2001). *The seven sins of memory.* Boston: Houghton Mifflin.

Schlegel, A., and Barry, H., III (1991). *Adolescence: An anthropological inquiry.* New York: Free Press.

Schmitz, S., Saudino, K. J., Plomin, R., Fulker, D. W., and DeFries, J. C. (1996). Genetic and environmental influences on temperament in middle childhood: Analyses of teacher and tester ratings. *Child Development* 67, 409–422.

Schneider-Rosen, K., Braunwald, K. G., Carlson, V., and Cicchetti, D. (1985). Current perspectives in attachment theory: Illustration from the study of maltreated infants. In I. Bretherton and E. Waters, eds., Growing points of attachment theory and research (194–210). *Monographs of the Society for Research in Child Development* 50, nos. 1–2 (serial no. 209).

Schofield, J. W. (1981). Complementary and conflicting identities: Images and interaction in an interracial school. In S. R. Asher and J. M. Gottman, eds., *The development of children's friendships* (53–90). Cambridge, England: Cambridge University Press.

Searby, A., and Jouventin, P. (2003). Mother-lamb acoustic recognition in sheep: A frequency coding. *Proceedings of the Royal Society: Biological Sciences* 270, 1765–1771.

Seeley, T. D. (1997). Honey bee colonies are group-level adaptive units. *American Naturalist* 150, suppl. no. 1, 22–41.

Segal, N. L. (1999). *Entwined lives: Twins and what they tell us about human behavior.* New York: Penguin.

Segal, N. L. (2002). Co-conspirators and double-dealers: A twin film analysis. *Personality & Individual Differences* 33, 621–631.

Segal, N. L., and Hershberger, S. L. (1999). Cooperation and competition between twins: Findings from a prisoner's dilemma game. *Evolution and Human Behavior* 20, 29–51.

Seligman, M. E. P., and Hager, J. L., eds. (1972). *Biological boundaries of learning.* New York: Appleton-Century-Crofts.

Senghas, A., Kita, S., and Özyürek, A. (2004, Sept. 17). Children creating core properties of language: Evidence from an emerging sign language in Nicaragua. *Science* 305, 1779–1782.

Serbin, L. A., Powlishta, K. K., and Gulko, J. (1993). The development of sex typing in middle childhood. *Monographs of the Society for Research in Child Development* 58, no. 2 (serial no. 232).

Shatz, M., and Gelman, R. (1973). The development of communication skills: Modifications in the speech of young children as a function of listener. *Monographs of the Society for Research in Child Development* 38, no. 5 (serial no. 152).

Sheldon, W. H. (1942). *The varieties of temperament.* New York: Harper & Row.

Sherif, M., Harvey, O. J., White, B. J., Hood, W. R., and Sherif, C. W. (1961). *Intergroup cooperation and competition: The Robbers Cave experiment.* Norman, OK: University Book Exchange.

Sherry, D. F., and Schacter, D. L. (1987). The evolution of multiple memory systems. *Psychological Review* 94, 439–454.

Simonoff, E., Pickles, A., Hervas, A., Silberg, J. L., Rutter, M., and Eaves, L. (1998). Genetic influences on childhood hyperactivity: Contrast effects imply parental rating bias, not sibling interaction. *Psychological Medicine* 28, 825–837.

Smith, A. (1776). *An inquiry into the nature and causes of the wealth of nations.* Reprinted in 1904 by Methuen and Co. (http://www.econlib.org/library/Smith/smWN.html).

Smith, J. D. (2002). Exemplar theory's predicted typicality gradient can be tested and disconfirmed. *Psychological Science* 13, 437–442.

Snibbe, A. C. (2003, Dec.). Cultural psychology: Studying the exotic other. *APS Observer* 16, 1, 30–32.

Spelke, E. (1994). Initial knowledge: Six suggestions. *Cognition* 50, 431–445.

Spinath, F. M., and Angleitner, A. (1998). Contrast effects in Buss and Plomin's EAS questionnaire: A behavioral-genetic study on early developing personality traits assessed through parental ratings. *Personality & Individual Differences* 25, 947–963.

Sroufe, L. A., Egeland, B., and Carlson, E. A. (1999). One social world: The integrated development of parent-child and peer relationships. In W. A. Collins and B. Laursen, eds., *Relationships as developmental contexts* (241–261). Mahwah, NJ: Erlbaum.

Staples, B. (2003, July 22). The politician, the mobster and the ties that bind them to each other. *New York Times*, A18.

Stattin, H., and Kerr, M. (2000). Parental monitoring: A reinterpretation. *Child Development* 71, 1072–1085.

Stattin, H. and Magnusson, D. (1990). *Pubertal maturation in female development: Vol. 2. Paths through life.* Hillsdale, NJ: Erlbaum.

Steinhausen, H.-C., Dörr, H. G., Kannenberg, R., and Malin, Z. (2000). Behavior profile of children and adolescents with short stature. *Developmental and Behavioral Pediatrics* 21, 423–428.

Steinmetz, H., Herzog, A., Huang, Y., and Hackländer, T. (1994, Oct. 6). Discordant brain-surface anatomy in monozygotic twins. *New England Journal of Medicine* 331, 952–953.

Stevens, M., Golombok, S., Beveridge, M., and the ALSPAC Study Team (2002). Does father absence influence children's gender development? Findings from a general population study of preschool children. *Parenting: Science & Practice* 2, 47–60.

Stevenson, M. R., and Black, K. N. (1988). Paternal absence and sex-role development: A meta-analysis. *Child Development* 59, 793–814.

Stipek, D. (1992). The child at school. In M. H. Bornstein and M. E. Lamb, eds., *Developmental psychology: An advanced textbook.* 3rd ed. (579–625). Hillsdale, NJ: Erlbaum.

Stocker, C., and Dunn, J. (1990). Sibling relationships in childhood: Links with friendships and peer relationships. *British Journal of Developmental Psychology* 8, 227–244.

Stone, A. A. (1997, Jan./Feb.). Where will psychoanalysis survive? *Harvard Magazine* 99, no. 3, 35–39.

Stoolmiller, M. (1999). Implications of the restricted range of family environments for estimates of heritability and nonshared environment in behavior-genetic adoption studies. *Psychological Bulletin* 125, 392–409.

Stout, R. (1951). *Murder by the book.* New York: Viking.

Sulloway, F. J. (1995). Birth order and evolutionary psychology: A meta-analytic overview (commentary on target article by Buss). *Psychological Inquiry* 6, 75–80.

Sulloway, F. J. (1996). *Born to rebel: Birth order, family dynamics, and creative lives.* New York: Pantheon.

Sulloway, F. J. (1999). Birth order. In M. A. Runco and S. Pritzker, eds., *Encyclopedia of creativity.* Vol. 1 (189–202). San Diego, CA: Academic Press.

Sulloway, F. J. (2000, appeared in print in 2004). Born to Rebel and its critics (reply to Townsend). *Politics and the Life Sciences* 19, 181–202.

Suomi, S. J. (1987). Genetic and maternal contributions to individual differences in rhesus monkey biobehavioral development. In N. A. Krasnegor, E. M. Blass, M. A. Hofer, and W. P. Smotherman, eds., *Perinatal development: A psychobiological perspective* (397–419). New York: Academic Press.

Suomi, S. J. (1991). Uptight and laid-back monkeys: Individual differences in the response to social challenges. In S. E. Brauth, W. S. Hall, and R. J. Dooling, eds., *Plasticity of development* (27–56). Cambridge, MA: MIT Press.

Suomi, S. J. (1997). Long-term effects of different early rearing experiences on social, emotional and physiological development in nonhuman primates. In M. S. Keshaven and R. M. Murray, eds., *Neurodevelopment and adult psychopathology* (104–116). Cambridge, England: Cambridge University Press.

Suomi, S. J. (1999). Attachment in rhesus monkeys. In J. Cassidy and P. R. Shaver, eds., *Handbook of attachment: Theory, research, and clinical applications* (181–197). New York: Guilford.

Suomi, S. J. (2002). Parents, peers, and the process of socialization in primates. In J. G. Borkowski, S. L. Ramey, and M. Bristol-Power, eds., *Parenting and the child's world: Influences on academic, intellectual, and social-emotional development* (265–279). Mahwah, NJ: Erlbaum.

Suzuki, D. T., Griffiths, A. J. F., Miller, J. H., and Lewontin, R. C. (1989). *An introduction to genetic analysis.* 4th ed. New York: W. H. Freeman.

Swim, J. K. (1994). Perceived versus meta-analytic effect sizes: An assessment of the accuracy of gender stereotypes. *Journal of Personality and Social Psychology* 66, 21–36.

Symons, D. (1992). On the use and misuse of Darwinism in the study of human behavior. In J. H. Barkow, L. Cosmides, and J. Tooby, eds., *The adapted mind: Evolutionary psychology and the generation of culture* (137–159). New York: Oxford University Press.

Tajfel, H. (1970, Nov.). Experiments in intergroup discrimination. *Scientific American* 223, 96–102.

Taylor, S. E., and Brown, J. D. (1988). Illusion and well-being: A social psychological perspective on mental health. *Psychological Bulletin* 103, 193–210.

Tesser, A. (1993). The importance of heritability in psychological research: The case of attitudes. *Psychological Review* 100, 129–142.

Tey, J. (1977). *The daughter of time.* New York: Pocket Books. Originally published in 1951.

Thorne, B. (1993). *Gender play: Girls and boys in school.* New Brunswick, NJ: Rutgers University Press.

Tibbetts, E. A. (2002, July 22). Visual signals of individual identity in the wasp *Polistes fuscatus. Proceedings of the Royal Society—Biological Sciences* 269, 1423–1428.

Tienari, P., Wynne, L. C., Moring, J., et al. (1994). The Finnish adoption family study of schizophrenia: Implications for family research. *British Journal of Psychiatry* 164, suppl. no. 23, 20–26.

Tooby, J., and Cosmides, L. (1990). On the universality of human nature and the uniqueness of the individual: The role of genetics and adaptation. *Journal of Personality* 58, 17–67.

Tooby, J., and Cosmides, L. (1995). Foreword to S. Baron-Cohen, *Mindblindness: An essay on autism and theory of mind* (xi–xviii). Cambridge, MA: MIT Press.

Townsend, F. (2000a, appeared in print in 2004). Birth order and rebelliousness: Reconstructing the research in *Born to Rebel. Politics and the Life Sciences* 19, 135–156.

Townsend, F. (2000b, appeared in print 2004). Taking *Born to Rebel* seriously: The need for independent review. *Politics and the Life Sciences* 19, 205–210.

Triandis, H. C. (1995). *Individualism and collectivism*. Boulder, CO: Westview Press.

Trivers, R. (1971). The evolution of reciprocal altruism. *Quarterly Review of Biology* 46, 35–57.

Trivers, R. (1985). *Social evolution*. Menlo Park, CA: Benjamin/Cummings.

Tully, L. A., Arseneault, L., Caspi, A.. Moffitt, T. E., and Morgan, J. (2004). Does maternal warmth moderate the effects of birth weight on twins' attention-deficit/hyperactivity disorder (ADHD) symptoms and low IQ? *Journal of Consulting and Clinical Psychology* 72, 218–226.

Turkheimer, E., and Waldron, M. (2000). Nonshared environment: A theoretical, methodological, and quantitative review. *Psychological Bulletin* 126, 78–108.

Turner, J. C., with Hogg, M. A., Oakes, P. J., Reicher, S. D., and Wetherell, M. S. (1987). *Rediscovering the social group: A self-categorization theory*. Oxford, England: Basil Blackwell.

Ullman, M. T., Corkin, S., Coppola, M., Hickok, G., Growdon, J. H., Koroshetz, W. J., and Pinker, S. (1997). A neural dissociation within language: Evidence that the mental dictionary is part of declarative memory, and that grammatical rules are processed by the procedural system. *Journal of Cognitive Neuroscience* 9, 266–276.

van Balen, F. (1998). Development of IVF children. *Developmental Review* 18, 30–46.

Vandell, D. L. (2000). Parents, peer groups, and other socializing influences. *Developmental Psychology* 36, 699–710.

Vandell, D. L., and Hembree, S. (1994). Peer social status and friendship: Independent contributors to children's social and academic adjustment. *Merrill-Palmer Quarterly* 4, 461–477.

Vandermeer, J. (2004, Jan. 23). The importance of a constructivist view (review of *Niche construction: The neglected process in evolution*, by J. Odling-Smee, K. N. Laland, and M. W. Feldman). *Science* 303, 472–473.

Vertegaal, R., and Ding, Y. (2002). Explaining effects of eye gaze on mediated group conversations: Amount or synchronization? *Proceedings of CSCW 2002 Conference on Computer Supported Collaborative Work* (41–48). New Orleans, LA: ACM Press.

Waring, N.-P. (1996, July 3). Social pediatrics. *Journal of the American Medical Association* 276, 76.

Watson, J. B., and Rayner, R. (2000). Conditioned emotional reactions. *American Psychologist* 55, 313–317. Originally published in 1920 in *Journal of Experimental Psychology*.

Weisfeld, G. E., and Billings, R. L. (1988). Observations on adolescence. In K. B. MacDonald, ed., *Sociobiological perspectives on human development* (207–233). New York: Springer-Verlag.

Wesseling, E. (2004). Judith Rich Harris: The Miss Marple of developmental psychology. *Science in Context* 17, 293–314.

White, K. R., Taylor, M. J., and Moss, V. D. (1992). Does research support claims about the benefits of involving parents in early intervention programs? *Review of Educational Research* 62, 91–125.

Whitfield, C. W., Cziko, A.-M., and Robinson, G. (2003, Oct. 10). Gene expression profiles in the brain predict behavior in individual honey bees. *Science* 302, 296–299.

Whiting, B. B., and Edwards, C. P. (1988). *Children of different worlds: The formation of social behavior.* Cambridge, MA: Harvard University Press.

Wierson, M., and Forehand, R. (1994). Parent behavioral training for child noncompliance: Rationale, concepts, and effectiveness. *Current Directions in Psychological Science* 3, 146–150.

Wilkinson, G. S. (1990, Feb.). Food sharing in vampire bats. *Scientific American* 262, 76–82.

Wilson, D. M., Killen, J. D., Hayward, C., Robinson, T. N., Hammer, L. D., Kraemer, H. C., Varady, A. and Taylor, C. B. (1994). Timing and rate of sexual maturation and the onset of cigarette and alcohol use among teenage girls. *Archives of Pediatrics and Adolescent Medicine* 148, 789–795.

Wilson, D. S. (2002). *Darwin's cathedral: Evolution, religion, and the nature of society.* Chicago, IL: University of Chicago Press.

Wilson, E. O. (1975). *Sociobiology: The new synthesis.* Cambridge, MA: Harvard University Press.

Wilson, M., and Daly, M. (1992). The man who mistook his wife for a chattel. In J. H. Barkow, L. Cosmides, and J. Tooby, eds., *The adapted mind: Evolutionary psychology and the generation of culture* (289–322). New York: Oxford University Press.

Winitz, H., Gillespie, B., and Starcev, J. (1995). The development of English speech patterns of a 7-year-old Polish-speaking child. *Journal of Psycholinguistic Research* 24, 117–143.

Withgott, J. (2002, Aug. 16). Birds spy on neighbors to choose nest sites. *Science* 297, 1107–1108.

Wood, J. V. (1989). Theory and research concerning social comparisons of personal attributes. *Psychological Bulletin* 106, 231–248.

Wright, K. (1997, October). Babies, bonds, and brains. *Discover* 18, 74–78.

Wright, R. (1994). *The moral animal.* New York: Pantheon.

Yan, H., Yuan, W., Velculescu, V. E., Vogelstein, B., and Kinzler, K. W. (2002, Aug. 16). Allelic variation in human gene expression. *Science* 297, 1143.

Young, A. W., Hay, D. C., and Ellis, A. W. (1985). The faces that launched a thousand slips: Everyday difficulties and errors in recognizing people. *British Journal of Psychology* 76, 495–523.

Zaslow, M., Tout, K., Smith, S., and Moore, K. (1998). Implications of the 1996 welfare legislation for children: A research perspective. *Social Policy Report, Society for Research in Child Development* 12, no. 3, 1–34.

Zimbardo, P. G. (1993). Pathology of imprisonment. In B. Byers, ed., *Readings in Social Psychology* (15–19). Boston: Allyn & Bacon. Originally published in 1972.

Index